COURTING DANGER

COURTING DANGER

INJURY AND LAW IN NEW YORK CITY, 1870–1910

Randolph E. Bergstrom

CORNELL UNIVERSITY PRESS

Ithaca and London

First published 1992 by Cornell University Press.

International Standard Book Number 0-8014-2607-3
Library of Congress Catalog Card Number 92-52744

Printed in the United States of America

*Librarians: Library of Congress cataloging information
appears on the last page of the book.*

♾ The paper in this book meets the minimum requirements
of the American National Standard for Information Sciences—
Permanence of Paper for Printed Library Materials, ANSI Z39.48-1984.

FOR MY FAMILY

CONTENTS

PREFACE

Accidental injury, which has always intruded violently into its victims' lives, has interjected itself hardly at all into our understanding of humanity's past. That may be because it seems a dismal story. It is morbid, true: a story of suffering, certainly. But not unmitigated suffering. Individuals and societies respond to accidents and have responded in different ways in the past. The incidence and nature of accidents have changed, as have knowledge about them and responses to them. The variety of experience makes the course of injury in the past something other than inevitable and therefore of value to historians. Understanding a society's response to destruction, such as that wrought by accidental injury, can be every bit as revealing as study of a people's complex feats of construction—physical, mental, or social. In fact, how a people answers adversity is perhaps a more exacting measure of their attainment than their most glorious endeavors.

That at least is a premise of this book. Turn-of-the-century Americans' changing responses to the danger of accidental injury tell as much about the history of the era, I believe, as many of the more prominent features of those years. Because the change involves the use of law, it is society's official, formalized response to danger that is the focus here. The perspective on law that I employ treats law in practice, rather than in principle and pronouncement (though considering the influence of both), as the best indicator of how the society ruled itself. While that has been the trend in legal history for decades, it needs to be declared up front because there are still many who disagree with this emphasis. Adopting a corollary of the "law in practice" perspective, I consider all the people of the

time as thinking beings, possessing ideas of law that mattered to their behavior. All, too, must be viewed as subjects of the rest of their historical
context—the physical, technological, cultural ("American culture," urban culture, ethnic, work, legal, and more), political, and economic conditions and developments of the day. Too often, we think of judges and
lawyers as moved primarily by ideas of law, and suitors and jurors as
moved by more economic and emotional influences. That may be true for
some people at some moment, but it is mostly an ahistorical assumption
that deserves further historical scrutiny.

I was drawn initially to this topic by the body of historical work that
has detailed how law directed the nation's development in the nineteenth
century. It is no secret that laws in the United States facilitated certain
sorts of endeavors while they disadvantaged others. Through law, the
country created and recreated itself in a particular vision. Although this
theme has been well explored for the nineteenth century, it has been less
examined for the years that followed, especially once one descends from
the realm of federal constitutional law. Just how law has shaped the nation's development in our own century, who has done that shaping, and
what it has meant for governance, ideas of law, and people's lives is a
story only beginning to be unraveled.

I owe a great debt to Stuart Bruchey, whose guidance and encouragement from the earliest stages of this work have been unerring and un-
flagging. I am similarly indebted to Eric Johnson for everything from
general inspiration to methodological criticism. James Shenton and Sig-
mund Diamond strengthened the work through their wide-ranging discussions of approaches to historical and social inquiry. Walter Metzger,
Rosalind Rosenberg, Donald Dewey, and Paul McNulty also contributed
valuable comments. Colleagues in the History Department at the University of California, Santa Barbara, have made helpful suggestions, and a
University of California Regents Junior Faculty Fellowship supported part
of my research.

Joseph Van Nostrand and Bruce Abrams, archivists of the New York
County Clerk's Records Office, could not have been more helpful to my
research. Their knowledge of the records, their insight into New York's
legal institutions, and above all, the hospitable reception they gave me
over nearly two years made the whole endeavor possible.

Debts to others accrued in the course of my work are too numerous to
list, but some of the deepest deserve special mention. Steven Deyle,
David Mattern, Doron Ben-Atar, and Peter Johnson provided historical

insight and searching criticism on all aspects of the project. Lynn Mather, Hendrik Hartog, and Robert Gordon commented on portions of the manuscript, and their suggestions have led to important revisions. Lawrence Friedman and Joyce Sterling have given the full manuscript close readings and are directly responsible for the most substantial improvements in its content and argument. Peter Agree, Kay Scheuer, and Nancy Moore have provided solid editorial guidance. All will discover their ideas throughout the book; where flaws remain it is despite their good advice.

Family and friends have been constant sources of support. My parents, Donald and Mary Bergstrom, have been especially encouraging. The biggest debt of all, though, I owe to Debra Bergstrom, who has not only given multiple drafts incisive readings and suggested alternative lines of approach to problems but has tolerated the company of a partner engaged in the study of random violence and the intrusion of word-processing noise in her home for more years than she cares to recall. Kate's contributions have been less tangible and limited to the recent past but have been real nevertheless.

RANDOLPH E. BERGSTROM

Santa Barbara, California

COURTING DANGER

INTRODUCTION

At the end of the nineteenth century, the inhabitants of New York pioneered the now common practice of suing when injured. Why did New Yorkers take so many more injury suits to the city's Supreme Court after 1870 than before? This book approaches that central question as a matter of social as well as legal history, merging the perspectives of current historical writing with those of recent legal scholarship. It tells one story, not two, treating legal and social developments simultaneously; society was shaping its legal culture even as that culture was affecting society.

Because the hybrid sociolegal approach to injury law frames the story, its basis requires some attention. The benefits of exploring society's use of legal processes (such as suing) have been heralded for the better part of a century, ever since the eminent legal scholar and proponent of sociological jurisprudence Roscoe Pound called for research of the law in action. Pound, the legal realists, and their progeny in the field of history encouraged such exploration by showing the importance of society's influences—economic, political, demographic, and intellectual—on legal development.[1]

1. Roscoe Pound, "Law in Books and Law in Action," *American Law Review* 44 (1910): 12. Lawrence Friedman concisely captures the historiography of American law in "American Legal History: Past and Present," in Lawrence Friedman and Harry Scheiber, eds., *American Law and the Constitutional Order* (Cambridge: Harvard University, 1988), 464–73, reprinted from *The Journal of Legal Education* 34 (1984): 563–76. Michael Grossberg argues that the expanding scope of recent legal history owes to the decline of the

As recently as 1982, J. Willard Hurst reported that historians still lagged behind legal researchers from other disciplines in studying the nexus of law and society.[2] That lag has since been cut sharply, however, by the appearance of several sophisticated social histories of law that are evidence of a union between the Law and Society movement and recent historical approaches. The Law and Society, or sociolegal, perspective is an interdisciplinary approach, a conceptually expanded offspring of sociological jurisprudence, legal realism, and most directly, the work of Hurst.[3] Hurst's view that "the most creative, driving, and powerful pressures upon our law emerged from the social setting" is the point of departure for sociolegal studies, in sharp contrast to the fundamental premise of traditional, doctrinally focused legal scholarship—that law's development is best understood as a wholly intellectual phenomenon, a story of great minds speaking across time to other great minds.[4] The problem with the traditional approach, sociolegal thinkers point out, is that it is highly unlikely that law developed free of any influence from other aspects of human existence. Hurst's metaphor puts it vividly: Legal studies of this sort treat law as though it was formed in a vacuum of abstraction.

Among the recurring, distinctive elements of sociolegal research is that it inquires into the parts played by the law's users, its practitioners, and its lower-level decision makers. It also pays attention to how the law is manifested, considering its absence and its indirect effects on routine behavior as well as its more obvious presence when mobilized in lawsuits. The events precipitating legal acts—injuries, grievances, and disputes—are thus opened for examination. As the troubles that have prompted

---

legal realist-influenced "Wisconsin School" of legal history, rather than its further development. Michael Grossberg, "Social History Update: 'Fighting Faiths' and the Challenges of Legal History," *Journal of Social History* 25 (1991): 191–201.

2. J. Willard Hurst, "The State of Legal History," in Stanley Kutler and Stanley Katz, eds., *The Promise of American History: Progress and Prospects* (Baltimore, Md.: Johns Hopkins University Press, 1982), 292–305.

3. For a brief introduction to the origins, aims, and accomplishments of the Law and Society Movement, see Felice Levine, "Goose Bumps and 'The Search for Signs of Intelligent Life' in Sociolegal Studies: After Twenty-Five Years," *Law and Society Review* 24 (1990): 7–35; and Marc Galanter, "The Legal Malaise; or, Justice Observed," *Law and Society Review* 19 (1985): 537–56.

4. J. Willard Hurst, *The Growth of the American Law: The Law Makers* (Boston: Little, Brown, 1950), 11. For bibliography and comment on Hurst's work, see Robert Gordon, "Introduction: J. Willard Hurst and the Common Law Tradition in American Legal Historiography," *Law and Society Review* 10 (1975–76): 9–55; and Harry Scheiber, "Public Economic Policy and the American Legal System: Historical Perspectives," *Wisconsin Law Review* 1980 (1980): 1159–89.

people to resort to the legal system are investigated, so too are the outcomes of the legal process—not only the immediate consequences of a legal event but its wider effects over time as well.

Those engaged in the social study of law are not satisfied with extrapolating a universal social meaning of law from the doctrinal assertions of judges.[5] They go beyond such pronouncements to seek the public's symbolic readings and perceptions of law and gauge the intensity of popular involvement with it. Law's social meaning is typically diverse rather than uniformly or consensually held, with different groups ascribing different significance to legal rules and process.

Trends in recent historical work complement those of the Law and Society movement. History has increasingly made ordinary people and everyday events central to its story. It has strived to learn how people lived, how they interacted, and how they assigned meaning to those interactions and the events surrounding them. In assessing how people interacted, historians are investigating their institutions—family and community, marketplace and workplace, formal and informal associations. Telling the story of society's institutions is nothing new; what has changed is the perspective. The less powerful are no longer assumed to have accepted the way society was structured for them by their dominant neighbors; they are no longer seen only as acted upon. As historian Clarke Chambers puts it, historians are working "to understand the ways in which populations . . . used institutions for their own ends."[6]

New historical approaches examine the array of subcultures that existed within the larger society, looking at how their distinctive needs, preferences, and practices meshed or clashed with those of other groups. They recognize that subcultures arose from different foundations, including economic (as broadly as class or as narrowly as occupational), geographical, gender, ethnic, and religious, and that people lived as part of more than one group at a time. The idea of a uniform and consensual American society has been supplanted by the idea of a multitude of societies, often

5. Galanter, "Legal Malaise," 543–49; and Stewart Macaulay, "Law and the Behavioral Sciences: Is there Any There There?" *Law and Policy* 6 (1984): 150–56. For a critique of social-legal studies suggesting that they have not moved far enough from the jurisprudential approach they reacted against, see Richard Abel, "Redirecting Social Studies of Law, *Law and Society Review* 14 (1980): 805–29. Critical Legal Studies scholarship has provided much of the impetus for closer attention to the meanings of law. See Robert Gordon, "Critical Legal Histories," *Standford Law Review* 36 (1984): 57–126; and David Trubek, "Where the Action Is: Critical Legal Studies and Empiricism," *Stanford Law Review* 36 (1984): 575–622.

6. Clarke Chambers, "Toward a Redefinition of Welfare History," *Journal of American History* 73 (1986): 420.

at odds over just what the nation's rules should be. This understanding makes writing the history of law an infinitely more complicated task; instead of presenting rules as "society's," the historian must dig deeper to find precisely whose rules they were and what legitimacy they carried for the rest of the population.

That development fits nicely with one of the great lessons of sociolegal research: that law differs little from other forms of policy. Legal historians have become more amenable to this way of thinking, discerning social division and contest where legal precepts had once been thought consensual (or contested only over matters of intellectual rigor, such as logic or consistency).[7] Understanding law as policy, as the play of interests, introduces the issue of power into its history.

Historians are considering power in policy-making in increasingly sophisticated ways, recognizing its influence upon law not only as blatant force or insidious manipulation but in more subtle forms. When those shaping legal development believed that what they were framing was the product of cool reason and universally shared principles rather than of their own norms or the interests of only a segment of society, more than rhetorical style was at stake. To the extent that others shared their belief, the framers won legitimacy and allegiance; they exerted power.

Historians and sociolegal scholars attend not only to the distribution of power but to how participants in legal processes utilized the power at their disposal. People had options and made choices; the possession of power did not compel its use toward any particular ends. For example, judges, the most visible policy makers and implementers in this book, upon learning through legislation and litigation that their ideas were not universally shared, could have yielded to the will of the community. Or they could have become rigidly defensive of their own views. The outcome was not inevitable. Deduction cannot tell us how people actually responded; close research is the only way of finding out.

My story of injury and law in New York at the end of the nineteenth century relies upon these recent scholarly developments. Current concerns, too, impose, themselves, but I have been vigilant against the danger of reading the present into the past or "ransacking the period for

7. Michael Grossberg, citing the influence of two decades of law and society research, notes that historians now think about the law " as an arena of conflict in which a variety of lay people and professionals contest its construction and use." "Social History Update," 195.

forerunners.''[8] Yet Marc Bloch's admonition to historians to know their own times ultimately prevails.[9] Ideas about injury and law today suggest interesting avenues of inquiry into past events.

That a "litigation explosion" plagues late twentieth-century America, a product (or progenitor?) of our "litigious society," is an idea that has wide currency. Culpability for this explosion is typically assigned to the tort suit. Many believe that the resort to the courts has become excessive and socially destructive.

Thoughtful observers have discredited the litigation-explosion thesis.[10] Yet the perception of explosion persists. The current gap between imagined and actual trends in court use suggests that historians should pay attention to perceived as well as real escalation in past court use. It suggests that for at least an influential minority of Americans, change in court use has been a cause for inordinate concern. That concern is evidence of the historical meaning of litigation. Understanding how people viewed the courts helps explain why they turned to or away from the courts over time.

Other corollaries of the current explosion thesis suggest avenues of historical analysis, especially the implication that there was once a golden age when tort law worked better than today and fostered, as a result, a less contentious society. That idea declares that law worked better when it discouraged legal actions, presumes that less court use signals social harmony, and assigns causality to law. It assumes that legal rules determined social relations. It says nothing about the distribution of the economic consequences of injuries during less contentious times, assuming either that such distribution remained constant whether there were many or few injury suits, or that such distribution does not matter. These are issues that history can help settle.

Sociolegal historians have made the field of injury law especially fertile since the mid-1970s. Lawrence Friedman's work has led thinking

8. E. P. Thompson, *The Making of the English Working Class* (New York: Vintage, 1964), 20.

9. Marc Bloch, *The Historian's Craft* (New York: Vintage, 1971 [1946]), 35.

10. For reasoned analyses of recent trends in court use and responses to the assertion that the rise is excessive, see Marc Galanter, "Reading the Landscape of Disputes: What We Know and Don't Know (and Think We Know) about Our Allegedly Contentious and Litigious Society," *UCLA Law Review* 31 (1983): 4–71; Lawrence Friedman, *Total Justice* (New York: Russell Sage, 1986); David Engel, "The Oven Bird's Song: Insiders, Outsiders, and Personal Injuries in an American Community," *Law and Society Review* 18 (1984): 551–82; and Jethro Lieberman, *The Litigious Society* (New York: Basic Books, 1981).

about nineteenth-century injury law. Friedman suggests in his *History of American Law* that injury suits were on the increase for two primary reasons: the number of injuries in urban, industrial, turn-of-the-century America was much higher than in earlier America; and prohibitive tort rules, established by judges in the mid-nineteenth century, were beginning to erode at the end. Friedman's explanation recognizes that social, economic, and legal trends affected one another and that the interaction of all these currents affected the course of injury law.[11]

In the middle of the nineteenth century, Friedman argues, judges shifted basic rules of liability to protect economically promising but physically dangerous activities. The change was most evident in shielding employers from work-accident liability through the invention of the fellow-servant and assumption-of-risk rules. Just as the rules beneficial to enterprise rose at mid-century, they declined at the turn of the new century in the face of "a conspiracy in which juries, judges . . . , and legislatures all joined in."[12] They did not disappear as abruptly as they had appeared, but their gradual demise encouraged a rise in injury suits. Injury law's prohibitive rules were short-lived, generated by and succumbing to socioeconomic pressure.

Others have plotted the historical path of injury law along different vectors.[13] Gary Schwartz's interpretation, which rejects the influence of

11. Lawrence Friedman and Jack Ladinsky, "Social Change and the Law of Industrial Accidents," *Columbia Law Review* 67 (1967): 50–82; Lawrence Friedman, *A History of American Law* (New York: Simon and Schuster, 1973); and Friedman, *Total Justice*.

12. Friedman, *History of American Law*, 423.

13. For four prominent alternatives to the sociolegal interpretation, see G. Edward White, *Tort Law in America* (New York: Oxford University Press, 1980); Morton Horwitz, *The Transformation of American Law, 1780–1860* (Cambridge: Harvard University Press, 1977), 203–10; Richard Posner, "A Theory of Negligence," *Journal of Legal Studies* 1 (1972): 29–96, and William Landes and Richard Posner, "The Positive Economic Theory of Tort Law," *Georgia Law Review* 15 (1981): 851–924; and Richard Epstein, "The Historical Origins and Economic Structure of Workers' Compensation Law," *Georgia Law Review* 16 (1982): 775–819.

White attributes end-of-the-century change in injury law to an intellectual shift in the upper reaches of the legal hierarchy. Horwitz believes the primary players came from those strata, but this crucial transformation occurs before mid-century and is moved by the legal elite's ideological preference to make law serve the interests of the rising business class. Posner thinks nineteenth-century judges (again, appellate) created and interpreted negligence rules to maximize social efficiency throughout the period. Epstein, too, finds "efficient," "moral" law in the nineteenth century, but in the era of strict liability rather than in negligence. Epstein reads the strict liability era just the opposite of Horwitz, characterizing it as prohibiting rather than enabling injury compensation, at least for workers. By implication, the move to negligence-based liability represented liberalization of the rules to Epstein.

socioeconomic forces, is the most notable. Opposing what he calls Friedman's "subsidy thesis," Schwartz argues that nineteenth-century law
was not protective of business enterprise or unduly prohibitive to injury
victims. In fact, excepting work injuries, it "tended to be generous in affirming the tort liabilities of emerging industry."[14] In Schwartz's vision,
injury law promoted no social or economic goal other than justice, judges
applied the law justly across the period, rules were not oppressive, and no
dramatic legal change transpired that could have impelled a rapid rise in
injury suits.[15]

Dispute over the course of injury-liability rules and the influence of socioeconomic developments upon them has encouraged researchers to
turn, as I have done, to court docket (or caseload) analysis for answers.
This approach asks what sorts of cases people took to courts, how those
cases were decided, and how the patterns changed over time. Trial-court
caseload studies have flourished since the mid-1970s and have been gaining special attention of late.[16]

When I began my research, only Robert Silverman had employed the
court docket approach to explain developments in injury law in the era.
His study of Boston trial courts between 1880 and 1900 concludes as
Friedman hypothesized in the *History of American Law* that injury suits
increased because the changing urban environment introduced new dangers into the lives of Bostonians, which in turn caused more injuries.[17] At
least 3 more such projects, started about the same time, however, apply
this approach to the problem addressed here, the use of trial courts in instances of injury in the late nineteenth century. Friedman and Thomas
Russell, pursuing Friedman's theories about the relationship between social change and accident law in the courts of Alameda County, California,

14. Gary Schwartz, "The Character of Early American Tort Law," *UCLA Law Review*
36 (1989): 641, 664–65.

15. Gary Schwartz, "Tort Law and the Economy in Nineteenth-Century America: A
Reinterpretation," *Yale Law Journal* 90 (1981): 1717–75; Gary Schwartz and Edwin Perkins, "Tort Law and Business Enterprise in Nineteenth-Century America," *Essays in Economic and Business History* 3 (1984): 218–30; and Schwartz, "Character of Early
American Tort Law."

16. The best indicator of this is the recent special issue of *Law and Society Review,*
"Longitudinal Studies of Trial Courts," ed. Frank Munger. It is a valuable starting point
for overviews of the history and accomplishments of the caseload study approach and an
excellent resource for considering its theoretical aspects. *Law and Society Review* 24, no.
2 (1990): 211–643. See especially the editor's introduction, Frank Munger, "Trial Courts
and Social Change: The Evolution of a Field of Study," *Law and Society Review* 24 (1990):
217–26.

17. Robert Silverman, *Law and Urban Growth: Civil Litigation in the Boston Trial
Courts, 1880–1900* (Princeton, N.J.: Princeton University Press, 1981).

provide a portrait of personal-injury suits and their outcomes between 1880 and 1910 that affirms the prohibitive character of the law in those years, contrary to Schwartz's assertions. Frank Munger's work on injury litigation in West Virginia from 1870 to 1940 discovers a general stability of injury-litigation rates over time amid a complex of contrasting trends for different types of defendants. Nancy Reichman, Joyce Sterling, and Patricia Wellinger explore Denver's injury-litigation suits between 1880 and 1917 and chronicle how social change affected changes in legal rules.[18]

This story of New Yorkers' uses of injury law at the turn of the century is written from the perspective of those using the law but also inquires into the contribution made by the agents of the courts. It asks what people sought in using the law and what they got. While focusing on lawsuits, it recognizes that this formal mobilization of the law was only one alternative for injury victims and an extraordinary one at that. It assesses the contribution of many factors to the creation and outcome of cases and examines the wider consequences of the outcomes on the lives of the injured and injurers and on the society. It looks at the conflicting visions of laws and duties different groups held and how those views contributed to the making and the determination of injury suits.

Finally, it considers the courtroom as a site where private lives enter the public arena. New York City's Supreme Court was a public forum, a meeting ground for the city's many social groups. By staking out the courtroom, we witness hundreds of individual contests, where private lives are opened to us for a moment through their recourse to a public institution. The contests were essentially battles over the policy that

18. Lawrence Friedman, "Civil Wrongs: Personal Injury Law in the Late 19th Century," *American Bar Foundation Research Journal* 1987 (1987): 351–78; Lawrence Friedman and Thomas Russell, "More Civil Wrongs: Personal Injury Litigation, 1901–1910," *American Journal of Legal History* 34 (1990): 295–314; Frank Munger, "Social Change and Tort Litigation: Industrialization, Accidents, and Trial Courts in Southern West Virginia, 1872 to 1940," *Buffalo Law Review* 36 (1987): 75–118; Nancy Reichman, Joyce Sterling, and Patricia Wellinger, "The Social Construction of Duty," paper presented at the 1988 Annual Meeting of the Law and Society Association Vail, Colorado; Nancy Reichman and Joyce Sterling "Constructing Order in the Frontier: The Case of the Missing Defendants," paper presented at the 1990 Annual Meeting of the Law and Society Association, Berkeley, California. Wayne McIntosh also reports statistics on injury suits as part of his study of civil litigation in St. Louis, in "A State Court's Clientele: Exploring the Strategy of Trial Litigation," *Law and Society Review* 19 (1985): 421–47; and Wayne McIntosh, *The Appeal of Civil Law: A Political-Economic Analysis of Litigation* (Urbana: University of Illinois Press, 1990).

governed the specific circumstances of each injury. This was the law in action.[19]

That is not to say that courts were the primary social institutions in New Yorkers' lives. At most times, for most people, courts sat on the periphery of society, resorted to only when more familiar social channels failed to deliver desired results. But in the period of this story, increasing use of New York's Supreme Court by the injured suggests that the court became a less peripheral social institution.

What is new about this story are the agents of change. Judges in the high courts and other legal luminaries have been given ample credit for their role in reshaping injury law. But others contributed to injury law's development—trial judges, lawyers, juries, and the injured themselves.

This book taps the previously unused cases of the Supreme Court for the City and County of New York at three intervals, 1870, 1890, and 1910.[20] I use one batch of the court's cases, a 10-percent sample of all cases, to show the trends in tort suits relative to the court's other sorts of suits. That cross-section of all the court's work is featured in Tables 1–3. I use a second batch, consisting of every injury case, to draw a more detailed picture of tort suits. It, or subsets of it, fill the columns of Tables 4–12. Chapter 1 provides this basic information.

Chapter 2 presents New York's population dynamics, then turns to a discussion of changes in the dangers and injuries that New Yorkers faced. Chapters 3, 4, and 5 probe the "internal" history of the legal process to show how changes occurred in rules and procedure and how those affected injury victims who used the court. The trial court's transcripts of tort cases provide much information on the process and on the character and predilections of the participants.

The sixth chapter looks at the problem faced by the injured in the aftermath of accidents. I study their economic plight relative to the sources of sustenance available to them, with lawsuits as one economic alternative. The book's concluding chapter opens by considering the contribution of the ideas of the injured to the rise in lawsuits. In the end, after following the story from the streets, houses, and workplaces of New York

19. I raise the public and meeting-place attributes of the courtroom to suggest its potential contribution to a sociopolitical synthesis. See Thomas Bender, "Wholes and Parts: The Need for Synthesis in American History," *Journal of American History* 73 (1986): 120–36; and Theodore Rabb, "Toward the Future: Coherence, Synthesis, and Quality in History," *Journal of Interdisciplinary History* 12 (1981): 315–32.

20. All tables in the book report these cases and use these dates unless otherwise noted.

City to the city's law offices and County Court House, that is where we wind up, in the thought processes of the injury victims.

The story of how New Yorkers changed their approach to coping with injury at the end of the nineteenth century is more than a history of law. It is a story of life in all its intricacy. It is as much a social, economic, and cultural history as a legal one. It is at the same time individual and institutional history, from the bottom up and the top down.

1. COURT USE, 1870–1910

Mary Isaacs rode the horsedrawn streetcars up and down the east side of New York, to work, to shop for her household, and to visit her married children. One November night in 1865 she boarded the Third Avenue Railroad's car with her daughter-in-law, bound along the Bowery for Spring Street. She recounts what happened next:

> I asked the conductor to put me out at the corner of Spring Street, and he said he would; . . . I rang the bell . . . and [rang it] again . . . and I got up and went to the door; and stood on the platform, and said to the conductor, "Now please stop the car." He said, "the car is stopped enough," and I said, "I will not get out until you have made a full stop to your car." He made me no answer, and took me by the shoulder and threw me out, and I fell on the pavement and broke my leg. I said, "Oh my God! My leg is broke; take the number of the car."[1]

The fracture was multiple, a bad break in more ways than one. It laid Isaacs up in a hospital bed for two months. The pain must have been excruciating, compounded as it was by anxiety for her family. Most of Isaac's eight children were still at home, dependent on her for their sustenance. So was her husband: He had been wounded in the Civil War and

1. *Mary Isaacs* v. *Third Avenue Railroad Company,* 1870 Number T96, Judgments of the Supreme Court for the County and City of New York, First Division, Archives of the County Clerk and Clerk of the Supreme Court, County of New York, New York (hereafter, "NYC Supreme Court").

had since been unable to "get a living" for the family. With Mary bed-ridden, he was forced back to work, scrambling to find odd jobs. Despite the severity of her injury, she did not stay down long and was soon back at her nursing work. But in the years that followed she repeatedly suffered periods of disabling pain in her leg, which incapacitated her for two to three weeks at a time.

Isaacs sued the Third Avenue Railroad Company for the suffering, the lost income, and the medical costs that resulted from the injury. Her suit went to trial in 1870 before Judge George Barnard in New York City's Supreme Court. Against Isaacs's version of the story, the streetcar company asserted that she got off the moving car of her own volition (how, the company's attorneys asked, could the conductor who was a small man have thrown Isaacs, "a large woman"?) and injured herself in the process. The company covered all contingencies by adding that even if their opponent's story was accepted, the fault was not theirs but the conductor's for acting as he did. The jury was not persuaded by the company's case and awarded Isaacs $3,500.[2]

Mary Isaacs's response to injury—to seek compensation through the courts—is the heart of this story. Few of her contemporaries in 1870 chose that response. In that year, in all New York City, only 13 people took personal-injury suits to the city Supreme Court. But more and more New Yorkers followed Isaacs's example over the next forty years. In 1910, those frequenting Manhattan were moved to use the court 595 times to settle their injury claims. (Although the bulk of cases involved New York City residents injured in New York, many situations could present the occasion for bringing suit in the city's court, as discussed below.) The change could hardly have been more dramatic: Over the forty-year span, the frequency with which the people of New York took injuries to the court increased 4,500 percent. That constitutes a "tort explosion" by anyone's standards.

Why did ever-increasing numbers of people resort to the court seeking redress for their injuries? An answer requires first a thorough understanding of how the city used the court and how that overall use changed. Toward that end, this chapter compares the trajectory over time of injury suits to other types of suits that New Yorkers took to the Supreme Court.

---

2. *Isaacs* v. *Third Avenue Railroad*. This was at least the third trial of the case; at its first in January 1867, a jury awarded Mary Isaacs $5,000, only to be overridden by the appellate term. "Another Action for Damages against a Railroad Company," *New York Times*, 14 November 1867 p. 3.

It then analyzes the rise in injury suits, looking at the circumstances that precipitated them. In the course of introducing the dimensions of the change in injury suits, this initial analysis proves that the increase in injury suits was not the product of a general rise in litigiousness.

Before presenting the basic findings, I must briefly clarify what the figures represent and where they come from. I have tracked change across four decades by plying two sets of data that chronicle the cases brought to a trial court, the Supreme Court for the City and County of New York. One set consists of a 10-percent sample of all the cases judged in the court at three intervals, 1870, 1890, and 1910. The other comprises all the tort cases that people took to the Supreme Court in those three years. The latter data provide information on the suitors, attorneys, judges, and the outcomes of the suits.

The day-to-day use of the legal system and the changes that stemmed from it are the historical phenomena this book seeks to explain. Previous court-use studies have proven the value of this approach.[3] They have probed the routine functioning of the legal system, showing the legal change discernible only with a view of a court's work over an extended period. From this perspective we discover obscure and incremental change. But while never as dramatic as the change wrought by landmark decisions, the gradual change revealed by attention to lower courts was just as formative in the making of society's laws.

The trial court has always been important as the point of popular entry to the legal system. In New York City, contrary to typical state court nomenclature, the Supreme Court was the primary court of initial jurisdiction, while the highest state court was the Court of Appeals. Amid other civil courts in the city, vestiges of colonial rule or arbiters of commercial concerns, the Supreme Court was the local representative of the uniform statewide civil justice system that the state's 1846 constitution created.[4]

3. See discussion of court-use studies in the Introduction.
4. The other civil courts in New York included the city Court of Common Pleas, which was the Mayor's Court of English origin, renamed and staffed with full-time judges in the 1820s; the city Marine Court, which had dispensed justice in maritime, mostly business, matters since the beginning of the nineteenth century; and the Superior Court, which in the mid-nineteenth century was "established as a commercial tribunal . . . [after] it became obvious that there should be a commercial tribunal in the city for the trial of mercantile causes" of all sorts, not limited to maritime business ("The Lawyers of New York," unattributed, circa 1865, Charles Daly Papers, Box 15, Scrapbook, New York Public Library). On the city courts, see Henry W. Scott, *The Courts of the State of New York; Their History, Development and Jurisdiction Embracing a Complete History of All the Courts . . . (New York: Wilson, 1909).*

The court's jurisdiction was not limited to particular classes of matters, nor did it have any thresholds or ceilings on the dollar value of claims it could decide. In addition to its trial docket, it also convened an appellate term (by 1890, an appellate division), which served as the intermediate appeals court for cases heard at the trial term and in the city's other courts.

New Yorkers whose accidents involved citizens or corporations from other states could elect to sue in the Federal District Court, and "foreign" defendants could remove to the federal court if sued in New York courts. The federal court's part in New York's injury litigation, therefore, requires some comment, because if the federal court experienced a very different pattern of use, to generalize about injury litigation in New York from the Supreme Court's work would be inaccurate.

Evidence suggests that the pattern of New Yorkers' federal cases should not alter conclusions based upon the city Supreme Court's work. First, most of the sorts of injuries New Yorkers sued over were wholly "domestic," outside the bounds of the federal court's diversity jurisdiction. That is, because in most instances both the accident victim and the injurer were New York residents, their case had no entry to federal court. Second, even when a prominent source of injury suit (such as transportation) fell into federal court bounds, the Supreme Court nevertheless drew many of them (out-of-state railroad, ferry, and steamship passenger suits). Edward Purcell has found that at the end of the nineteenth century, corporations generally found removal to federal courts favorable to their interests.[5] But in New York, neither injured nor defendant turned automatically to the federal court in such cases, indicating that neither found

---

The fact that the Supreme Court was one of part of the civil justice system in New York rather than its whole is important. Richard Lempert and Stephen Daniels have warned scholars to heed differences between different levels of trial courts and not assume that all experienced the same trends. Richard Lempert, "More Tales of Two Courts: Exploring Changes in the 'Dispute Resolution Function' of Trial Courts," *Law and Society Review* 13 (1978–79): 91–138; Stephen Daniels, "Ladders and Bushes: The Problem of Caseloads and Studying Court Activities over Time," *American Bar Foundation Research Journal* 1984 (1984): 751–95; and Stephen Daniels, "Continuity and Change in Patterns of Case Handling, A Study of Two Rural Counties," *Law and Society Review* 19 (1985): 384–86. The justification for focusing on the city Supreme Court in light of this is twofold. First, since its jurisdiction was general and unbounded, it provides the most unrestricted body of litigation in the city; and second, its designation as a state court of record meant that its full output of judgment rolls was preserved, while that of the other city courts, except the Superior, was not.

5. Edward A. Purcell, Jr., *Litigation and Inequality: Federal Diversity Jurisdiction in Industrial America, 1870–1948* (New York: Oxford University Press, 1992). $\sqrt{}$

an overpowering advantage in federal doctrine, procedure, or judicial predisposition that would remove a whole category of cases from the Supreme Court.

A third point in support, not compelling but suggestive, is the absence from the contemporary press, legal periodicals, lectures, treatises, and bar-association reports of any mention about state-federal "jurisdiction shopping" in New York, or about stark differences in the administration of tort law that would foster it. Lawyers, judges, and other commentators scrutinized the law at the turn of the century and readily reported any tendency in the administration of justice that displeased them, but they did not notice any problem of this sort.

Ultimately, the only way to know how federal courts' patterns of litigation fit into the picture is to chart their business. This is what Lawrence Friedman did in his study of injury litigation in turn-of-the-century Alameda County, California, investigating federal trial-court business alongside the work of state courts. He found the federal cases to be quite similar to the local court's in topic, disposition, and recoveries. Purcell's exploration of diversity jurisdiction shows no great disjunction between what the federal and state courts were doing. The litigation system of the time benefited sued corporations who removed their cases to federal courts, he found, but the advantage was diminished in the Northeast.[6] In short, while research is needed before we can know conclusively, no extant evidence suggests that the federal court in New York had a remarkably different experience with injury law than the city's court.

As might be expected given the character of the city it served, the New York City Supreme Court adjudicated disputes that emanated from every imaginable human interaction. Cases sprang from battles with intimates and from chance meetings with strangers, from connubial conflicts and from streetcar collisions. From every quarter, from every class, the city's populace brought disputes to the court.

The tables that follow chart the changes in the types of injuries New Yorkers took to the Supreme Court across the forty years. The first tables present data on all the cases brought to the court. These highlight the dramatic rise in injury suits compared to trends in the other types of suits (such as debt cases) that were part of the court's business, establishing that the rise in injury suits was not simply the product of a general increase in litigiousness.

6. Friedman, "Civil Wrongs," 351–78; and Friedman and Russell, "More Civil Wrongs"; and Purcell, *Litigation and Inequality.*

TABLE I
TABLE I

Cases by issue of law: Number of cases and percentage of total caseload

Issue	1870		1890		1910	
	n	%	n	%	n	%
Debt and contract	498	97.4	431	91.1	243	39.5
Real property	0	0	1	0.2	1	0.2
Corporation and partnership	2	0.4	2	0.4	2	0.4
Torts	5	1.0	22	4.6	70	11.3
Public law (City)	3	0.6	12	2.5	295	47.9
Family and estate	1	0.2	5	1.0	1	0.2
Other	2	0.4	1	0.2	3	0.5
Total	511	100	474	100	615	100

Source: Data drawn from Judgments, New York County Clerk Office of Old Records. Categories borrowed from Robert Kagan et al., "Business of State Supreme Courts," *Stanford Law Review* 30 (1977–78) 133–35.

n = number of cases (10-percent sample of all suits before the court)

The next tables move from viewing the trend in injury suits within the larger pattern of litigation to detailing the component developments within the trend. As was true for all torts, personal-injury suits from every kind of cause were on the increase, though some categories of accidents—work, traffic, and sidewalk-roadway, most notably—rose more sharply than others. Later tables examine trends within each category of accident, providing the information with which to assess the role of larger forces—industrialization, most notably—in the rise of injury suits.

Table I presents a breakdown by category of all the cases New Yorkers took to the city's Supreme Court.[7] While claims spilled into all categories, they concentrated more in some than in others. These areas of concentration changed over time; the mix of cases New Yorkers brought to the court was quite different in 1910 from what it had been in 1870. Debt and contract cases, which nearly filled the court's docket in 1870, com-

7. To enable comparison of the findings here with previous and future research, I employ the schema Kagan and colleagues used to categorize their state supreme courts studies. They group cases according to the following headings: debt and contract (including mortgages, promissory notes, sales contracts, insurance), real property (land ownership and use), corporations and partnerships, torts (negligent injuries, property damage, defamation), family and estates (divorce, trusts, wills), and public law (taxes, elections, land condemnation). Robert Kagan, Bliss Cartwright, Lawrence Friedman, and Stanton Wheeler, "The Business of State Supreme Courts, 1870–1970", *Stanford Law Review* 30 (1977–78): 121–56, and "The Evolution of State Supreme Courts," *Michigan Law Review* 76 (1978): 961–1005.

TABLE 2

Contested cases by issue of law: number and percentage of all contested cases

Issue	1870		1890		1910	
	n	*%*	*n*	*%*	*n*	*%*
Debt and contract	110	93.3	82	71.9	91	53.2
Real property	0	0	0	0	1	0.6
Corporation and partnership	2	1.7	2	1.8	2	1.2
Torts	5	4.2	21	18.4	70	40.9
Public law	0	0	4	3.5	6	3.6
Family and estate	1	0.8	5	4.4	1	0.6
Total	118	100	114	100	171	100

Source: See Table 1.

prised less than half of its work by 1910. In sharp contrast, public law issues, arising from acts of governance, provided less than 1 percent of the court's cases in 1870 but generated almost half of the suits by 1910. In the midst of these shifts, tort suits' portion grew steadily, from 1 percent to 11 percent of the total.

On the surface, the change was dramatic. But the two chief components of the change, the rise in public lawsuits and the fall in debt and contract cases, were not as significant as numbers make them appear. For example, of the 295 public law cases in the 1910 sample, 280 were initiated by the city to collect property taxes. Not one of these 280 was contested; no defendant ever showed up to dispute her or his tax charge.[8] The court's work in these cases was minimal. It amounted to validating the debts by noting the defendant's defaults. This is an important point; not all cases made equivalent demands on the court. As those now refining studies of court dockets point out, claims or cases cannot be treated as having equal weight. Since one of the purposes of studying popular use of courts is to gauge the changing social pressures upon the courts by tracking changes in their caseloads, it is important to distinguish the cases where the court actually resolved disputes from those where the disputes effectively resolved themselves.

Examining the city court's work by considering only contested cases, in which the defendant responded to the plaintiff's complaint, reveals a very different distribution of lawsuits. In Table 2, the sharp growth in public law cases of Table 1 disappears, as do the overwhelming majority

8. In going through all the cases I turned up about 5 contested tax cases, but none fell within the 10-percent sample.

of debt and contract cases. A sizable body of contested debt and contract cases remains, though, which showed only a slight decline over the forty years. The picture of cases actually contested before the court is one of continuity in public law and debt and contract cases. That is a significantly different portrait from the one painted by looking at all cases, contested or not. Winnowing away the uncontested cases also magnifies the importance of the growth in tort suits. Though the number of contested debt and contract suits fell only slightly, they shrank significantly as a portion of the court's contested cases because contested tort issues rose so sharply. In contrast to debt suits, defendants fought every tort in the sample.

Comparing contested cases with uncontested highlights the changes that occurred in the functions that the court performed at the time that injury suits were multiplying. From the research of Friedman and Percival into the work of Alameda and San Benito County, California, courts, we might have anticipated increases in routine use of New York's court. There, although contract and property disputes declined after 1890 (more evidently after 1910), as they did in 1890 and 1910 in New York, in the California trial courts, routine administration cases rose (though again the trend is somewhat ambivalent before 1910).[9] In the New York court, just the opposite was happening at the turn of the century. Businessmen stopped turning to the court for routine debt service. Creditors brought fewer and fewer "rubber stamp" debt cases, those in which they anticipated no opposition but sought the power of the state behind their pursuit of repayment. At the very least, it is clear that contrary to expectations, there was no uniform trend toward routine use of the Supreme Court, coursing ever upward as society grew more complex and rigorously legalistic.

When a group stopped using the courts routinely, they did not necessarily stop using the courts altogether. While the court's administrative role of sanctioning recovery of debts for businessmen dwindled toward

9. Lawrence Friedman and Robert Percival, "A Tale of Two Courts: Litigation in Alameda and San Benito Counties," *Law and Society Review* 10 (1975–76): 267–301. Perhaps the difference in findings is explained by the longer span of time that Friedman and Percival studied. Following the business of the New York City court to 1970 might uncover a trend of routinization akin to that discovered in the California courts. Or the difference might lie in the nature of the records examined. The "civil casefiles" of the California county courts may be a more comprehensive heading than the "civil judgments" file of the New York County court, which does not include issues filed solely as "writs." Including this category, which comprised routine administrative tasks, might have shown greater similarity in the use of the two states' trial courts.

TABLE 3
Contested cases as percent of all cases

	1870	*1890*	*1910*
Contested cases as percent of all cases	23.1%	24.0%	27.8%
Contested cases except torts as percent of all cases	22.2%	20.0%	16.4%

Source: See Table 1.

insignificance, businessmen still needed the judiciary. Creditors continued to look to the court to settle their more intricate, irresolvable debt and contact disputes. In New York, businessmen did not—could not—turn entirely from the courts, no matter how vociferously they decried the system's inefficiencies. Contrary again to what the routinization thesis would lead one to expect, it was the court's work resolving disputes that would not resolve themselves that merchants continued to require.

The increase in tort suits took place in this court context. The court's work was in large part administrative but was becoming more adjudicative, as Table 3 reveals. The move to more adjudicative tasks was due wholly to the increasing number of tort suits being filed. Tort suits excepted, the court's work in resolving contested cases was falling. Of course, the decline in suits in other categories cannot be considered apart from the rise in torts, because it could have been that increase and the incumbent pressure it placed on the system that encouraged those with debt and contract disputes to look elsewhere for solution.

The jump in injury suits was not the whole but was the most dynamic part of the rise in torts in the New York court. Table 4 moves to the larger tort database, which includes every tort judged in the city Supreme Court in the years 1870, 1890, and 1910, to present the trend in injury suits.

While people took more of every form of tort suit to the court, personal-injury suits grew by far the fastest. Injury suits had not been the majority of torts in 1870, comprising only 41 percent of torts then. Their escalation to 82 percent in 1910 was indeed dynamic, considering that their portion among torts doubled even as the other categories of tort were increasing. Property-damage claims rose over time and in proportion to the rest of the court's caseload but declined in the portion of tort cases they represented. The populace increased its filing of intentional tort suits—such as assaults, libels and slanders, false arrests—as well, to

TABLE 4

Tort cases by category: number, percentage of torts, and percentage of all cases

Issue	1870			1890			1910		
	n	% tort	% all	n	% tort	% all	n	% tort	% all
All personal injuries	13	40.7	0.3	112	66.3	2.4	595	81.7	9.7
Malpractice	0	0	0	1	0.6	<.1	8	1.1	0.1
Other personal injury	11	34.4	0.2	110	65.1	2.2	573	78.7	9.4
Personal injury and property damage*	2	6.3	<.1	1	0.6	<.1	14	1.9	0.2
All property damage	16	50.1	0.3	15	8.9	0.3	37	5.1	0.6
Property damage only	14	43.8	0.3	14	8.3	0.3	23	3.2	0.4
Personal injury and property damage*	2	6.3	<.1	1	0.6	<.1	14	1.9	0.2
All intentional torts	5	15.7	0.1	43	25.5	0.8	110	15.0	1.8
Assault	2	6.3	<.1	13	7.7	0.3	19	2.6	0.3
False arrest and malicious prosecution	1	3.1	<.1	12	7.1	0.2	32	4.4	0.5
Defamation	2	6.3	<.1	9	5.3	0.2	41	5.6	0.7
Breach of marriage promise	0	0	0	1	0.6	<.1	12	1.6	0.2
Other intentional	0	0	0	8	4.7	0.2	6	0.8	0.1
Total torts:	32	100	0.6	169	100	3.6	728	100	11.8
Total all cases:	5,102			4,748			6,144		

Source: Data drawn from manuscript Judgments, Archives of the County Clerk of New York County (Division of Old Records).

* = Cases asking compensation for both personal injury and property damage are included in both categories.

TABLE 5

Personal injury cases by type of cause: number and percentage of all personal-injury cases

Issue	1870		1890		1910	
	n	%	n	%	n	%
Work	—	—	24	21.4	160	26.8
Traffic	1	7.7	8	7.2	114	19.2
Railroads	—	—	10	8.9	19	3.2
Streetcars	5	38.4	29	25.9	92	15.4
Bad roads and sidewalks	1	7.7	16	14.3	111	18.7
Buildings	3	23.1	15	13.4	61	10.3
Other causes	3	23.1	10	8.9	38	6.4
Total	13	100	112	100	595	100

Source: See Table 4.

110 in 1910, setting the same pace of increase as the tort category as a whole but not matching the pace of growth in injury suits.

That, in a nutshell, was the nature of the change in lawsuits that New Yorkers took to the city court at the turn of the century. The most salient point was that change was not general to all kinds of disputes; the swelling of injury suits was not merely riding a larger wave of litigiousness. The increase came as other causes, even related ones such as property damage, grew less sharply, remained stable, or declined as generators of lawsuits.

Clearly, the tort explosion at the turn of the century was essentially an explosion of personal-injury suits. Personal injuries encompassed an array of very different sorts of accidents. Which prompted lawsuits, and when? Table 5 categorizes personal-injury suits at the three points in time by the type of activities that caused the injuries.

Some of the findings are not surprising. Railroad and streetcar injuries (though streetcars were all horsedrawn until after 1890) and industrial casualties fit our general idea of the dangers that lurked in the late-nineteenth-century American landscape. It is well known that the machine age delivered progress only at a cost assessed in flesh. As the cost mounted, the standard story goes,[10] the victims of progress turned "naturally" to the courts for compensation.

10. For a description and critical evaluation of the "normative effects" social development model implicit in much of the historical litigation research, see Frank Munger, "Law, Change, and Litigation: A Critical Examination of an Empirical Research

Whether or not that thesis proves true for industrially caused injuries, it does not explain other causes that appear prominently here. Pedestrian and vehicular traffic accidents, strolling or rolling into cracks and crevices in sidewalks and streets, and disabling stumbles in dimly lit buildings are not the stuff of machine-age horror stories. Their sizable part in the rise of injury suits compels reconsideration of the "natural social development" explanation of the rise.

As was the case with every category of tort, the number of suits under each personal-injury heading climbed between 1870 and 1910. People were bringing their injuries to court more frequently, no matter what the cause. The rise in injury suits was broadly based, fueled by injuries from all walks of life. At the same time, some activities definitely produced a greater, growing share of injury suits, while others produced a diminishing portion. Work injuries rose more steeply, to pile up larger numbers than any other form of personal injury. From no such suits in 1870 to the most by 1910 (27% of all personal injuries), work-injury suits led the way into the courtroom.

Right behind work wounds in contributing to the growth of lawsuits came injuries from the city's streets and sidewalks. Traffic accidents, where a vehicle was involved, were at cause in only one injury suit (8% of all injury suits) in 1870; by 1910, they were responsible for 19 percent. Injuries that arose from walking or driving into holes in the city's imperfect pavement propelled another 19 percent of injury-suit plaintiffs into court in 1910. Combined, work, traffic, street, and sidewalk accidents accounted for 385, or 65 percent, of 1910's 595 injury suits and over half (53%) of all that year's 728 torts. What makes this especially noteworthy is that they had generated only 2 suits (15% of injury cases, 6% of all torts) just forty years before.

Meanwhile, the mechanized movers of Manhattan's masses—the streetcars, elevated trains, subways, and mainline railroads—contributed a growing number but shrinking share of the city court's injury suits. Injury suits that involved railroads, including elevateds and subways, declined from 9 to 3 percent between 1890 and 1910. Streetcars had been the largest single generator of court-bound injuries in 1870 and 1890. But their

Tradition," *Law and Society Review* 22 (1988): 58–101; Frank Munger, "Trial Courts and Social Change: The Evolution of a Field of Study," *Law and Society Review* 24 (1990): 217–26; Daniels, "Ladders and Bushes"; Stephen Daniels, "A Tangled Tale: Studying State Supreme Courts," *Law and Society Review* 22 (1988): 833–63; and Samuel Krislov, "Theoretical Perspectives on Caseload Studies: A Critique and a Beginning," in Keith Boyum and Lynn Mather, eds., *Empirical Theories about Courts* (New York: Longman, 1983), 161–87.

portion of the court's injury suits fell over the two-decade span, from 38 to 26 percent. Over the next two decades, streetcar-injury cases multiplied three-fold, yet came to comprise only 15 percent of 1910's injury suits.

The city's buildings were the other source of a large number of lawsuits. The number of cases that stemmed from accidents in residences and business places jumped twentyfold. All other sorts of causes not encompassed in any of the preceding categories, taken together, prompted an increasing number but declining percentage of injury suits. The small number and decrease in the share of these suits indicates that the sources of injuries that triggered injury suits, although broadening, were ultimately limited.

Can a general pattern be detected in this collection of trends in sources of injury suits? The linear idea inherent in the standard interpretation, that the industrial ascent of society created more accidents and more accidents created more lawsuits, is logical, plausible, and best of all, testable. How well does it fit what we know about the injury suits New Yorkers took to the court?

Of the causes one would expect to dominate in an industrially driven rise in tort suits, two of the most prominent categories were not on the rise. On the contrary, though their numbers increased, railroad-injury suits and streetcar suits were shrinking in proportion to all other injury torts. This occurred despite constant expansion of the rail network in Manhattan and the Bronx and despite technical advance that enhanced the speed and size of the machines. Another sort of injury suit that would be expected to rise under this interpretation gains support from the statistics: work-injury suits proliferated. But work injuries, even in New York City, were not necessarily industrial work injuries. The same is true of traffic accidents. The arrival of the automobile brought more injuries and lawsuits, as the industrialization interpretation would predict, but was not the only source of traffic injuries. Moreover, two other kinds of cases that contributed to the growth in injury suits—sidewalk and street, and buildings injuries—had little to do with industrialization.

Additionally, the timing of the rise in injury suits was too sudden to support the idea that suits rose in direct proportion to industrial injuries. The court judged almost no injury cases in 1870, but almost 600 just a short forty years later. While the years 1870–1910 were ones of tremendous industrial growth and advances in transportation, they did not mark the advent of industrialization in New York; its move to machines had been by going on for at least half a century before and was a much more gradual process than would be required for the theory to explain the rapid rise in torts.

TABLE 6

Work-injury cases by cause: Number and percentage of personal-injury cases

Issue	1870		1890		1910	
	n	%	n	%	n	%
Industrial manufacturing	—	—	1	4.2	26	16.2
Transport-mechanized	—	—	2	8.3	14	8.8
Transport-horse	—	—	1	4.2	4	2.5
Construction	—	—	3	12.5	65	40.6
Mining	—	—	1	4.2	—	—
Seaman-longshoreman	—	—	11	45.8	7	4.4
Other mechanized work	—	—	2	8.3	12	7.5
Other non-mechanized work	—	—	1	4.2	20	12.5
Work injury, not	—	—	2	8.3	12	7.5
by own employer						
Total	0	0	24	100	160	100

Source: See Table 4.

Delving deeper into the sources of injury suits in the Supreme Court provides further cause to question the association between industrialization and the rise in tort suits. Table 6 looks at the nature of the work that injured New Yorkers and gave rise to lawsuits. Suits from industrial manufacturing injuries and from other machine-related accidents did increase substantially. Industrial injuries and those attributable to machines grew from 0 in 1870, to 5 in 1890, to 52 in 1910. As a portion of work injuries, they also grew, rising from 21 percent in 1890 to 32 percent in 1910. Yet a much larger group of work injuries was not directly connected to industrial work or machines. Those New Yorkers employed in construction, transportation, and other businesses brought more suits in 1890 (19) and in 1910 (108) than their mechanized counterparts, twice as many suits in 1910 as from industrial accidents. As Table 6 shows, the great growth in work-injury suits came from accidents at almost every sort of job. In 1910, construction casualties led to the most suits and represented the greatest gain in suits, while only in the maritime trades did suits decline between 1890 and 1910.

Numerous railroad activities, not all from machine-borne dangers, were responsible for injuries and lawsuits (Table 7). Riding on these machines, for example, did not promote injury litigation. Passenger-injury suits against mainline railroads, elevated roads, and subways were rare and did not experience the growth that visited most other types of per-

TABLE 7

Railroad-injury cases by cause: Number and percentage of personal-injury cases

Issue	1870		1890		1910	
	n	%	n	%	n	%
Railroad passenger	—	—	3	30	4	21.1
Railroad collision with pedestrian or vehicle	—	—	2	20	8	42.1
Elevated railroad or subway passenger	—	—	4	40	1	5.2
Elevated railroad or subway station	—	—	1	10	6	31.6
Total	0	0	10	100	19	100

Source: See Table 4.

sonal injury suits. Actions that arose from railroad collisions with pedestrians and vehicles increased but not as much as other sorts of personal-injury suits did.

The railroad-accident suits that showed the most growth were only peripherally related to the mechanical nature of trains. These were station accidents, mostly injuries that occurred in trying to board or exit stationary trains. Occasionally, people fell into gaps between trains and platforms and made those falls the subjects of lawsuits. Such accidents were hardly the product of man contending with machine, bearing more kinship to hallway or sidewalk accidents than to railroad-passenger or collision injuries.

Injury suits brought against street railroads show another complication in the relationship between the mechanization of transportation and court use in New York. As noted above, the peak for this category of suit came in 1890, when street-railroad suits represented 26 percent of all personal injury suits; in 1910 they contributed only 15 percent of injury suits. The decline in percentage, as Table 8 shows, coincided with the adoption between 1890 and 1910 of the electric streetcar, or trolley, an important step forward in the mechanization of New York's transportation system. Though introduction of the trolley did produce more accidental injury suits than the all-horsecar system had, street transit's portion of the court's injury suits declined upon entry to the electric era.

The pattern of cases New Yorkers brought against street-railroad companies illustrates that the relation of injury suits to technological change was laced with subtlety. The increase in danger that accompanied the

TABLE 8

Street-railroad injury cases by cause: Number and percentage of personal-injury cases

Issue	1870		1890		1910	
	n	%	n	%	n	%
Horsecar: passenger	2	40	5	17.2	4	4.3
Horsecar: entry/exit	1	20	5	17.2	2	2.2
Horsecar: pedestrian	2	40	17	58.7	5	5.4
Horsecar: vehicle	—	—	2	6.9	2	2.2
Trolley: passenger	—	—	—	—	7	7.6
Trolley: entry/exit	—	—	—	—	33	35.9
Trolley: pedestrian	—	—	—	—	22	23.9
Trolley: vehicle	—	—	—	—	17	18.5
Total	5	100	29	100	92	100

Source: See Table 4.

introduction of a new form of mechanization was not the same (or at least was not perceived similarly) for all who encountered it. People discovered different degrees of threat as they met the machine in different roles. For New Yorkers who used the cars as passengers and those who battled the cars as drivers of other vehicles, the street railroads' shift from animal to electrical power raised the number of injury suits.[11] For New Yorkers walking the streets, the transition had no such effect. Injured pedestrians took street railroads to court a few more times in 1910 than in 1890, but as a portion of all streetcar suits, pedestrian cases declined.

A good portion of the rise in traffic-injury suits is attributable to a cause that was also of industrial-mechanical origin: the automobile (Table 9). Motor vehicle injuries added a sizable group of cases to 1910's personal injury suits (55 suits, 48% of traffic-injury suits or 9% of all injury suits). Even excluding those cases caused by motor vehicles, the growth of traffic-injury suits exceeded the growth of personal injury suits as a whole (8 suits in 1890, or 7% of all personal-injury cases that year, to 59 suits in 1910, or 10% of the year's injury suits). So while injury suits that came

11. See Table 8. Horsecar-passenger suits, including those rising from entry and exit accidents, numbered 10 in 1890. Electric trolley passenger-injury suits, including entry and exit suits, were four times as numerous in 1910. Suits from injuries in vehicular collisions with streetcars multiplied eightfold between 1890 and 1910 as modes of power changed (2 cases from horsecar/vehicle collisions in 1890, 17 cases from electric trolley/vehicle collisions in 1910).

TABLE 9

Traffic-injury cases by cause: Number and percentage of personal-injury cases

Issue	1870		1890		1910	
	n	%	n	%	n	%
Horse-pedestrian collision	I	100	6	75	47	41.2
Horse-horse collision	—	—	2	25	5	4.4
Miscellaneous horse accident	—	—	—	—	I	0.9
Horse-motor vehicle collision	—	—	—	—	5	4.4
Motor-pedestrian collision	—	—	—	—	46	40.4
Motor-motor collision	—	—	—	—	4	3.4
Passenger, vehicle unknown	—	—	—	—	6	5.3
Total	I	100	8	100	114	100

Source: See Table 4.

Horse = horse-drawn vehicle

Motor = motor vehicle

from industrial-mechanical causes contributed to the rise of torts, suits precipitated by accidents wholly removed from such causes contributed just as much to that rise.

Buildings provided the setting for a range of accidents that ultimately entered the Supreme Court as injury cases (Table 10). A small group of these suits involved an industrial-advance component. Elevators transformed the buildings in which New York's populace worked, and for a small number of people, the buildings in which they resided. But the new vertical transit system claimed its victims as well, and the injuries that those victims took to the court formed an increasing portion of the cases in the building category (1 case or 7% of building-injury suits in 1890, to 10 cases or 16% of building suits in 1910). Still, the overwhelming majority of cases in 1870, 1890, and 1910 originated in simple stumbles and falls or in falling pieces of building. These accidents also accounted for most of the growth in numbers in the category. Overall, industrially promoted change had a minimal part in the rise of building-injury suits, and these suits grew at the same pace as personal-injury suits in general.

Another prominently ascending group of cases, which outpaced the growth of injury suits in general, started literally on the streets of New York. Roadways and sidewalks in varying states of levelness, cratering, and cracking tripped walkers and tipped wagons, causing injuries that growing numbers of citizens took to the Supreme Court. As Table 11 shows, the growth of the category was reflected in every case.

Table 10

Injury cases from accidents in buildings, by cause: Number and percentage of personal-injury cases

Issue	1870		1890		1910	
	n	%	n	%	n	%
Elevator injury						
in residential buildings	—	—	1	6.7	—	—
in business buildings	—	—	—	—	10	16.4
Tenements-halls, stairs	1	33.3	6	40.0	31	50.8
Tenements-grounds	—	—	—	—	4	6.6
Business buildings	—	—	5	33.3	5	8.2
Passersby-building construction	—	—	1	6.7	6	9.8
Other passersby	2	66.7	2	13.3	4	6.6
Other building injury	—	—	—	—	1	1.6
Total	3	100	15	100	61	100

Source: See Table 4.

Table 11

Sidewalk- and roadway-injury cases by cause: Number and percentage of personal-injury cases

Issue	1870		1890		1910	
	n	%	n	%	n	%
Pedestrian						
Bad road-sidewalk	—	—	6	37.5	35	31.6
Icy road-sidewalk	—	—	3	18.7	18	16.2
Excavated road-sidewalk	1	100	—	—	9	8.1
Obstructed road-sidewalk	—	—	3	18.7	10	9.0
Sidewalk openings	—	—	2	12.5	11	9.9
Vehicle						
Obstructed road	—	—	1	6.3	10	9.0
Bad road	—	—	1	6.3	18	16.2
Total	1	100	16	100	111	100

Source: See Table 4.

Though the number of these suits was new, there was no novelty in the causes of injury behind them. Most cases involved people stumbling over curbs, over cracks and dips in pavement, into coal chutes or gaping excavations (the latter usually at night), and over piles of rubble or other material left on the public way. Pedestrian injuries were at issue in 1 case

TABLE 12.

Miscellaneous injury cases by cause: Number and percentage of personal-injury cases

Issue	1870		1890		1910	
	n	*%*	*n*	*%*	*n*	*%*
Travel over water						
Ship travel	I	33.3	3	30	—	—
Ferry travel	2	66.7	I	10	5	13.2
Explosion	—	—	2	20	6	15.8
Items thrown and fallen	—	—	3	30	5	13.2
Recreation–public & amusement parks	—	—	—	—	3	7.9
"Servant" assault	—	—	—	—	I	2.6
Industrial discharge	—	—	—	—	I	2.6
Product liability	—	—	—	—	I	2.6
Other	—	—	I	10	16	42.1
Total	3	100	10	100	38	100

Source: See Table 4.

in 1870 (7.7% of personal-injury suits for that year), 14 in 1890 (12.5%), and 83 in 1910 (13.9%). Injuries to drivers or riders of vehicles (horse-powered in every instance) lay behind 2 injury suits in 1890 (1.8%), and 28 suits in 1910 (4.7%). Here was a group of torts where mechanization and industrialization played almost no part, yet the injured were coming to court in numbers that rose faster than the numbers for almost every other type of personal injury.

Table 12 presents the rest of the injury suits that New Yorkers initiated, those that fit in none of the preceding categories.

Considering the evidence from this examination of personal-injury suits, the industrialization theory does not provide a satisfactory explanation, for two reasons. First, many of the injuries apparently tied to industrialization actually did not connect to matters industrial or mechanical. Construction and other "machine-free" work-accident cases are one example, elevated train and subway station injury cases another. Some industrial and mechanical injury suits occurred, from such causes as motor vehicle and elevator accidents, sitting in the nonindustrial injury categories, but they were small in number.

Second, over time, people were making cases from a broader, rather than narrower, range of circumstances. Most of the pioneering cases in these new areas came in 1910, though some can be found in 1890. The variety of injurious circumstances in the cases before the court would be accentuated by further subdivision of the cases. For example, New York's construction workers' suits resulted from injuries on large-scale projects (e.g., midtown tunnels for the new Pennsylvania terminal) and small-scale projects (e.g., renovating the facade of a small building), for injuries in highly skilled work (e.g., creating and setting decorative masonry or erecting armor ceilings in bank vaults) and in unskilled work (pick-and-shovel excavation).[12] As this demonstrates, it does not take much digging to verify the broadening of causes of injury suits.

Pulling the pieces together produces a more complete picture of how New York was using its court as personal-injury suits were escalating. While the rise in court use for redress of injuries was mirrored in every area of tort law, it was not replicated in debt, contract, property, family, and public law trends. Among torts, the rise in personal-injury suits outstripped that in intentional torts and far outstripped that in property damage.

The broadening range of causes that produced torts suggests that attention be directed at how litigants broadened the use of the legal system for injury compensation and how they began to see similarity between their situations and others where liability was clearly defined. Injuries did not always become lawsuits; for those that did, the translation to a lawsuit was never automatic. The rise in suits, therefore, needs to be viewed in the context of trends in accidents in New York.

12. See *Pauline Drazdowski* v. *Roebling Construction Company et al.*, 1910 Number D275, N.Y.C. Supreme Court; *Thomas Garrett* v. *National Fireproofing Company* 1910 Number N126, N.Y.C. Supreme Court; *Dagny Anderson, Administrator* v. *Pennsylvania Steel Company*, 1910 Number P101, N.Y.C. Supreme Court; and *Pasqualina Bertolami, Administrator* v. *United Engineering & Contracting*, 1910 Number U88, N.Y.C. Supreme Court.

2. DANGER AND INJURY

Danger: New York teemed with it at the turn of the century. It sped through the streets, spun on industry's shafts, fell from the buildings above, grabbed from the ground below. Because New York was the nation's greatest city, danger loomed larger there. New Yorkers marveled as inventions in transportation, construction, production, illumination, and communication remade the city around them. But even as invention worked its wonders, its new forms threatened the well-being of the city's dwellers.

The challenge presented by change was compounded by the intensity with which life was lived in New York. If the city was active in 1870, it was frenetic by 1910. Technological change wrested the island's inhabitants from their neighborhoods and thrust them into the larger city, forcing them rapidly to master unfamiliar surroundings and situations. The steady rhythm of the neighborhoods of the walking city gave way to the impatient starts and stops, the commotion, and the hurry of the Industrial Age city.

Historians have asserted that the growth of population and physical environment, the intensification of pace, and the heightened complexity of life introduced by technological advance combined to create new levels of danger in society. This idea was current, too, at the turn of the century, as the observations of a contemporary businessmen testify: "The various and continually multiplying uses of steam and of electricity are surrounding us with a thousand dangers which not only were not known to our fathers,but which were strange to the boyhood and to the early manhood of those who have hardly reached middle age."[1]

The scholars who share this view see the increase in danger directly producing more injuries. Danger promulgated legal change by spurring increased use of legal processes and the consequent adaptation of the law. They detect a straightforward relationship: A rise in injuries begot a rise in injury suits. Lawrence Friedman stated the idea most succinctly: "The modern law of torts must be laid at the door of the industrial revolution, whose machines had a marvelous capacity for smashing the human body."[2] Study of the Boston courts at the turn of the century convinced Robert Silverman that injury lawsuits increased because "Bostonians lived in the midst of thousands of machines, which, when carelessly operated, maimed and killed."[3]

How accurate is this attribution of cause? Was escalating danger the root of climbing court use? Was danger, in fact, escalating? The industrial-mechanical interpretation is premised upon such a change. But where is its proof? Admittedly, New York was growing, and life in it was becoming more demandingly complex and fastpaced. The impression that the city was dangerous rings true. But the thesis that increased mechanization led to more injuries posits more than the concurrence of change and danger; it asserts a change in the amount of danger. That change cannot be extrapolated from the coexistence of danger and change. Evidence has just begun to be gathered toward this end.[4]

One possible explanation exists for the increase in personal-injury suits that is still more elementary than a rise in accidents: population growth. Was the multiplication of personal injury suits simply the product of more persons? If population grew at the same pace as injury suits, there would be no need to look further for the cause of the rise; it would be a simple matter of demographics.

1. James R. Pitcher, "Accidents and Accident Insurance," *Forum* 12 (September 1891): 136. Reforming lawyer George Alger, creator of New York's Employer's Liability Act of 1902, had the same impression as Pitcher: "Accidents were increasing as the machine age advanced and as steam and electric power came into industry. . . . There were more and more accidents and no effective law either to prevent or redress injuries." George Alger, "Reminiscences of George W. Alger," in the Columbia University Oral History Collection New York, 1951–52, vol. 2, p. 196.

2. Friedman, *History of American Law*, 409.

3. Silverman, *Law and Urban Growth*, 100.

4. The only other work I have found that has sought to measure changes in accidental injuries to assess their effect on litigation is Frank Munger's study of West Virginia: "Social Change and Tort Litigation," 75–118. Munger's analysis works despite the limitation of industry-reported accident data and finds that the litigation-to-accidents rate fluctuated across time.

New York's population climbed, but not the 4,500 percent that city Supreme Court injury suits did (13 cases in 1870 to 595 in 1910; see Table 5). The city's population nearly doubled in the twenty years before 1870 and nearly tripled over the forty years that followed. The 942,000 New Yorkers of 1870 (in 1870 the city was coterminous with the county, comprising Manhattan and part of the Bronx) were joined in the next forty years by 1,800,000 more in the city court's jurisdiction (i.e., in Manhattan/New York County and the Bronx but not including Brooklyn, Queens, and Staten Island).[5] So population growth was substantial, 200 percent over the forty years, but it did not begin to approach the much steeper ascent of injury suits.

Furthermore, the increases in cases was not synchronous with that of population gains. The population of the city grew 61 percent (from 950,000 to 1,500,000; see note 5) between 1870 and 1890 and 82 percent (from 1,500,000 to 2,750,000) between 1890 and 1910. Meanwhile, the growth in the number of injury suits was proportionally stronger in the earlier decades than the later. Between 1870 and 1890, the number of injury suits filed annually grew by 762 percent, whereas from 1890 to 1910 the growth was 431 percent. Growth in injury suits was greater, then, in the decades where population increase was smaller (from 1870 to 1890).[6]

5. The population within the jurisdiction of the Supreme Court of the City and County of New York was as follows: 1870, 942,292; 1890, 1,515,301; 1910, 2,761,522. Ira Rosenwaike, *Population History of New York City* (Syracuse, N.Y.: Syracuse University Press, 1972), 55, 58. New York City outgrew its Manhattan Island county with the annexations of 1874, 1895, and 1898 and thus grew beyond the jurisdictional boundaries of the Supreme Court for the County and City of New York. These annexations brought southern Westchester County (the Bronx), Kings (Brooklyn) and Queens Counties, and Staten Island into the city but not all into this court's purview. The 1874 annexation joined the towns of Morrisania, West Farms, and Kingsbridge to the city and to the court's terrain. This added only 36,000 people to the 1,000,000 then residing in Manhattan. As the Census Office noted, in this newest part of New York "scarcely a hundred inhabitants can be counted to the square mile," compared to the density of 220,000 people per square mile in lower Manhattan. U.S. Census Office, *Report on the Social Statistics of Cities, Part I* (Washington, D.C.: U.S. Government Printing Office, 1886), 568. The 1895 annexation of the rest of what is now the Bronx brought another 130,000 citizens under the court's jurisdiction. The 1898 "consolidation" was much larger, making the nation's fourth largest city, Brooklyn, along with Queens and Staten Island, part of New York. This annexation doubled the city's population, but did not expand the universe of potential litigants for the court (Kings and Queens counties already had their own Supreme Court, which retained its separate jurisdiction after annexation). A comprehensive analysis of the peopling of the city can be found in Rosenwaike, *Population History*.

6. This was less obvious for tort cases. Tort suits grew 482% from 1870 to 1890, and 330% from 1890 to 1910.

So population growth does not explain the advance of injury cases. Heightened danger (or an increase in injuries) becomes the next most logical explanation. Was the city becoming more dangerous? Were accidental injuries becoming more frequent in New York? One way to get at the question is to reconstruct the environment of danger in New York in the period and chronicle its changes. For example, while the growth in population has been discounted as the primary, direct cause of the rise in injury suits, the rising numbers of people did contribute indirectly by altering the city's web of danger. To accommodate its newcomers, the city adapted in two ways: It spread north up Manhattan Island, and it packed more people into already densely populous areas in the southern part of the island.

The concentration of population came about in two basic ways that affected the prevailing level of danger. Architects and engineers turned sky into real estate by constructing steel-framed, elevator-accessed megaliths. At the same time, owners of older buildings intensified the use of their properties by converting houses into apartments and by subdividing apartments into grossly overcrowded, single-room family residences, as Jacob Riis graphically chronicled in *How the Other Half Lives.*[7] The result was that by 1910, densities reached 290,000 to 500,000 people per square mile in lower Manhattan.[8]

How did the concentration of population abet danger? More people seeking a limited amount of shelter made continued use of decrepit buildings as profitable as the building of new ones. There was no need to improve facilities to entice tenants. Buildings were subdivided to pack in more rent-payers, which subjected the buildings to harder and harder use. Deterioration of existing stock accelerated, making New York's housing ever more dangerous. The tolerance of new New Yorkers for cramped quarters encouraged builders to construct new tenements according to the intensive floorplans of the old ones. They built cheaply and quickly in the face of constant demand, more interested in quantity and profit than quality and safety.[9] In 1870 there were 18,000 tenement buildings in Manhattan. That number doubled by 1890. Of the city's 81,000 dwellings in 1890, 35,000 were tenements, home to 1 million of the 1.5 million

7. Jacob Riis, *How the Other Half Lives* (New York: Hill and Wang, 1957 [1890]).

8. Riis proffered the 290,000 people/sq. mi. figure, *The Other Half*, 8; 500,000 is cited in Raymond Mohl, *The New City: Urban America in the Industrial Age, 1860–1920* (Arlington Heights, Ill.: Harlan Davidson, 1985), 51.

9. Mohl, *New City*, 47–52; Edward Kirkland, *Industry Comes of Age: Business, Labor, and Public Policy, 1860–1897* (New York: Holt, Rinehart, 1961), 255–61.

people inhabiting Manhattan. By 1901, the date of the New Tenement Law, the number of such buildings had more than doubled again to 82,000.[10]

Another important aspect of the press of population on housing is that New Yorkers became overwhelmingly a renting population. By 1910, 87.9 percent of the inhabitants rented their shelter from someone else.[11] This contributed to the ill use of tenement buildings by diffusing responsibility for their maintenance. It also placed a growing portion of the population in an environment that was partly the legal responsibility of another person. This did not increase danger so much as it changed where danger and the duty of care against that danger resided. It brought a common, heretofore privately absorbed source of injury—residential accidents—into the public realm.

The city also grew skyward. The same technology that availed the heavens to the builder opened new possibilities for injury to workmen and habitants. Full steel-frame construction brought new materials to the construction site by the mid-1890s to strike or fall upon the construction worker or for the worker to fall from once in place. And any falls were likely to be longer plunges than those taken in building masonry wall-supported or wood-framed structures. Injury could result from short drops as readily as from longer ones but usually did not have the same physical consequences. Steel-frame structures were typically erected frame first, creating a many-storied skeleton before the building was fleshed out with floors and walls. Thus men worked well above any fall-breaking barriers, and nimbleness became as important to longevity in the trade as were building skills.[12]

As buildings rose to new heights, a vertical transit revolution occurred that was as important as its horizontal counterpart. Elevators made building growth beyond a few stories feasible. They, like railroads and trolleys, had their dangerous aspect, presenting the possibility for accidents in

10. Mohl, *New City:* 50; David Brody, introduction to Roy Lubove, "The Tenement Comes of Age," in David Brody, ed., *Essays on the Age of Enterprise, 1870–1900* (Hinsdale, Ill.: Dryden Press, 1974), 122.

11. Kirkland, *Industry,* 255–61. For the history of that development, see Elizabeth Blackmar, *Manhattan for Rent, 1785–1850* (Ithaca, N.Y.: Cornell University Press, 1989).

12. In the 1880s, iron- and masonry-bearing walls began to carry buildings to new heights; New York's first full steel-frame building, the American Surety Building, was constructed 1894–1895. Three years later, the Park Row Building, using the steel-frame design, became the world's tallest building and set off a race for new heights that ended only with the Great Depression. See Carl Condit, *The Port of New York: A History of the Rail and Terminal System from the Beginnings to Pennsylvania Station* (Chicago: University of Chicago, 1980).

entry and exit, in striking those in their path, and in injuring passengers when their mechanisms failed. Cars were not always fully enclosed, so passengers also stood to lose fingers if they inadvertently grasped the sides of the lift.

The danger of elevators was real. But again, we must consider whether its advent represented a heightening of danger when compared to its alternative—stairways. Stairs were notorious for precipitating injuries. By installing elevators, stairway use was lessened, thereby reducing the frequency of stairway injuries and offsetting to some extent any rise in accidents that elevators might have caused.

Territorial spread, the other product of a proliferating population, meant that crop and pasturelands had to be filled with the buildings people required to house themselves, their work, and the merchants servicing them. Building starts grew rapidly, peaking in 1890 and plateauing at a high level thereafter.[13] Construction, whether steel-frame or a more traditional form, harbored potential for danger to those involved in or passing near it. Excavation brought cave-ins and flying rock from overcharged blasts and set traps for passersby. Construction posed similar threats from above. By putting men and materials overhead, it tempted gravity to mischief. Both could fall and did. The tools construction required to cut, pound, and weld materials into shape occasionally turned on their masters, cutting, pounding, and injuring them.

Sprawl also forced residents to traverse greater distances within the city to work and to provision their homes. The development of spatial specialization—the emergence of central business and manufacturing districts, and the relocation of residences as commercial and industrial uses restructured property values—removed the bedroom from proximity to the workplace, ensuring that the populace would need to cross the greater distances of the expanded city. Whereas in 1870 only about one quarter of the population lived above 42nd Street and more than half lived below 14th Street, by 1890 more than half the population resided north of 42nd Street. Business remained clustered south of it.[14]

Entrepreneurial purveyors of mobility responded innovatively to New Yorkers' transit needs at mid-century with horse-drawn streetcar lines

13. The number of building permits issued in 1890 was greater than for any year before 1925. Kirkland, *Industry*, 255–61.

14. Charles Cheape, *Moving the Masses: Urban Public Transit in New York, Boston, and Philadelphia, 1880–1912* (Cambridge: Harvard University Press, 1980), 21, 40; and Rosenwaike, *Population History*, 55–58.

along the city's main thoroughfares.[15] These cars offered a cheaper and better ride than the stagecoach or omnibus. The number of horsecar riders tripled to 115 million in 1870. Charles Cheape says this demonstrates the first axiom of urban transit: "Betterment of facilities generated greater traffic, which in turn swamped the improvement."[16]

Horsecars crossed the threshold of injury-causing danger for pedestrians despite the constraint of operating on already congested streets, which Cheape believes kept their net speed below 5 miles per hour. While the speed itself was not dangerous, since most people could comfortably respond to it and avoid danger, the horsecars achieved it irregularly. The pace was jerky, composed of moments at a standstill and moments racing to the next point, of tedious ascents up Manhattan's many hills and rapid descents back down. So despite low average speed, horsecars did increase danger for pedestrians. At the same time, they probably did not add noticeably to danger for their own passengers or other vehicles.[17]

After 1870, transportation innovation flourished. Previously, inanimate motive power had not been adapted to the city's transit needs. Steam railroads had been deemed too dangerous for the risk they posed to pedestrians, their frightening of horses, and the possibility of their boilers exploding; they were outlawed below 42nd Street before 1870. A way around this injunction was found; transit took to the air, one of the few uncongested places left in New York, and created new rights-of-way for elevated steam railroads.[18]

Their lofty perch afforded the elevateds freedom from hitting other vehicles or knocking pedestrians about. They added two elements to the

15. The New York and Harlem Railroad opened the new era of transportation in 1831–32 laying down a line connecting the city to villages miles outside it; it operated with steam power as well as horses. Within the city, its popularity grew rapidly, and it was hard pressed to extend its service as quickly as demand warranted. The Hudson River Railroad was chartered next in 1846, and the race to charter new lines took off in the next decade. By 1913 the city and state had chartered 726 railway companies to operate surface, elevated, subway and steam rail routes in New York City. Harry Carman, *The Street Surface Railway Franchises of New York City* (New York: Columbia University Press, 1919), 9, 11–77.

16. Cheape, *Moving the Masses*, 25. James Blaine Walker verified the axiom in *Fifty Years of Rapid Transit, 1864–1917* (New York: Law Printing Company, 1918), ii. In 1870 travel amounted to 115,000,000 passengers; by the 1910s it was in the neighborhood of 1,900,000,000 passengers. Rides per resident of the city had climbed 3½ times. Blaine's reading of the numbers anticipated Cheape: "In other words the more traveling facilities provided, the more people make use of them."

17. Cheape, *Moving the Masses*, 26.

18. Ibid., 31–32; Walker, *Fifty Years of Rapid Transit*, 60–86.

danger of the city, nevertheless: traffic- and vision-obstructing poles in the streets and the same risks to passengers that afflicted ground-bound railroad travel (station accidents, boarding and disembarking dangers, quick starts, and abrupt stops). By 1890 elevated railroads rivaled the horsecars for numbers of passengers. But their carrying capacity had been reached; ridership on horsecar lines began to ascend again.

In the early 1890s the means of moving about the streets became more mechanized, as street rails began to carry cable and electric cars. These promised to haul more citizens at greater speeds, though the promise was not met: again, Cheape's saturation axiom and increasing congestion of the streets from other sources prevailed. Heavy traffic kept operating speeds in most parts of town at the same levels at which horsecars had run. The speed was less constant, though, than that which horsecars had delivered. These machines of much greater power and acceleration achieved their average speed even more by lurching starts and sudden stops, a pattern familiar to us in the late twentieth century but disconcertingly unfamiliar to contemporaries. Passengers seem to have been the most susceptible to the new dangers posed by the improved street transit, though those driving other vehicles now had to contend with greater danger from the more powerful streetcars as well.

Innovation took transportation underground to avoid street congestion. By 1910, private money had added subterranean roads to the city's mass transit network. The first stretch of subway in Manhattan opened in 1904. Removal from the streets freed the new motive means from many of the dangerous aspects of street transit: danger to pedestrians, to vehicles, and to the cars themselves from obstacles set in their path. As with the elevated trains, though, none of the dangers of mainline roads abated. Passengers still fell victim to entry/exit mishaps and start/stop injuries. And building the subways intensified danger for those involved in it, more so than for street or elevated lines because of the added element of danger involved in excavation.

Transportation needs for New York's burgeoning population included the need to move goods and people in and out of the city as well as within it. Here the railroads figured prominently. The proliferating use of steam locomotion, more so than any change in its use, heightened danger in the city. True, the steam engine was banned below 42nd Street by city ordinance, but population north of that line grew rapidly, to over 1 million by 1910. And while railroads did not run through Manhattan, they made it their terminus. The New York Central, for example, had extensive and expanding operations on the west side of Manhattan from 60th Street north. Other lines—the Erie, Lackawanna, Ontario, Pennsylvania, and West Shore railroads—carried passengers and freight into Manhattan, but they did so primarily through an extensive ferrying system.[19]

Railroads brought all the dangers of mainline railroads into the city: crossing accidents, work accidents, fires, and explosions. To get into Manhattan posed special problems for railroads, too, requiring bridges or tunnels, both especially dangerous construction projects at the turn of the century. Accidents from construction of the Pennsylvania Terminal and its connecting tunnels appear prominently among the 1910 work-injury suits.[20]

Since Manhattan was a major business center, many railroads without so much as one engine on the island located offices there. This created the potential for suits against railroads to grow well out of proportion to the physical danger they presented to the city. While the victims of railroad injuries might sue the corporation at the location where the accident occurred or the victim resided, they could also bring suit at the location of the corporation's offices. Translocal transportation companies of all kinds faced the possibility of "venue shopping" by those suing them, although the defending company could contest the venue. Nevertheless, with a few exceptions, the cases from accidents outside Manhattan never materialized to any great extent in the city Supreme Court.[21]

While steam locomotives changed the movement of goods into New York, the movement of goods within the city changed little between 1870 and 1910. Motor vehicles had entered the city, providing some personal transportation by 1910, and figured in a number of lawsuits.[22] But motor

19. Condit, *Port of New York,* 110.

20. The story of railroads and railroad construction in New York City is well told in John Stilgoe's *Metropolitan Corridors* (New Haven, Conn.: Yale University Press, 1985) and Condit's *Port of New York. Thomas Garrett v. National Fireproofing Company,* 1910 Number N126, N.Y.C. Supreme Court, was one suit stemming from accidents related to the construction of the Pennsylvania Terminal.

21. One quite apparent instance of venue shopping was *Pietro Pietraroia v. The New Jersey and Hudson River Railway and Ferry Company,* the case of Carmario Galiaza, a Palisades Park, New Jersey, woman who was run over and killed by a trolley of a wholly local company. Despite her husband and children's continued residence in New Jersey, the surrogate proceedings to appoint an administrator of Galiaza's New York estate (a bank account) had come under New York County jurisdiction. Galiaza's father, who resided in Manhattan, was made executor so that the wrongful death suit could be filed in New York. *Pietraroia v. New Jersey and Hudson River Railway and Ferry,* 1910 Number P63, N.Y.C. Supreme Court.

22. Automobile fatalities first registered in the national mortality statistics in 1905, causing 0.4 deaths per 100,000 population that year. By 1910, that figure had already grown four times larger, to 1.8 deaths per 100,000. See Chapter B, "Vital Statistics, Health and

freight transport was slower to evolve. The main way of moving merchandise remained the horse-drawn truck. Their number and size grew, but they posed no new threat to pedestrians or other vehicles.[23]

The actual level of danger in any situation is not inevitable; people can and have intervened to lessen risks. So the amount of danger any situation posed was, to a degree, the result of choice. The potential for injury in hazardous activities was often reduced by countermeasures, such as restrictive rules for doing the deed, for protecting against its side-effects, and for warning those likely to be put at risk. The city and state's attention to precautionary safety was greater for some types of activities than for others. For example, steam railroads and the use of explosives drew many safety regulations, while tenement and workplace conditions were only beginning to. The effectiveness of measures varied as well. Since potential danger does not equal actual danger, accidents, or injuries, figures on the incidence of accidental injuries in New York are the only way to determine if the potential hazards had any real consequence.

The best data on accidental injuries comes from the city coroner's annual tallies in the Board of Health reports.[24] These give a detailed accounting of the causes of all deaths that occurred in the city during each year. One of the major causes, grouped with homicide and suicide under the heading "Violence," was death by accident. The value of the coroner's statistics lie in their morbid completeness. We can be sure that every accidental death that occurred in Manhattan (and the Bronx in 1910) is in the count. This is not true of most injury statistics, which are subject to the problem of "dark figures," those injuries unreported or selectively excluded. Unlike injury, death was indisputable; corpses were tough to deny.

Medical Care," U.S. Bureau of the Census, *Historical Statistics of the United States, Colonial Times to 1970, Part I* (Washington, D.C.: U.S. Government Printing Office, 1975), 58.

23. See Francis V. Greene, "An Account of Some Observations of Street Traffic," *Transactions of the American Society of Civil Engineers* 15 (1886): 123–38; and Clifford Richardson, "Street Traffic in New York City, 1885 and 1904," *Transactions of the American Society of Civil Engineers* 57 (1906): 181–90. Greene, Richardson, and colleagues counted vehicles passing various points in the City in the two years and found increased traffic at each place. In 1885, for example, only 9 percent of the vehicles passing 34th Street on Fifth Avenue were larger than one ton; by 1905, more than 21 percent were that large.

24. New York City Department of Health, *Report of the Board of Health of the Health Department of New York City, First Annual Report, April 11, 1870 to April 10, 1871* (New York: David Gildersleeve, 1872); *Annual Report of the Board of Health of the Health Department of the City of New York for the Year Ending December 31, 1890* (New York: Martin B. Brown, 1890); *Report of the Board of Health of the Department of Health of the City of New York for the Years 1910 and 1911* (New York: J. W. Pratt, 1912).

TABLE 13

Deaths, accidental deaths, and death rates in New York City

	1870	*1890*	*1910*
All deaths	27,175	31,937	45,646
Death rate (all deaths, per 100,000 population)	2,880/100,000	2,490/100,000	1,640/100,000
Accidental deaths	834	1,449	2,189
Accidental death rate (accidental deaths per 100,000 population)	88/100,000	90/100,000	79/100,000

Source: New York City Department of Health, *Second Annual Report of the Board of Health of the Department of Health of the City of New York, April 11, 1871 to April 10, 1872* (New York: David Gildersleeve, 1872); *Annual Report of the Board of Health . . . for the Year ending December 31, 1890* (New York: Martin B. Brown, 1890); and *Report of the Board of Health . . . for the Years 1910 and 1911* (New York: J. W. Pratt, 1912).

Table 13 compiles some of the New York City coroner's accidental death figures for the years 1870, 1890 and 1910. The table tells us that first, despite the introduction into New York of more potential hazards, accidental death rates did not rise at all across these forty years. Relative to population, they were stable or decreasing. But as a portion of the overall mortality, accidental deaths were growing, from 3 percent of the total in 1870 to 5 percent in 1910. But this relative growth was due to a decline in other causes, not an increase in the rate of deaths by accident, which comprised a small portion of all deaths throughout the period.

Second, while the number of fatalities from accidents did increase from 834 to 2,189, that number did not grow anywhere near as much as the number of injury suits did. As Table 5 in Chapter 1 shows, personal-injury suits climbed from 13 in 1870, to 112 in 1890, to 595 in 1910, a forty-fivefold increase. By comparison, accidental deaths in 1910 were only 2½ times their 1870 number. This is hardly the explosive sort of growth that could have propelled the forty-fivefold rise in injury suits.

But, did particular types of accidental deaths increase faster than others? The category "accidents" included a large number of drownings, poisonings, and other causes that seldom became the subject of lawsuits. The constancy or decline of these could have obscured a sharp rise in other sorts of accidents that lay behind the fastest growing categories of injury suits.[25]

25. The coroner's statistics, as good a source as they are, pose two problems for this analysis. First, the coroner's accident categories were not the same as those grouping accident lawsuits here. The reports categorized cases by the cause of death first, then

That was not the case. The trends in casualties from the sorts of accidents (except railroad accidents) isolated by Table 14 did indeed move ahead of the pack. However, with the exception of motor vehicle accidents, these trends were still not of the magnitude to account for the rise in injury suits from railroads, streetcars, and traffic.

The number of people fatally injured by the city's railroads fluctuated, not coinciding with the trend in the number bringing personal-injury suits against the railroads. Rail injuries on the island were not the only injuries out of which city Supreme Court suits could arise (e.g., suits could be lodged against lines with offices in Manhattan), which partly explains why railroad-injury suits developed differently than fatal injuries from Manhattan's railroads.

The railroads' circumstance does not apply to wholly local streetcar and traffic suits. Thus, it does not explain why the same pattern—more growth in injury suits than in injuries—held true for them. The net growth in streetcar deaths was roughly 33 percent, about the same as for deaths from railroads. Streetcar suits, meanwhile, grew much faster. Similarly, there were three times as many deaths from horse-vehicle accidents in 1910 as in 1870, but sixty times as many horse-traffic suits. In these leading categories, as in general, injury suits amassed faster than did injuries.

In contrast, the increase in subway and elevated railroad deaths was greater than the increase in lawsuits, and the increase in motor vehicle injury suits just kept up with the increase in deaths. Why did the people

---

subcategorized by the circumstances that gave rise to the fatal injury, with occasional aberrant categories. The categories for 1871 (New York City Department of Health, *Report of the Board of Health . . . April 11, 1870 to April 10, 1871*, table XXVIII) included burns and scalds; drowning; explosion of boiler of the steamer "Westfield" (with subcategories drowning, fractures, and scalds); fractures and contusions; wounds; poison–accidental; run over; and suffocation–accidental. The reports were not marvels of consistency; when these data were summarized for the "Consolidated Abstract" (ibid., table XIV) the categories became bone lodging in bronchus; burns and scalds; drowning; explosions; falls; effects of immersion; killed by vehicles, &c., in streets; neglect and exposure; poison; suffocation; medical operations; wounds (various); and gunshots. Coroners did not isolate work fatalities in their tallies; those must be extracted from other categories that rely upon information that is inadequate for the task. For purposes of comparing the incidence of work deaths in New York to that of Pittsburgh or London, these figures will not work.

The other problem is the lack of consistency in how coroners categorized and presented the data from one year's report to the next. Categories utilized in one report disappeared by the next. Where categories remain consistent, we can only assume that the classifying of cases did not change drastically so that the distinction made in 1870 between an explosion of gunpowder under the heading "burns and scalds" and one under "fractures and contusions" was made similarly in 1910.

TABLE 14
Deaths and lawsuits* from railroads, streetcars, and traffic in New York City

Cause	1870	1890	1910**
Railroad deaths	34	56	44
Railroad injury suits	0	5	12
Subway and elevated railroad deaths	—	3	27
Subway and elevated railroad suits	—	5	7
Streetcar deaths	61	12	83
Streetcar injury suits	5	29	92
Horse vehicle deaths	41	44	120
Horse-vehicle injury suits	1	8	59
Motor vehicle deaths	—	—	76
Motor-vehicle injury suits	—	—	55

Source: See Tables 4 and 13.
*Lawsuits brought before the Supreme Court for the City and County of New York.
**Deaths within the jurisdiction of the Supreme Court for the City and County of New York (Manhattan and Bronx).
Note: Because the purpose of this table is to provide comparison between trends in lawsuits and deaths, percentages (e.g., railroad deaths' % of all accidental deaths, railroad-injury suits' % of all injury suits) do not pertain here and have been omitted.

of New York respond differently to these sorts of accidents than to other transportation mishaps?

The answer is that they did not respond differently. The element common to elevated subway and motor vehicle accidents is the timing of their appearance. These sources of injury did not exist in 1870, when overall there were few lawsuits emanating from the great number of injuries. They came into being at a later point when the frequency of injury suits relative to the number of injuries was higher for all kinds of accidents than it had been in 1870. New Yorkers responded to injury from automobiles or subways in the same way they were responding to injuries from all other kinds of causes after 1890, invoking the law with greater frequency then they would have a few decades before.

Table 15 presents the data on building, sidewalk, and roadway injuries. The coroner's statistics for these are not as strong as for the transportation deaths. The figures for 1890 are wholly inadequate. Consistency exists for a few types of building accidents and for road and sidewalk spills, but there is no guarantee of completeness. As a result, the figures are fine for our comparison across time within the city, but again, are useless for comparison with figures from other locales.

Table 15

Deaths and lawsuits* from buildings, sidewalks and roadways in New York City

Cause	1870	1890	1910**
Building deaths	70	na	244
Elevators	5	36	47
Stairway falls	31	na	109
Falls from building	21	na	58
Falls from fire escape	5	na	30
Other building deaths	8	na	na
Building-injury suits	3	15	61
Elevator injury suits	0	1	10
Falls: stairs, halls, building suits	1	11	40
Other building suits	2	3	11
Sidewalk and road deaths	20	na	102
Pedestrian falls	16	na	60
Falls from vehicles	4	na	42
Sidewalk and road injury suits	1	16	111
Pedestrian injury suits	1	14	83
Falls from vehicle suits	0	2	18

Source: See Tables 4 and 13.
*Lawsuits brought before the Supreme Court for the City and County of New York.
**Deaths within the jursidiction of the Supreme Court for the City and County of New York (Manhattan and Bronx).
na: Number not available.
Note: See note to Table 14 on the omission of percentages.

Sidewalks, roadways, and buildings were causing a sizable number of fatal injuries in 1870, but they precipitated very few lawsuits. Fatal injuries from these causes rose through 1910, but as with most types of transportation accidents, injury suits rose still more. Deaths from building accidents, for instance, grew somewhat faster than the population. In part, the growth was due to the spreading use of elevators, but surprisingly, much of it came from more mundane and timeless sources, such as stairway falls. The growth in building accidents was surpassed by the twentyfold rise of lawsuits from such accidents, with the most dynamic change, a fortyfold rise, occurring in lawsuits stemming from hall and stairway falls.

The same relationship between trends in accidents and lawsuits characterized sidewalk and roadway injuries. They also grew just ahead of population growth; even pedestrian falls killed four times more people in 1910 than in 1870. Meanwhile, increases in lawsuits by wounded walkers

far eclipsed fatality trends, jumping to eighty times their 1870 level by
1910. The growth in suits by New Yorkers injured in their vehicles by bad
roads was even greater.

Work injuries generated the most phenomenal growth among injury
suits in the city Supreme Court. But work accidents are also the cause of
injury for which reliable figures are most difficult to get.[26] From the
highly detailed 1871 coroner's report, I have made an approximation of
work deaths for that year, which is reliable for our purpose (Table 16).

When a person was sliced by a circular saw, fell from a ship's mast, or
was buried by a trench cave-in, it is highly unlikely that this was anything
other than a work injury. If a person was burned or fell from a ladder, the
injuries may or may not have come in the course of employment. There
were 425 of these indeterminable cases. And if injury resulted from a
"musquito bite," "cutting a corn," or suffocation "by artificial teeth,"
work could safely be ruled out as the cause. There were 269 such "not
work related" deaths. The fatalities assigned to other causes (e.g., railroads, buildings) amounted to 242 in 1871.[27]

There were approximately 94 deaths from work accidents in 1871,
compared to 34 from railroads, 61 from streetcars, 70 from buildings, and
41 from traffic. The 94 work fatalities themselves tell us that the absence
of work-injury lawsuits in 1870 was not due to a dearth of work injuries.

Unfortunately, the coroner's early manner of reporting did not carry
through to 1910. For 1890 and 1910, the coroner's categorizations of
cause for the most part were just too general to be of use in separating
work injuries from others. Nevertheless, coroners did report figures in
1870 and 1910 for machinery deaths, which might serve as a partial
proxy for work injury. The number of people who died after getting
caught in machinery decreased from 14 to 8 between 1871 and 1910.[28]
This decline poses fundamental questions: Were there less machines, or
less people working with machines, in Manhattan in 1910 than forty
years before? Was the mix of work performed in the city changing, perhaps becoming less mechanized? Work, after all, encompasses a range of
activities that varied widely in potential for injury to life and limb. A shift
in the distribution of the working population across that range could significantly have altered the likelihood for injury.

26. See note 25.

27. New York City Department of Health, *Second Annual Report of the Board of Health
of the Department of Health of the City of New York, April 11, 1871 to April 10, 1872* (New
York: David Gildersleeve, 1872), 228–30.

28. *Annual Report of the Board of Health for 1910 and 1911,* 185.

TABLE 16

Deaths from work accidents in New York City, 1871

Cause	Number
Accidental deaths, total	1,071
Work accidents, total	94
caught in machinery	14
caught in hawser, hoist rope	2
caught in linch pin of car	1
fall from scaffolding	12
fall from sawhorse	1
fall from theatre scenery	1
fall from awning	2
fall from beam	1
fall from telegraph pole	1
fall from truck	7
fall from ship mast or yardarm	3
fall into ship hold, through hatch	11
fall between barges	1
fall onto meat hook	2
fall into vat of hot beer	1
fall into vat of boiling soap	1
struck by falling derrick	1
struck by falling dummy elevator	2
struck by falling bar of iron	4
struck by falling grindstone	1
struck by falling hand barrow	1
struck by levers	2
struck by circular saw or splinters from	5
struck by burst flywheel	1
struck by propeller blade	1
struck by lifted wagon	1
struck by threshing machine	1
crushed by block of marble	2
crushed by barrel, pilings	2
crushed by caving embankment	7
crushed between streetcars	2

Source: New York City Department of Health, *Second Annual Report of the Board of Health of the Department of Health of the City of New York, April 11, 1871 to April 10, 1872* (New York: David Gildersleeve, 1872), 228–30.

The economy of New York was changing in this period from one centered on commerce to an economy that mixed manufacturing, finance, and management with commerce. New York has never been renowned for its industry the way Chicago, Detroit, or Pittsburgh have, but throughout this period New York remained the nation's leading manufacturing center. There were more than 16,000 factories operating in the city in 1890, according to the Board of Health.[29] Most important to the question of mechanization, roughly twice the number of workers toiled in industry in 1910 as in 1880 in Manhattan, Brooklyn, Queens, and the Bronx. Since more workers came into contact with machines, the decrease in machine deaths cannot be attributed to declining contact with machines.[30]

Machine-caused work injuries must be considered only a partial proxy for all work injuries because manufacturing was only one of the "dangerous trades" in New York. Other less mechanized jobs injured their practitioners at different rates. In construction, for example, "getting caught in machines" was a small threat. Yet construction was one of the most hazardous of occupations at the turn of the century, as it is today. Its prominence among the causes of work-injury lawsuits in the city Supreme Court is evidence of that. But the trend in construction-worker lawsuits does not tell us about the trend in construction accidents. The coroner's reports, unfortunately, do not present a likely proxy for assessing change in construction or other less mechanical types of work accidents.

At the end of the nineteenth century, the Assembly of New York faced the same lack of information. Sensing an increase in work accidents, it created in the 1880s the state Bureau of Labor Statistics to provide the information. With the power to prosecute recalcitrant noninformants, the bureau began collecting data on industrial, mining, and construction accidents in the state. Ostensibly then, we should have at our disposal a longitudinal series on work injuries that corresponds to the time frame of this study. But as those collecting the data were the first to acknowledge, the reported statistics did not resemble actual levels of work injury. They were amassed through industry self-reporting, supplemented by the prodding of the state's factory inspection force, which consisted of two men.

29. *Annual Report of the Board of Health for 1890*, 74–75.
30. David Hammack, *Power and Society: Greater New York at the Turn of the Century* (New York: Russell Sage, 1981), 37–42. Using the U.S. censuses of manufactures, Hammack found that there were 275,000 manufacturing workers in Greater New York (Manhattan and the other soon-to-be boroughs) in 1880 and 554,000 in 1910. Within the region, Manhattan was losing large plant manufacture to the periphery, so we cannot be sure that the population trend for manufacturing workers in Manhattan conformed to that for the whole region. But the manufacturing taking place in Greater New York was increasingly concentrated in clothing, printing and publishing, custom and specialty manufacture, metal working, and food processing, all industries not in need of large plants, and many located in Manhattan. These manufactures accounted for 89 percent of new industrial jobs between 1880 and 1910, and their share of industrial employment rose from 41 percent to 55 percent.

Business firms were neither assiduous in discovering all accidents on their premises nor forthright in reporting those they discovered.[31]

Adna Weber, the director of the bureau at the turn of the century and an ardent advocate of a state response to the "industrial carnage," labored hard to give as accurate an estimate as possible of the extent of work injury.[32] Yet he found the bureau's statistics unsatisfactory. "The incompleteness of these figures," he wrote, "has been so patent that no statistician has ever undertaken to use them for the measurement of the relative hazard of occupation."[33] In a special study to better estimate the toll of accidents in the work force, Weber produced an improved figure of 7,400 injuries per year for 450,000 workers whose employers were included in the reports. Since that represented less than half of the state's workers, he figured that of the state's entire working population, roughly 16–20,000 workers met injury per year. Weber believed this still underestimated the incidence of work accidents, though it was closer than the estimate found in the bureau's regular 1899 report: 1,626 injuries for 700,000 workers.[34]

Since as few as a tenth of the state's work injuries were reported in the Bureau of Labor Statistics' annual reports, comparison of figures from decade to decade would yield little of value. Changes in the numbers were more likely to be products of variance in reporting than indicators of an increase or decrease in work injuries. The bureau made an effort to more comprehensively measure work injuries in 1912 and 1913 and found 72,789 injuries in the state's factories (50,704), mines (736), and construction sites (21,349) per year.[35] That figure could be compared to the

---

31. The state Labor Law of 1887 required employers to report all work injuries. But as the factory inspectors testified, the law was honored mostly in the breach: "I do not think that the tables given contain more than a small fraction of the accidents which happened in New York City. Notwithstanding that it is a misdemeanor punishable by severe penalties for an employer . . . not to report accidents, the information that such accidents have occurred is carefully suppressed from the inspectors, and it is by accident that the facts are oftentime obtained. We are aided by the newpapers to a considerable extent in learning of accidents, but this is not the case in New York City, where such items are not printed unless the result is fatal, or the facts are out of the ordinary." From *Factory Inspectors' Report for 1890* (Albany: J. B. Lyon, 1890), 51; cited in Adna Weber, "The Compensation of Accidental Injuries to Workmen," the *Seventeenth Annual Report of the Bureau of Labor Statistics of the State of New York* (Albany: J. B. Lyon, 1900), 563–64.

32. See Weber, "Compensation," 561–1162.

33. Ibid., 563.

34. Ibid., 565, 570–77.

35. State of New York, Department of Labor, *Statistics of Industrial Accidents in 1912 and 1913, Bulletin no. 68* (Albany: J. B. Lyon, 1914), 10–19. Frederick Hoffman compiled and categorized work deaths reported in the *New York (State) Department of Labor*

16–20,000 estimate extrapolated from Weber's undercounted figure for 1899, but there would be no way of knowing how much of the three to four fold increase would be due to enhanced reporting and how much to actual increase in injury.

Frederick Hoffman of the Prudential Insurance Company made what was intended to be the definitive independent estimate of the nation's work injuries and deaths for the U.S. Bureau of Labor Statistics in 1913. He arrived at 25,000 deaths and 700,000 long-term disabilities nationally that year, but he said nothing about trends in accidents over time.[36] Even if he had, national trends might or might not have taken the same direction as work injuries in New York City. And much of Hoffman's estimation was based on the data reported by the New York Bureau of Labor Statistics and its counterparts in Massachusetts, Wisconsin, Illinois, and other states, all of which were suspect for the same reasons as were New York's.[37]

Bulletins (nos. 48–55) for the 18 months from September 1911 to March 1913, giving us some additional information about the relative danger of types of work in the state at the end of the period:

Open excavations	96
Excavation in shafts, tunnels	93
Track laying	82
Iron and steel	55
Electric wiring and installation	51
Manufacture of vehicles	44
Construction: iron and steel structures	42
Construction: wood	38
Construction: masonry	34
Painting and decorating	31
Manufacture of paper and pulp	20
Mining	20
Total	606 of 925 total work fatalities

F. Hoffman, *Industrial Accident Statistics, U.S. Bureau of Labor Statistics, Bulletin no. 157* (Washington, D.C.: U.S. Government Printing Office, 1915), 45–47.

36. Hoffman, *Industrial Accident Statistics,* 6.

37. Another insurance company statistician, Louis I. Dublin, drew upon a different source, the statistics for deaths to industrial policyholders of the Metropolitan Insurance Company, to research work danger for the U.S. Bureau of Labor Statistics. But he, like his peers, was more interested in obtaining an accurate static portrait than in a moving picture; he did not compare the 1911 death rates he found for the various occupations with similar statistics from earlier decades. So while we learn that 42 percent of the railroad engine and train men who died, died from "accidental violence," while that was the cause of the demise of only 3 percent of saloonkeepers, we do not find out whether these were higher rates than in the past, whether there were more workers dying of work accidents or not. Louis I. Dublin, *Causes of Death by Occupation; Occupational Mortality Experience of the Metropolitan Life Insurance Company, Industrial Department, 1911–1913, U.S. Bureau of Labor Statistics, Bulletin no. 207* (Washington, U.S. Government Printng Office, 1917).

Social analyst and reformer Crystal Eastman, in her studies for the New York State Employer Liability Commission, came the closest to a usable figure for work fatalities for 1910. Eastman was interested in the impact of work injury on the family. In the course of portraying the sad consequences to the household economy of losing a main breadwinner, she reported 48 work-related deaths to married men in Manhattan in 1908.[38] Doubling that figure estimates the work deaths for the entire population to have been 96 in 1908. If this estimate and the 92 work-related deaths of the 1871 coroner's count are accurate, then work deaths remained at the same level.[39] The change did not keep pace with population growth and does not come close to the gain in work-injury lawsuits.

For a rise in injuries to explain the rise in injury suits, injuries would have had to show much greater growth. With 92 work deaths in 1871, for fatal work injuries to have grown at the rate of injury suits, nearly 15,000 New Yorkers would have had to succumb to work deaths in 1910.[40] Nothing like that occurred.

New York's fatal accidents in this period did not all happen in streetcars, traffic, tenements, and the workplace, or in any of the other locales we have examined so far. Many occurred in places and from causes that seldom appeared in lawsuits. Drowning, suffocation, surgery mishaps, asphyxiation from illuminating gas, and building fires fostered few injury cases from 1870 to 1910 (see Table 17) but killed many New Yorkers. Despite their rare appearance in the courtroom, these accidents were no different than train accidents in that they, too, caused losses and hardship. Thus they had the potential to be seen by victims as the basis of lawsuits.

That they were not so perceived in 1870 does not mean they would not be thereafter. After all, no type of accident was widely held to be courtroom material in 1870. None produced more than one or two injury suits a year. Some of these activities were soon causing lawsuits in other jurisdictions,[41] and others would precipitate considerable legal

38. Crystal Eastman, *Work Accidents and the Law* (New York: Charities Publication Committee, 1910), 271.

39. Weber, in the New York Bureau of Labor Statistics study, found that half of those injured at work in 1899 were married men. "Compensation," 574–75.

40. I arrived at the 15,000 figure as follows: 92 deaths in 1871 multiplied by the growth rate for injury suits in the city Supreme Court, 1870–1910 (from 0 [1] to 160, or 160x); 92 × 160 = 14,720.

41. One cause of injury that was producing lawsuits in other courts, but not in New York's, at the time was asphyxiation from illuminating gas leaks. These were a regular fixture in Boston's courts by 1900. See Silverman, *Law and Urban Growth*, 106.

TABLE 17

Deaths from drownings, fires, illuminating gas, and surgery in New York City

Cause	1870	1890	1910*
Drownings	190	222	250
Fires	5	3	38
Illuminating Gas	3	33	142
Surgery	63	122	na**

Source: See Table 13.
*Deaths within the jurisdiction of the Supreme Court for the City and County of New York (Manhattan and Bronx).
**Data not available.

action in New York later in the twentieth century. The controversy over medical malpractice cases in the 1970s and 1980s demonstrates the point vividly.

That these accidents only rarely ended up in court by 1910 had to do with something other than the frequency of their occurrence. As Table 17 reports, the trends in these accidents were the same as for railroad, street-car, building, or sidewalk accidents. After falls, drownings were the second most frequent fatal accident of this sort in 1870. Their number increased but not as fast as population (in other words, their rate of occurrence declined) over the next forty years. Fatalities from fires and from illuminating gas grew well ahead of population growth rates (8 times and 47 times their 1870 levels by 1910, respectively; population grew 2.8 times over this span). Here, an increase in accidents induced by technological change in household lighting led to no flurry of lawsuits.

It was not that gassed New Yorkers sought compensation through legal channels and lost; they did not seek compensation in court at all. This further undermines the industrial-technological hypothesis of the rise of injury suits. The populace did not automatically consider the injurious consequences of new technologies to be lawsuit material.

Other accidental deaths would never become lawsuits because the injurer and victim were one and the same. In 1870 and 1890, a significant number of accidental deaths resulted from overly rigorous parenting. Fourteen infants died from being overlaid with covers in their beds in 1870, and seven more were smothered at their mother's breasts or in their arms. Fifty died from these causes in 1890. In these circumstances, legal rules considered the parents both the injured and injurer, a situation unlikely to promote many lawsuits.

*prior to / w | a
decision of commission
of medicine*

Injuries and deaths from medical procedures were another apparently
unlikely source of lawsuits, though they did make their way onto the
court's docket in a handful of medical malpractice cases.[42] The unlikeli-
ness of medical injury being taken to court stemmed from he nature of the
activity. Medicine was applied when the patient's health had already de-
teriorated, meaning that a preexisting condition was responsible for some
damage before the physician even got his chance. The original condition,
if left untreated, might have caused more damage than the doctor's intervention. But the doctor's intervening hand left a clear path of causality for
injured persons to follow to compensation in the future, clearer than that
available to family and victims of drownings or fires. This might explain
why medical malpractice suits eventually did make their way to court,
though in this period, very few of these injurious activities produced injury suits.

To this point, the growth of accidental injuries has been indexed using
accidental fatalities. But can rates of accidental injury be inferred from
rates of accidental death? Did the incidence of injury follow the same pattern over time as the incidence of fatal injury? The answers are probably
no and yes, respectively. Common sense tells us that accidents from some
causes are more deadly than others and that the relative rates of injury
among causes therefore will not correspond to the relative rates of fatal
injury.

For example, injuries from stumbles in tenement hallways certainly
happened far more regularly than injuries from explosions. Yet there were
probably relatively more deaths from explosions than from tripping in
halls, explosions having a higher ratio of death to injury. Were relative
injury rates from deaths for these two categories to be projected at the
same rate, we would misrepresent the relative occurrence of injury.

---

42. See *Francis Pryor* v. *Manhattan Eye and Ear Hospital,* 1890 Number P218, N.Y.C.
Supreme Court, where Pryor had entered the hospital with lye in his eye. Hoping for the
removal of the lye, Pryor wound up with the removal of his eye. He had his suit dismissed
on demurrer. See also *Joseph Bickstein* v. *Michael Schiller,* 1910 Number B518, N.Y.C.
Supreme Court; *Alexander Brak* v. *John F. Buckley,* 1910 Number B520, N.Y.C. Supreme
Court; and *Antoinette Shea* v. *New York Post Graduate Medical School and Hospital,* 1910
Number N177, N.Y.C. Supreme Court. Peter O'Hara sued the city for an assault and bat-
tery, which might be considered as an extreme malpractice suit. When his son tried to leave
Gouveneur Hospital after seeking treatment for an injury to his knee, a house surgeon
stopped him by "blackening both his eyes, bruising him and wounding him, . . . placing
him in a straight jacket, gagging and smothering him," which wound up killing him. *Peter
O'Hara, Administrator* v. *Philip O'Hanlon et al.,* 1890 Number M9, N.Y.C. Supreme
Court. None of the cases cited here won their claim. For the history of malpractice, see
Kenneth A. DeVille, *Medical Malpractice in Nineteenth-Century America* (New York:
New York University Press, 1990).

What about drawing conclusions concerning changes in the occurrence of injury over time? Unless there is evidence of increasing deadliness for a particular type of injury, it is reasonable to assume that the rise in deaths attributed to a cause reflects a rise as well in the number of injuries that were not fatal. So if accidental deaths grew twofold in most categories but fourfold in one particular category, it is most likely that the latter injuries also grew faster than injuries from other causes. The alternative is that the latter cause was suddenly killing a greater portion of those it injured than before, while other sources of injury were not.

Returning to the explosions/hallway-falls comparison, the assumption is that if explosions were more deadly than hallway falls in 1870, they would remain more deadly throughout the following forty years. No evidence exists that one cause grew more deadly than others in proportion to injuries. Since that did not occur, then using change in deaths as a proxy for change in injuries should work well.

The comparability of change in injury rates does not assume that the relation between injuries and deaths stayed constant over time. The rates might well have diverged. Improvement in medical techniques that saved more severely injured patients probably diminished the ratio of fatal injuries to all injuries.[43] Comparability merely assumes that any divergence in trends occurred evenly across all causes. This makes sense; medical improvements were not selectively applied to victims of one sort of accident, while denied to similarly injured victims from accidents of another sort.

Little substantive information on numbers of accidental injuries exists with which to test these ideas. Louis Dublin, who devoted a lifetime to the study of mortality and morbidity, noted at the end of his career in the 1960s that the incidence and causes of accidents were still "not fully known."[44] Dublin continued to use rates of accidental death as the most reliable source to study trends in accidents.

Other indices of accidents are fraught with problems. One industrious reporter tallied the accidents reported to the New York police in 1891, counting 5,223 "resulting in serious or fatal injury."[45] Unless the reporter was using stringent criteria to define serious injury, though, the

---

43. See David Rosner, *A Once Charitable Enterprise: Hospitals and Health Care in Brooklyn and New York, 1885–1915* (New York: Cambridge University Press, 1982).

44. Louis I. Dublin, *Factbook on Man from Birth to Death* (New York: Macmillan, 1965), 242.

45. Pitcher, "Accidents and Accident Insurance," 135.

number that was reported to the police must have been a small fraction of all the city's accidents that year. Why? Because the city coroner found an average of 1,300 deaths by accident in Manhattan the years around 1890. Are we to believe that one of every four (1,300 of 5,200) accidents in the city resulted in a death? Weber's 1899 study of industrial accidents in New York found only 1.5 to 5.8 percent to be fatal.[46] The number of accidents reported to the police, then, was far from the true number of accidents that befell the citizens of New York City.

There is no way to reliably assess the incidence of accidental injury over these forty years apart from counting accidental deaths. Paul Uselding has compared mortality rates among occupations at the turn of the century to prove that what he calls "the muckraker thesis"—that industrialization increased workers' mortality rates—was fallacious.[47] He reaches the conclusion that contemporary concern over danger at work was unwarranted, because "manufacturing and mechanical employments . . . had a lower death rate . . . than several other non-industrial occupational categories."[48]

The use of death rates is innovative—and the essential flaw in Uselding's study. As Table 13 shows, accidents were one small, though growing, cause of death at the turn of the century. Treating mortality rates as indicative of accident rates buries stark differences among occupational accident rates under the more frequent causes of death common to all men, which are irrelevant to the consideration of industrial violence. Mortality rates are broad measures that obscure the picture of danger in the workplace.

Roger Ransom and Richard Sutch suggest another problem with using mortality rates as a surrogate for accident rates. Mortality rates are higher for occupations that individuals stay in into old age. As they point out, individuals do not retain high-risk occupations into old age. This made the mortality rate for high-risk jobs lower than for other work, despite high accident rates.[49] The experience of injury victims' return to work in New

46. Weber, "Compensation," 571. Another tally of accidents, this for the entire country by the American Medical Association, reported that for three months in 1910, there had been 22,328 people hurt in accidents (excepting railroad accidents), 2,948 of them fatally. Fatalities by this account were the result of about 13 percent of all injurious accidents.

47. Paul Uselding, "In Dispraise of the Muckrakers: United States Occupational Mortality, 1890–1910," *Research in Economic History* 1 (1976): 334–71.

48. Ibid., 348–49.

49. See Roger Ransom and Richard Sutch, "The Labor of Older Americans: Retirement of Men On and Off the Job, 1870–1937," *Journal of Economic History* 46 (March 1986): 1–30. This is shown plainly by an example Ransom and Sutch drew from closer

York bears this idea out. Almost invariably, they moved to safer, less demanding (and less remunerative) jobs. Their misfortune accelerated the job-to-job odyssey characteristic of the life-work cycle that Ransom and Sutch find.[50]

Ostensibly, Uselding's use of death rates captures more fully the risk posed by particular kinds of work because deaths from job-related disease also make the tally. This, admittedly, is a shortcoming of representing work injury by fatal work accidents as I do. Deaths from industrial disease do not get included because the workplace cause is so far removed from the fatal consequence. The remedy is to more closely study smaller populations, disease by disease, to learn what portion of various diseases might be attributable to industrial, mining, and other types of work. This could then be added to information on accidental injury to form a well-rounded picture of the consequences of industry on health. In contrast, to employ all-encompassing measures of death like mortality rates on national populations so overloads the statistical portrait that the effect of industrial disease is lost together with that of industrial accidents.

My contention, based on accidental death figures, is that accident rates were not rising, which must be distinguished from Uselding's conclusion,

---

categorization of the same data Uselding employed, comparing the mortality rates of professors and quarrymen. Professors rank high on an occupational mortality scale, while quarrymen do not (32.4 deaths per thousand for professors, compared to 5.3 per thousand for quarrymen).

50. Four cases exemplify this pattern. Harshaw Scott had been a chrono-lithographer, making $2,000 per year before being struck by a train. Afterward he became a night watchman at Franklin Bank Note Company. *Harshaw Scott* v. *Pennsylvania Railroad*, 1890 Number P111, N.Y.C. Supreme Court.

George Huber made $18 per week as a stevedore until his leg was destroyed by a sling full of logs. His employer Ocean Steamship paid him $10 per week for four months. After a year he found a job at $13 per week. *George Huber* v. *Ocean Steamship Company et al.*, 1890 Number W57, N.Y.C. Supreme Court.

John Toner had been a motorman for the New York City Railway Co. at $18 per week for eight years before losing a leg in a multitrolley accident. He had trouble finding other than sporadic employment after that, serving as a night watchman for a couple months at $10 per week and for six weeks at $12 per week. *John Toner* v. *New York City Railway*, 1910 Number N139, N.Y.C. Supreme Court. Charles Schwartz lost his skilled trade after having his feet crushed by an elevator in a building he was constructing: "Before the accident I could not be any better. I never was sick in my life. My earnings were from Twenty-five to Thirty dollars a week. My trade was iron work. I always acted as foreman. I done several buildings. . . . Since my injury I have not done any work. At my trade I can't get any more. I cannot go in a building. I cannot get up or down a ladder and another thing I could not stand it all day on the feet. I tried to be a night watchman but I could not stand it all night." *Charles Schwartz* v. *Onward Construction Company*, 1910 Number O109, N.Y.C. Supreme Court. All four plaintiffs won their cases and received sizable awards.

drawn from mortality rates, that industrial work was not especially injurious. On the surface, the two points seem mutually supportive. But my finding does not declare work in New York to have been "safe." While I have shown that work injuries could not have grown as fast as work injury suits did, their slower growth, stagnation, or decline occurred at a high level of work injury.

The best sources on work injury in the period—Eastman, Hoffman, Dublin—concur that work accidents were taking a high toll. Uselding recognizes this but writes, "Surely any form of mortality and morbidity has the capacity to shock. It is impossible to form a balanced appraisal from this kind of discursive evidence." What is needed is "an appropriate set of accident frequency and severity rates over time."[51] That certainly would be desirable. But until that set is constructed, the evidence supports the proposition that Uselding discounts, that work accidents "significantly increas[ed] the incidence and severity of mortality and morbidity of the occupied population."[52] The research of Hoffman and the others also makes clear that there were especially risky occupations: in New York City, construction and the maritime trades; elsewhere, railroad work and mining.[53]

Finally, Uselding concludes from the unexceptional mortality rate he found among manufacturing and mining workers that work conditions and injuries in these industries drew an inordinate amount of society's attention, implying that public action was unwarranted. My finding that injury suits climbed more quickly than injuries should not be construed as supporting that proposition. The goal here has been to explain what caused the rise in injury lawsuits, not to determine whether that rise was justifiable. That it was not simply a rise in injuries that propelled the rise in injury suits does not imply that the rise in injury suits was therefore

51. Uselding, "Dispraise," 350.

52. Ibid. As just one indicator of the significance of work injury, Hoffman estimated that of all fatal accidents, one-third happened at work (25–35,000 of 82,000 per year, 1912). Hoffman, *Industrial Accident Statistics*, 1–55.

53. Hoffman's study for the Bureau of Labor Statistics reported that the average rate for fatal work injuries across all occupations was .73 per 1,000 population. For miners, the figure was over five times as high, for sailors over four times. Railroad workers were over three times as likely to be killed as the average worker, and construction workers nearly twice as likely. Interestingly, Uselding's thesis concentrated on manufacturing workers, whom Hoffman found to have a lower than average work-injury rate. But industrialization affected work at more places than the factory, as discussed in Chapter 2. The equation of manufacturing workers with industrial workers was fortuitous for the use of mortality statistics but limits the effects of industrialization and mechanization on work to those that occur in factories. Hoffman, *Industrial Accident Statistics*, 1–55.

excessive or unwarranted. That would require a further step involving a normative assessment comparable to deeming today's court use "excessive litigation." The study of numbers of injuries and injury suits is different than the study of the perceptions of those numbers.

Contemporaries' perceptions of numbers of injuries and injury suits did have effects on the rise of those suits. One of the effects was what Uselding dispraised: a change in society's rules in an effort to lessen the number of accidents or provide compensation for the injured. Since the change in numbers of injuries was not the driving force behind the rise in injury lawsuits, perhaps the impetus came from these changes in rules. That is where this study turns next, to the legal process itself, to see whether changes in the structure or rules of that process catalyzed the increase in court use.

3. THE LAW

Since injury suits climbed more steeply than either demographics or danger could account for, other factors must have played a part in that ascent. Logic says that the next place to turn to is the legal system itself. Perhaps something in the system had become more enticing, pulling more suits from injurious circumstances. Changed rules might have been the lure. Had suits with little previous chance for success now become compensable under new law? Alterations in court structure or procedure might have been the draw: Had access to the court become easier or its procedures simpler, making use of a court more amenable to the people of New York City?

The answers to these questions wait inside the legal system. This, especially the focus on rules, is what legal history had been exclusively about for so long—"internal" legal history. The law's story told of the evolution of rules, procedure, jurisdiction, and other topics "distinctively legal."[1] As legal scholars became realists, these topics lost primacy to the social influences and consequences of law. Yet the weight of the internal logic and heritage of the law—its culture—upon the application of the law was very real. In downplaying it, the realists undervalued an important component of history. Ideas and traditions can carry power enough to perpetuate institutions. They can mute, or even override, current social values and the personal values with which the institution's agents might otherwise imbue the law. Individuals can rise above their own immediate

---

1. Gordon, "Introduction: J. Willard Hurst and the Common Law Tradition," 10–11.

interests to be guided by greater principles, logic, or heritage, though such transcendence has been claimed more often than it has actually occurred throughout the course of history.

Even the most empirically minded social scientists who study legal ways have found that change in the law cannot be attributed entirely to the power of societal forces.[2] Those legal historians who emphasize society's influence are regularly admonished by critics who say that law has developed from internal as well as external forces.[3] The admonition may be gratuitous, because historians who examine the law in society continue to recognize the effects of substantive doctrine, structure, and legal culture upon the law's development.[4]

Reconstructing the governing ideas of injury liability as the judges of the New York court in the era comprehended and acted upon them, the ruling principle of tort law in 1870 was that every citizen owed a general duty of reasonable care to the rest of society. Judges believed that care and its opposite, neglect, governed tort liability. They assigned liability by determining whether the parties to a suit had fulfilled their duties of care. Scholars now argue that this was not uniformly so. In particular sorts of injurious acts, other considerations ruled, even where the terminology still followed negligence. Yet the idea was so central that injury law was as often called negligence law as it was tort law.[5]

2. See James Gibson, "Environmental Constraints on the Behaviour of Judges: A Representational Model of Judicial Decision Making," *Law and Society Review* 14 (1979–80): 343–70. Gibson concluded that only one sixth of the variance between courts in judging similar issues could be explained by judges' responsiveness to a direct social force, the influence of local norms.

3. Mark Tushnet, "Perspectives on the Development of American Law: A Critical Review of Friedman's 'A History of American Law'," *Wisconsin Law Review* 1977 (1977): 81–109.

4. See Kagan et al., "Business of State Supreme Courts," 123–24; Lawrence Friedman, "Legal Culture and Social Development," *Law and Society Review* 4 (1969–70): 34. *Change in substantive doctrine* occurs when courts establish a new rule of law or when a legal question is "settled" by legislation. *Structure* refers to such factors as the number and level of courts in a system, their jurisdiction, and the number of judges serving on them. *Legal culture* includes attitudes within the law system, absorbed by attorneys and judges in their training and interaction with other lawyers and jurists.

5. Robert Rabin points out that the term *negligence* was employed two distinct ways: as the term that referred specifically to the fault principle on the one hand and as the more general label for the field or cause of action on the other. The latter included the principle but also involved other aspects of determining liability, such as proof of cause, damages, and the duty itself. Rabin blames this dual usage for misleading scholars into believing that the principle has been more pervasive than it actually ever was. New York City's judges evinced Rabin's idea; they confounded the two meanings regularly, so that their references to negligence often had nothing to do with the breach of the duty of due care. Robert Rabin,

The negligence rule was based on fault. Injury did not by itself give right to sue, as Judge George Barrett explained: "It stands to reason that a person cannot recover from what is in its nature an inevitable accident. There are plenty of misfortunes to which people are subjected where they must suffer without recompense. It is only when the accident was caused by someone's negligence that an action will lie."[6]

To ascertain fault, a court measured two elements: the care the injurer displayed in doing the deed that inadvertently led to injury, and the care with which the injured person had comported himself at the time of injury. For an injury to be compensable under the negligence rule, the injurer must have been negligent in his action, and the victim completely free of any negligence. One New Yorker might have caused the injury of another, and if the injurer was cautious and the injury happened despite his efforts to safeguard from such an event, no liability existed.[7]

Alternately, by the rule of contributory negligence, the injurer might have been grossly negligent and still have no liability, if the victim of the injury had contributed in any way to the accident. Judge Thomas O'Gorman put it bluntly to the jury in *Bail* v. *New York, New Haven, and Hartford Railroad:* "Wherever it appears that there has been fault on both sides, then even though one of the two careless persons has been injured, he or his representatives are without redress."[8] The rule directed that a lapse of care of even the slightest degree made injury victims fully responsible for the accidents that befell them.[9]

"The Historical Development of the Fault Principle: A Reinterpretation," *Georgia Law Review* 15 (1981): 931–33. See also James P. Murphy, "Evolution of the Duty of Care: Some Thoughts," *DePaul Law Review* 30 (1980): 147–79, especially 147–53, which offers a similar corrective about the development of the duty of care.

6. *George Morison* v. *Broadway and Seventh Avenue Railroad Company,* 1890 Number B190, N.Y.C. Supreme Court.

7. For more detailed discussion of negligence law in the nineteenth century, see Friedman, *History of American Law,* 409–27; Charles Gregory, "Trespass to Negligence to Absolute Liability," *Virginia Law Review* 37 (1951): 359–97; Rabin, "Historical Development," 925–61; Richard Epstein, "The Historical Origins and Economic Structure of Workers' Compensation Law," *Georgia Law Review* 16 (1982): 775–819; and White, *Tort Law in America.*

8. *Abraham Bail* v. *New York, New Haven, and Hartford Railroad,* 1910 Number B607, N.Y.C. Supreme Court.

9. On contributory negligence, see especially Wex Malone, "The Formative Era of Contributory Negligence," *Illinois Law Review* 41 (1946): 151–82; and David Kretzmer, "Transformation of Tort Liability in the Nineteenth Century: The Visible Hand," *Oxford Journal of Legal Studies* 4 (1984): 46–87. Malone viewed contributory negligence as a nineteenth-century creation, appearing at the beginning of the century in England, but in the United States "it lay dormant until about the middle of the last century; then suddenly it sprang to life" (p. 151). Malone counted the appearances of contributory negligence in

The other requirement of negligence law, so apparent that it might easily be overlooked, was that the injury had to occur by accident. An injurer who knowingly acted to injure another (or did not act to avoid injuring another) was no longer subject to the rules of negligence but to the laws of malicious or willful injury. There was a substantial difference: The injured person's contribution to her or his own injury was not considered in the determination of liability in instances of willful injury.[10]

Judge and jury still faced a number of issues that required decision. An important one was, what constituted enough care to fulfill one's social duty? New York courts settled on a standard that required of both parties the care that an "ordinary," reasonable man would exhibit in the situation. Of course, this did not resolve much, for the definition of ordinary care depended upon the norms of those judging each incident. And the ordinary care standard was not universally applied; it was relaxed for children, according to age.[11] For the very youngest, those not having the ability to care for themselves (*non sui juris*), their requirement of care was passed on to a supervising adult. This doctrine, imputable negligence, Lawrence Friedman considers "one of the most offensive rules" of the era, because in practice it impeded recovery for children's injuries.[12]

---

appeals courts cases and discovered that the rule showed up five times more often in the decade after 1870 than just twenty years before. Kretzmer found, to the contrary, a principle closely akin to contributory negligence operating a century earlier in England.

10. An example of what the difference could mean: in the 1867 case of *John Whittaker* v. *Eighth Avenue Railroad,* Whittaker recovered a $2,500 verdict for an injury, despite the judge's declaration that Whittaker's negligence had clearly contributed to the injury. The judge had instructed the jury that "if the accident resulted from the willful act of the driver—he knowing at the time that if he kept the car moving he must necessarily run into the plaintiff—the company were liable." The evidence showed that Whittaker had been standing "on a plank . . . over an excavation in the street. While standing, looking at the workmen employed in the excavation, he was run into by one of the [defendant's] cars and knocked . . . into the excavation." The driver had not slowed down and after hitting Whittaker was heard to yell "Damn him, it served him right." The evidence persuaded the jury to find the railroad company liable for malicious injury. "Damages against the Eighth Avenue Railroad for Malicious Injury," *New York Times,* 22 June 1867, p. 3.

11. As Judge Peter Hendricks presented it: "The law is not so unreasonable as to require from a child five years of age the same amount of prudence and care on the streets as it would require from an adult who was of mature age and of mature experience. The care which a person is bound to exercise is to be measured by the intelligence, the age and the experience of the person who is involved." This attenuated care ruled right up to the verge of adulthood, in this case "a boy of 18." *Margaret Hayden, Administrator* v. *Adrian Joline et al., Receivers of the New York City Railway Company et al.,* 1910 Number H483, N.Y.C. Supreme Court.

12. Friedman, *History of American Law,* 417–18; see *Ellen Delahunt, Administrator* v. *Southern Boulevard Railroad Company,* 1910 Number S696, N.Y.C. Supreme Court, for an example of the application of imputed negligence. The plaintiff, a widow caring for four

The elderly were accorded no special status that required extra care on the part of those who interacted with them. In fact, the court required special care by the elderly themselves. If an old person "because of infirmity or old age . . . was unequal to the little effort that a younger man might find easy" to perform a task safely, then he or she would be liable for any injury that resulted from attempting the feat, O'Gorman told a jury. The measure of freedom from contributory negligence for the elderly became, "Did the plaintiff act with reasonable care considering his years and his capacity?"[13]

Other people with reduced physical capabilities fared better. One Supreme Court judge charged a jury that the "reasonable time" a streetcar driver owed Caroline Rexford, injured while trying to board the car, was longer than for ordinary passengers because she was an invalid on crutches. "What is a reasonable time," he instructed, "depends on circumstances—a cripple should have more time than a well person."[14]

The care one exercised to stay out of harm's way could be imperfect and still not constitute contributory negligence. For example, Judge George Barnard left the question to the jury in *Henrietta Conz, Administrator* v. *Hudson River Railroad* whether the victim, her husband, "suddenly surprised with an ox-team on the track and an express train running down upon him at the rate of thirty miles an hour," could have been expected to have "use[d] his best faculties and make the very best move possible to escape the threatened danger." Barnard did not hide his reading of the situation. "Something must be allowed," he suggested, "for human nature under such circumstances."[15]

The court also established rules for how directly one's acts had to contribute to an accident for those acts to be considered causal. The basic rule was that the act or condition must be the immediate cause of the injury, with no other person or act between it and the accident. This was more easily stated than applied in practice, as injury often resulted from

---

daughters, recovered $2,000 for the death of her youngest child when the jury absolved her of fault in response to a specific question by the judge, Henry Dugro. Because the child had done nothing that would have been negligent for an adult, there was no negligence that Delahunt should have prevented by closer vigilance. Thus there was no negligence imputed back to the daughter and no bar to recovery.

13. *Herman Crueger* v. *F. Whitridge as Receiver of the Union Railway Company of New York City*, 1910 Number W478, N.Y.C. Supreme Court.

14. *Caroline Rexford* v. *Seventh Avenue Railroad Company*, reported in "The $20,000 Suit Against the Seventh-Avenue Railroad . . .," *New York Times*, 12 December 1866, p. 2.

15. "Action against a Railroad Company for Alleged Negligence," *New York Times*, 13 November 1867, p. 2.

a concatenation of acts by different parties. Life was untidy that way; there could be many contributors to an injury, each an equally likely cause.[16] But the law would not countenance complexity: "It will not do to bring into Court a case of mixed or compound negligence. . . . The action must be for the negligence of the defendant, and the plaintiff . . . is bound to make out that he suffered the injury from the negligence of the defendant exclusively."[17]

Further complicating the court's task of affixing cause was that at the end of the century, courts were applying that one word "cause" to two distinct operations: determining simple cause, or "cause-in-fact," and deciding legal, or "proximate" cause. Simple cause evaluated the facts in asking whether the relationship between a defendant and an injured person was one of direct cause and effect. Proximate cause applied policy to the relationship to ascertain if the simple cause was one where a legal responsibility lay. Once simple cause was established in a case, proximate cause asked about the considerations that limited or extended legal liability. Jurists and prominent legal thinkers were moving to disentangle the two operations, primarily to get the jury as far away from rules as possible. Judges' instructions and lawyers arguments from 1910 reflect some effort to realize the distinction.[18]

Along the same line, the rule of *respondeat superior* (literally, "let the master answer") specified the liability of New Yorkers for accidents caused by those acting as their agents. By this rule, individuals and corporations bore full responsibility for the acts done for them by others in the course of agency. For example, a streetcar conductor's rough treatment of passengers was held to be the legal responsibility of his employing streetcar company rather than of the conductor himself.[19] The

16. Attorney Nelson Zabriskie argued (to no avail) that his client's injury passing by a construction site was caused by a group of conditions, including failure to warn on the ground as well as by lowering a boom. "There may have been a number of proximate causes," Zabriskie argued. The lift "might have been lowered with the greatest possible care and the accident never would have happened if there had not been negligence down on the sidewalk." Judge Henry Dugro did not view the event the same way, and Zabriskie lost his case. *Angelino Sartirana* v. *New York County Bank et al.*, 1910 Number S243, N.Y.C. Supreme Court.

17. Judge E. Darwin Smith in *John Schappner* v. *The Second Avenue Railroad Company*, 1870 Number S392, N.Y.C. Supreme Court.

18. See case cited in note 16, for example. Wex Malone, "Ruminations on Cause in Fact," *Stanford Law Review* 9 (1956): 60–99, reprinted in Robert Rabin, ed., *Perspectives on Tort Law* (Boston: Little, Brown & Co., 1976), 44–59.

19. Employers did not concede this rule gracefully. In the *Isaacs* case, the Third Avenue Railroad sought dismissal on the grounds that the railroad company was not responsible for

employer's liability was at issue most often in transportation and traffic accidents, where responsibility for drivers' carelessness was assigned to the drivers' companies.

Not all agent-caused accidents fell under the employer's responsibility rule. Two very different rules governed such situations. An employer was responsible to anyone except his employee for the negligence of his agents; to employees, themselves agents, there was no liability. This points out the special legal conditions under which workers labored. Because almost every work accident could be attributed in some way to the action of co-workers, orders of a foreman, or failure of a supervisor to enforce reasonable precautions, employers escaped all responsibility. While, in principle, negligence was also the law of the workplace, negligence and contributory negligence were interpreted uniquely for workers' injuries to effectively bar their recovery for their injuries.[20]

Special rules were concocted to apply to liability for accidents in the workplace; the rules had no validity in any other context.[21] The fellow-servant provision was the first of these: If an accident was in any part the responsibility of another employee, directly or indirectly, the employer could not be held responsible. This was how *respondeat superior* was taken away from workers. Judges had made into law a personal contact model of the workplace appropriate to an age (fast becoming past in the 1840s when Lemuel Shaw invoked it) when the owner/employer and the worker occupied the same shop, when orders and supervision moved directly.[22]

---

the "willful trespass" upon Mary Isaacs by the conductor. They opined that "the act of the conductor in intentionally shoving the plaintiff from the car . . . was not a matter of negligence in the course of his employment." The judge, George Barnard, did not agree. *Isaacs* v. *Third Avenue Railroad*. See also *Albert Scott* v. *Central Park North and East River Railroad*, 1890 Number C39, N.Y.C. Supreme Court. Scott, trying to get off a Belt Line car near the Cortland Street Ferry, was "assisted" by the driver of the car "who . . . without any provocation . . . struck [Scott] a violent blow in the mouth with a clenched fist, thereby knocking out two of [Scott's] front teeth, cutting open his left eye and pushing him off the car." The company was held liable, though the original jury award of $880 was overturned on appeal as excessive; a subsequent jury's reduced award of $500 was not challenged by the defendant. A similar incident on a mainline railroad also brought a recovery for the plaintiff under the *respondeat superior* rule. See *John O'Brien* v. *New York, New Haven, and Hartford Railroad*, 1890 Number N41, N.Y.C. Supreme Court.

20. Rabin is more direct: "In short, the fault principle was a foreign element in the industrial injury context." "Historical Development," 947.

21. "No validity" is not entirely true; Rabin notes that the assumption-of-risk doctrine was adopted in the decades after 1910 to govern accidents in some forms of recreation. Rabin, "Historical Development," 943.

22. Work-injury liability rules are concisely and clearly presented in Friedman and Ladinsky, "Social Change and the Law of Industrial Accidents," and are also discussed in the

The fellow-servant rule's application to an age of remote ownership, management by intermediates, and an increasingly segmented work process required creative interpreting: Who on a construction site, in a factory, or at a railroad yard was the worker's "fellow," and who was her or his employer? The courts treated the question as if the answer was natural: The employer was only the person or entity that owned the business. All others, managers and workers alike, were employees. By the fellow-servant rule, they were the ones responsible for injuries, not the employer.

That interpretation combined with the personal contact model of the workplace to block workers' injury recoveries in two ways. First, in focusing attention on the acts of other workers, it directed attention away from the basic conditions and practices of a workplace, components of injury that could be more readily seen as the employers' responsibility. Second, if a case ever got as far as looking at the conditions and practices of the workplace, it attributed them, especially work commands, to immediate supervisors rather than to the ultimate determiner of those conditions, the employer. If employers could not be credited with commands, they could not be held liable for the consequences of commands.

The second special rule applied to workers' injuries was the assumption-of-risk doctrine. In accepting a job, the courts decided, a worker assumed all the ordinary risks incidental to the job, whether evident or not. In addition, they assumed all extraordinary risks that were "open and obvious." This proved a powerful weapon for employers, as it virtually negated their common-law duty to provide workers with safe workplaces. Not that the safe-workplace rule was so exacting that it cried to be overridden. As Judge George Andrews presented it in 1890, "The rule is that the master does not owe to his servants the duty to furnish the best known or conceivable appliances, . . . simply safe and suitable [ones]."[23] But the value of the assumption-of-risk rule was that it could be applied to virtually any circumstance to stop workers from successfully bringing suit.[24]

---

sources cited in note 7. For New York's rules in particular, see Robert Asher, "Failure and Fulfillment: Agitation for Employers' Liability Legislation and the Origins of Workmen's Compensation in New York State, 1876–1910," *Labor History* 24 (1983): 198–222; and Robert Wesser, "Conflict and Compromise: The Workmen's Compensation Movement in New York, 1890–1913," *Labor History* 12 (1971): 345–72.

23. *Albert Eldridge* v. *Atlas Steamship Company,* 1890 Number A11, N.Y.C. Supreme Court.

24. The justification for this rule was that a person who voluntarily entered danger must suffer the consequences (in Latin, as was the popular judicial practice of the day, *volenti non fit injuria* or "to a willing person no injury is done").

The uniqueness of the assumption-of-risk doctrine to work-injury cases is made starkly apparent in comparing the allotment of risks in the workplace to the same apportionment in other places in the city. On Manhattan's sidewalks, for example, "No one is bound to anticipate that the sidewalks are in a dangerous condition[;] those using them have the right to assume that they are in proper and safe condition, and also the right to use them in the usual manner."[25]

Applying the tort-liability rules in the courtroom, the injured person faced the task of proving all the required propositions, the fact of injury, the defendant's negligence in causing it, and the victim's freedom from contributory negligence, by a preponderance of evidence. This requirement of New York tort law was a source of difficulty to injured litigants.[26] First proving that the alleged injurer had in fact caused the injury, and then that he was negligent in causing it, required evidence that an injury victim was in a poor position to obtain. Collecting witnesses' names could be difficult from a prone position.[27] As a result, injured persons often served as the sole eyewitness for their own cases.

Meanwhile, injurers learned quickly to collect names of witnesses, to note conditions at the scene, and to record accounts of accidents. Repeat

25. Loran Lewis, "The Law of Icy Sidewalks in New York State," *Yale Law Journal* 6 (1896–97), 262. This is just one affirmation of what contemporaries found evident: It was not that principles were evenly applied to all injuries to injured workers' detriment but that different laws ruled injuries in the workplace. See Weber, "Compensation," 645–46.

26. Not every state assigned the burden of proof to the plaintiff; Gary Schwartz notes that the burden resided with defendants to disprove negligence under California law, perhaps explaining his conclusion that injury law was reasonably favorable to victims. See Schwartz, "Tort Law and the Economy," 1717–75.

27. Mary Isaacs had the presence of mind to start gathering evidence immediately after being thrown from a streetcar (see p. 11), but her actions were exceptional in this regard. Typically, amassing evidence posed real problems for potential plaintiffs. Police occasionally collected names of witnesses at accidents but just as often did not. See *Jennie Flax* v. *New York Taxicab Company*, 1910 Number N171, N.Y.C. Supreme Court. Occasionally a friend, relative, or other person at the scene would take names of witnesses, or neighborhood witnesses would volunteer their testimony at the home of the injured. See *Annie Baum* v. *Giuseppe Gallo et al.*, 1910 Number G315, N.Y.C. Supreme Court; and *Benjamin Stein, Administrator* v. *Grand Ice Cream Company*, 1910 Number G320, N.Y.C. Supreme Court. In the latter case, it took an astute peddler to gather names after police dispersed witnesses. "A few minutes after [the accident]," witness Daniel White recalled, "an officer came and there was quite a few gathered in the drug store by that time and the officer asked what we all wanted and chased everybody out." The neighborhood lemon peddler, Max Kriegsberg, stepped in. The policeman did not ask for any names, Kriegsberg recounted, so "I went outside and I got a few names of witnesses." Having witnesses' names did not end plaintiffs' problems. It was only after two trials and a room-by-room search of the neighborhood that Stein's lawyer managed to find witness Fanny Gross, and then he had to locate an interpreter to interview her.

injurers, such as streetcar companies, required it of their employees. A New York streetcar conductor testified that the company's "awful book of rules and regulations" required the immediate deployment of this defensive action; failure to perform would bring "a fine and a threat of dismissal." The steetcar conductor, he explained, "has to be most careful in case of accidents, whether they are serious or trivial. If John Smith sprains his foot in alighting from the car, the conductor must interview John Smith, and, if possible examine his ankle; and he must secure the names and addresses of five or six persons who saw John Smith sprain his ankle"[28]

Proving negligence in work-injury cases was especially difficult, as all witnesses were typically employed by the defending company. This did not dispose those witnesses interested in preserving their jobs to readily volunteer testimony for the injured person. Usually an injured worker could only count on those witnessing co-workers who had left the company since the accident. And arrayed against the worker's witnesses would be a collection of supervisors and other workers to affirm the defendant's story.[29]

If proving negligence was difficult, proving one's own freedom from contributory negligence was more so. Defense attorneys constantly complained that plaintiffs introduced "negative proof"—witnesses testifying to *not* hearing any bells, whistles, or verbal warnings before an accident, for example. Yet the contributory negligence rule invoked by the same defendants forced plaintiffs to show the absence of negligence, which was entirely an exercise in negative proof.

Documenting the negative proposition posed unique problems. It was difficult to find witnesses to testify that the injury victim exercised reasonable care at the moment of the accident. Anything else—for instance,

28. Anonymous conductor, interview published in the *Independent* 55 (1903): 1920–24, reprinted as "Experiences of a Streetcar Conductor," in David Katzman and William Tuttle, eds., *Plain Folks* (Urbana: University of Illinois Press, 1982), 16–17.

29. See for example *Kate Hogan* v. *David Henderson et al.*, 1890 Number H74, N.Y.C. Supreme Court; *William Jenkins* v. *Mahopac Iron Ore Company*, 1890 Number J3, N.Y.C. Supreme Court; *Thomas Riley* v. *Quebec Steamship Company*, 1890 Number Q1, N.Y.C. Supreme Court; *Abraham Bloom* v. *Schwarzenbach, Huber, and Company*, 1910 Number B556, N.Y.C. Supreme Court; *Bernard Ford* v. *Joseph Moses and Arthur Stern*, 1910 Number F271, N.Y.C. Supreme Court; and *Edward Kerman* v. *Pennsylvania Steel Company*, 1910 Number K218, N.Y.C. Supreme Court. One case unusual for its number of plaintiff witnesses was *Susie Bambal, Administrator* v. *Michael Breen*, 1910 Number B549, N.Y.C. Supreme Court. Bambal was able to get three of her husband's fellow trench diggers (a real ethnic montage: Peter Krulder, Genaro Vigilante, and Joseph Davidowitz) to testify about the fatal accident and won a $1,000 verdict for the effort.

the general carefulness of the injured person—was not considered pertinent proof. The injured's own testimony was always suspect, and the
opposition invariably subjected anyone else testifying to the injured's
care to skeptical examination: Why did they happen to be watching the
injured person's behavior at the precise moment that accident was immi-
nent? Was the behavior so out of the ordinary as to attract attention? With
such questions, defense attorneys impugned both witness and plaintiff in
short order.

Successful defense required planting only the smallest seed of doubt
with judge and jury, according to contemporary observers. That would
not take much discrediting, because many judges and jurors were predis-
posed to believe that the injured contributed to their own injuries, Crystal
Eastman discovered in her investigation of work accidents in New York.
They had already "made up their minds about this accident question from
what they have heard employers, superintendents, and casualty managers
say . . . . They believe that 95 per cent of the accidents are due to the
carelessness of the men."[30]

The state legislature contributed another important part of injury law.
It created the right to bring suit for a fatal accident through the wrongful-
death statute in 1847. Previously, New York judges voided lawsuits
brought for fatal injuries on the premise that under the common law, the
person's right to sue died with that person.[31] After the wrongful-death
statute, the city Supreme Court judges often informed juries that a dece-
dent's administrator's right to bring suit was statutory, though this distinction—that the rule was not judge-made—was completely extraneous
to the juries' task. It neither directed nor informed the juries' job of applying the law. It was as if judges were impugning the right as unnatural
because it was of legislative rather than common-law origin, and at the
same time as they were noting what a benevolent concession it was to
otherwise unentitled suitors. Judges were less subtle in emphasizing the
award limitations that the legislature had imposed.[32] These limitations

30. Eastman, *Work Accidents*, 84.
31. Lawrence Friedman, drawing upon an argument made by Wex Malone, points out
that the common-law basis for excluding next of kin from the right to compensation had
been that killing a man was a felony and upon conviction the victim's kin had a claim
against the felon's forfeited possessions. Though that form of compensation had vanished
by the nineteenth century, the block on civil lawsuits as an alternative means to compensation was retained to fend off railroad-injury cases, Friedman believes. Friedman, *History
of American Law*, 414–15.
32. An especially lengthy example of this is Josiah Sutherland's exposition to the jury
in *John Ihl* v. *Forty-Second Street and Grand Street Railroad Company*, 1870 Number F69,
N.Y.C. Supreme Court; for further discussion of Sutherland's instructions in *Ihl*, see
Chapter 5.

were two: Only pecuniary loss to the next of kin could be considered in fixing an amount, with no award to be made for pain and suffering; and the ceiling for any award, no matter the magnitude of the loss, was $5,000.[33] *indeed*

These were the general attributes of injury law from 1870 to 1910, but they were not timeless attributes. While debate continues over the origins of the negligence rule and its supporting doctrines, most students of the problem agree that the law changed in the nineteenth century, and some believe the change was dramatic.[34]

That the rules had not been long-settled in 1870 might lead us to suspect that they were susceptible to continued alteration. Charles Gregory and Lawrence Friedman have said as much; Gregory has demonstrated that in one area, extra-hazardous works (e.g., the use of explosives), the battle between fault and strict liability principles never ceased. "The New York Court," he concludes, "was inconsistent and utterly confused in trying to evolve a theory of liability for unintentionally caused harm."[35]

Friedman agrees. In the last two decades of the century, he writes, doctrine "began to wobble." Courts created exceptions such as the vice-principal doctrine that made employers liable to employees for the negligence of the employers' managers, and a tighter safe-workplace duty that held employers directly responsible for a minimum level of workplace safety. These combined with legislated safety standards and railroad liability statutes to mitigate injury law's harshness. The latter applied the vice-principal doctrine to railroads and made them strictly liable to injured workers for discoverable defects in the railroads' equipment and facilities. The exceptions and statutes piled on top of existing rules but did not supplant them. By 1900 this coexistence of contrary principles produced a confusing, "wildly nonuniform" body of negligence law.[36]

Contemporaries recognized that both wobble and nonuniformity were present in decisions of the many state appeals courts and the U.S.

33. The 1847 statute placed no ceiling on recovery; that came soon thereafter (1849) to keep juries from becoming "the uncontrolled judges of the pecuniary injury." Sutherland, in *Ihl*.

34. See Introduction, note 13, and Robert Kaczorowski, "The Common Law Background of Nineteenth Century Tort Law," *Ohio State Law Journal* 51 (1990): 1127–99.

35. Gregory, "Trespass," 372. Though not addressing rules change, and disagreeing with Gregory over what principles were contending, Rabin's discussion of the tension between negligence and non-tort (contract) principles in work-injury law supports the point of susceptibility to change. Rabin, "Historical Development," 925–61.

36. Friedman, *History of American Law*, 423–25.

Supreme Court.[37] But if we shift the focus from the pronouncements of
high courts to the day-to-day applications of doctrine in trial courts, the
picture of change gives way to one of continuity. The work of the New
York City trial court shows that the attention to high courts has exaggerated the amount of change in the doctrine that decided injury suits. Doctrinal change was of little consequence in promoting the use of the legal
system by the injured.

In contrast to the picture of injury rules in flux in high courts throughout the land, intellectual life was much more stable for the judges of New
York City's Supreme Court. Tort rules proved much less volatile. To
gauge by their explanations of the law to juries in 1870, 1890, and 1910,
injury law barely changed at all in the city court. As will be shown in
Chapter 5, judges' instructions to juries could vary widely from judge to
judge and from case to case for any one judge. Yet the range of variance
held quite steady throughout the forty years.

Negligence and contributory negligence remained the essence of the
judges' law. In 1870, Judge Albert Cardozo explained the basic principle:
"The omission of any act which human skill, care and foresight could
have done to prevent this catastrophe is negligence, and makes the defendants liable."[38] Judge E. Darwin Smith's definition of negligence agreed
with Cardozo's, "consist[ing] in the omission of some legal duty, or the
doing of some act carelessly and improperly."[39]

Smith clearly set forth the other half of the liability equation, contributory negligence, in the same case: "If the injury he has sustained is produced by his own negligence, why, then, of course he has no right to
complain, and he has no cause of action. If he has suffered an injury by
his own misconduct, carelessness, or heedlessness, although the defendant may be negligent, too, he has no right to ask a jury to say how far the
defendant was negligent, and divide the negligence between them."[40]

37. See Lindley Clark, "The Legal Liability of Employers for Injuries to Their Employees," *U.S. Bureau of Labor, Bulletin no. 74* (1908), 1–120; and Editorial, *New York
Times,* 19 July 1887, p. 4. Clark's survey gave examples of the variance. In New York,
contrary to most states, a worker's violation of an employer's rule did not in itself constitute contributory negligence by the injured worker. Conversely, while an employer's violation of workplace safety and inspection laws was held as negligence in itself in federal
and other states' courts, it was not in New York's. And while seven states modified the
fellow-servant doctrine through the vice-principal or similar rules and sixteen states eliminated the fellow-servant rule altogether, New York retained it.

38. *Nathaniel Caldwell v. The New Jersey Steamboat Company,* 1870 Number N77,
N.Y.C. Supreme Court.

39. *Schappner v. Second Avenue Railroad.*

40. Ibid.

The rules prevailing in 1890 and 1910 were indistinguishable from 1870's law. Judge Abraham Lawrence spoke for the court of 1890: "Before a plaintiff can recover in an action of this character, she must establish . . . two facts. In the first place, that the accident from which she claims injury resulted to her was caused by the negligence and want of care of the defendant, and that she herself did not contribute to the accident by want of care or negligence on her own part."[41] Judge Samuel Greenbaum hit upon the same points in delivering a typical negligence instruction to his 1910 jury: "It is incumbent upon the plaintiff in a negligence case to establish not only that the person sued was the one who was guilty of the particular act of negligence that caused the injury, but that [the plaintiff] himself did not by any act of negligence on his part contribute to the injury."[42] The doctrinal equivalence of the 1910 exposition to that of 1870 is surprisingly consistent, given the lapse of forty years. Clearly, the fundaments of the law remained constant throughout this period.

The ancillary rules held just as steadily. The standard of care had two basic traits in 1870: It was based on common sense, that of a "rational, intelligent, and careful man," and it was relative to the context of the injuring incident.[43] The same two traits defined the care standard in 1890 and 1910. In 1890, George Andrews explained it as "the reasonable care which prudent men should exercise under [the] circumstances," interchangeable almost word for word with Judge John Brady's 1910 definition: "that degree of care which the average man of ordinary prudence would use and would deem adequate to the circumstances."[44]

41. *Hedwig Blaechinska* v. *Howard Mission and Home for Little Wanderers*, 1890 Number H49, N.Y.C. Supreme Court. In another case, Judge Andrews's exposition of the guiding principles was almost identical to Lawrence's: "The plaintiff cannot recover ordinarily, simply because he has been injured by an accident. In order to succeed in this action it is necessary that . . . the accident has been caused by the negligence of the defendant, and that the plaintiff's own negligence did not contribute to the injury." *Lauris Tendrup* v. *John Stephenson Co., Ltd.*, 1890 Number J37, N.Y.C. Supreme Court.

42. *Francesco Latargia, Administrator* v. *Frederick Whitridge, Receiver of the Third Avenue Railroad*, 1910 Number W472, N.Y.C. Supreme Court.

43. Judge Smith elaborated the standard for the *Schappner* jury: "The rule of caution and care which should govern the conduct of men depends upon the place, the time, and the circumstances which surround him. Every man must exercise his common sense, and common intelligence, and common prudence in respect to the care of his person, and in the exercise of his rights of locomotion." See also *Angelina Seabrook* v. *John Hecker*, 1870 H100, N.Y.C. Supreme Court, where Judge Barnard highlighted the relative nature of the care required of builders. The appropriate standard, Barnard explained, was "the care and caution that all other persons engaged in the line of buildings he is engaged in, use."

44. The 1890 instructions come from *Tendrup* v. *Stephenson Co.*; see also George

The judiciary's standard of cause remained similarly unaltered. Smith's express requirement of exclusive, not mixed or compound, causation was an 1870 emanation.[45] Judge Edward McCall's 1910 instructions invoked the same rule, that the injury must have "resulted directly and immediately from the cause of this accident. By immediately it is not meant point of time. It means in direct line of causation."[46]

The mitigating rules Lawrence Friedman presents were not all post-1870 arrivals in the New York City Supreme Court. Attorneys were already employing the *res ipsa loquitur* (the thing speaks for itself) doctrine in 1870 as they would in 1910 to shift the burden of proof onto the defendant. The doctrine assumed that especially dangerous acts that led to injury were negligent and left it to the defendant to show otherwise. As Cardozo explained to a jury in 1870: "The law presumes from the fact of explosion that the defendants have been guilty of negligence, and it rests with them to show that they have not been, and that this misfortune was not attributable to any cause which human skill, care, and foresight could, in the condition of science at the time of this occurrence, have prevented."[47]

It is possible that judges became more reluctant to apply the doctrine over time. Attorney Joseph Hlavac's inclusion of a full explanation of the defendants' negligent acts at the same time he was invoking *res ipsa loquitur* in the 1910 case *Rokos* v. *Astoria Marble Company et al.* suggests as much.[48] Hlavac hedged his bet because he was not sure the judges would accept the rule's application; *res ipsa loquitur* should have obviated the detailing of negligence. Elsewhere, in the vast majority of cases where *res ipsa loquitur* was not applied, the burden of proof of both the defendant's negligence and the plaintiff's reasonable care remained fully with the plaintiff and was so stated to juries in 1870, 1890, and 1910.

The rules that guided the determination of awards are an important part of tort law, for if rules in this area had become more liberal, they might well have attracted more wounded Manhattanites to the courtroom.

Ingraham's nearly identical instruction in *Catharine Cowan* v. *Third Avenue Railroad Company*, 1890 Number T22, N.Y.C. Supreme Court. The 1910 version was exposited in *Patrick Jordan* v. *Timothy Phelan*, 1910 Number P60, N.Y.C. Supreme Court.

45. See text at note 16.

46. *Mary Corcoran, Administrator* v. *Union Railway Company*, 1910 Number U89, N.Y.C. Supreme Court.

47. *Caldwell* v. *New Jersey Steamboat*.

48. *Frank Rokos* v. *Astoria Marble Company and Voska, Foelsch, & Sidlo*, 1910 Number R139, N.Y.C. Supreme Court.

Again, though, judges' instructions show that the rules for setting awards did not alter. For example, in 1870, Smith told the jury to base any award ''upon the simple principle of what it has cost [the plaintiff] to cure this injury, the expenses of taking care of him, and what will make him good for the remainder of his days.''[49] Barnard instructed the jury to consider ''the amount of the physicians' bill paid, the length of time, if she has been a laboring woman, that she has been taken away from her labors and the sickness she may have suffered either in body or mind. All of these are to be taken into consideration because the damages are not for the mere naked injury.''[50] Closely related to this, almost every judge in 1870 emphasized the jury's discretion in setting awards.[51]

Other than stating more routinely that suffering in body and mind should be part of the award equation, nothing sets 1910 instructions apart from their 1870 counterparts. Joseph Newburger's instructions to the jury in *Finkelstein* v. *Kramer* typify the rule as it was applied in 1910: ''You have a right to consider first the pain and suffering, the time that he was deprived of any work, [and] the fact that the injuries are permanent. . . . You have a right to consider his age, his station in life, the amount he was earning, and all that he might have earned if his hand had not been injured in the way that it was.''[52] On the issue of discretion, as his 1870 predecessors were wont to do, Newburger told the jurors, ''You are the sole judges [of the] proper sum.''[53]

So judicial readings of the law changed little. But the judiciary was not the only possible source of changes to injury law. The most important of the other sources was the New York State legislature. By the beginning of the twentieth century, labor leaders and progressive reformers made the legislature aware that they found courts' work-injury liability rules seriously flawed. From the mid-1890s on, they prodded the state representatives to restructure work-injury law. The legislature certainly could have changed the law; though they had never exercised it, the legislators held real power over injury rules. They could controvert any aspect of the judges' law, from the smallest rule all the way to the entire edifice of negligence rules.

49. *Schappner* v. *Second Avenue Railroad*.
50. *Isaacs* v. *Third Avenue Railroad*.
51. A typical statement of this point is Albert Cardozo's, that the amount of damages ''rests entirely within your reasonable discretion.'' *Catharine Ann Doran* v. *The East River Ferry Company*, 1870 Number E59, N.Y.C. Supreme Court.
52. *David Finkelstein* v. *David Kramer*, 1910 Number K46, N.Y.C. Supreme Court.
53. Ibid.

That they did not desire to do so until labor raised its voice in the final decade of the nineteenth century tells us that no group had ever perceived injury law as a problem for public debate. Injury law had not been political. That began to change when people hurt at work started to seek compensation for their injuries. The pace of politicization accelerated as more New Yorkers injured at work sought recompense in the courts. There they ran into the unique rules, created to govern such cases, which ensured that wounded workers fared far worse than people injured in other ways. This inequity goaded labor leaders and progressives to campaign hard against those rules after 1890.

In 1902 the New York legislature rewarded the reform advocates' persistence with an Employers' Liability Act. The central feature of the new law made employers liable to workers for the negligence of employees who acted as supervisors. Under the fellow-servant rule, New York courts had held employers liable only for the direct acts of supervisors who bore the title supervisor and had usually limited liability to the acts of the one manager charged with overall supervision of a plant or project. Another part of the Liability Act lessened the comprehensive reach of the assumption of risk by making employers liable for hazards of employment created by the negligence of management, unless the defect was known to the worker alone.[54]

This last provision brought a change in the requirement on workers to report danger in the workplace and showed the confusion workers must have faced adapting their behavior to meet the contingencies of the law. Before, if a worker had reported a workplace flaw to an employer and did not quit the job if the employer did nothing to fix the flaw, judges considered the worker to have assumed the risk of the condition.[55] Under this regime, it was unlikely that workers would rush to report faulty work conditions, only to ensure their own liability in case of an accident. Under the

54. Chapter 600, "The Liability of Employers for Injuries to Employees," New York Legislature Acts of 1902 (reprinted in Clark, "Legal Liability," 74–76). See Clark, "Legal Liability;" Asher, "Failure and Fulfillment," 214–15; Wesser, "Conflict and Compromise," 348–49; Friedman and Ladinsky, "Social Change and the Law of Industrial Accidents," 50–82; Claire Walker, "A History of Factory Legislation and Inspection in New York State, 1886–1911" (Ph.D. dissertation, Columbia University, 1969), 111–13, 255; and Irwin Yellowitz, *Labor and the Progressive Movement in New York State* (Ithaca, N.Y.: Cornell University Press, 1965), 108.

55. For a case where the New York Court of Appeals applied this rule, see *Knisely v. Pratt, New York Court of Appeals Reports* 148 (Albany, N.Y.: Smith and Sons, 1897), 372 (hereafter cited as *New York Reports*). Discussed in William Hard, "The Law of the Killed and Wounded," *Everybody's Magazine* 19 (September 1908): 364.

Employers' Liability Act, if the worker failed to report a flaw that he could be proven to have been cognizant of, the liability was his.

So the new law reversed prudent practice for the worker, making it safest to report every flaw in the work environment. But it did not deny to employers the assumption-of-risk defense. It merely altered the conditions under which workers assumed the risks of the workplace.

On the whole, however, the Employers' Liability Act did not substantially remake work-injury law. Intended to remedy the defects of the common-law injury rules, the act did not challenge the common-law principle of fault as the basis of liability and left most of the judicially created rules of that law wholly intact.[56] Further, any advance that the act might have represented was soon turned back by judicial interpretation.[57] And by the best measure of change, comparison to the law as it had previously worked in practice, the act did not accomplish much. The provisions that were hailed by proponents as significant change were nothing more than statutory versions of palliatives that judges had been plying for decades.

The assumed-risk and fellow-servant rules that labor and progressives had sought to reshape in the Liability Act were already somewhat eroded before the legislature began its work. That is not to say that the rules were weak; they were still strong enough to prevent two out of three attempts by injured workers to get compensation. But the one case out of three that resulted in an award did so because in practice judges deviated already from the strictest interpretation of the work-injury rules. They applied a work-injury law that featured a relaxed version of the assumption-of-risk doctrine and the vice-principal rule that modified the fellow-servant doctrine.

Judges relaxed the rule that allocated risk between employer and employee by finding exceptions and adding qualifiers to it. Before 1890, possibly before 1870, the legal acquiescence to the dangers of the workplace imputed to workers—their "assumption of risk"—had been eliminated where the courts decided that employers rather than nature had created the dangers. Judges put particular risks back upon employers and

---

56. This assessment of the Employers' Liability Act was originally made by the Wainwright Commission in their 1909–10 investigation of New York's work-injury law. Seven years of the 1902 Liability Law was enough to convince the investigators that it had changed nothing. See New York State, *Commission to Inquire into Employers' Liability, First Report* (Albany: J. B. Lyon, 1910), 14.

57. Robert Asher offers evidence that the bill changed liability laws little: the state Workingmen's Federation, authors of the 1902 Law, were so disappointed with the lack of effect of the law that by 1904 they were campaigning for a new law to replace it. Asher, "Failure and Fulfillment," 214–16.

exempted workers in certain trades from the rule.[58] The 1902 Liability Act's modification of the assumption-of-risk doctrine did no more than what trial judges had already been doing.

The fellow-servant principle also met with exception, in the form of the vice-principal rule. Judges' application of the fellow-servant doctrine treated managers as workers' "fellows" rather than as agents of employers. The effect was that almost no workplace act or instruction could be traced directly to the employers. The vice-principal rule changed that in part; under it, employers became liable for any negligent supervision or management by their foremen and supervisors (the employer's vice-principals).[59] This was precisely how legislators sought in the 1902 act to de-fang the fellow-servant principle. The statute merely confirmed the practice of the preceding thirty years.

When exactly these mitigating rules came into play before 1890 is difficult to pin down. Since no work-injury cases appeared before the city court in 1870, I have no record of proceedings from which to extract the operative principles of work-injury law at that point. The very fact that there were no work-injury cases then might be seen as evidence that the strict assumption-of-risk and fellow-servant rules must still have been in effect, deterring the many New Yorkers injured at work (see Table 16, Chapter 2) from suing. But that is weak, circumstantial, and speculative evidence. At the same time, fairly strong evidence in the other direction suggests that the rules had already been loosened by 1870. Judge Andrews's 1890 search for precedent for the vice-principal rule led him to conclude that its basic idea—"that where a master owes a duty in regard to a particular matter to the servant, that he cannot get rid of that duty by delegating it to somebody else"—was "laid down a great many years ago."[60] To back up his assertion, Andrews cited the rule's appearance in Court of Appeals cases from two decades before.

58. For example, see *Eldridge* v. *Atlas Steamship*, where Judge George Andrews ruled that sailors did not fully assume the risks of employment because they were subject to the commands of superiors under the Maritime Law.

59. A good example of a case where the vice-principal doctrine ruled is *Tendrup* v. *Stephenson Co.*

60. Ibid. Andrews finds ample substantiation for a liberal vice-principle exception to the fellow-servant doctrine: "There are cases which I have made a note of beginning back in the 53 N.Y. [volume 53 of the *New York Reports* for 1873] and 59, 81, 91, 99, and 100 N.Y., all stating the same doctrine, that where a master owes a duty, then it does not make any difference what the position of the individual who is guilty of the actual negligence may be, whether he is the superintendent or whether he is the lowest man in the service, . . . if he is negligent, that is the negligence of the master."

This suggests that the Employers' Liability Act of 1902 simply codified work-injury rules that had been substantially in place by 1870. In their application, rules that had remained constant through the last decades of the nineteenth century remained unchanged in the first decade of the twentieth, despite legislation.

The legislature's other attempt at correcting the problems of the work-injury law was more successful. The Barnes Act of 1906 eliminated the broad interpretation judges had taken of the fellow-servant rule in railroad-injury suits. Instead, it made the acts of supervisors and all workers who controlled trains, switches, and signals the responsibility of the railroads. This was a significant rule change: Under the old practice, virtually every railroad-worker's injury suit was dismissable as the doing of a "fellow servant."[61]

The Barnes Act's other important provision was that the condition of all machinery and materials became the company's responsibility. Any defect in trains, switches, or even tools served as *prima facie* evidence of negligence on the railroad's part. This was a big step, essentially a merging of *res ipsa loquitur* with another idea of the courts', constructive notice. *Res ipsa loquitur* said that the occasion of an injury showed negligence. The rule of constructive notice said that if a dangerous condition could have been discovered by reasonable inspection or if it had existed for long enough that it should have been discovered, then the defendant was considered to have been informed of the defect.[62] Claiming ignorance was no longer a viable defense; failure to inspect and know of defects was now itself negligent. As an earlier New York Court of

61. Chapter 657, "The Liability of Railroad Companies for Injuries to Employees," New York State Legislature Acts of 1906 (reprinted in Clark, "Legal Liability," 76). See *Michael McGovern* v. *Adrian Joline et al., Receivers of the New York City Railway,* 1910 Number M66, N.Y.C. Supreme Court. In this case, McGovern's lawyer Thomas Keogh argued that the Railroad Law applied to street-railroad employees. Judge Edward McCall accepted its applicability but found another means to dismiss the suit: that Keogh had proven no defect in the company's equipment.

62. Judge James Gerard defined constructive notice as follows: "You may find that a person has notice of a defect when it has remained in that condition for such a length of time that a reasonable man of ordinary prudence, in the exercise of reasonable care, would have had an opportunity to discover and remedy it." *Jordan* v. *Phelan.* The case was over a work accident that cost Jordan his arm. The issue of notice was raised by the defense lawyer seeking a way out of his client's responsibility. He asked Gerard to instruct the jury that the defendant was not negligent unless it had notice of dangerous conditions in the workplace. Gerard agreed to make the charge but then added constructive notice to the definition of notice. *Max Deener* v. *Heyman Rosen,* 1910 Number R184, N.Y.C. Supreme Court is another case where constructive notice was invoked.

Appeals judge put it, defendants "can no longer fold their arms and shut their eyes, and say they have no notice."[63] The merger of *res ipsa loqui-tur* with constructive notice meant that the railroad should know the condition of its equipment; because it should have known, if its equipment's defects caused an injury, the company was responsible.

The Barnes Act made "very serious inroads" into the obstacles to railroad workers' recoveries for injuries.[64] It was so much a change, however, that it did not have a major effect on workers who were bringing lawsuits. Railroads learned immediately of the courtroom consequences of playing by new rules and became more magnanimous in settling claims and more persistent in pushing money in return for releases among those less aggressive injured workers who had not filed a lawsuit. This avenue for escaping lawsuits did not have to be built from scratch by the railroads. They simply adapted their time-tested strategy for avoiding passenger-injury suits to work injuries. The consequence was that railroad work injuries produced more compensation but no more cases than under the older, more restrictive rules.

So for very different reasons, the two legislated revisions of liability law were not generators of litigation. The Employers' Liability Act of 1902 ultimately effected no significant changes in the law as the judges of the city Supreme Court applied it, and the Barnes Act promised so much change that the railroads acted to circumvent it.

The state legislature did not have to attack tort rules or procedures directly to alter the process of determining liability. Other legislation affected the adjudication of injury suits indirectly by prescribing safety measures for machines, buildings, or the performance of hazardous but socially desirable acts (such as operating a railroad or blasting during the course of excavation). The safety standards these statutes set were analogous to standards of care in negligence law. At least the analogy was clear enough to attorneys who frequently claimed that the safety standards should be the measures of care in injury cases.

Protective legislation thus had great potential to alter the administration of injury law without directly addressing the existing rules at all. The potential rose as the number of such statutes mounted in the years after 1870. By the turn of the century, statutes regulated more and more types of danger in New Yorkers' lives, most prominently in the areas of work, transport, and housing.

63. Judge Earl in *Todd* v. *City of Troy, New York Reports* 61, 506; quoted in Lewis, "Law of Icy Sidewalks," 259.
64. Walker, "History of Factory Legislation," 255.

New York's state labor laws, in establishing maximum hours and minimum conditions for safe work, promised to affect the outcome of work-injury suits. The first Labor Law (1886) limited the number of hours children and women could work per week. A child or woman injured while working more hours than the rule allowed might claim that her or his overwork demonstrated the employer's negligence. The connection was logical; the employer had exceeded a standard of care explicitly defined by the state and was thus negligent.

Subsequent versions of the Labor Law of 1886 expanded the statutory coverage of work-safety standards and made the link between safety standards and injury law's standard of reasonable care even more evident. The Labor Law of 1887 mandated for the first time safety devices on machines in the workplace. It required guards on gears, belts, and elevators, as well as strips to prevent slipping on stairs. It also required that employers report to the state all accidental work injuries and deaths. The Labor Law of 1895 required permits for all children between the ages of 13 and 16 who worked. The next year's iteration inaugurated regulation of mercantile establishments and the conditions under which their workers, predominantly women, could labor. In 1897 the legislature further defined the employer's responsibility to provide workers with a safe workplace. The Labor Law was amended and extended again in the laws of 1899, 1903, 1907, and 1909.[65]

The utility of these provisions is clear. Like an injury to a worker while the employer was breaking the rule on maximum hours, an injury resulting from any failure to guard machines or otherwise provide a safe workplace in accordance with the Labor Laws might be posited as a violation of the duty of care. The link between safety law and standard of care came easily. As lawyers for injured workers argued, nothing was a more reasonable measure of the care society expected than one derived from the legislature's edicts on a safe workplace.[66]

---

65. Ibid., 79–90. The 1907 version of the law dealt specifically with safety at the construction site: "A person employing or directing another to perform labor of any kind in the erection of, repairing, and altering or painting of a house, building, or structure shall not furnish or cause to be furnished or erected in the performance of such labor scaffolding, hoists, stages, ladders, or other mechanical contrivances which are unsafe, unsuitable, or improper and which are not so constructed, placed, and operated as to give proper protection to the life and limb of a person so employed or engaged." Thomas Garrett successfully invoked the law's standards for scaffolding after he lost a couple inches of his leg in a scaffolding collapse while working on the new Pennsylvania Terminal. *Garrett v. National Fireproofing.*

66. Workers used legislation other than the Labor Laws to show that defendants failed to conform to society's standards of care. For instance, Susie Bambal cited the defendant

Achille Oishei built the case for injured drill-press operator Michele Pirolo on such logic. Pirolo had been working his press when it shattered, shooting shards of metal into one of his eyes. Oishei asserted that Pirolo's employer, the Hinkle Brothers' Iron Company, was negligent because it "failed to provide safe and suitable machinery, . . . failed to keep [it] in proper condition, [and] . . . failed to provide necessary safety apparatus."[67] In short, the Hinkles failed to comply with the Labor Law of 1899 and were thus negligent. The first judge and jury agreed with Oishei and awarded the verdict to Pirolo. The iron company appealed to the Appellate Division and won a reversal and retrial. On retrial, Judge McCall and a second jury delivered a verdict for the company. Pirolo lost not only his award, but $394 in court costs to the defendants.[68]

Pirolo's experience demonstrates why the Labor Laws did not act as an unequivocal lure to work-injury suits. Trial judges occasionally recognized the Labor Laws as standards of care but more often did not. Judges who were inclined to place responsibility for accidents with workers did so just as easily under the Labor Laws as before. In fact, they had the sanction of the state's highest court backing them. The Court of Appeals ruled in 1897 that "there is no reason in principle or authority why an employee should not be allowed to assume the obvious risks of the business as well under the factory law as otherwise."[69] So while the Labor Law mandated that workplaces meet minimum safety requirements, the high court decided that employers who disregarded the law were not necessarily negligent when injury resulted from that contraven-

---

employer's violation of the city building code along with the 1902 Liability Law to claim employer negligence when her husband died because of a trench cave-in. *Bambal v. Breen.*

67. *Michele Pirolo* v. *Eugene and Terry Hinkle,* 1910 Number P92, N.Y.C. Supreme Court.

68. Some injured workers had more success using the Labor Law. Thomas McDowell won a $9,000 award after being knocked seven stories down a hod-elevator shaft at a construction site. McDowell's lawyer William Carey charged that the absence of guard rails around the lift, in violation of the Labor Law, showed the contractor's negligence. In combination with other circumstances, that charge prevailed. *Thomas McDowell* v. *A. Robinson Co. and Henry Tinker,* 1910 Number A244, N.Y.C. Supreme Court.

69. *Knisley* v. *Pratt, New York Reports* 148 (1897), 372, in Hard, "Law of the Killed and Wounded," 364. This case is an especially good example because the judges in the Appellate Division of the Supreme Court had reached just the opposite conclusion, that the worker did *not* assume the risks incidental to the failure of the employer to guard gears and shafts as the labor law required. *Knisley* v. *Pratt, New York Supplementary Reports* 26 (1894): 1010, cited in *American Lawyer* 2 (1894): 517.

tion. As a result, the Labor Laws did not change the standard of care in work-injury torts.[70]

The story of safety legislation in that most regulated of workplaces, the railroad yard, began similarly. Congress passed a strong railroad Safety Appliances Act in 1893, which was intended to reduce the high incidence of car-coupling accidents by requiring airbrakes and uniform automatic couplers on all rail cars. But railroad management resisted the new law. They successfully sought strings of extensions that exempted them from the rules; they were still stalling a decade later. As a result, the Safety Appliances Act had no impact on injury suits for over a decade. Only Congress's passage of the Employers' Liability Act of 1908 (applying to interstate common carriers) finally forced the railroads into compliance with the 1893 safety law.[71]

The new act exacted compliance with the safety law by making it too expensive for railroads not to use the safer mechanisms in the same way that the Barnes Act in New York forced state railroads to repair defective equipment and facilities. The Federal Liability Act virtually eliminated the fellow-servant doctrine and cut into the defenses of contributory negligence and assumed risk as well. With the new rules and with the remarkable effectiveness at saving lives that the safer couplers were providing, judges began to find the absence of new couplers evidence of railroad negligence. A care standard taken from a safety statute came to

70. That judges interpreted safety statutes to avoid change in injury law is an important addition to the reviving debate about the role of state courts in the Progressive Era. Melvin Urofsky recently concluded that because state supreme courts upheld protective legislation more often than they overturned it, the courts at the turn of the century did not really block progressive reform (though he points out New York's high court was more obstructionist than most). The problem with this conclusion is that sheer rejection of statutes was only the most blatant way state courts countered reform. Contemporaries recognized this; George Alger, New York's leading workmen's compensation advocate, demonstrated that state appeals courts effectively blocked reform by keeping the results of cases from becoming favorable to plaintiffs, no matter what negligence rules were applied. Alger discovered that the New York Court of Appeals impeded reform by reversing verdicts where juries had given reasonably sizable awards to injury victims. The court did this with remarkable consistency, reversing 28 of 30 work-injury cases that came to it between 1891 and 1898. George W. Alger, "The Courts and Factory Legislation," *American Sociological Review* 6 (1900–01): 406. In the present study, the work of the city trial court shows that judges' creative interpretation of legislation also blocked reform effectively. So before we dismiss the idea that courts hindered reform, we ought to look at just what happened to the protective legislation that was allowed to stand, as the courts applied it. See Melvin Urofsky, "State Courts and Protective Legislation during the Progressive Era: A Reevaluation," *Journal of American History* 72 (1985): 63–91.

71. See Kurt Wetzel, "Railroad Management's Response to Operating Employees' Accidents, 1890–1913," *Labor History* 21 (1980): 351–68.

rule, but only after twenty years had elapsed and a statutory revision of
the entire structure of railroad workers' liability had facilitated that
adoption.[72]

The legislature prescribed safety provisions for other aspects of transportation as well. In fact, the safety of passengers and pedestrians had
drawn government regulatory attention well before the safety of workers.
Legislators set down rules in this area well before the period of this study.
In 1852, for example, the U.S. Congress passed "An Act to Provide for
the Better Security of the Lives of Passengers Propelled in Whole or in
Part by Steam" (applying to steamboats), which established standards of
practice against which an astute attorney might prove negligence.

The state legislature and city followed suit, passing rules for the protection not only of passengers but of others who had to contend with
powerful steam locomotives, such as pedestrians and wagon drivers.
Crossing rules mandated the sounding of bells or whistles and the presence of a flagman or a fence or gate, as well as dictating maximum train
speeds at crossings and in built-up areas.[73] Government at various levels
created rules to guide not only steam transportation but vehicular transport in general. The city had speed ordinances that governed all forms of
movement on its streets.[74] These were often cited by injured individuals to
show that their injurers had not lived up to society's standards of reasonably careful behavior.[75]

The creation of the Metropolitan Board of Health in 1866 was the occasion for the passage of most comprehensive protective statute the legislature would author in this period. Section 2 of the Code of Health
Ordinances declared that "no person shall carelessly or negligently do or
advise or contribute to the doing of any act dangerous to the life or det-
rimental to the health of any human being . . . nor shall any person omit

72. See ibid., 357–368; and John R. Commons and John B. Andrews, *Principles of Labor Legislation* (New York: Harper and Brothers, 1927), 414.

73. The New York City ordinances directed at the operation of railroads date back to the
1850s. See, for example, the string of rules cited in *Scott* v. *Pennsylvania Railroad*.

74. New York City Corporation Ordinances, 1880 Revision, Section 205, 199. Cited in
Lawrence Leonard v. *Second Avenue Railroad Company*, 1890 Number L13, N.Y.C. Supreme Court. The ordinances kept speed limits low, regardless of type of vehicle. Even in
1910 the limit remained 8 miles per hour for "bicycles, tricycles, velocipedes and motor
vehicles however propelled, or by passenger and other vehicles drawn by horses." *Richard
Cummings* v. *New York and Long Island Traction Company*, 1910 Number N50, N.Y.C.
Supreme Court.

75. See *Laura Overton* v. *Horace DeLesser*, 1910 Number O50, N.Y.C. Supreme Court;
Marie Bayone, Administrator v. *New York Taxicab Company*, 1910 Number N112, N.Y.C.
Supreme Court.

to do any act or take any precaution reasonable and proper to prevent or remove danger . . . to the life or health of any human."[76] The language of that provision was general enough to outlaw nearly every injurious act imaginable. If it was ambiguous, Section 6 of the code got more specific, listing locations where New Yorkers would have to exercise this care: every "place, water, ground, room, stall, apartment, building, erection, vessel, vehicle, matter, and thing."[77] The law basically reiterated the common-law duty of care in statute form. That might explain why lawyers did not invoke it in any of the cases that I read: It was too general to be of help. While seemingly of great potential, it did not further clarify what constituted a dangerous act, the sort of measure that lawyers could invoke to establish opponents' negligence.

In contrast, injured New Yorkers and their attorneys promoted housing statutes as potential standards of care in building-related injuries brought to the city Supreme Court. The first of New York City's Tenement House Laws was passed in 1867. Though its provisions were minimal and ill defined, when considered in conjunction with the 1866 Health Law, it demonstrated that society was coming to see a public interest and right to set standards in what had previously been intensely private realms. Proponents sought tenement laws to force owners to bring their housing to a minimum standard of safe habitability. In so doing, it defined standards to which tenants could compare their landlords' acts. As historian Roy Lubove put it, the enactment of the first Tenement House Law "represented the acceptance in principle of the community's right to limit the freedom of the tenement landlord and builder."[78]

Initially, that right was not exercised in negligence suits. The statutory standards for housing existed in 1870, yet they brought few tenement-injury suits into the court. The existence of legally defined standards for housing had not been enough to turn the injuries that occurred in those buildings into lawsuits.

Once the potential inherent in statutory standards had been ascertained, though, those suing for injuries began to argue that housing regulation set the appropriate standard of care. Elizabeth McPartland, for one, claimed that her injury from a fall in Mary Healy's 16th Street apartment building resulted from Healy's negligent violation of the Tenement

76. Metropolitan Board of Health, *Code of Health Ordinances and Rules and Sanitary Regulations* (New York: John W. Amerman, 1866).

77. Ibid., Section 6.

78. Roy Lubove, *The Progressives and the Slums: Tenement House Reform in New York City, 1890–1927* (Pittsburgh, Penn.: University of Pittsburgh Press, 1962), 25–48.

House Law of 1901.[79] The part of the Tenement House Laws that
McPartland and others suing for injuries cited most often was a hall-
and stairway-lighting requirement. Diana Rawlins relied on this after
falling through rotted flooring in the dark hallway of an East 61st
Street tenement.[80] Likewise, Loretta Morton claimed her fall down the
stairs of a Bronx tenement happened because owner Louis Peroni and his
partners failed to provide the lighting that the Tenement House Law
called for.[81]

The lighting requirement was meager at first; the 1867 law said every
room must have a window to the outside—or a window into a room that
had outside light. The "Dumbbell" Tenement House Law of 1879 raised
the requirement, though not by much: All rooms, hallways, and stairs
were to have light from a window to the outside, though the outside might
only be the narrow airshaft that gave the dumbbell its characteristic shape
and its name. The Tenement House Law of 1901 raised standards con-
siderably, requiring not only windows but direct artificial illumination in
halls and stairways after dark.[82] It is likely that injury victims increased
their use of the Tenement House Law standards over time precisely because of this toughening of the standards.

The injured were not the only ones who made use of safety statutes.
Injurers called upon them as well. Astute defendants tried to use the standards to prove their own freedom from negligence. They argued that by
conforming to often minimal statutory safety regulations, they fulfilled
their duty to be careful. They owed no more care than that, they said. This
was a typical posture taken by the street railroads but was by no means
limited to them.

The 1870 suit *Caldwell* v. *New Jersey Steamboat* is one example of a
defendant invoking statutory standards. The lawyer for the steamship
company tried to avert liability to passengers injured in a boiler explosion
by claiming that since the company's pilots and engineers had been li-
censed according to the national law, the company had fully met its duty
of care.[83]

79. *Elizabeth McPartland* v. *Mary Healey*, 1910 Number H366, N.Y.C. Supreme
Court.
80. *Diana Rawlins* v. *Jonas Weil et al.*, 1910 Number W273, N.Y.C. Supreme Court.
81. *Loretta Morton* v. *Louis Peroni et al.*, 1910 Number P81, N.Y.C. Supreme Court.
82. Lubove, *Progressives and the Slums*, 25–48.
83. *Caldwell* v. *New Jersey Steamboat*. The effort was unsuccessful in this case: Judge
Albert Cardozo refused the defendant's request to charge the jury that "if the jury find
from the evidence that the defendants have in all respects complied with the act of Congress, there is to be no further presumption of neglect indulged against them, by virtue of
that act." Caldwell won the suit and was awarded $20,000.

The claim that safety laws limited employers' liability was probably most infamously exercised by the owners of the Triangle Shirt Waist Company in the aftermath of the deadly fire at their Washington Square loft factory in 1911. "We did everything the law said," Triangle Company owner Max Blanck told reporters over and over, hoping this would exonerate him of fault in the 141 deaths. Joseph Asch, the owner of the building in which the company had operated, protested that he was not responsible, for he, too, had "obeyed the law to the letter."[84] Blanck and his partner Isaac Harris were found not guilty of criminal charges, not because they had followed the law, but because the jury was not certain that they had knowledge of the violations of law at their factory at the moment of the fire.

Those charged with causing injury did not just use statutes defensively. They also used them the same way the injured did, to impugn the care and attentiveness of their opponents. For example, defense lawyer James Quackenbush claimed that his client was not liable for its trolley car crashing into a slow-moving horse-drawn van because the van was not showing lights, as required by city ordinance. The court accepted the application of this requirement, but it did the defendant no good; the jury found, counter to the defendant's claim, that the van had been running with lights visible.[85]

Other legislation had some bearing on the amount of injury litigation. A city statute enacted in 1886 set specific procedures for suing the municipality for negligence. It required injury victims to file claims with the city comptroller's office and to formally notify the city of their intention to sue within a set time limit. While it was strictly a procedural edict, having no effect on doctrine whatsoever, its consequence for injured citizens could be just as substantial. The rule, in effect, denied courtroom standing to those who were not aware of their need to move expeditiously. Minnie Hyde, crippled by a defective sidewalk in late 1886, was one who learned of the rule too late. The city won a dismissal in the lawsuit because the jury found that Hyde had not filed within the statutory time limit—this after deciding that the city had been negligent and Hyde had not.[86]

---

84. *New York Times,* 26 March 1911; and *New York Evening Post,* 27 March 1911. Cited in Walker, "History of Factory Legislation," 7. On the trial of Triangle Shirtwaist owners Blanck and Harris, see Leon Stein, *The Triangle Fire* (New York: Carroll and Graf, 1985 [1962]), 177–203.

85. *Richard Cummings* v. *New York and Long Island Traction Company,* 1910 Number N50, N.Y.C. Supreme Court.

86. *Minnie Hyde* v. *Mayor et al., City of New York,* 1890 Number H43, N.Y.C. Supreme Court. The story had a better ending for Hyde than was usually the case. After the

For the most part, then, liability rules did not change. Negligence and its auxiliary rules, whether new in the middle decades of the nineteenth century or not, continued to prevail in court in 1910 as they had in 1870, offering prospective plaintiffs no more encouragement. As Minnie Hyde's experience demonstrated, the changes that did occur did not necessarily abet the bringing of suits.

Judges interpreted and applied the legislature's new rules to maintain continuity with old rules. Thus here, too, the consequence on injury actions was only to continue what was already underway. One piece of evidence is especially telling: work-injury suits climbed as fast, relatively, from 1870 to 1890 as from 1890 to 1910, showing gains as great before the Employers' Liability Act and the myriad Labor Laws as after they had been enacted.[87] The one piece of legislation that truly changed the working of injury law, the Barnes Act, did not precipitate any more lawsuits than before, because railroads recognized its potential to do just that and practiced a sort of preventive compensation to avoid the courtroom.[88]

Courts usually held that safety statutes did not set standards of care. However, when they did, it was for defendants as frequently as for plaintiffs; injurers found standards derived from statutes as useful for limiting responsibility as the injured did for extending it. Taken together with the stability exhibited elsewhere in liability law, this situation could hardly have encouraged a significant rise in lawsuits.

But rules were not the only feature of the process that determined how the law worked. Lawyers, judges, and juries all affected the outcome of cases independent of the rules of law. Changes in their roles and practices, far more than changes in rules, altered the functioning of the law.

---

dismissal, the city consented to vacate the judgment and allow a settlement of $250 to Hyde. The reasoning for this, whether magnanimous recognition of responsibility despite the outcome of the suit or a more practical desire to avoid appeal by the plaintiff, was not expressed in the judgment.

87. See Chapter 2, Table 6.
88. See Chapter 2, Table 7.

4. LAWYERS

The formal rules of the legal system in 1910 were essentially those of 1870. This does not necessarily mean that the working of the law was the same at both points. Rules were but one component of the legal process. The application of general rules to particular situations was a human act. People were as important as rules and procedures in determining how the law worked and what resulted from its use. Operating with effectively the same rules and procedures, lawyers, judges, and jurors changed the working of the law markedly every time they altered their ideas and practices. That is the basic issue of this and the next chapter. Did lawyers, judges, and juries do things differently in 1910 than they had twenty or forty years before, so differently that these changes encouraged the rise in torts?

The question sends the inquiry into the less formal regions of the legal process. Lawyers, judges, and juries were involved in that process from the initiation through the decision of lawsuits. What power did each of those parties have in the legal process? Did the power of the different players change relative to one another? How much discretion did each have in applying rules?

Injured New Yorkers started their legal odyssey in the lawyer's office. Obtaining legal representation was the initial step in translating injury into injury suit.[1] As the gateway to the legal system, hiring a lawyer was

---

1. The question of how disputes such as accidents get translated into lawsuits has drawn much research. See Herbert Kritzer, W. A. Bogart, and Neil Vidmar, "The Aftermath of

so important that any difference in injured New Yorkers' ability to do so might have had great impact on how many of them took their grievances to court.

One factor that had the potential to affect access was the number of lawyers. There were more lawyers in New York in 1910 than 1870. But this did not avail more legal service to injury victims, because after 1880 the population grew at an even faster pace than the number of lawyers.[2] While the increase in the number of lawyers did not make a difference in access to the law, a change in the way many of them contracted for their services in injury suits opened the courtroom doors to more New Yorkers. This change was the rise of contingent-fees advocacy.

The idea was a simple one. Instead of paying set fees for a lawyer's work, the client promised the lawyer a percentage of whatever money was won. A person who could not afford a lawyer under the traditional pay-as-you-go type of retainer could hire a lawyer who was willing to await payment until the case was over. This was not all: The biggest attraction of contingent fees was that the client paid only for success. If the lawyer lost the case, the plaintiff owed him nothing. Contingency compensation "was intended to help a poor man, with an honest claim, who could not afford to pay counsel for commencing or conducting a suit to collect it," as Judge Irving Vann of the state Court of Appeals explained.[3]

Injury: Cultural Factors in Compensation Seeking in Canada and the United States," *Law and Society Review* 25 (1991): 499–543; William Felstiner, Richard Abel, and Austin Sarat, "The Emergence of Disputes: Naming, Blaming, and Claiming . . . ," *Law and Society Review* 15 (1980–81): 631–54; Richard Miller and Austin Sarat, "Grievances, Claims, and Disputes: Assessing the Adversarial Culture," *Law and Society Review* 15 (1980–81): 525–66; generally, "Special Issue on Dispute Processing and Civil Litigation," *Law and Society Review* 15, nos. 3–4 (1980–81); Herbert Kritzer, "Political Culture and the 'Propensity to Sue'," *Institute for Legal Studies Working Papers* 9, no. 1 (July 1988); Richard Lempert, "Mobilizing Private Law: An Introductory Essay," *Law and Society Review* 11 (1976): 173–89; and Matthew Silberman, *The Civil Justice Process: A Sequential Model of the Mobilization of Law* (Orlando, Fla.: Academic Press, 1985).

2. The ratio of lawyers to population in New York and surrounding states showed a net increase from 1870 to 1910, but most of that occurred before 1880; from 1880 the lawyer-to-population ratio declined. See Terence Halliday, "Six Scores and Ten: Demographic Transitions in the American Legal Profession, 1850–1980," *Law and Society Review* 20 (1986): 53–78. Roscoe Pound claimed that New York had about 4,000 lawyers in 1870, but he gave no figures for later dates. Pound, *The Lawyer from Antiquity to Modern Times* (Minneapolis: West, 1953), 255.

3. Vann made it clear that the practice had not lived up to the intention: "Although passed for a good purpose, [legalizing contingency arrangements] opened Pandora's Box and let out evils which the ancient law against champerty was designed to prevent." Irving G. Vann, *Contingent Fees: An Address in the Hubbard Course on Legal Ethics* (Albany: Albany Law School, 1905), 7.

Attractive as this arrangement was, it had its cost for the plaintiff. As insurance against the contingency of losing, the lawyer retained under these terms charged a sizable percentage of the amount won. In the last decades of the nineteenth century, contingency-fees lawyers typically worked for 15 percent to 40 percent of the winnings "with 50 percent not uncommon."[4] In New York City, the high end of the scale soon became the norm. In the first years of the twentieth century the state Court of Appeals decided that 50 percent would be the maximum allowable fee, which had the effect of cementing that figure as the standard arrangement.[5] In fact, 50 percent of the award was probably the typical agreement in the city even before the new century arrived; it was the only figure mentioned in 1890 cases.[6]

Contingent-fees advocacy is presented here as a change in legal practice because there is no evidence of these arrangements in any of the 1870 cases, even though it was an option available to plaintiffs. The practice appeared in the 1890 cases, and the 1890 evidence of contingent fees indicates that the city Supreme Court was regulating the practice at the time. In *Riley* v. *Quebec Steamship,* the plaintiff's attorney motioned for judicial approval of his fees, and in both *Gallagher* v. *Anchor Line Steamship* and *Henderson* v. *Anchor Line Steamship,* the plaintiffs' attorney filed notice of his retention on a contingent-fee basis.[7] If the court required attorneys to file notice of contingent-fees agreements in 1890, it is likely that it would have required the same in 1870. Since no contingency-retainer agreements appear in the 1870 judgments, and contingent fees are never mentioned anywhere else in the rolls, the most reasonable conclusion is that they were not common in 1870.

By 1910, case-by-case regulation had all but disappeared, though general rules like the 50-percent fee ceiling remained. The practice had become pervasive. Judicial oversight of contingent fees remained only in cases involving children. There the court retained the right to pass on the

4. Frederick B. MacKinnon, *Contingent Fees for Legal Services: A Report of the American Bar Foundation* (Chicago: Aldine, 1964).

5. *In the Matter of Fitzsimons, New York Reports* 174 (1903), 15. See *John C. Herrman* v. *Ernest Christian et al.,* 1910 Number H466, N.Y.C. Supreme Court; and *Bridget Norton* v. *Mayor et al., City of New York,* 1910 Number M389, N.Y.C. Supreme Court.

6. In *Riley* v. *Quebec Steamship,* Riley's lawyer Edmund Terry received 50 percent of Riley's $1,000 award on the approval of judge George Barrett. In separate cases, Daniel Gallagher and John Henderson hired lawyer James T. Williamson on the same 50-percent basis. See *Daniel Gallagher* v. *The Anchor Line Steamship Company,* 1890 Number G29, N.Y.C. Supreme Court and *John Henderson* v. *The Anchor Line Steamship Company,* 1890 Number H50, N.Y.C. Supreme Court.

7. See note 6.

amount of fees.[8] Otherwise, the 1910 judgments rarely mentioned contingency contracts. Rather than indicating scarce use, though, the absence of notice now attested to their commonness. When they were mentioned, they were treated as typical, as "the usual contract of contingency."[9] Lawyer Andrew Hirschl confirmed that society had so far "passed the condemnation of the contingent fee" that it had come to "the debatable stage of what is popularly—or rather, unpopularly—spoken of as 'ambulance chasing.' "[10]

While the use of the contingent-fees arrangement only became commonplace after 1870, it had been legitimated and was available to lawyers and injury victims decades before. The watershed year was 1848 for the practice in New York. Before that date, under the common law, such an arrangement constituted the crime of champerty.[11] By enacting David Dudley Field's 1848 Code of Procedure, the New York legislature repealed all limits on fees and all restrictions on agreements between lawyers and clients. The state courts upheld the law in face of challenge in the next decade, thereby eliminating a possible barrier to the procurement of legal services on a contingency basis. The Court of Appeals made the message crystal clear: "What was before not only illegal but disreputable is now lawful, if not respectable."[12]

    8. See *Wilhelmina Schleiter, Administrator* v. *John H. Stearns and Company and Gustave Hurliman,* 1910 Number S71, N.Y.C. Supreme Court; *James Satore* v. *New York Central and Hudson River Railroad,* 1910 Number N134, N.Y.C. Supreme Court; and *Anna Speck* v. *Mayor et al., City of New York,* 1910 Number M390, N.Y.C. Supreme Court.

    9. The comment was defense attorney Jacob Rieger's in *Solomon Levy, Administrator* v. *Michael Henig and Solomon Henig,* 1910 Number H461, N.Y.C. Supreme Court.

    10. Andrew Hirschl, "Personal Injury Actions: The Plaintiff's Standpoint," *Illinois Law Review* 1 (1905–06), 17.

    11. The illegality of contingent fees rested on the idea that it corrupted lawyers to have an interest in the outcome of a case. This idea continues to prevail in Britain and most common-law nations, where contingent fees remain illegal. In New York, the common-law champerty rule had been adopted by statute in 1813. An 1830 revision of statutes eliminated the champerty law, but judges kept it a crime until the 1848 Code. For decisions maintaining contingent fees, see *Merritt* v. *Lambert, Paige's New York Reports* 10 (New York: Paige, 1843), 352; *Wallis* v. *Loubat, Denio's New York Reports* 2 (New York: Denio, 1845), 607. Otto Sommerich, "The History and Development of Attorneys' Fees," *The Record of the Association of the Bar of the City of New York* 6 (1951): 369–74; MacKinnon, *Contingent Fees for Legal Services,* 42–43; and Howard Karshan, *Contingent Fees in Personal Injury and Wrongful Death Actions in the United States* (New York: Institute for Judicial Administration, 1957), 9.

    12. *Rooney* v. *The Second Avenue Railroad Company,* in *New York Reports* 18 (1858), 368. The legislature reaffirmed the right to work for contingent fees in Section 66 of the 1877 Code of Civil Procedure and Sections 474 and 475 of the Judiciary Law of 1909. See Sommerich, "History and Development of Attorneys' Fees," 370, 371, 374; and MacKinnon, *Contingent Fees for Legal Services,* 42–3.

So the contingency retainer was available to attorneys in 1870. Its availability did not incite the populace to inundate the Supreme Court with injury suits. Among the small number of New Yorkers at the time who did take to the court seeking compensation for injuries, contingent-fees advocacy was not used. This adds to the evidence that it was not so much legal change—in this instance, contingent-fees lawyering—that prompted a rise in injury suits, as it was the rise in injury suits that ushered in legal change, here making the contingent fees retainer common practice.

Contemporary commentators, primarily judges and prominent lawyers, claimed just the opposite: that the number of injury suits climbed because contingent-fees lawyers promoted them. New York's elite lawyers, often serving the defendants of suits brought under contingent-fees arrangements, were certain that the practice produced scores of lawsuits that would not have otherwise appeared in the courts. Unethical lawyers at the lowest rungs of the profession were stirring up lawsuits for the sole purpose of making money, they claimed.[13]

This perception must be taken for what it was, part of a campaign against the contingent-fees lawyer. The lawyers and judges who thought this way, the members of the New York State Bar Association, were so antagonistic to contingent fees that it was not long after the practice had become established that they were hard at work trying to eradicate it. The bar's antagonism ran so deep that when a bill to curtail such arrangements came up for discussion at the association's meeting, many of the brethren criticized it as insufficiently harsh.[14]

The extent to which the spread of lawyers willing to work for contingent fees encouraged more injured people to go to court will never be fully known. The most often claimed contribution of contingency compensation is that it availed legal counsel to those who had not had access to the law before, those who were not wealthy. While this is reasonably accurate, it must be qualified: The poorest New Yorkers had always had the right to sue *in forma pauperis* and have a lawyer appointed to represent them. They exercised this right and continued to do so after contingency payment had become the regular practice, though they did so rarely.[15]

13. See, for example, Vann, *Contingent Fees.*

14. New York State Bar Association, "Report of the Committee on Contingent Fees," *Proceedings of the Thirty-First Annual Meeting* (Albany: Argus Company, 1908), 99–136.

15. Plaintiffs brought suits *in forma pauperis* in both 1890 and 1910. See *Nellie Fowler v. The Broadway and Seventh Avenue Railroad Company,* 1890 Number B224, N.Y.C. Supreme Court; *William Doyle v. Manhattan Railway Company,* 1890 Number M158, N.Y.C.

Two other developments also had at least the potential to promote the
rise of injury suits by affording increased access to law. The New York
Legal Aid Society presented a new way for the working poor to get their
troubles adjudicated, and its work grew rapidly (providing, incidentally,
further evidence of the tremendous latent demand for legal services
among ordinary New Yorkers in this era). When it opened its doors in
1876, 200 people sought its assistance. By 1890 over 4,000 did. By 1910,
that number had grown to 30,000.

But the legal aid movement had no escalating effect on injury suits,
because while the society assisted average New Yorkers in all other sorts
of matters for which they needed law, it refused to handle accident cases.
The society seems to have had three reasons for doing this: a belief that
contingent-fees advocacy already covered the poor who had this need; a
principle of avoiding competition with existing private provision of services; and a desire not to have the opprobrium associated with injury suits
stain the reputation of their fledgling institution. To the extent that the
last point motivated the society's refusal to assist in accident cases, the
legal elite's publically aired dislike for accident victims' litigation can be
seen to have had an effect in retarding the rise of injury suits by chasing
away a potential provider of legal counsel. Ironically, the society's refusal
to handle accident cases also increased injured New Yorkers' reliance on
contingent-fees lawyering.[16]

Much of the notoriety of injury suits drew from critics' close association of contingency lawyering with another practice that had the potential
to increase litigation: ambulance chasing. The potential returns from injury suits did inspire some lawyers to innovative marketing practices, hiring agents to solicit business or creating networks of people to guide

---

Supreme Court; *Samuel Friedman* v. *New York City Railway Company,* 1910 Number N31,
N.Y.C. Supreme Court; and *David L. Singer* v. *Isaac Garlick,* 1910 Number S407, N.Y.C.
Supreme Court. To qualify for representation under this provision, the injury victim had to
show "that she is a poor person, and is not worth one hundred dollars, besides the wearing
apparel and furniture necessary [to live]." *Fowler* v. *Broadway and Seventh Avenue Railroad.* The petition in *Friedman* v. *New York City Railway* mentioned another qualification:
"that neither this infant nor his guardian has any rich friends or relatives."

16. J. P. Schmitt, *History of the Legal Aid Society of New York, 1876–1912* (New York:
Legal Aid Society, 1912); and Harrison Tweed, *The Legal Aid Society of New York City,
1876–1951* (New York: Legal Aid Society, 1954). Reginald Heber Smith reported that
"one of the best attorneys of the New York Legal Aid Society" explained to Smith in 1912
that "there is about the negligence case an atmosphere that is totally different from any
other kind of case, and as a matter of fact [they] have taken on an atmosphere of gambling." Reginald Heber Smith, *Justice and the Poor* (New York: Carnegie Foundation for
the Advancement of Teaching, 1919), 157.

injured co-workers and neighbors to their offices.[17] In fact, this solicitation could be more insidious than "chasing" implies; it could occur "inside the ambulance," through medical caregivers, including doctors.[18] This "chasing" was no more, of course, than what accident-prone companies like street railways were doing simultaneously. Agents of the companies, again often doctors, sought out the freshly injured in an effort to get liability releases from them for little or nothing, before victims learned of their legal rights.[19]

The extent of ambulance chasing in these years will probably always be subject to question. As with contingent fees, though, more important than the extent of the practice to the argument here was the timing of the invention and its diffusion. If, as its appearance in the literature and on New York bar association agendas indicates, its advent is best dated between 1900 and 1910, while it may well have contributed to the magnitude of the rise in injury suits, it thus followed rather than led the trend.[20]

17. Charles Banfi testified that he found his first lawyer through an intermediary. He was "directed to one James Sullivan who was a stranger to [Banfi]. . . . Sullivan represented himself as an attorney and [Banfi] paid to him the sum of $50. . . . Thereafter Sullivan brought [Banfi] to the office of Charles Zerbarini, an attorney." *Charles Banfi v. Davis Brown,* 1910 Number B587, N.Y.C. Supreme Court.

18. From his testimony, it was evident that sailor Michael Finnie had, at the very least, had his lawyer, Don Almy, recommended to him by a doctor at the Hudson Street Hospital, though Finnie was emphatic under rigorous defense examination that the initiative to sue was his own: "None of the doctors in the hospital gave me advice about [the idea of suing the railroad company]." The line of questioning suggests that defense counsel Herbert Smyth was trying to discredit the suit as being instigated by someone else. *Michael Finnie v. Central Park, North, and East River Railroad Company,* 1910 Number C436, N.Y.C. Supreme Court.

19. Or as the State Bar Committee on Contingent Fees put it, "unscrupulous agents of railroad corporations" using "chicanery and fraud" gained from the injured "in the moment of their pain and suffering, releases of insufficient consideration." New York State Bar Association, "Report of the Committee on Contingent Fees," 103. This could also occur after the injured person had obtained a lawyer, if the lawyer for the injuring company was not averse to a bit of "chicanery and fraud." In August 1908, fruit vender Pietro D'Ancona had contracted with lawyer Achille Oishei to sue for injuries to his daughter from an accident with a Borden's Condensed Milk wagon. Working through a vender friend of D'Ancona's, Borden's lawyer, LeBarbier, convinced D'Ancona to accept a $450 settlement, though he knew Oishei was his attorney. As Oishei had been slow about initiating suit, LeBarbier was able to file an alternate suit earlier. He filed as D'Ancona's lawyer in Municipal (akin to a small claims) Court, accepted Borden's offer of a $450 judgment for D'Ancona, and Oishei was beaten. *Achille Oishei v. Pietrina D'Ancona et al.,* 1910 Number 0108, N.Y.C. Supreme Court.

20. For example, Andrew Hirschl's 1905–6 article, "Personal Injury Actions," refers to legal practice as entering the stage of ambulance chasing, and the New York State Bar Association's Committee on Contingent Fees of 1908 refers to the arrival upon the scene of "unprofessional solicitors of litigation" and "runners." The tone of the 1908 report is

Clearly the development of contingent-fees lawyering, ambulance chasing, and legal aid were not the key events in injured New Yorkers' move to the courtroom. If they had been, the rise in suits would have come decades earlier. New York City had both accident victims and contingent-fees representation in 1870 but few injury lawsuits. Contingent-fees law was not the leaven in the rise of injury cases in the New York City Supreme Court.

Contingent fees availed the law to the injured; it did not insure them success in their pursuit of compensation. How the injured fared in court depended partly upon whether the circumstances of the injury warranted compensation under extant rules and upon the disposition of judge and jury. Courtroom success depended equally upon the attorney's prowess— his or her ability to construct a tenable claim from the circumstances of the injury and to persuade a judge and jury of its validity.

A lawyer had many tactics to persuade the court to accept the plaintiff's version of facts and law, even when faced with the worst case, New York lawyer Thomas Hubbard proposed. Suppose a lawyer "burdened with a cause that is urged by the client's caprice or anger, has found in neither the facts, nor the law, weapons to give him the victory the client expects." He might unsheath other weapons:

> He may open his case, or his defense, by stating with warmth and exaggeration, the things his client wishes to have proved. He may impugn the motives of the adverse party. He may harass the opponent's witnesses. He may lay traps for them and lead them into apparent contradiction. He may lay stress on immaterial matters and obscure the material. He may exclude the evidence known only to himself and his client, that favors the other side. He may amuse the jury by bright or caustic personalities in respect to matters not relevant to the cause. He may use the weapon of eloquence in

more one of annoyance than of threat to the legal system, which characterizes the tone of a Supreme Court investigation of twenty years later. The 1908 report finds the practice "unseemly," more problematic for the rivalry it produces and for attorneys' initiative in proposing bargains than for the 1928 investigation's ominous exploitation of those "easily imposed upon" and its barratry through "high-powered salesmanship." New York State Bar Association, "Report of Committee on Contingent Fees," 100–101; New York State, Appellate Division of the Supreme Court, *Report of the Investigation Ordered by the Appellate Division of the Supreme Court in and for the First Judicial Department, by Order Dated February 7, 1928, upon the Petition of The Association of the Bar of the City of New York, New York County Lawyers Association and Bronx County Bar Association for an Inquiry by the Court into Certain Abuses and Illegal and Improper Practices Alleged in the Petition* (New York: M. B. Brown, 1928).

summing up and may give it keener edge, by ingenious misapplication of facts, misconstruction of facts, sophistical criticism of testimony, [and] undeserved denunciation of parties.[21]

Lawyers had means to persuade. Given these means and the willingness to exercise them, it was no wonder, Hubbard concluded, "that the profession has earned a reputation for disingenuousness."[22] Though there was difference of opinion over which part of the bar most contributed to that reputation—not even the self-righteous bar association contingent was immune from criticism—critics often blamed lawyers engaged in personal-injury litigation.[23] Judge Vann reported that "all over the State of New York . . . the bar is suffering to-day in the mind of the public on account of the general belief that in actions involving personal injuries the practice of bribery and perjury is common."[24]

The reputation was earned largely between 1870 and 1910. In these years the lawyers representing the injured and their adversaries continually tested new strategies and tactics in pursuit of courtroom success. That lawyers' methods of advocacy and their approach to their trade changed should not come as a surprise. The turn of the century was a period of changing thought and practice in business, government, and the sciences[25]; certainly lawyers were not immune to the influences that wrought "revolutions" in organization, strategy, and professional outlook within those neighboring realms.[26] The professionalization of law

21. Thomas Hubbard, *Legal Ethics: Lectures Delivered Before the Students of the Law Department of Union University* (Albany: Albany Law School, 1903), 22. Lawyer Hubbard's description is confirmed by observations from the bench. Judge John Wesley Donovan reported that " 'playing with the jury' is often indulged in to an excess by our leading trial lawyers. Questions are asked that are clearly objectionable. Their only purpose seems to be an argument directed to the jury. The result is that even though the answer is excluded the jury has received the benefit of the argument." John Wesley Donovan, *Modern Jury Trials and Advocates* (Albany: Banks and Brothers, 1881 [1924]), xvii.

22. Hubbard, *Legal Ethics*, 22.

23. A *New York Times* editorial cited "the growth of corporations" as having "had much to do with the degradation of legal practice" and faulted the bar association for only pretending to promote ethical practice. "The Ethics of Legal Practice," *New York Times*, 21 November 1886, p. 8.

24. Contrary to the *Times* attribution, Vann blamed lawyers working for contingent fees for the public's disillusionment with lawyers. *Contingent Fees*, 11.

25. On the transformation of business, for example, see Alfred Chandler, *The Visible Hand* (Cambridge: Harvard University Press, 1977).

26. Contemporaries realized this. The *American Lawyer* compared the lawyer of the previous generation with its own: "The practitioner was isolated from the wide-awake

at that juncture is manifest in the creation of bar associations, the tightening of bar-admission standards, and the growth of formal training in law schools.[27]

Pressed by social and economic change and learning from observation and experience, lawyers were able to devise ways to prosecute their work more effectively. But demonstrating change in injury-law advocacy is not simple. The problem is twofold: First, there is no neat formula for assessing effectiveness of lawyers. It would be a formidable enough task to erect an apparatus for measuring the effectiveness of present-day lawyers, let alone those removed by a century. Introduce the element of *change* in effectiveness, and the dimensions of the problem become clear. The second problem is the paucity of source material upon which such an assessment can be based.[28]

In using trial-court records, especially case transcripts, this study is drawing upon one of the best existing resources for the historical study of lawyers' work. These records yield information on lawyers' innovative

---

business world. . . . His course was that of a plodder, his work was unfacilitated by invention, and his hereditary conservatism caused the profession to lag far behind in the procession of life. Today all that is changed. The revolutions which have occurred in the business world, have produced corresponding changes in the professional life and methods of the lawyer." "The Evolution of the Law Office," *American Lawyer* 2 (1894), 78.

27. The professionalization of law has been the subject of much attention by historians lately. It is not a new discovery; Roscoe Pound addressed it in *Lawyer from Antiquity to Modern Times*, Minn. 249–255. Hurst talked about it in *Growth of American Law*, 249–293. Richard Hofstadter chose it to exemplify the changes professionals faced in *The Age of Reform* (New York: Vintage, 1955), 154–64. For recent treatments, see Wayne Hobson, *The American Legal Profession and the Organizational Society, 1890–1930* (New York: Garland Press, 1986); and Robert Gordon, "Legal Thought and Legal Practice in the Age of American Enterprise, 1870–1920," in Gerald Geison, ed., *Professions and Professional Ideologies in America, 1730–1940* (Chapel Hill: University of North Carolina Press, 1983), 70–110. Hobson, in another article, ("Professionals, Progressives and Bureaucratization: A Reassessment," *Historian 39* [1977], 639–58) makes the point that professionalization took many forms and varied from one profession to the next due to the different cultural background and social function of each. While most historians argue that professionalization brought marked change to law at the end of the nineteenth century, Maxwell Bloomfield finds the professionalism of late nineteenth-century lawyers more continuous with that of antebellum lawyers; see Maxwell Bloomfield, "Lawyers and Public Criticism: Challenge and Response in Nineteenth-Century America," *American Journal of Legal History* 15 (1971), 269–77; and Maxwell Bloomfield, *American Lawyers in a Changing Society, 1776–1876* (Cambridge: Harvard University Press, 1976), 136–90, 346–47.

28. Leading legal scholars have lamented this lack. Hurst pointed it out in *Growth of American Law* (pp. 334–35). Jerold Auerbach wrote, "I was unable to discover any collection of papers from a country lawyer, an urban solo lawyer, [or] an ambulance chaser." Jerold Auerbach, *Unequal Justice: Lawyers and Social Change in Modern America* (New York: Oxford University Press, 1976), 312.

TABLE 18

Lawyers' experience: Number of injury cases by number of injury cases each lawyer served on, New York City Supreme Court

| | Injury suits per lawyer | | | | | | | |
| | *1* | | *2–4* | | *5–9* | | *10 or more* | |
	n	%	n	%	n	%	n	%
Defendant	133	22.7	118	20.1	87	14.9	248	42.3
Plaintiff	302	42.5	277	38.9	79	11.1	53	7.5

Source: See Table 1.

manipulation of law and procedure, their courtroom strategies, their "presence," and their persuasiveness.

Lawyers did not respond uniformly to the rise in injury suits. The most telling differences are between defense lawyers and plaintiff lawyers. It is significant in itself that the profession was divided this way, with only a handful of practitioners straddling the divide. It has long been recognized that a plaintiffs' bar emerged quickly in injury law to abet the rise in tort suits; that a defendants' bar was just as quick to evolve may come as a surprise. In fact, the defendants in injury suits tended to draw upon a smaller number of attorneys than did their accusers. The relative concentration of defense business among fewer counsel is partly explained by multiple cases against single defendants, such as the city. But even with the city removed from the picture, defendants were still more likely to draw upon a small circle of lawyers—specialists—than were plaintiffs. Table 18 shows that over 40 percent of these injury cases were defended by attorneys who appeared in ten or more cases per year. By contrast, the plaintiffs' attorneys in over 40 percent of the cases only worked on one injury suit in the year studied. In only 7 percent of cases were plaintiffs represented by lawyers who had handled ten or more injury suits (again, effectively in one year).

The key question about the rise of specialization is whether those working one side of the courtroom developed more successful strategies for achieving results than those on the other side. The concentration of injury-suit defense in the hands of a few attorneys gave defense attorneys an advantage in experimenting with new tactics. As Marc Galanter has pointed out, experience and thus skill in advocacy have not been evenly distributed in our legal system. Galanter's suggestion that advantage accrues to those who appear in court frequently—the "repeat players"—appears to fit the situation of injury-suit defendants in the New York courts at the turn of the century.[29] Because the work of defending injurers went mostly to a handful of lawyers—eight lawyers defended 40 percent of the work-injury cases studied—even those defendants who were not frequently in court benefited from the lessons their attorneys learned by defending similar cases.

What did plaintiffs' and defendants' attorneys learn, and how did it change their approach to injury suits? Changes in lawyers' contributions to the disposition of injury claims fell into four basic categories: gathering facts and organizing them into viable cases, guiding those cases to trial through the procedural maze, suggesting ruling principles and precedents to the judge, and convincing judge and jury of the rectitude of the lawyer's facts and reading of the law. In all four categories, lawyers made adaptations in practice that became peculiar to injury suits. Practices rare in 1870 became commonplace by 1910.

Lawyers altered their case-building practices. We often forget that constructing cases was a work of creativity by the lawyer. As historians well know, facts are not immutable bits of truth, which when pieced together faithfully recreate the circumstances of injury, imparting cause and consequence to the passive observer. Facts only become facts after a person extracts them from the background and deems them significant. The lawyer had to decide which facts were essential to the case. Then he had to find someone to attest to the fact. No witness to an event could see every aspect of it, and when more than one person witnessed the occurrence they were bound to see it in different ways. Lawyers realized this and reconstituted events by stressing some particulars while ignoring others. This structuring was as crucial as procuring facts. Facts did not organize or interpret themselves; lawyers did. Opposing lawyers typically presented contrary accounts of the same incidents, equally founded on the facts.

The reconstruction of an injury was a work of the lawyer's mind. To create a lawsuit, the lawyer had to discern and distinguish important pieces of information from background events and impose order on the information so collected. In framing injury suits, lawyers learned to forsake tradition—and often ethics—to select, arrange, and interpret information in ways particular to this type of suit so as to increase their chances of success.

Innovation came quickly to the process of garnering facts. As mentioned in the preceding chapter, people involved in accidents learned to

29. Marc Galanter, "Why the 'Haves' Come Out Ahead: Speculations on the Limits of Legal Change," *Law and Society Review* 9 (1974): 95–160.

collect names of witnesses. The advantage inhered to the injurers over the injured in this; at the scene of the injury, the latter was occupied while the former was free to seek witnesses. Corporations that repeatedly caused accidents made good use of claims agents and doctors who could gather evidence at the same time as they could offer settlements to the injured.[30]

With experience, attorneys learned to tailor the fabric of facts to fit the measurements of injury law. This evolved from screening witnesses and selecting only those favorable to the case, to "coaching" witnesses, instructing them how to testify most favorably.[31] While seeking to construct the most favorable case possible was not unique to attorneys in injury suits, the means employed to accomplish that goal in these suits were singularly declaimed as unethical and illegal.

One approach was to eliminate unfavorable evidence; key witnesses were paid to leave town. Frank Russell, a subway worker, testified in a co-worker's injury case that payoffs to witnessing workers by railroad companies were common in work-injury cases. Russell was double-crossed in his own effort to sell his silence; he signed an agreement in defense lawyer Quackenbush's office to leave the state or testify for

30. See *Anna Flynn* v. *New York Taxi Cab Company, et al.,* 1910 Number N104, N.Y.C. Supreme Court; and *Herrman* v. *Christian et al.,* for examples of injury victims being visited by representatives of the defendant soon after their accident.

31. The evidence for this comes from lawyers' questioning of the oppositions' witnesses. They asked whether answers had been suggested or revised upon their lawyers' advice. Attorneys also asked their own witnesses such questions preemptively. Collusion was never admitted, but the frequent appearance of the question and the occasional acknowledgement of discussions of evidence in lawyers' offices suggests that "coaching" was a regular occurrence. See *Delahunt* v. *Southern Boulevard Railroad;* and *Corcoran* v. *Union Railway.* The contemporary literature associates doctoring of evidence with plaintiff attorneys, but the New York judgments show defendants at least equally guilty of the practice. Judge Greenbaum noted this in refusing to overturn a jury verdict for the plaintiff in *Latargia,* v. *Whitridge:* "While there are certain features of the testimony adduced in behalf of the plaintiff that tend to cast doubt upon the credibility of some of the plaintiff's witnesses, the same observations may be equally made respecting the testimony presented on behalf of the defendant."

Defense attorneys complained about collusion, as Theron Strong did to Judge George Benton: "Your honor knows what we are exposed to on these cases." *Bertolami* v. *United Engineering and Contracting.* But there is clear evidence that defendants exposed injured plaintiffs to the same tactics. In *Cummings* v. *New York and Long Island Traction ,* Cummings' lawyer showed that the defendant's chief witness had intended to sue the trolley company until he received a settlement; now he was swearing that the defendant was guiltless. Street railroad lawyer Quackenbush was involved in the doctoring of a statement made by the plaintiff in *Finnie* v. *Central Park, North, and East River Railroad.* Finnie could not read, and after giving his statement to Quackenbush's investigator, the investigator altered it and added a few sentences to say that Finnie was drunk and that he had jumped off the train (rather than being jerked off it with a sudden start, as Finnie stated).

the railroad in return for $500. Quackenbush never paid Russell but instead used the agreement to impugn his testimony for the plaintiff. Thus, in a slick maneuver the defense lawyer neutralized an adverse witness at no cost.[32]

If the subtraction of evidence was insufficient, lawyers undertook addition. Alteration, augmentation, and the outright manufacture of the facts to fit the law offered a less difficult, if still unethical, method to the same end.[33]

There was no complaint or evidence of this sort of lawyering in the 1870s. In the early 1890s, a journal's warning about limits to the lawyer's professional duty to the client signals that these practices were beginning to appear. What the editor of the *American Lawyer* worried about was that the lawyer "so absorb[ed] the [client] as to induce him to either seek legal ends by illegal means or illegal ends by legal means."[34] By 1910, evidence of "sharp practices" was everywhere. The outcry against them was still loud. But now while some commentators kept trying to invoke the higher ethical obligation of the lawyer to fulfill his or her role as an agent of the court, bar leaders counseled acceptance of the new ways.

Justification emanated from the highest legal circles. Connecticut judge Simeon Baldwin, founder of the American Bar Association, stressed, for example, that while attorneys as officers of the court had public obligations, their primary duty was to their client. Even if a lawyer knew that right resided on the other side of the courtroom, in personating the client the attorney was required to mobilize all means available to achieve a favorable outcome.

> A lawyer may in full conformity with legal ethics plead . . . some defect having no relation to the merits of the cause, and when to dismiss the cause is to defeat what would be justice were there no law to support the plea. The lawyer who thus carries out his client's will by claiming for him a strict legal advantage, on which a client with a higher sense of honor might disdain to lean, is, I believe, in the line of professional duty, and therefore, of professional honor."[35]

32. *Ernst Wartenberg* v. *Interborough Rapid Transit Company,* 1910 Number W479, N.Y.C. Supreme Court.

33. See note 31 for examples; and Vann, *Contingent Fees,* 8–9.

34. *American Lawyer* 1 (April 1893): 4.

35. Simeon Baldwin, *A Lecture in Legal Ethics Delivered before the Students of the Law Department of Union University* (Albany: Albany Law School, 1903), 46.

While Baldwin was probably most interested in defending another group, the rapidly growing body of corporation lawyers, the message fit the situation of injury lawyers as well.

Concern about sharp practices in constructing cases passed when these means became recognized as common to both plaintiff and defense attorney alike. In the early 1890s, lawyers, including those who served the injured, generally associated "accute [*sic*] and trained trickery" solely with the lower-class practitioners.[36] For the elite bar, the blame for all sharp practices—those of defendants' lawyers as well as plaintiffs'— lay in the lap of unscrupulous plaintiffs' counsel.[37] By the end of the decade, even the most conservative observers had to apportion blame more evenly.[38]

Trained trickery was not limited to the building of cases. It abounded in lawyers' imaginative uses of procedure as well.[39] Early in the new century, Judson Landon, a former justice of the state Court of Appeals, noticed and registered his displeasure with lawyers' procedural machinations:

> I sometimes think our methods of administering justice—I mean the procedure, . . . not the weightier matters of the law—are unworthy of an intelligent and justice-loving people. The lawyers are largely responsible for it. We inherited something like these methods from England, and have

36. Gilbert Hawes, "Winnow the Bar," *American Lawyer* 1 (April 1893): 5. Hawes, a New York City lawyer who appeared in cases in this study, wrote: "The rules of admission are too lax and the consequence is that we are disgraced every day by the admission of men who are better fitted to be mechanics, tradesmen, or clerks, than members of what should be a learned and exalted profession. . . . In consequence the standard of the profession has sunk very low and we are obliged to recognize as brother lawyers men who are capable of every kind of chicanery and trickiness, or on the other hand, men who are incapable of writing or speaking the English language properly." Hawes, "Letter to the Editor," *American Lawyer* 1 (October 1893): 7.

37. "It would be strange if . . . [among defense] lawyers dependent for livelihood upon their practice and afraid to report disaster to their clients . . . there should not be found some willing to adopt the methods used against them, to sacrifice means to ends, and to defend this course by persuading themselves that their act was unavoidable." E. Parmalee Prentice, "Where Jury Bribing Begins," *Arena* 22 (1899): 313–14.

38. See, for example, Eli Hammond, "Personal Injury Litigation", *Yale Law Review* 6 (1896–97): 328–29.

39. The imaginative use of procedure has long been recognized as a lawyer's tool in getting cases before appellate courts. Frank C. Smith, the editor of *American Lawyer*, presented to the American Bar Association statistics on the deciding issue in state court appeals. He found that of the 14,000 cases reported in West's *Reports* for 1894, 48 percent had been decided on points of procedure. In New York the percentage was slightly less but still quite sizable: 43 percent. See Frank C. Smith, "Practice and Procedure," *American Lawyer* 3 (1895): 17–18.

manipulated our inheritance—sometimes for sinister purpose—into a sort
of maze, so beset with perplexing details that the honest suitor seeking the
straight road to speedy justice finds himself mired in its by-paths.[40]

Defense lawyers introduced most of the innovations here. The busiest
and most sophisticated of the injury-defense specialists, Frank Verner
Johnson, arrayed in 1910 an entire "procedural defense" that plaintiffs
had to overcome just to get their case to the courtroom.

The first of Johnson's battlements was the bill of particulars, a seemingly innocuous request for clarification of the charges injured suitors
made in their complaints. Defense lawyers ostensibly sought information
on the precise events that caused injury, the proof of negligence, the nature of the injury, and the losses the injury wrought upon the plaintiff.
The bill of particulars put to Alexander Sved, for example, required information on fourteen points, including how the printing room Sved was
working in was unsafe, how the machine he used was unsafe, how the
machine was improperly guarded, how the lighting at the machine was
deficient, how printshop owners Geza Spitzer and Victor Heller were negligent, and what work rules the defendants had failed to promulgate.[41]
The wording in defendants' demands for bills of particulars tried to pin
plaintiffs down as tightly as they could. For example, one of Johnson's
six questions in the bill submitted to Thomas Thornton demanded "a definite explanation of the manner in which some of the wheels fell against
and upon this plaintiff as alleged in paragraph 'Sixth' of the complaint
herein, explaining clearly and definitely the exact manner in which plaintiff claims the alleged accident occurred."[42]

The rationale behind allowing the defense to ask such questions was
that only the plaintiff was privy to such information and had to disclose
it to the defendant so that the charges could be answered and surprise
avoided. The defendant had to provide an affidavit that stated that the
defendant was "utterly unable to obtain any information asked for in
the motion . . . and the facilities for so doing and the knowledge there-
of are peculiarly with the plaintiff" before a judge would grant the

40. Judson Landon, *Legal Ethics: The Hubbard Course on Legal Ethics* (Albany: Albany Law School, 1905), 16.
41. *Alexander Sved, by Guardian* v. *Geza Spitzer et al.*, 1910 Number S269, N.Y.C.
Supreme Court.
42. *Thomas Thornton* v. *The Steamship Company of Savannah*, 1910 Number T208,
N.Y.C. Supreme Court.

motion.[43] That this was the defense's need in *Sved* was belied by the request for the name of Sved's supervisor. Could the employers not have discovered this themselves?

Surely they could have. But Johnson had other reasons to demand specifics. Once a bill of particulars was granted, only information or charges used in the bill could be used in trial in response to the same question. Thus, the bill limited the proof a plaintiff could use in trial. If Sved identified one supervisor, for example, but not the one the court considered legally responsible, that second supervisor could not be incorporated into the suit at that point because he had not been part of the original complaint, as later narrowed by the bill of particulars.

It was not only information that defense lawyers sought through bills of particulars but limits on the scope of plaintiffs' attacks. They had taken a procedural tool intended for one purpose and bent it to another: the hindrance of those trying to bring injury suits. Its widespread use confirms this as defense lawyers' purpose. For Johnson and many of his fellow defense specialists, the bill of particulars became a routine step in defending an injury suit, requested in every case.

Plaintiff lawyers responded in a variety of ways to these bills. The most astute tried merely to restate the complaint, keeping the answers as broad as possible to leave alternatives open once the case got to court. Defendants might then return the bill as unsatisfactory and a fight would ensure. Judges occasionally let the vague answer suffice over defendants' complaints. When they did not, the plaintiff provided more specific information or the judge dismissed the suit.[44]

43. Samuel Sargent, counsel to Johnson, in *Thornton* v. *Steamship Company of Savannah*. Judges granted most requests for bills of particulars. Occasionally, they would modify the request, excluding one or two demands; Cuthbert Pound did this in *Thornton*, denying Johnson's demand for the names of "other persons entrusted with and exercising superintendence." Sometimes, motions for bills of particulars were wholly denied. This happened in *Nicholas Sullivan* v. *Frederick Hoyt*, 1910 Number S634, N.Y.C. Supreme Court. Ironically, the Sullivan's victory in this procedural skirmish ultimately lost him his case. He waited patiently to be paid the $10 cost of the failed motion and had the defendant stayed from proceeding until the costs were met. After a lapse of two years, the defendant paid, vacating the stay, then moved immediately for dismissal for failure to prosecute. Sullivan's lawyer LaMott Hartshorn argued, "The defendant's attorney having been guilty of gross laches and delay cannot come before this Court and ask a dismissal of this complaint because of any delay on the part of deponent." Judge James Gerard thought otherwise and granted the motion. The sly defender who worked this stratagem was Frank Verner Johnson.

44. See *Amelia Traub* v. *Saks and Company*, 1910 Number T214, N.Y.C. Supreme Court. A plate of glass from a storm door fell on Traub as she entered Saks. She com-

Other lawyers responded in great detail to the original demand. This approach did not always protect the plaintiff from further obstructions, as Jeremiah Walsh found out. Injured at work when some iron pipe was unloaded from a truck onto his head, Walsh fully complied with Johnson's bill of particulars and gave Johnson notice of trial. Johnson returned the notice on the technicality that it was served less than fourteen days before term. Johnson then demanded a second bill of particulars; Walsh again complied.

This time, though, Walsh could not file for trial because he was out of work and could not come up with the $4 fee (his lawyer Hector Robichon could not provide the sum either, or he would have been guilty of the crime of maintenance). Johnson moved for dismissal for failure to prosecute, and Judge Alfred Page granted it over the plaintiff's objections.[45]

While Walsh's fate demonstrates the effectiveness of the tactical use of bills of particulars, the bill was most effective when a plaintiff's attorney unfamiliar with the bill just ignored it. The defense attorney then simply submitted a motion to the court to exclude all evidence requested in the bill, and the plaintiff was blocked from prosecuting the case.[46] When a case was filed after the plaintiff's lawyer appeared in court, the defendant could move for dismissal for failure to prosecute, and the case was done.

The obstructive use of the bill of particulars was only the first procedural barricade that injury-law specialists erected. Two others came out in

---

plained that it bruised and wounded her, and she wanted $25,000. Bertrand Pettigrew, Saks's lawyer, was granted a bill of particulars asking "the nature, extent, location, and duration" of Traub's injury. Traub's lawyer Arthur Henning gave what he thought was a reasonable answer: "Injury to the side, hip, and back of a permanent nature, and severe shock." Pettigrew moved for another bill of particulars, the first being inadequately answered, and Henning contested the claim. He prepared a brief citing the state courts' rulings on bills of particulars: "While the power exists of requiring Bills of Particulars of all descriptions of actions, caution should be exercised in requiring Bills of Particulars in actions for negligence. . . . The Courts have also repeatedly held that a party may be excused from giving minute particulars. . . . Before the defendant can succeed in his motion, he must show this Court that the facts he demand are necessary for him to prepare his case." Judge Cuthbert Pound did not agree with this reasoning, and granted Saks the second bill. In the end, Traub lost her suit on a jury verdict after a three-day trial and paid Saks $180 in costs.

45. See *Jeremiah Walsh* v. *J. C. Rodgers and Son,* 1910 Number W406, N.Y.C. Supreme Court. Judge Irving Vann, no great proponent of legal change, defined the lawyer's maintenance of a client (by advancing filing fees) as "the intermeddling of a stranger in a suit in which he has no interest by assisting one party to continue a litigation against another without lawful authority." Vann, *Contingent Fees,* 6.

46. See *Morris Katz* v. *Henry Koester,* 1910 Number K39, N.Y.C. Supreme Court; *John Brady* v. *Jeremiah Carey et al.,* 1910 Number B562, N.Y.C. Supreme Court; *Salvatore Fertita* v. *Degnon Contracting Company,* 1910 Number F261, N.Y.C. Supreme Court.

the illustrations above: delay and dismissal. Delaying tactics were used by both plaintiff and defendant, by the former typically to gain negotiating time and by the latter in the hope of exhausting the plaintiff's patience and money. There is little evidence of this happening in 1870, but by 1910 it is apparent.

Delay is difficult to pick out in the judgment rolls. The only real evidence of it is a longer than normal lapse of time between the initiation of a suit and its final disposition where no multiple trials, appeals, or other events intervened.[47] This evidence is rife with problems, though. Silence in the record hides all sorts of events along with deliberate delay, such as backlogs of cases in the court. The distinction is important; delay as a tactic to effect desirable outcomes is different than simply waiting one's turn on the court's calendar.

Evidence exists of deliberate delay in 1910, though, thanks to the impatience of Judge John Goff. After running through forty cases on his calendar one morning and finding not a single one ready to proceed, the exasperated Goff vented his anger in an impromptu lecture to the courtroom. The subject was the problems injury-law specialists—"lawyers [who] have made the practice of bringing such actions [(injury suits)] a specialty"—were causing to the administration of justice. The "Accident Trust," as these lawyers were known at the court house,[48] earned Goff's disapproval for agreeing among themselves to delay suits: "The Court expresses the opinion that the way the attorneys answered in the various cases bears evidence of a general understanding between the attorneys to put their cases off, and hereafter by consent, have them restored to the calendar."[49]

Defendants often sought the dismissal of a suit even while delaying it, as *Walsh* v. *Rodgers and Son* illustrated. Dismissal was the defendants' preferred end to cases because it saved time and avoided traumatic encounters with juries. Johnson developed the dismissal strategy to its highest form, employing lawyer Louis Cohn strictly to work for early

47. One exception is *John Conlon* v. *Edison Manufacturing Company and National Phonograph Company*, 1910 Number C444, N.Y.C. Supreme Court, where an affidavit by the defendant's lawyer stated that the case had come up for trial five times, only to be put off each time, presumably by the plaintiff's lawyer. The last time it came up for trial, it had definitely been the plaintiff's lawyer who took it off the calendar.

48. The *New York Times* reported the nickname in common use at the County Court House, where it referred to a "little group of lawyers . . . [that] has a monopoly of about 80% of the prosecution and defense of accident cases." "Justice Goff Raps Accident Lawyers," *New York Times*, 16 December 1911, p. 7.

49. Ibid.

dismissals. Cohn watched the filing dates of the cases coming to trial, and as soon as a case appeared that had been filed after a suit Johnson was defending, Cohn moved for dismissal of the suit Johnson was defending for plaintiffs' failure to prosecute their case.[50] Even when plaintiffs countered by claiming that they were in the midst of negotiations with the defendant as the defendant was making this move, they seldom won.

The motion for dismissal also became a regular feature at another point on the lawsuit's procedural journey, the trial. After the plaintiff presented his case, the defense attorney would routinely ask the judge to dismiss on the grounds that the evidence did not constitute a cause of action, that it did not show the defendant negligent, or that it did not show the plaintiff free from negligence. Like the other procedural tactics, this was not common practice in 1870, but it was by 1910. Demurrers, a pleading that asserted a plaintiff had not made a sufficient case in law, had appeared occasionally in injury suits,[51] but motions to dismiss for failure to prosecute did not show up with regularity until 1910.

The reflexive call for dismissal appears to have come into use in the 1890s. Lawyer Eli Hammond noted in 1897 that repeat defendants, such as railroads, always asked judges to take the case from the jury, regardless of the merits of the suit.[52] Hammond's disdain for the automatic nature of the maneuver suggests that the practice had only recently become commonplace, because he still expected defendants to refrain from seeking dismissal unless it was well founded. By 1910 none of the judges of the New York court would have expected that. In almost every injury case they heard, defense lawyers sought dismissal at least once and typically three times (at the opening, after the plaintiff's case, and after the defendant's case). Facing this every day, few judges retained their hope that lawyers would act as disinterested agents of the court rather than as ruthless partisans.

A final procedural defense tactic was to strain plaintiffs' financial resources in any way possible to force the end of the suit. If $4 could stymie an injured person from moving his proceedings forward, as it did in the Walsh case, it is easy to imagine the effect of requiring a $200 deposit of the plaintiff. That is precisely what defense attorneys Stetson, Jennings,

---

50. See, for example, *William Curran* v. *Max Weinberg et al.*, 1910 Number C410, N.Y.C. Supreme Court.

51. See *Edward Bennett* v. *Harold Sanderson et al.*, 1890 Number B225, N.Y.C. Supreme Court; and *Thomas Cavanagh, Administrator* v. *Oceanic Steam Navigation Company*, 1890 Number C144, N.Y.C. Supreme Court.

52. Hammond, "Personal Injury Litigation," 328.

and Russell did to Stanley Belleas, moving the court to require of him a $200 surety against the possibility of his default on any costs awarded to the defendant.[53]

Procedural defenses were designed to trip up plaintiffs short of trial; if cases reached trial, attorneys from both sides unveiled new tactics developed for this stage of the game. One place in the trial where lawyers retained a surprisingly large role was in the determination of the law. This was not new. The practice had long been that the lawyers presented to the judge the principles that they believed ruled in the situation before the court. From these and his own experience, the judge then decided the appropriate law for the case and instructed the jury.

Lawyers developed a strategy here, too. The more alert lawyers learned to submit some charges but hold others in reserve so that they could request them orally at the close of a judge's instructions. The ploy was fairly transparent: Juries then associated points of law with one party's case, and the lawyers' law was then the last law that juries heard before deciding the suit. Only occasionally did judges complain about the irregularity of the practice.

The judiciary encouraged this opportunity to lawyers by its own inconsistency; the accepted way for lawyers to request that points of law be charged varied markedly from judge to judge. Some judges accepted only written requests before instruction and then merged all valid requests into one set of instructions. Others read the charges directly to the jury with full attribution to the respective attorneys. Many retained the practice of oral requests for charges at the end of the judges' instructions. In this last form, the instructions became essentially a debate about matters of law that the jury witnessed. Jurors saw the law not as consensual and constant but as a subject of contention and interpretation, as "plaintiff's law" and "defendant's law." Of course, even in extreme cases, the judge provided a final ruling on the law. But lawyers were planting ideas along the way.

Lawyers developed a tactic for promoting their cause through the instructions of law, by requesting the same charge more than once or requesting the same charge with a slight twist. Typically, the judge would hear or read the request and charge it again. Or finding that he had already charged it, he would announce this to the requesting lawyer. Despite the apparent rebuff, the benefit went to the side that had made the request.

---

53. This was not universally applicable; Belleas was required to put up the surety because he was not a citizen of New York state. *Stanley Belleas* v. *Pittsburgh Construction Company,* 1910 Number B559, N.Y.C. Supreme Court. See also *Edwin Hall* v. *Erie Railroad Company,* 1910 Number H424, N.Y.C. Supreme Court.

They had their position declared and confirmed by the judge once more, the declaration came just before the jury retired to decide the case, and subtle twists in wording might even have extended the rule beyond the principle the judge had originally charged.

For example, in *John Buhrens v. Drydock, East Broadway, and Battery Railroad,* Judge Morgan O'Brien instructed the jury on the basis of charges the two lawyers requested. At the close of his instructions, plaintiff's lawyer William Townley asked for an additional charge, to which O'Brien agreed. The charge asked that pain and suffering be added to the factors in determining damages, which O'Brien had neglected to mention. The defense lawyers, Robinson, Scribner, and Bright, responded with a series of requests of their own.

Henry Robinson appealed to the judge, "There are some propositions which I requested the Court to charge which your Honor has omitted to charge, whether intentionally or otherwise." "I intended to cover them all," O'Brien defended. Robinson presented his propositions again, point by point. O'Brien complied with the requests, agreeing to charge each after reading them in the defense's own language to the jury. The content of the requests had clearly been included in his initial instructions; Robinson's law was consequently presented twice to the jury, the second time more favorably.[54]

Lawyers tried hard to make their cases foregone conclusions before they ever reached the instruction stage. One way to do this was by extending existing rules to cover new situations or parlaying particulars into exceptions to the rules. Candy-factory worker Rose Cerighino's lawyers, Smith and Bowman, successfully employed the latter, asserting that her lack of skill on machines should absolve her of any contributory negligence. Her unfamiliarity with technology and its dangers, they argued,

---

54. *John Buhrens v. The Dry Dock, East Broadway, and Battery Railroad Company,* 1890 Number D9, N.Y.C. Supreme Court. To give an idea of the similarity of the requests to what had already been charged, here are two of Robinson's requests, related by Judge O'Brien: "I am asked to charge you that 'The defendant's car had the right of way and the defendant was entitled to the exclusive possession of its track for the unrestricted passage of the car in question'. . . . [and] 'In the exercise of the franchise conferred by the Legislature, the defendant's right to its track was paramount and superior to the right of the plaintiff to cross the same.' I so charge."
The judge had already instructed the jury: "A street railroad company has not the exclusive right to the use of its tracks but simply a paramount right and . . . a person lawfully driving on the tracks may not recklessly, carelessly or wilfully obstruct the passage of its cars. . . . Inasmuch as the railroad company itself is confined to its tracks, and persons, vehicles or passengers having the capacity to move to one side or the other, the law gives the company on its own tracks such paramount right."

should exempt her from the ordinary standard of care.[55] Frederick Van-Zant, lawyer for Tillie Mattson, tried to extend the clear warning requirement that applied to inherently dangerous activities (e.g., trains approaching grade crossings, use of explosives) to elevator-construction employment to get around the assumption-of-risk doctrine. VanZant claimed that the defendant "failed to provide for a warning being given to Oscar Mattson of the peculiar dangers he was thus subjected to." Judge Nathan Bijur was not persuaded and dismissed the suit after five days of trial.[56]

Neither did Edward Hall's lawyer Strassman convince Judge James Gerard that the Erie Railroad was liable to Hall because it had "failed to provide a proper and suitable place for its employees to come and go from work." Strassman had sought to extend the safe-workplace concept, but the idea did not fall upon sympathetic ears.[57] Defendant attorneys Blandy and Hatch were more successful in convincing Judge George Ingraham to dismiss a tenement building-injury suit against their client William Clark, arguing in part that it was unreasonable for someone "of [as] unusual weight" as the plaintiff Honoria Ryder to be shaking rugs on the building's roof.[58]

This probing and pushing of the rules, even in the majority of cases where it amounted to naught, was important for its longer-run effects. These constant tests of the law, repeated often enough or suggested in the right case in the right courtroom, fomented numerous small changes in injury-law rules over the decades. Rule changes have been almost solely attributed to judges; reading the trial record suggests that lawyers should share some credit or blame. It is probable that many of the new ideas judges are credited with were initially suggested by lawyers groping for an advantageous reading of the rules. In attempting only to win their immediate cases, lawyers served as rule innovators.[59]

55. *Rose Cerighino* v. *David Auerbach et al.*, 1910 Number A282, N.Y.C. Supreme Court.

56. *Tillie Mattson, Administrator* v. *Otis Elevator Company*, 1910 Number 055, N.Y.C. Supreme Court.

57. *Hall* v. *Erie Railroad.*

58. *Honoria Ryder* v. *William Clark*, 1890 Number R33, N.Y.C. Supreme Court.

59. The contributions of lawyers to rule evolution has received little systematic assessment. See Jonathan Lurie, "Lawyers, Judges and Legal Change, 1852–1916: New York as a Case Study," *Working Papers from the Regional Economic History Research Center* 3 (1980): 31–56; and Stanley Katz, "Law and Economic Development in Antebellum America: A Comment," *Working Papers from the Regional Economic History Research Center* 3 (1980): 90–99.

adversary system

Rules were not the only targets of lawyers during trials. In their efforts to develop more effective strategies of winning over judges and juries, lawyers experimented, loosing all sorts of tactics on their opponents. Defense lawyers attacked plaintiff complaints at the roots. They had learned quickly that it was as easy to take the offensive and challenge the essence of the plaintiff's claim—that they had been injured, or injured to such an extent that they truly had sustained a measurable loss—as it was to defend their own client's acts.[60] Where injury was too evident to disprove, a defendant might claim that the plaintiff had always been in poor health anyway or that the injured person should be able to get some kind of work despite the injury.

Defense lawyer John Platt's questioning of a plaintiff's witness combines both tactics, though witness Joseph LaSelle appears to have the better of the exchange:

> PLATT: Is there no other branch of that business [hatmaking] that he could work at sitting? [The plaintiff's leg had been crushed in a streetcar accident.]
>
> LaSELLE: No; There is not, because what is done by sitting is done mostly by girls.
>
> PLATT: Still, he could do that?
>
> LaSELLE: A man has not got the skill of girls sewing and felting, and a man would not earn half as much as a girl does, and the girl earns little enough.
>
> PLATT: He was rather a delicate man, always, was he not?
>
> LaSELLE: He was by his looks; he was stronger than he looked.[61]

The lawyers for the injured developed a graphically convincing counter strategy to this line of questioning. At every opportunity, they had witnesses describe injuries in bloody detail, and when they could get away with it, had the victim display the wounds—mangled and missing limbs, scars, and oozing sores.[62] The goal was evident. As defense lawyer Her-

---

60. See, for example, *Orlando Barrelle* v. *Pennsylvania Railroad Company,* 1890 Number B110, N.Y.C. Supreme Court; *Sarah Uransky* v. *Drydock, East Broadway, and Battery Railroad Company,* 1890 Number D16, N.Y.C. Supreme Court; and *Walter Smith* v. *Orlando Potter,* 1890 Number S504, N.Y.C. Supreme Court, all cases where the defendant claimed that the plaintiff had never been injured at all.

61. *Schappner* v. *Second Avenue Railroad.*

62. See, for example, *Patrick Cronin* v. *Manhattan Transfer Company,* 1910 Number M698, N.Y.C. Supreme Court, where the defending lawyer's slowness of response allowed the plaintiff's mother to get in some gory and sympathy-evoking testimony before an

bert Smyth protested to Judge Warren Hooker, "The plaintiff can have no other object than to inflame the minds of the jury."[63]

Lawyers on both sides attempted to maintain a certain demeanor in the courtroom, incisive yet civil. In doing so, they were keeping with long-standing practice. Lawyers had always played to a dual audience, judge and jury. Civility and avoidance of contentiousness was commended by the bench, while stridency was frowned upon. It simply did not fit judges' images of professional conduct. Judges noted with displeasure the combativeness that seemed to fill the courtroom in 1910, which they believed had not characterized trials forty years before.[64]

Recognizing this, attorneys tried to bring out the unsavory side of their opponents' personalities to lower them in the eyes of both judges and juries. This seems to have been plaintiff's lawyer Gilbert Ray Hawes's goal in the 1910 case *Harry Schultz* v. *New York Transportation*. Hawes prodded his opponent George Wing to anger repeatedly with off-hand remarks ostensibly to the judge, clearly out of order, but nevertheless not restrained in any way by the judge. Early in the trial, Wing objected to a statement by a witness. Judge Henry Dugro allowed it to stand, and Hawes threw in a gratuitous comment to which Wing again objected.

HAWES: That was only a little colloquy with the Court.
JUDGE DUGRO: We all know that some [vehicles] do go terribly fast.
HAWES: Certainly, and this is a silly objection and simply is made to influence the jury.
WING: I except to that remark.

Hawes waited a few minutes then resumed his irritating tactics. Again he triggered an outburst by Wing, who was quickly becoming exasperated. Wing had been badgering witnesses throughout the case, and the judge was stepping in to reword Wing's questions, blocking his ploy.

---

objection cut it off. Mary Cronin testified: "He was undressed, all covered with blood, just as he was born, when I saw him at the hospital." See also *Delahunt* v. *Southern Boulevard Railroad*.

63. *Finnie* v. *Central Park, North, and East River Railroad*.

64. Frank Verner Johnson was the epitome of civility, which may have contributed to his exceptional record of success (he won 72 of 93 cases). See, for example, *Schwartz* v. *Onward Construction*. Judge M. Warley Platzek recorded the judges' preference for brevity and civility: "Counsel on both sides are entitled to your commendation and my gratitude for having in these heated days of trial tried this case with such few objections and in so remarkably short a time." *Garrett* v. *National Fireproofing*.

Hawes joined in, too, responding to a Wing question. This was the last straw for Wing, who wholly lost his composure.

> WING: I move for a mistrial of this case because of Mr. Hawes' actions. Mr. Hawes is trying to anger me by his frequent interruptions and I will not stand it; and he is telling the witness what to say. I insist on my motion.
> JUDGE DUGRO: Motion denied. . . . We are wasting time this way. If Mr. Hawes does things like those you say the jury will see it.
> WING: They ought to.
> JUDGE DUGRO: Then you are not so badly hurt by it.[65]

Again, the judge chastised Wing rather than Hawes, though it was Hawes who had transgressed. Wing's tone appears to have annoyed Dugro; in any event, Hawes was benefiting from flustering Wing. Twice more Wing stopped the proceedings, once after Hawes indirectly accused him of doctoring a transcript from the previous trial and finally in the lawyers' closing statements to the jury. Wing was harried and neither Dugro nor the jury gave him any quarter; the former refused Wing's repeated requests to dismiss, and the latter returned a verdict with a sizable award for Schultz.

Innovative lawyering did not touch every attorney involved in injury suits, to be sure. Some of the advocacy was uninspired and ineffective, and some was worse than that. Anton Skvor and Giovanni LoBravico, for example, lost their cases because of their attorneys' incompetence. In the case of Skvor's lawyer Lewis Goebel, the suit was dismissed after "the papers were filed away in the cabinet and the matter slipped [Goebel's] mind."[66] LoBravico's attorney William Deane had a better excuse. He could not attend his client's trial because he (Deane) had fled town in the face of criminal charges.[67]

Though there were no instances of defense lawyers fleeing, this group was not exempt from charges of ineffectiveness. Defense counsel Smith Multer, for example, lost two objections in one case that he could have won: "The Court would have excluded it had you objected," Judge War-

65. *Harry Schultz, Administrator* v. *New York Transportation Company,* 1910 Number N171, N.Y.C. Supreme Court.

66. Deposition by Lewis Goebel, *Anton Skvor* v. *George Schumann,* 1910 Number S237, N.Y.C. Supreme Court.

67. *Giovanni LoBravico* v. *Mayor et al., City of New York,* 1910 Number L165, N.Y.C. Supreme Court.

ren Hooker told him. But by the time Multer realized he might lodge an objection, he had missed the opportunity.[68]

Having surveyed the practice of lawyers involved in injury lawsuits and finding that changes in that practice did emerge between 1870 and 1910, are we any closer to an explanation of the rising use of the Supreme Court by injured Manhattanites? Were the changes ones that would have induced lawsuits where there had been none before?

The developments proved ambivalent: One practice that encouraged plaintiffs to sue emerged in an environment of other developments bound to discourage. Of the three trends that interacted to produce the overall effect of changed lawyering on litigation—the spread of contingent-fees retainers, the rise of injury-defense specialists, and the developments in the construction of injury cases—the first stands out for its impact on amounts of litigation. The practice became so widespread that we would expect it to have had an effect on the increase in lawsuits. Yet as this chapter argues, chronology shows that contingent-fees law practice was more likely to have been encouraged by rising use of the courts than vice versa. The relationship became symbiotic. Once afield, contingent fees probably did contribute to the rise in the number of injury suits, just as more injury suits contributed to the further spread of the contingency contract. But the path to the court was already well worn by the time contingent fees came into wide use.

In the meantime, defense lawyers who specialized in injury suits were sharpening the weapons they would use to thwart those suits. The concentration of injury-suit defenses in the hands of a small number of lawyers gave an advantage in litigation not only to the oft-sued company over the typical "one-shot" injury victim but to the defense specialists' occasional or first-time clients as well. Defense specialists drew upon their resource advantage and accumulating experience in ways that presented an increasingly formidable opposition to potential opponents.

Lawyers for plaintiffs and defendants experimented in the same ways with advantageous case construction, but the results of innovation did not distribute evenly. In gathering, selecting, and organizing information, in learning through repeated exposure the predilections of the different judges, in practicing procedural ins and outs regularly, and in subtle other ways, the repeat-playing defense specialists were better prepared to construct successful cases than their opposing brethren.

68. *Jennie Sabath* v. *Interborough Rapid Transit Co.*, 1910 Number 180, N.Y.C. Supreme Court.

Of course, information on the city's Supreme Court procedure was probably not widely disseminated, especially news on lawyers' subtle alterations in that procedure. There was no publicity for cases that were lost because of failure to respond adequately to bills of particulars; these were arcane, mundane events. Casualties of the legal process went largely unnoticed, and lawyers' procedural changes and their consequences did not get emblazoned on the public consciousness, either in an encouraging or discouraging way.

The changes in lawyers' practice did not gain compensation for the injured any more often than before. This would have been the primary way changes in lawyers' work would have become known and stimulated more suits: to win more often and have the populace recognize it. As long as the vital ingredient—greater success—was lacking, no new courtroom methods plaintiffs' lawyers deployed would encourage more law suits.

The advocacy of injury suits changed but not enough to explain New York City's sudden, sharp rise in the numbers of those suits. Except for contingent retainers, the practices of lawyers did not visibly change people's pattern of court use. But two other groups of players in this legal drama wielded considerable power over injury lawsuits: judges and juries. If the balance of power between them or their use of that power shifted, then the administration of injury law changed. Any new direction in the rendering of the law by these participants held the potential to make going to court a more attractive option for the city's injured.

5. JUDGES AND JURIES

Judges have always played a prominent role in the telling of the law's history. But rather than assuming that the law that emerged from lower courts was simply trial judges' rote application of existing rules, or conversely was wholly those judges' inventions only tenuously connected to precedent and statute, we will probe deeper into just what the men in this post contributed to the legal process.

Historians have much to learn about the particulars of what judges did in their courts.[1] Clearly, judges wielded real power over the fate of the suitors before them, in a system of countervailing powers where other participants were also invested with authoritative roles. The trial judge's rule was shared, was under the close scrutiny of contending parties, and was ultimately subject to higher judicial sanction.

The judges' control over individual cases and cumulatively over the general direction of injury law was not absolute, nor was control exerted evenly. The way judges used their power differed from man to man. Their legal philosophies, abilities, personal styles, and social views were not uniform. The work of the individual judge varied from case to case as well; the rules and procedures a judge adhered to in one case might be disregarded in the next. Given this, it is only to be expected that the exercise of judicial power yielded varying results from case to case.

1. Robert Gordon notes that historians and legal scholars remain "in a wilderness almost completely devoid of knowledge or apparent interest in knowledge about what courts . . . in this society actually do." Robert Gordon, "Historicism in Legal Scholarship," *Yale Law Journal* 90 (1981): 1052.

The judge's most basic power in trying injury suits was to serve as arbiter of the law: He determined what rules applied to each case. This set the bounds within which the dispute could be argued. Of course, there were restraints on the trial judge's freedom here. Precedent and statute had to be followed, because consistency was the intention of law. Law was intended to remove the whims of men from the administration of justice, to make the resolution of disputes objective.

While this had always been the goal, belief in the possibility of attaining consistency had risen and fallen from age to age. In the science-conscious intellectual milieu of the late nineteenth century, the ideal was believed to be one and the same with reality; belief in the attainability of objective law was at its apogee.[2] The comments and instructions of the New York City court's reigning officers confirm that this view permeated the bench.

Judges' quest for consistency in setting forth the law was limited by their knowledge of and capacity to remember the law. Their capabilities in this regard varied not only from judge to judge, but from day to day. A set of one judge's cases typically reveals omissions of pertinent rules cited only weeks or months before in other cases.[3] The judge had this knowledge but did not consistently recall it, possibly because it was so evident to him that he occasionally forgot the need to bring it to the jury's attention or because the right cues were not present to elicit its recall.[4] The crucial part of this fallibility is that it opened a window of opportunity for the contending advocates, providing one of their real sources of power—arguing the laws.[5]

2. White, *Tort Law in America*, 60–62; and Grant Gilmore, *The Ages of American Law* (New Haven, Conn.: Yale University Press, 1977), 41–67.

3. Compare, for example, Judge Henry Dugro's instructions in *Baum v. Gallo et al.; Schultz v. New York Transportation; Sartirana v. New York County Bank;* and *Delahunt v. Southern Boulevard Railroad.*

4. Dugro failed to mention in his instructions to the jury in *Sartirana v. New York County Bank* that the defendant was engaged in a hazardous activity and had a duty to protect the public. When asked to do so by Sartirana's lawyer Nelson Zabriskie, Dugro derisively answered that the proposition was too evident to require instruction: "Why, there cannot be any sensible man that does not think that. Lowering a platform on a public street certainly has an element of danger in it, and any one that does so must exercise ordinary care for the public in doing it. The jury know that without my charging it, and they would not be reasonable men if they did not think so." Obviousness apparently did not apply equally to the plaintiff's duty to be careful around hazards; Dugro thought this sufficiently extraordinary to bring to the jury's attention without being prodded.

5. See Chapter 4. Again Henry Dugro's work confirms the significance of judicial abdication of responsibility to lawyers' power to shape the law in practice. Dugro's instructions in *Sartirana v. New York County Bank* presented just four brief charges before turning to five pages of the lawyers' requests. In considering those requests, he was not shy about commenting upon their merit, as the excerpt in note 4 demonstrates.

Judges melded the rules of the contending parties with varying degrees of skill. Some presented well-synthesized, consistent, and complete sets of instructions, while others presented ambiguous, contradictory sets of rules. As a reporter to *American Lawyer* noted:

> In many cases [the jury] receives three charges [of the law]—one by the plaintiff's attorney, one by the defendant's attorney and one by the court. . . . A juror was asked why the jury were unable to agree on a verdict, since the case was so plain. "Well," said he, "we found if we went according to the plaintiff's instructions, we would have to find a verdict for him; and if we were guided by the defendant's instructions, we should have to find a verdict for him, and if the judge's instructions were to be our guide, then the devil himself could not tell which party ought to have the verdict."[6]

This response provides a clue to why cases coming to the court from nearly identical events could exit the court with such diverse outcomes.

The other important power judges held was presiding over trials. In this role they structured the way evidence was given, established the range of issues attorneys were allowed to raise, and determined the extent to which flourishes and dramatics would be tolerated. In other words, they determined how many of Thomas Hubbard's "weapons" the lawyers would be allowed to wield.

Law prescribed the general procedural format for the presentation of cases: opening statements; evidence presented via examination, cross-examination, and rebuttal; summations; and instructions to the jury. New York's rules of practice were codified first in Field's Code of 1848, then again more comprehensively in the Code of Civil Procedure (Throop's Code) of 1876. Neither of these, however, set strict guidelines that governed how a case could be waged. The latter's "phraseology was so confusing that the judges were constantly perplexed by the task of interpreting it."[7] As might be expected, in practice, trials varied greatly. Much of the variance was due to decisions made by the judges, which set the tone of each proceeding somewhat differently from all others.

In this role, the judge was effectively a censor, screening the presentation of the facts to the jury. In theory he sought to keep all extraneous information from the determiners of fact, especially information intended

---

6. "Jurors and Trials by Jury," *American Lawyer* 4 (1896): 200.

7. Henry Taft, *Legal Miscellanies: Six Decades of Changes and Progress* (New York: Macmillan, 1941), 32–36. Other problems included its size (3,296 sections after amendment in 1880) and disorganization.

to prejudice them. In practice, he did both more and less than this. By 1890, trial judges were frequently keeping entire cases from juries, dismissing suits and directing verdicts on the grounds either that precedented standards of conduct were at issue (rather than determination of what transpired in the accident) or that insufficient evidence existed to warrant juries' consideration.[8] In so doing, these judges effectively usurped the jury's duty.[9] In applying set standards of conduct, judges were admittedly determining facts; in deciding that cases were insufficiently substantiated, judges set evidential thresholds that might or might not have coincided with the amount and quality of evidence the ordinary citizen would have found persuasive.[10]

Judges were aware of this discrepancy. Their drive to dismiss suits was fueled at least in part by the idea that their threshold of proof was more appropriate than that of the laymen serving on juries. Their belief that juries reached decisions on inadequate evidence or against the evidence was voiced frequently in the professional and popular press.[11]

The opposite of this complete censorship was to allow total freedom to the contending parties in presenting their cases. Judges did this—relinquished their power to control—as often as they dismissed suits. In trials this translated into judges failing to sustain any objections; attorneys on both sides decided for themselves what was relevant to the issue at hand.

8. Samuel O. Smith, "Judges and Justice—the Judge's Role in Personal Injury Cases," *University of Illinois Law Forum* 1962 (1962), 175. For the extent of this practice in New York, see Table 19.

9. Kenneth Krasity has pointed out that, technically, the term "usurped" is incorrect; under the common law, judges had held the power to comment upon evidence and express an opinion on the credibility of witnesses. While most states stopped this practice by 1900, New York was one of nine that did not. I use "usurped" because as Krasity illustrates and as the evidence from New York shows how the legal community understood and explained it, the finding of fact was considered to be wholly the jury's domain by right of long-standing principles. It was strictly separable from the determination of law, which was rightly the judge's duty. Kenneth Krasity, "The Role of the Judge in Jury Trials: The Elimination of Judicial Evaluation of Fact in American State Courts from 1790 to 1913," *University of Detroit Law Review* 62 (1985), 595–632.

10. The criterion for dismissal or direction of verdict was declared by the common-law scintilla doctrine to be that no evidence, however slight a trace (hence the doctrine's name, scintilla), was offered and that no inference from the facts could support the plaintiff's cause. The N.Y.C. Supreme Court opened that somewhat in 1872, requiring only that "no evidence upon which a jury can properly proceed to find a verdict" be available. Krasity, "Role of the Judge," 620.

11. For further discussion of this point, see Chapter 7. Hammond, "Personal Injury Litigation," 328–32; and Samuel Page, "Personal Injury Actions: The Defendant's Standpoint," *Illinois Law Review* 1 (1906–7): 27–38, present judges' and other legal opinion leaders' views on juries in injury cases.

In the typical trial of this sort, only at the end of the case would the judge lament the lack of proper restraint on the part of the attorneys and suggest to the jury which evidence pertained and which did not, far too late to keep the jurors free from the influence of that which was to be disregarded. This approach drew the judge into the uncomely situation of joining the ranks of the advocates, pushing upon the jury his rendering of the facts. The intrusion into the duties of the jury was usually preceded or followed by a disclaimer, stating that the jury should not be guided by the judge's version of the facts.[12]

The extent to which judges could violate the spirit of the general prohibition against the bench deciding the facts of a case was great and was an issue in many jurisdictions. As B. M. Ambler reminded his fellow lawyers: "The Supreme Court of the United States has held more than once that as long as a federal judge will say to a jury, 'Gentlemen, I don't bind you by what I think about the facts of this case, though my mind is clear that the plaintiff ought to have a verdict,' that this is not invading their province."[13]

It is difficult to assess the impact of this aggrandizement by judges: Did juries think that judges, when they propounded their versions of facts, were encroaching on jury powers? Or did they assume that it was the proper domain of the judge or perhaps even welcome the overstepping of bounds for the assistance it lent them in executing their unfamiliar duty?

The potential importance of judges' informal, indirect power over decisions is clear, rivaling in importance their enumerated powers. If juries were regularly swayed by the rhetoric of judges, then the jury was simply another controllable aspect of the legal system, and the judiciary deserves that much more attention. The actuality lies somewhere between the jury as instrument of the mesmerizing judge, and the jury as oblivious

12. Judge Peter Hendrick led off his instructions to the jury of *Hayden* v. *Adrian Joline et al.* with this disclaimer: "Whatever I may say in relation to the facts is simply for the purpose of making such a statement as will enable me to formulate upon that statement the principles of law wich you are to follow. . . . You are the sole judges of the facts in this case, as I am the sole judge of the law, and you must resolve the facts for yourselves irrespective of the statement which I will make to you in relation to them." Hendrick recounted the facts but editorialized on the victim's choice in the incident, thereby adding his conjecture on the contribution the victim made to his own demise. He reinforced this with a lengthy paragraph on the defendant's many theories on the plaintiff's contributory negligence and added reminders on contributory negligence every couple pages throughout the instructions.

13. B. M. Ambler, from "Proceedings of the West Virginia Bar Association," *American Lawyer* 1 (June 1893): 41.

to the judge (and the law, as many commentators within the legal community charged).

The best way to get at judges' role in shaping the law at this nearly invisible day-to-day level is to look at some examples of their work. Judges' instructions to juries in three 1870 cases, *Isaacs* v. *Third Avenue Railroad, Ihl* v. *Forty-Second Street and Grand Street Railroad*, and *Doran* v. *East River Ferry,* give a sense of the range of judicial styles and the latitude that judges had in fulfilling their role.[14]

In *Isaacs,* Judge George Barnard delivered a fairly short set of instructions to the jury. He briefly reviewed Mary Isaacs's complaint, explained that for Isaacs to be entitled to compensation she must have been free from negligence and the conductor must have been negligent, posed the issue again in terms of whether the jury believed Isaacs's story as corroborated by her witnesses or believed the story of the conductor and driver of the car, and presented the items to be considered in determining damages. His instructions filled less than three pages (probably 6 to 8 minutes delivered orally), a model of brevity from the bench.[15]

By contrast, Josiah Sutherland's instructions to the jury in *Ihl* ran twice as long, filling six pages. He devoted more than two pages to explaining the wrongful death statute of 1847 alone (Ihl's young son had been run over by a horse-drawn streetcar and killed). He explained the issue of negligence on Ihl's part and on the part of the defendant by stating the findings under which Ihl would be entitled to compensation. He defined negligence, and then took the jury through the evidence against the driver of the car, in great detail, for the final two pages.[16]

Judge Albert Cardozo took a different tack in explaining negligence to the jury in the *Doran* case, where the issue was liability for an East River ferry that crushed passenger Catharine Doran's hand. The first portion of Cardozo's instructions dwelled upon the conditions that should bar Doran

14. I select 1870 cases because they provide a chronological base against which to measure change over the ensuing decades, even though it means drawing upon the work of the notoriously corrupt judges Albert Cardozo and George Barnard for illustration. (Because there were so few injury suits in 1870, there were even fewer appealed cases, and so fewer cases with full transcripts are available for analysis; Barnard and Cardozo presided over two of them.) Barnard and Cardozo's susceptibility to monetary persuasion is of no consequence to the value of their instructions for our purposes. By a number of indicators—topics (not) covered, consistency, operability, length, citations—their instructions were representative of those other judges presented to juries in 1890 and 1910. See the discussion of changes over time in judges' presentations of rules in Chapter 3, text with notes 33–48.

15. *Isaacs* v. *Third Avenue Railroad*. See Chapter 1 for the details of this case.

16. *Ihl* v. *Forty-Second Street and Grand Street Railroad*.

from compensation, a very different emphasis than Sutherland's presentation in *Ihl* of the circumstances under which the jury should decide for the plaintiff. The standard of care required of the ferry company was treated next, briefly, before Cardozo highlighted for the jury the evidence he thought most important.[17]

It is plain from these three examples alone that cases ruled in theory by the same law could be decided in fact according to very different versions of the law. Judges' instructions were the juries' sole source of the law and their last provision of information before they sequestered off to decide their cases. The variance in the content, ordering, and emphasis of instructions as well as differences in tone and style were bound to affect verdicts and awards and thus the course of injury law's development.

Barnard's directions in *Isaacs* were subtly laced with the judge's favorable opinion of the plaintiff's case; the tone of his instructions imparted a sense of inclination but no blatant evidence of it. Barnard betrayed his position only in small ways: in the use of concrete illustrations for his explanations, in the elements he included and left out, in his order of presentation, and in his instructions for assessing damages.

Barnard first broached the possibility and legal consequences of Isaacs's own negligence but quickly left that behind. As he moved from the issue of Isaacs's negligence to that of the Third Avenue Railroad's, Barnard shifted from speaking of negligence in the abstract to casting it in the concrete. Isaacs's responsibility was defined abstractly (though formidably) as freedom "from all fault and from negligence or carelessness of every kind and description." But Barnard undermined the firmness of this definition immediately as he clarified the absolute freedom from negligence to mean doing "all that a prudent person should do."

By contrast, he assessed the possibility of the railroad's liability in more tangible terms: "If she made her request to the conductor to be left off at a certain place; and if he, in his regular practice as conductor, failed to accede to her request, and was guilty of negligence or carelessness, then she would be entitled to a verdict."[18]

At this point, the order Barnard chose for his instructions became important. Rather than returning to the testimony that would show the passenger's negligence, Barnard pursued the testimony that showed the railroad's negligence. And when the railroad's case for Isaacs's carelessness was mentioned later, Barnard premised it with "I am requested to

17. *Doran v. East River Ferry.*
18. *Isaacs v. Third Ave Railroad.*

charge . . . ," thus distancing the judge from the defendant's story and reinforcing his association with the injured's. Further, in considering the railroad's version of facts and liability, Barnard interjected "That would be true, gentlemen, if she was not thrown off the car by the conductor."[19]

Barnard's explanation of how the jury was to decide damages also worked to the victim's benefit. The criteria he proposed as a guide were not extraordinary: "the amount of the physician's bill paid, the length of time, if she has been a laboring woman, that she has been taken away from her labors and the sickness she may have suffered either in body or mind," taking into consideration "the circumstances, age, appearance and position in life of the party who appears at your hands."[20] Had this been the whole of the criteria, the instructions on damages would have benefited the defendant by making it liable for less in damages than the law required, as Barnard failed to make explicit mention of compensation for pain and suffering. Barnard had probably intended to indicate that the jury should compensate pain and suffering in the "sickness she has suf- fered" phrase, but it would have taken a juror versed in the law to extract that and translate it to terms his fellows could use.

The subsequent paragraph was not so typical; Barnard changed the whole color of the award instructions by suggesting that punitive damages might be in order, a rare event. "Damages are not for the mere naked injury," he charged. If the injury was "done wickedly and maliciously" by the act of another, the jury "would have a right to give such damages as in the future would have a tendency to stop a perpetration of what a jury considered to be an outrage."[21] The language was vivid, likely to stand out in the load of information the jury carried into the decision pro- cess. The terms were ambiguous, leaving much to jury standards of "out- rage." Though he stopped short of saying the defendant had been malicious, his suggestion must have spoken loudly. The message could only work in one direction: to increase the award.

Encouraging punitive damages was rare in 1870 and became rarer with time. Judges seldom encountered a case where they detected malice. One reason was that judges wanted to make the law as predictable and "sci- entific" as possible. Because punitive damages were not tied closely to measurable criteria, as lost wages and medical costs were, judges con-

19. Ibid.
20. Ibid.
21. Interestingly, Barnard did not mention that if the jury found that the injury was a product of malice, consideration of contributory negligence should be suspended.

sidered them especially subject to abuse. Further, judges were concerned that juries had a natural tendency to punish even when punishment was not called for; judges wanted to restrain that retributive impulse rather than encourage it. By 1910, warnings were common against juries that tacked extra sums on awards to punish defendants, especially when defendants were corporations.[22]

As encouraging as Barnard's instructions were for a plaintiff's verdict in Mary Isaacs's case, Albert Cardozo's were as discouraging to that outcome in *Doran* v. *East River Ferry*. It is worth noting, though, that Cardozo declined to dismiss the case outright when requested to do so by the defense at the end of the trial. Doran had presented a solid enough case to warrant jury consideration in the judge's mind. There was none of the outright dismissing of cases that would come to characterize the work of some judges by 1910.

The instructions worked to subvert the plaintiff's cause right from the outset. Of the three short pages of directions, the first page and a half were dedicated to the possibility of the Doran's own negligence. Like Barnard did in *Isaacs*, Cardozo first considered Doran's contribution to her own injury abstractly: "If any act or omission of hers has tended in your judgment to the happening of this disaster; then, however much you may sympathise with her, she cannot recover in this case." Then he took to the particulars: "If her hand were lying over the rail, extending beyond the rail itself, that will be a circumstance from which the jury will have a right to infer negligence upon her part."[23]

The defendant's negligence was treated in some detail as well, with its duty posed as the exercise of "human skill, prudence, and foresight." Cardozo pointed out specific facts for the jury to heed. He also emphasized that it was the plaintiff's task to convince the jury both of her own

22. Disparagement of punitive damages was strongly in evidence in Judge Miles Beach's warning to a jury in 1890: "The circumstances of this case will not authorize, and the jury will not be justified in awarding to the plaintiff in any event, anything by way of punitive or vindictive damages, otherwise known as smart money." *Barrelle* v. *Pennsylvania Railroad*. In a case of a workman killed on a railroad construction project, Judge Edward McCall warned the jury: "The fact of the plaintiff being a widow and the defendant a corporation is of no concern in a Court of Justice. If we were to allow our minds to be swayed in the slightest degree by such thoughts the results reached would indeed cause Court proceedings to be mere hollow mockeries of justice and would make our legal tribunals objects of derision and of scorn." *Ann Grant, Administrator* v. *Delaware, Lackawanna, and Western Railroad et al.*, 1910 Number D287, N.Y.C. Supreme Court. See also Judge Warren Hooker's instructions in *Finnie* v. *Central Park, North and East River Railroad*.

23. *Doran* v. *East River Ferry*.

freedom from negligence and of the ferry company's carelessness. Short of that, she could not be compensated.

In contrast to the detailed discussion of damages in the *Isaacs* instructions, Cardozo gave the *Doran* jury no guidelines for determining compensation. "That rests entirely within your reasonable discretion," he instructed them, though he followed that with two qualifications, "Without prejudice or passion, or undue sympathy, you will determine [the amount], if you reach that question."[24] In one sense, this could be read as granting the jury tremendous latitude. But another reading is that Cardozo did not expect the jury to get to the question of damages. And when they ultimately did, the lack of guidance might have had an effect just the opposite of the license that full latitude implies. The absence of suggestions that the sum should compensate suffering might have diminished the award.

The final component of Cardozo's instructions that gives pause is his language of inadvertence. He refers to the injuring event not as "accident," the most commonly employed term among his fellow judges, but as "misfortune," connoting inevitability as well as personal responsibility for the burden that followed the event. A small point? Not in the late nineteenth century, when rules such as assumption of risk reinforced fatalism. This was the moment when an expanded view of causality and responsibility was just beginning to challenge fatalism.

Cardozo did not use "misfortune" neutrally. With it, he planted the idea that "however free from fault the plaintiff may have been" she might just have to accept injury as her fate.[25] It was possible, he suggested, that the accident might be "one of those misfortunes to which all human beings are liable, and for which there is no legal responsibility."[26] This idea, so foreign to the late twentieth-century mind, must be considered in historical context and in its use in the instructions. It was quite reasonable in 1870 for Cardozo to raise "no responsibility" as a possibility. What is noteworthy is the continued use of "misfortune" throughout the instructions. After Cardozo's initial equation of misfortune with self-liability, all later ostensibly neutral appearances of the term evoked this unfavorable (from the plaintiff's standpoint) connotation.

Josiah Sutherland's instructions in *Ihl* v. *Forty-Second Street Railroad* demonstrate that the differences between judges' instructions cannot be fit to a simple linear "pro-plaintiff/pro-defendant" model. While the in-

24. Ibid.
25. Ibid.
26. Ibid.

structions in the *Isaacs* and *Doran* cases were selective in content, were structured differently, and were counter to one another in tone, both were concise, logically constructed, and clearly accessible to the juries. By contrast, Sutherland's directions were digressive, disorganized, and bombastic. At issue here is quality. Were Sutherland's instructions as useful to his jury as Barnard's or Cardozo's were to theirs? Did his instructions help the jury in reaching a verdict or did they have to be overcome? The distinction is important, for a jury's inability to understand a judge's instructions was another source of variance in the law. It was as much an avenue of legal change as judges' selective reading of the law and probably more so than juries' deliberate disregard for rules.

Sutherland launched into his task with a two-and-a-half page discourse on the genesis, modification, and application of the wrongful death statute. It was all extraneous. The jury was well aware of the point: The next of kin had a right to sue for damages in the death of a family member. Sutherland cited at length from the statute and its judicial interpretation. The prose was laden with jargon; the style was verbose and redundant.[27] Here, in a trial court, in instructions to the jury we have almost a perfect example of the "formal style" Morton Horwitz has found characteristic of the appellate opinions of this era.[28] Whether it was used by Sutherland for the conservative ends Horwitz attributes to it or was simply a stylistic affectation emulating the style of the higher courts' work, we cannot be sure, although the content of the instructions supports the latter view.[29]

Two examples of confusing, run-on prose illustrate the trouble a jury might encounter as it searched for meaning in formalist-style instructions. Here is Sutherland's effort to clarify the rules of recovery in a fatal injury:

> The Act of 1847 provided that, whenever the death of a person should be caused by wrongful act, neglect, or default, and the act, neglect, or default is such as would if death had not ensued, have entitled the party injured to maintain an action and recover damages in respect thereof, then, and in every such case, the person who, or the corporation which would have been liable if death had not ensued, should be liable to an action for damages to be brought by and in the name of the personal representatives of such deceased person, notwithstanding the death of the person injured, the sum recovered to be for the exclusive benefit of the widow, and next of kin

27. *Ihl* v. *Forty-Second Street and Grand Street Railroad.*
28. Morton Horwitz, "The Rise of Legal Formalism," *American Journal of Legal History* 19 (1975): 251–64.
29. *Ihl* v. *Forty-Second Street Railroad.*

of such deceased person, and to be distributed to such widow and next of kin in the proportion provided by law in relation to the distribution of personal property left by persons dying intestate.

With the jury thus enlightened, Sutherland turned to elucidate the central issue of law. "What is negligence?" he asked.

It may be defined to be the absence or want of that care or caution which is required of a person in any particular situation to prevent injury to the person or property of others. Whether it be the agent or the principal, it is the question of proper conduct, under the circumstances of the case. You are to consider the situation of the agent, what his duty was and the circumstances of the case calling upon him for caution and care. If he omits or neglects to observe that care and caution, as the agent of the defendants, whose servant he was, and whose property he had control of, or whose railroad car he was driving, which was required of him from human experience and the ordinary affairs of men, then he is guilty of negligence.[30]

Not only was this instruction redundant, but it introduced an amazing standard of negligence: that level of care that causes injury. This was pure tautology. By that standard, the very fact that defendants were involved in injuries proves that they were negligent, because they did not exercise enough caution to avoid an accident. Every plaintiff should have been compensated under this pronouncement. That such a definition could make its way into judges' instructions shows the power that judges bore over rules.

The evidence suggests that judges' instructions did not become any more uniform over the decades. The first decade of the new century brought the stirrings of a move to standardize courtroom instructions, which suggests that judges continued to exercise their power to "personalize" the law. While the movement made little headway until the bar associations took up the cause in the 1920s, it nevertheless offers proof that judges' instructions were continuing to vary widely. What is more, it signals that some in law viewed the variance as such a flagrant deviance from the ideal of consistency that it warranted intervention in the sacrosanct realm of judicial autonomy. At the same time, the instructions of the city court judges betray no awareness of their inconsistency. To the contrary, judges' repeated references to the clarity and singularity of the law

30. Ibid.

reminds us that judges were no less sure in these decades that they were uniformly applying one set of rules than they would become later under the regime of standard instructions.[31]

How influential were instructions—particularly judges' implicit opinions—to the outcome of the injury cases? In the three preceding cases, the juries decided for the injured person each time, despite the judge's confusing instructions in *Ihl* and flatly unfavorable ones in *Doran*. Examples abound of juries deciding counter to the tenor of judicial instruction. In *Jonas Van Praag v. Third Avenue Railroad Company,* for example, the jury received a brief lecture from Judge James on juries' growing inability to deliver "righteous verdicts" when corporations' negligence was at issue. James concluded with an instruction to "give such a verdict that for once it can be said that one jury have decided a case of this kind according to law and evidence." The jury decided quickly for Van Praag.[32]

Even where a judge's leanings in the administration of a case were in concert with the jury's decision, we cannot assume that the judge's rendering of facts and law carried the day. Juries heard the same facts that judges did and were perfectly capable of reaching the same conclusions as the judges, before or independent of input from the bench. On the other hand, where twelve men of differing disposition sat down to decide a case with convictions on the truth of the testimony ranging from the highly skeptical to the totally persuaded, a judge's implicit conclusion could carry weight. It probably gave the necessary support to those on the jury already tending toward the outcome the judge favored. And for those who were hesitant, it could promote one view over another by cloaking it in expert sanction, turning their uncertainty into resolve.

An analysis of the outcomes of injury suits, judge by judge, also shows that in 1870 there was no clear tendency for any of the judges to decide for plaintiffs more than defendants, or for defendants more than plaintiffs. Daniel Ingraham was the only judge to preside over more than five tort suits, and the decisions in those cases went to plaintiffs and defendants in equal numbers. The same held true for 1890. Of the seven judges who were in charge of more than five tort cases that year, five showed no

31. This is mentioned to make sense of the discrepancy between judges' rhetoric and performance. They idealized precision and consistency no less than later commentators who, through the lens of time, would see the judges' work as "the slanted instructions of yesteryear." Smith, "Judges and Justice," 184.

32. "Another Verdict against a City Railroad Company for Negligence," *New York Times,* 20 March 1866, p. 8.

pattern of outcomes that favored plaintiffs over defendants or vice versa. In Abraham Lawrence's courtroom, plaintiffs won twice as many suits as defendants, and in George Ingraham's defendants won six out of ten.

The unbalanced records of Lawrence and Ingraham became the norm by 1910. Of the 21 judges who handled more than 10 tort suits in 1910, for only 8 did outcomes divide fairly evenly between plaintiff and defendant. Eleven judges had records where defendants prevailed more than 55 percent of the time; of the 11, 8 recorded decisions for defendants 65 percent or more of the time. Defendants succeeded 69 percent of the time in M. Warley Platzek's court, 76 percent of the time in Nathan Bijur's, 82 percent of the time in Joseph Newburger's, and 92 percent of the time in Henry Bischoff's. Of the 11 tort suits that came before Edward Whitney, not 1 was decided for a plaintiff. At the other end of the spectrum, plaintiffs' claims were upheld over 55 percent of the time by 2 judges. With those 2 judges, Charles Dayton and John Goff, plaintiffs were successful over 70 percent of the time.[33]

The patterns in the disposition of cases suggest that the predilections of individual judges so suffused the administration of the law that they affected outcomes. Of course, the fate of these cases may not indicate judges' work at all. The judges may have administered the law in precisely the same way, and the outcomes varied from judge to judge wholly as a product of the merit of the cases and "the luck of the draw." However, the likelihood is remote that only one-quarter of the suits that many of these judges were randomly assigned were valid complaints, while three-quarters of the suits that Dayton and Goff happened to draw were clearly meritorious.

33. The records for the judges with the greatest imbalances were

	Decision for Plaintiff		Decision for Defendant	
1890	*n*	*%*	*n*	*%*
George Ingraham	10	38	16	62
Abraham Lawrence	15	65	8	35
1910				
Edward Whitney	0	0	11	100
Henry Bischoff	1	8	12	92
Joseph Newburger	2	18	9	82
Nathan Bijur	4	24	13	76
Mitchell Erlanger	12	29	30	71
Alfred Page	18	29	44	71
M. Warley Platzek	12	31	27	69
P. Henry Dugro	9	35	17	65
Charles Dayton	15	71	6	29
John Goff	15	71	6	29

The mix of issues was the same for judges at both ends of the decision spectrum, which further reduces the likelihood that the difference were due to chance. Judges with records of high success for plaintiffs in their courtroom had roughly the same proportions of suits for injuries from traffic, street-railroad, building, and other accidents as did judges with records of low success for plaintiffs.

The lone difference was that judges with records of low success for plaintiffs had proportionately more work-injury suits than other judges.[34] That could support the "luck of the draw" thesis, but it would require believing that the work-injury suits had no intrinsic merit. By this thesis, defendants won more often in the courts of Erlanger, Bijur, Bischoff, Page, Platzek, Dugro, Whitney, and Newburger than in the courts of Dayton and Goff because those judges presided over more work-injury suits that were without merit than did Dayton and Goff. The converse is just as plausible: that work-injury suits fared so poorly in the Supreme Court in part because they went disproportionately to judges who favored defendants.

Comparison of the backgrounds of these men shows that while there were real ambiguities, there was enough difference between judges with low rates of plaintiff success and those with high rates of plaintiff success to support the idea that judges' predisposition did matter to the outcome of injury claims. Among the frequent claim-defeaters, for example, Bischoff had inherited one banking firm, founded another, and retained his interest in them during his judicial tenure; Platzek had been rich even before entering the profession; and Bijur's private practice before election to the judiciary had included defending corporations sued for negligence.[35] In contrast, Goff, in whose court plaintiffs prevailed with much greater frequency, had migrated from Ireland, had "had to work for a living," gained a workingman's education at Cooper

34. Typically, work-injury suits made up 19.8 percent of a judge's tort cases. Work injuries comprised 28.6 percent of the cases for judges with records of strong defendant success (i.e., in which defendants won 65 percent or more of their cases). While these judges presided over 27 percent of all tort suits they handled 39 percent of work-injury claims.

35. Bischoff had even more direct personal experience with negligence and injury than Bijur. In a truth-is-stranger-than-fiction irony, Bischoff, who had overseen the demise of so many negligence claims, had his judicial career terminated abruptly with a 150-foot plunge down the judicial office building's elevator shaft. Bischoff's widow could not have carried a claim in her husband's former workplace since Bischoff, "whose eyesight was poor," contributed mightily to his own end by failing to check for an elevator car before stepping into the shaft. "Justice Bischoff Plunges to His Death," *New York Times,* 29 March 1913, p. 1.

Union, and learned the law via law office "apprenticeship" rather than in a law school.[36]

While economic heritage tended to differentiate the two groups of judges, political beliefs did not. Goff, Lawrence, and Dayton, the three judges under whose adjudication claims of the injured fared the best in 1890 and 1910, had Democratic politics in common. But they shared that trait with many of their less plaintiff-abetting colleagues, including George Ingraham, Dugro, and Whitney. Goff and Dayton had been active in anticorruption movements, Dayton in the anti-Tammany Hall Citizens Movement of the early 1880s and the anti-Tammany Municipal League (1890) and Goff as the "persistent, merciless" counsel for the State Senate's Lexow Commission investigation of New York City police corruption. But Whitney, too, had been an ardent reformer. As counsel to the New York Tenement House Commission in 1900, he had drafted the landmark Tenement House Law of 1901, and he went on to fight street railroads and defend a state utility price-setting law before the U.S. Supreme Court. Lawrence, meanwhile, had felt no compunction about running for mayor as Tammany Hall's candidate in the immediate wake of the Tweed Ring.[37]

These records of plaintiff and defendant success were amassed under varying degrees of judicial influence. When juries determined verdicts, judges' influence over outcomes was indirect. By the 1890s, judges had grown less patient with their indirect role and developed dismissal as a way to decide suits themselves. Of course, this only allowed judges to decide cases in one direction. But the direction apparently fit well judges' predilections at the time, and the innovation gained adherents. Judges rarely dismissed tort suits in 1870 (see Table 19). By 1890, whatever reluctance they had shown in the past had disappeared. Judges dismissed a quarter of the torts that came to trial that year. Defendants won over twice as many suits through judge dismissal at trial (28) as they did by jury verdict (12).

36. Ibid., and 31 March 1913, p. 13; *American Lawyer* 2 (1894), 212–13; *Patrick Kenney* v. *Ocean Steamship Company of Savannah*, 1890 Number 052, N.Y.C. Supreme Court; *Charlotte Miller* v. *Ocean Steamship Company of Savannah*, 1890 Number 016, N.Y.C. Supreme Court; *New York Law Journal* 3, no. 46 (May 23, 1890), 409; and *New York Times*, 10 November 1924, p. 17.

37. The characterization of Goff comes from the *New York Times*, 10 November 1924, p. 17. *New York Times*, 15 February 1917, p. 11; 22 October 1887, p. 10; 8 December 1910, p. 13; 25 January 1931, p. 28; and 6 January 1911, p. 9; and Charles Daly Papers, Box 17, Scrapbook, p. 9, New York Public Library; and Box 19, Scrapbook, p. 77.

TABLE 19
Personal-injury suits dismissed by judges

Disposition	1870		1890		1910	
	n	%	n	%	n	%
Personal-injury suits	13	100	112	100	595	100
Suits dismissed for plaintiff's lack of prosecution, or default	0	—	6	5.4	125	21.0
Suits dismissed at trial	0	—	28	25.0	94	15.8

Source: See Table 4.

The justification for the increase in this practice was twofold: the first argued progress in the law, the second, deterioration in the quality of claims. The logic of the first was that the increase in negligence cases produced an increase in precedents that defined appropriate standards of conduct for more and more sets of circumstances. As these situation-specific standards of conduct solidified as rules, deciding the appropriate levels of care became more an act of invoking law than of deciding facts, moving it into the realm of the judge. That migration was viewed with judicial approbation because it increased consistency and took a stride toward the scientific, "mechanical application" ideal that had such force at the turn of the century. Holmes expressed the importance of the practice in the negative: "Every time that a judge declines to rule whether certain conduct is negligent or not he avows his inability to state the law."[38] The pace of dismissal at trials declined somewhat by 1910, though this may have been due to defendant lawyers' strategy of seeking "preemptive dismissals."[39] These dismissals were initiated for lack of prosecution or failure to appear when the case came up on the calendar. They climbed to 22 percent of all torts by 1910. Combining both the "preemptive" dismissals and the dismissals at trials, judges dismissed over a third of the tort suits filed in 1890 and 1910.

Personal-injury suits were the only kind of suit judges dismissed at trial; not one instance of any other type of case in the sample ended in dismissal. The practice was not widely hailed even by those who wanted juries constrained. Eli Hammond decided that dismissal had grown out of

38. Oliver Wendell Holmes, "Law in Science and Science in Law," *Harvard Law Review* 12 (1899): 443–57.
39. See Chapter 4.

the "evil of jury injustice" in personal-injury suits, yet was troubled by its own potential for abuse:

> It is mostly this personal injury litigation that has developed so actively the practice of directing verdicts by the court. That the power exists there can be and never was any question, but that it was for a long time . . . almost dormant in this country is also true. . . . In personal injury cases, there is a possibility of "straining the timbers of the law" and pressing perilously near the danger line in directing the verdicts of juries.[40]

Short of dismissing cases, judges developed a method of controlling juries by asking them specific questions about their determinations of fact on particular issues rather than by asking for a simple verdict. Typically, these questions took the form of asking the jury if a particular act of the defendant had been negligent and whether the plaintiff had exhibited reasonable care.[41] These questions could earnestly seek to focus a jury's deliberations. Or a judge's intention could be to narrow juries' criteria and misguide them into peripheral issues. As a contemporary commentator noted: "Our practice of submitting special questions . . . has a tendency to injustice, especially . . . where these questions have been drawn for the purpose of entrapping [the jury] into a position on one of these special questions and thereby avoiding the real merits of the case."[42]

In examining the part played by judges in the shaping of injury law, the jury is never far from view. Indeed, the judges' and juries' work is separated only with difficulty. Yet the jury had powers and limitations that have to be considered in their own right. Today, juries come under heavy fire for their alleged irresponsibility in fueling the litigation explosion and for their retention of so much power in the legal system despite their biases and lack of "expertise." This same critique of juries was current at the turn of the century. Hammond criticized juries for their "general prejudice against the companies." Judge Samuel Page concurred in a

40. Hammond, "Personal Injury Litigation," 330–31.

41. See *Julius Sagebiel* v. *New York City Railway Company et al.,* 1910 Number S223, N.Y.C. Supreme Court. Judge James O'Gorman put three questions to the jury: Was the defendant, the city of New York, guilty of negligence? Was the defendant, the New York City Railroad, guilty of negligence? Was the plaintiff, Sagebiel, free from contributory negligence? The jury answered all three in the affirmative, but the judge overrode their specific answers to dismiss the suit against the city and direct a verdict against the railroad for $1,200.

42. J. A. Hutchinson, from "Proceedings of the West Virginia Bar Association," *American Lawyer* 1 (June 1893): 42.

more scathing tone: Jurors were "ignorant, unqualified men, some of them possibly vicious and even anarchistic in their ideas," and were "ignorant and prejudiced, especially against capital and vested interests, whether railway companies, manufacturing institutions or otherwise." Herbert Spencer's characterization of the jury as "twelve people of average ignorance" was mild by comparison.[43] Though we might dismiss these assessments as themselves tending toward the "ignorant and viscious," they do testify that juries were important contributors to the direction of the administration of injury law.

The importance of the jury in late nineteenth-century injury law came from three powers it held. It was the sole judge of facts in a trial, meaning that in theory it set the threshold of proof necessary to prove a claim. It was the determiner of awards, again theoretically sovereign in fixing monetary values on pain and loss. And it was the body that ultimately defined what the general duty of care to others was in the rapidly changing environment of New York City.

The powers of juries were the product of change over the years, as were the limits upon those powers. The juries of the late nineteenth century worked in a system where judges had extensive power to keep the decision making of juries within bounds compared with just a century before. Judges monopolized the definition of law in the courts after the middle of the nineteenth century. Before, juries could hear lawyers argue the law or would receive instructions on the law from bodies of multiple judges, both of which heightened the likelihood of a jury carrying conflicting ideas of the rules into their deliberations. At the end of the nineteenth century, juries also began to have their verdicts set aside by judges when the judges found verdicts inconsistent with their interpretations of the law.[44] By the mid-nineteenth century the jury was a tightly constrained institution.

Yet the jury of the late nineteenth-century Supreme Court was not as restricted as this picture would lead us to expect. While judges were toiling to shore up their power, other forces were freeing juries so that by 1900 they were again exhibiting some of the empowering attributes William Nelson found characteristic of the eighteenth-century trial courts.

43. Hammond, "Personal Injury Litigation," 330; Page, "Personal Injury Actions," 29; Spenser cited in Harry Kalven and Hans Zeisel, *The American Jury* (Chicago: University of Chicago Press, 1971), 6. For an equally intemperate assessment, see Prentice, "Where Jury Bribing Begins," 312–19.

44. William E. Nelson, *The Americanization of the Common Law: The Impact of Legal Change on Massachusetts Society, 1760–1830* (Cambridge,: Harvard University Press, 1975), chapter 1.

The proliferation of precedents combined with the vagaries of judges' instructions and lawyers' advocacy of rules to unsettle the law in the eyes of the jury. Though ostensibly *the* (singular) law guided juries, the variety of and vagueness in the rules gave them the opportunity to select law to fit their conceptions of duties.

Combine this implicit lawmaking power with the three enumerated powers of the jury—setting standards of proof, setting standards of care, and determining levels of compensation—and the potency of the jury begins to emerge. Juries were still subject to the real constraints of a judge's power to dismiss or reverse a jury's decision. But judges, too, were subject to constraints. Other than taking cases from juries, judges could not coerce juries to conform with judicial conceptions of care, proof, and damages. And with the unprecedented extent that judges were forced to drastic measures of dismissal or reversal, jurors were unconsciously activating public attention to the problem of injury law. A growing number of episodes like the "remarkable case" of *Henry Ernst* v. *Hudson River Railroad* gradually brought to popular attention disagreements between juries and judges over injury lawsuits. The *New York Times* reported the story of the Troy, New York, case because only after twelve years and three trials, twice concluding with dismissals, and once with a jury verdict for the plaintiff which was overturned upon appeal, a trial judge finally allowed the injured Ernst the jury's verdict. By 1900, the accumulation of such reports starkly showing the difference between judges and juries suggested a problem for public policy and initiated the politicization of the issue before it was ever discussed in the halls of New York government.[45]

The jury was the sole judge of facts in all injury suits, at least in theory. This responsibility involved determining the level of evidence required to prove a case of injury liability. Judges gave juries only the most general guidance here. The standard they mandated was that injured suitors prove their case with a "preponderance of the evidence."

Further explanation of that standard still left much of the definition and decision making to jury discretion because judges left the standard ambiguous or introduced their own nuances into the instruction about "preponderance of evidence." For Judge Leonard Giegerich, the evidence standard was "that which satisfies the conscience and carries

45. "Twelve Years' Litigation—Heavy Verdict for Plaintiff," *New York Times,* 26 May 1867, p. 3.

conviction to an intelligent mind.''[46] For Judge Edward Amend, preponderance meant ''such evidence as carries conviction to your mind; such evidence as impresses you with its truthful character.'' The plaintiff was not ''required to prove her case beyond a reasonable doubt, but what is required of her is that the evidence in support of her case shall outweigh the evidence in opposition.''[47] Within the same general definition, Judge Dayton imposed a tougher guideline: ''The plaintiff cannot recover one single penny unless she satisfies you . . . absolutely that the defendant was guilty of negligence.''[48] Despite the obviously higher threshold to demonstrate liability, the jury had no problem finding a verdict for the plaintiff.

Ordinary common sense guided jurors to their conclusion of what comprised a preponderance of the evidence. If they did not do this because they were instructed to, they did it out of habit or for lack of any other faculty to guide them. Amend gave the jury in *Rubinsky* v. *Joline et al., Receivers* an interesting mix of perspectives to apply to the task: ''You are to look at the testimony as businessmen would look at a business proposition. . . . [Consider] the matters you would consider in every day life, if a proposition were submitted to you.'' Finally he added, ''A common sense view will undoubtedly lead you to a correct conclusion.''[49]

Jurors' exercise of their common sense was not merely tolerated, it was encouraged. As judges of fact, jurors also had to decide what standards of behavior and vigilance they would require of the suitors. What comprised reasonable care? What acts or omissions constituted negligence? Judges again gave broad guidelines that emphasized ''everyday'' community norms and the relative nature of the standard. The appropriate standard of care was that of the ordinarily prudent man, which varied according to the person and situation involved.[50]

46. *Morris Levy et al.* v. *James Roosevelt et al.*, 1910 Number R334, N.Y.C. Supreme Court.

47. *Alice Dunsford* v. *Ralph Jacoby*, 1910 Number J172, N.Y.C. Supreme Court.

48. *Rosa Krombach* v. *Adrian Joline et al., Receivers of the New York City Railway Company*, 1910 Number J171, N.Y.C. Supreme Court.

49. *Mary Rubinsky* v. *Adrian Joline et al., Receivers of the New York City Railway Company*, 1910 Number J174, N.Y.C. Supreme Court. Edward Amend proposed the same guideline to the jury in *Amanda Landon* v. *Baker Smith and Company*, 1910 Number B615, N.Y.C. Supreme Court: ''In determining the facts submitted to you, you are to judge the testimony as a business man judges matters submitted to him in every day life.''

50. Judge Amend stressed the relative nature of care and neglect in his instructions to the jury in *Thomas Williams* v. *Interborough Rapid Transit Company*, 1910 Number I82, N.Y.C. Supreme Court. ''Now what is negligence?'' he asked. ''That is a relative term,

Ordinary care was entirely relative, which gave great responsibility to juries. The standard the courts applied could be interpreted by juries as verging on absolute care in the midst of a very dangerous set of circumstances, to near obliviousness in less threatening situations. And this does not exhaust the interpretive range. As explained by Judge Peter Hendrick, the degree of care also varied relative to the physical abilities of the person: "The law imposes on every person the obligation of prudence for their own safety. The amount of care which a person is bound to exercise is not always the same. . . . [It] is to be measured by the intelligence, the age and the experience of the person who is involved."[51]

Along with relative standards of care doubly dependent on place and person for their degree of rigor, and a charge from the bench to apply "common sense" of "everyday life," a third avenue of flexibility to the jury's imposition of its values on the law can be seen: the appropriate level of care was dependent upon the times. As new forms of transportation, housing, communication, and work became commonplace, the definition of ordinary care had to be tailored to fit the new dangers being encountered. This was especially true in an era and place as full of change as New York at the turn of the twentieth century.

Juries adapted their definition of reasonable care to new conditions. They were not locked into the past in setting their standards. Street railroads, for example, were not held to horse-drawn levels of speed and acceleration when they converted to electric locomotion. The level of vigilance applicable to the general populace was adjusted upwards as well. As mass transit changed its mode of power, pedestrians were expected to learn to judge the speed of the new vehicles.

Juries were also the assessors of damages. The "commonsense view" reigned in this field as well.[52] However, while supposedly the sole judges of award size, trial or appellate judges frequently overrode the juries' decisions. A trial judge, by holding a motion to dismiss in reserve, could dismiss a case after the jury announced its award. The judge could also threaten to dismiss the suit unless the plaintiff stipulated that the verdict

---

and what may be negligent under one state of circumstances may be consistent with prudence under another state of circumstances; so that an act is or is not negligent, according to the peculiar circumstances surrounding the case."

51. *Hayden* v. *Joline et al.*

52. In *Flynn* v. *New York Taxicab*, the jury was instructed to decide damages according to their good judgment: "There is no sum which the Court can lay down for you, it is whatever you think in your good judgement adequate and reasonable. A common sense view will undoubtedly lead you to a correct conclusion as to this question of damages."

be reduced.[53] With the prospect of a second trial opposed to the option to accept a reduced award, few plaintiffs opted for the retrial. Where judges imposed stipulations, they made themselves the sole judges of damages, which was a usurpation of a jury's duty.

The justification for this invasion of the jury's domain was that juries regularly awarded excessive verdicts. Because judicial intervention in setting awards was seen as an intrusion upon the jury's fact-finding responsibility, the criterion for judicial action had to be that the compensation was more than an affront to the judge's sense of reasonableness. As established by Chancellor Kent early in the century, the call to remit was to issue only when "the damages [are] so excessive as to strike mankind . . . as being beyond all measure unreasonable and outrageous, and such as manifestly show the jury to have been actuated by passion, partiality, prejudice, or corruption. In short, the damages must be flagrantly outrageous and extravagant, or the court cannot undertake to draw the line.[54]

The Supreme Court judges discerned a pattern of outrageousness on the part of juries. As Hammond put it, judges acted "because juries will not do the right thing toward corporations."[55] If that was the judges' rationale, it was based on an inaccurate perception. In fact, juries did do the right thing, if the right thing was to treat corporations no differently from individuals who either were engaged in business or not acting in a business capacity at the time of injury. Table 20 illustrates the evenhandedness juries brought to their determination of responsibility. The ratio of cases juries decided for plaintiffs to those decided for defendants was roughly 2:1, no matter who the defendant was. The exception was the municipal government as a defendant; plaintiffs prevailed in jury trials against the city by the ratio of 3:1. Corporations and the city departed

53. This power was known as *remittitur;* that is, the ability to require the recipient of an excessive verdict to remit part of it. Typically, it was posed to the plaintiff as a choice; she or he could accept the reduction of the verdict to the "reasonable" level of the judge's choosing, or wait and gamble with a new trial. For example, Judge Edward Patterson sustained the defendant's motion to set aside Frank Dietz's award of $1,500 unless Dietz "consented in open court that said verdict be reduced to $1,000." Dietz consented. *Frank Dietz v. Mayor et al., City of New York,* 1890 Number M70, N.Y.C. Supreme Court. In theory, the complementary power to *remittitur* was *additur,* or the power to increase an inadequate verdict. In New York, the judges had no power of *additur;* the only action the judge so inclined could take was to grant a new trial upon the plaintiff's request. See Smith, "Judges and Justice," 186–88.

54. *Coleman v. Southwick, Johnson's Reports* (New York) 9 (New York: 1812): 45, 52; cited in Smith, "Judges and Justice," 187.

55. "Personal Injury Litigation," 331.

TABLE 20

Means of disposition of tort suits by type of defendant

Disposition	Private Individual		Business Individual		Corporation		Government	
	n	%	n	%	n	%	n	%
Jury decision, plaintiff	37	27	70	30	121	28	37	27
Jury decision, defendant	17	13	35	15	67	16	12	9
Defendant settles	2	2	6	3	62	15	37	27
Judge dismisses, lack of prosecution	39	30	54	23	70	17	17	12
Judge dismisses, trial	11	8	43	18	76	18	19	14
Miscellaneous disposition	26	20	26	11	28	6	15	11
Total	132	100	234	100	424	100	137	100

Source: See Table 4.

most significantly from other defendants in reaching settlements before trials. The city settled over a quarter of the claims against it before trial, and corporations settled 15 percent of the suits against them, while individuals settled very few.

Another way to assess the claim of contemporaries that juries were ignorant, prejudiced, and driven by sympathy is to look at the effort that they put into performing their assignment. Harry Kalven and Hans Zeisel found in their controversial landmark study of juries in the 1950s that contrary to the general supposition, juries typically understood the facts and issues of law that confronted them and that their decisions "by and large moved with the weight and direction of the evidence."[56] The New York City Supreme Court transcripts hint that the same was true for juries there fifty years before.

New York jurors' questions revealed a working knowledge of the law and the central issues of the injury suits. What is more important, their queries demonstrate that juries made serious efforts to understand the law and legal process. The critics' sympathetic, emotional jury was nowhere in evidence. In its stead stood a jury attentive to the law and facts before it. The occasional glimpses of jurors gained from the case transcripts show jurors actively involved in the legal process.

56. Kalven and Zeisel, *American Jury*, 149.

For example, enthusiastic jurors joined in the questioning of witnesses from time to time.[57] Juries in the middle of their deliberations often called for further information or a rereading of testimony. The jury in *Schappner v. Second Avenue Railroad* sent out for an actuarial table to aid in its calculations of an award. The jury in *Emanuelli v. Milliken Brothers* requested the transcripts of a key witness's testimony.[58] Sometimes a jury would move beyond informational questions to inquire into how evidence was to be interpreted. One juror asked Judge George Ingraham about the validity of a piece of testimony and how it might be challenged or confirmed.[59]

Juries took their charge seriously to carefully weigh the testimony. In *Caldwell v. New Jersey Steamboat*, the jury was on its second day of deliberation when it notified Judge Albert Cardozo that there was disagreement over the testimony of three witnesses. "We ask you to decide for whose benefit the doubt should be extended according to law," the jury enquired. Cardozo instead lectured the jury on their duty and threatened to "keep them together until they agreed, even if it be until next Monday." The testimony was read again to the jury, and the question about doubt Cardozo answered in favor of the defendant. Apparently the jury overcame its doubts, because it returned a verdict of $20,000 for the plaintiff.[60]

The bearing of particular evidence on questions of liability was the subject of a question the jury put to the judge in *Cronin v. Manhattan Transit*.[61] The trouble that the jury met in *Schornstein v. The Mayor et al.* demonstrates the determination of those twelve to follow the law and shows the latitude that remained to them in doing so. In the midst of deliberations, the jurors asked to have Judge Mitchell Erlanger's instructions again. Instead, Erlanger brought them back into court and asked them, "What seems to be the difficulty?"

"The gentlemen of the jury do not seem to be able to agree as to what is reasonable care," the foreman stated. Erlanger reiterated the standard. "Will your Honor define contributory negligence?" another juror asked. Erlanger did. The questions show that the jury was wrestling with the

57. *Schultz v. New York Transportation.*
58. *Schappner v. Second Avenue Railroad;* and *John Emanuelli v. Milliken Brothers,* 1910 Number M14, N.Y.C. Supreme Court.
59. *Cowan v. Third Avenue Railroad.*
60. *Caldwell v. New Jersey Steamboat.*
61. *Cronin v. Manhattan Transit.*

central issues of liability law and having a hard time reaching agreement on their meaning.[62]

Most of the questions juries asked were about setting awards, attesting to the difficulty of the task and paucity of guidance they were given. A juror's question in *Sartirana* v. *New York County Bank* suggested that judges' brief treatment of the criteria for determining awards might have allowed the jury more license than intended. The juror asked, "Will it be fair to consider in arriving at a verdict for damages at all the financial standing of the defendants?" "Of course not!" Henry Dugro answered. Common sense had not naturally led the jury to the law's criteria for fixing awards.[63]

Other juries wondered what exactly the bounds were to their discretion. One jury's foreman asked, "What are the limitations governing us? Your Honor has not exactly touched upon that. It is not quite clear to me what the limit of our power is, so to speak, which tells us that we shall go so far and no further."[64] The answer he received could not have been very satisfactory. Judge Edward McCall fumbled around in issues tangential to the question before arriving at the obvious: "If I understand the purport of your question, whatever judgment you reach must be based upon the same proof offered in the case."[65]

The jury in *Reynolds* v. *Ireland* wanted to make sure its formula for figuring damages was reasonable and asked the judge if it was proper to consider future decrease in earning capacity. Judge Erlanger was noncommittal, deciding to leave his charge to the jury as it stood. The jury persisted. It returned to court in the middle of its deliberation to ask sanction for their specific calculation; could it reach its verdict by calculating six years at $3 loss per week? "That is entirely a question for the jury," Erlanger replied.[66] The jury's methodical approach and concern for the legitimacy of its decision stand in sharp contrast to critics' accusations that juries' decisions were acts of emotion and sympathy.

This information on juries and judges delivers some insight into why injury cases in the New York City Supreme Court climbed. Judges' applications of rules, though generally consistent across the decades, were inconsistent from case to case. Juries retained considerable power in de-

62. *David Schornstein* v. *Mayor et al., City of New York,* 1910 Number M90, N.Y.C. Supreme Court.

63. *Sartirana* v. *New York County Bank.*

64. *Stein* v. *Grand Ice Cream.*

65. Ibid.

66. *Dora Reynolds* v. *John Ireland,* 1910 Number I78, N.Y.C. Supreme Court.

termining the meaning of the general principles judges expounded. Judicial inconsistency and jury interpretation meant that even within an unchanged set of rules, room remained for variance in the application of the law.

The margin for variation allowed juries to apply their values and their community's standards to define the central principles of injury law: responsibility (or fault) and reasonable care.[67] Juries established the levels of fault and care that would determine liability. This left to those who filled the juries, the people of New York, much influence over just what the law of injury would be. While no two juries defined the standards of care and fault in precisely the same way, there was a clear shift in the pattern of juries' definitions across the forty years. Juries consistently extended the responsibility of people who established conditions that promoted injury, people who caused injury indirectly. Jurors also adjusted their ideas of what constituted "reasonable care" to require more stringent care of those who created danger.

The terms remained the same—reasonable care, proximate cause, negligence—but the meaning had shifted. As historian Marc Bloch once pointed out, "To the great despair of historians, men fail to change their vocabulary every time they change their customs."[68] Juries did just that at the turn of the twentieth century. They changed the law to fit their changed customs without any proclamation or fanfare and without rules or procedures showing any sign of the change.

Injury victims came from the same body of people that jurors did. Those who were deciding responsibility and reasonable care in the cases of others met injury themselves, and an increasing portion of them elected to seek compensation in the court. The change in their response to injury shared origins with the change in juries' behavior. The seedbed for both was the shift in public conceptions of responsibility and reasonable care.

Two pieces of evidence attest to change in popular thinking about injury at the end of the nineteenth century. First, New Yorkers began litigating injuries from causes that had long existed but had never before produced many lawsuits, such causes as broken sidewalks, dark hallways, loose floorboards, and horse traffic. These were not new sources of injury, but they were new sources of contested injury. What had formerly

67. Sociologists have recognized that the determination of fault is dependent on "cultural values, social norms, and culturally shared rules of interpretation." Peter Berger and Thomas Luckmann, *The Social Construction of Reality* (New York: Anchor, 1967).
68. Bloch, *Historian's Craft*, 34.

been thought of as the injured individual's own fate and responsibility was suddenly transformed into a compensable event, the fault and financial duty of another.

Second, juries' views on just verdicts began to diverge regularly from judges' views. Judges began to overturn juries' conclusions of fact and awards, although they never missed an opportunity to speak reverently of juries' absolute domain in these areas. Judges' dismissals of jury decisions occurred very rarely in 1870 but were regular occurrences by 1890. This could only signal either that judges' ideas about injury law were changing or that jurors' ideas were changing. Since judges' application of the law proved stable across time over the long term despite variance and inconsistency among judges, stable to the point that judges even interpreted new rules to conform to old practices,[69] it must have been jurors who were thinking differently than before.

Disagreement between judge and jury bluntly revealed itself. Judges reserved judgment on defendants' motions to dismiss, allowing juries to rule. When juries returned verdicts favorable to plaintiffs, judges negated the juries' decisions by exercising their reserved right to dismiss. In other words, when juries ruled counter to judges' views on cases, the judges suddenly discovered that the facts had not really been at issue. The cases should never have gotten to juries in the first place, they ruled, either for lack of evidence or for clear plaintiff negligence.[70]

Divergent conceptions were just as apparent when cases were tried more than once. The typical pattern was that the jury would decide for the plaintiff, be reversed when the defendant took the case to the Appellate Division, be vindicated when another jury decided again for the plaintiff, and again be reversed upon appeal. The final decision almost always went to the defendant, as the judge at the third trial tightly circumscribed the issues that the jury could decide, based on the decisions of his Appellate Division brethren. When this limitation was still not apparent to the jury on the third (or later) trial, the judge might intervene to take the case from

69. See Chapter 3.

70. See, for example, *Bail* v. *New York, New Haven, and Hartford Railroad;* and *Hartley Haigh* v. *Edelmayer and Morgan Hod Elevator Company,* 1910 Number H401, N.Y.C. Supreme Court. In *Schultz* v. *New York Transportation,* Judge Dugro ultimately decided to abide by the jury's verdict for Schultz, though he heard arguments on the defendant's motion to overturn the verdict because "it is a very close case. I am not at all clear that a verdict in favor of the plaintiff can stand because of the question of contributory negligence." In *Anderson* v. *Pennsylvania Steel,* Judge Charles Guy also decided to uphold a jury verdict for the plaintiff after reserving decision on the defendant's motion to dismiss. In doing so, he felt compelled to justify his choice with a five-page opinion.

the jury.[71] By the final trial, the jury's inclusion in the process was mere formality. Outcomes were foreordained. The judges had levered juries out of the decision process and had done it for a reason; juries disagreed with them on the basic tenets of injury liability.

The popular and judicial conceptions, rooted in the same principles, parted ways most significantly on the question of responsibility: Was the individual presumed liable for any injury that befell her or him if someone had not directly caused it? Or was the person liable who set preconditions that were necessary to the accident's occurrence? Clearly, causality was tightly bound to the issue of responsibility. The traditional ideas embodied in the law—self-responsibility and immediately direct causation—came into conflict with public perceptions of cause and responsibility. A new view rose to challenge the traditional, emphasizing individuals' social responsibilities as people came to think in terms of longer chains of causation.

71. This was the plaintiff's fate in *Haigh* v. *Edelmayer and Morgan Hod Elevator*. The defeat was a costly one for Haigh. Haigh, a mason, was working on a construction site on West 96th Street, removing a wheel barrow from a lift operated by the defendants when the lift fell apart and Haigh with his load of bricks plunged four floors. He suffered broken bones, numerous gashes, a dislocated shoulder, and internal bleeding. In his first trial in 1907, a jury awarded him $2,500. After the Appellate Division overturned the jury's decision, another jury reached the same conclusion, this time to the figure of $2,000 for Haigh. Reversed again, the suit was tried before yet a third jury, which arrived at the same finding as the earlier juries and awarded $1,000 to Haigh. Judge Charles Dayton, having reserved his decision on defense attorney Frank Johnson's standard motion to dismiss, decided that Johnson was right; the plaintiff did not have a case sufficient to put to the jury after all. He dismissed the suit. Haigh lost not only the $1,000 award, but $991 in costs that were granted to the defendant.

6. THE INJURED:
NEED AND COMPENSATION

Not inevitably driven by socioeconomic forces, not fomented by an institutional imperative, the rise in injury suits must be studied as the handiwork of human decision of those who made the lawsuits in the first place: the injured. Since their acts of seeking redress built the increase in suits, they are the logical source of the decisions that changed the course of injury litigation. This chapter will look at the process of suing from the perspective of the injured to assess what in their line of vision might have made legal recourse more necessary or attractive by 1910 than forty years before.

While the physical trauma of injury did not change between 1870 and 1910, other aspects of injury were less fixed. Two of those variable aspects in New Yorkers' experience, which might have influenced them to sue more frequently than before, are changes in the need for compensation and in the likelihood of gaining it. Either by itself could have driven injured New Yorkers' decisions to sue; they pose such a potent possibility because they complemented each other. The need for compensation could have propelled people to sue, while the chance of success could have attracted potential suit-bringers to the court. In turn-of-the-century New York, however, neither moved decisively to promote lawsuits.

That injury created need does not require much proof. Injury wreaked havoc on the tenuous solvency of most victims' existences. A breadwinner struck down for even a short period of time lost precious income. And income was precious; few of these people were rich. Table 21 reports the

TABLE 21

Weekly income of plaintiffs at time of injury

Income	1870		1890		1910	
	n	%	n	%	n	%
Under $5	—	0	—	0	2	3
$5–10	—	0	1	17	7	10
$10–15	1	100	1	17	35	49
$15–20	—	0	2	33	5	7
$20–30	—	0	—	0	14	19
$30–40	—	0	2	33	4	5
Over $40	—	0	—	0	5	7
Total	1	100	6	100	72	100

Source: See Table 4.

incomes of the people taking injury suits to the city Supreme Court who testified about their income.

The range of incomes shown for 1910 is probably representative of injured suitors' incomes in that year, since other contemporary studies attested to a similar range. Among those studies are U.S. Census wage figures for the city, the New York State Bureau of Labor Statistics figures on the average wages of injured workmen, and journalist Francis McLean's report on the spread of incomes of injured workers in New York.[1] According to the Census Office, men in unskilled jobs in light industry earned from $10 to $12 per week, women averaged $7, and children $4 in 1890. By the state's compilation, the average income of men injured at work was $9.93 per week in 1899; the average number of days lost was 29, translating to five six-day weeks. Over half of these injured workers were married and had children.[2] McLean's information about the income of the city's work-injury victims mirrors almost exactly the distribution presented in Table 21. He found 20 percent of work-injury victims made less than $10 per week (compared to 13% of those in Table 21,

1. The U.S. Census figures are cited in Rosner, *A Once Charitable Enterprise*, 24–26, and come from "Statistics of Cities," *Report on Manufacturing Industries in the U.S. at the Eleventh Census: 1890, Part II* (Washington, D.C.: U.S. Government Printing Office, 1895). The New York State statistics are from New York State Bureau of Labor Statistics, Weber, "The Compensation of Accidental Injuries to Workmen," 570–77. Francis McLean reports his findings in "Industrial Accidents and Dependency in New York State," *Charities and the Commons* 19 (1907–8): 1203–12.

2. "Compensation," 571, 576.

year 1910), 40 percent between $10 and $15 (compared to 49%), and another 40 percent over $15 (compared to 38%).[3]

Moreover, the similar distributions of income of 1910 tort plaintiffs (Table 21) and of McLean's work-injury victims suggest that suing was not exclusive to any particular income group. Apparently, people at each level of income initiated lawsuits in about the same proportion to the numbers of injuries that struck them.

Before their injuries, workers tried to live on these wages in a city where the minimum cost of living for a family of five was $16 to $22 per week.[4] Obviously they were in a tenuous economic position, and the loss of any income brought immediate trouble to most families. The injured and their dependents needed food, clothing, and other basic provisions in the interim between injury and return to work. Even short lapses of income brought "underfeeding, insufficient clothing, and uncertain tenure of home."[5] Robert Coit Chapin discovered that families who fell even slightly below the minimum income level for subsistence in New York ($14–$15 per week) experienced "some manifest deficiency"—overcrowded housing, inadequate food, less clothing, scavenging the streets for heating fuel, and foregoing most health and dental care.[6]

Severe injury, however, required medical attendance that could not be put off. While the poor had typically relied upon public dispensaries rather than hospitals for even their most serious medical problems, by 1900 the treatment of severe injury increasingly required hospitalization. In an unfortunate coincidence, at the same time, the injured were becoming more reliant on specialized medical services and medical costs were

3. McLean's statistics come from 241 incomes verified out of 396 instances of injury, and the statistics in Table 21 come from 72 incomes reported out of 596 lawsuits. The incomes of Table 21 are from victims of all sorts of accidents, McLean's are from work-injury victims. "Industrial Accidents," 1210.

4. Cost-of-living figures from "What It Costs to Live," *New York Tribune,* 19 November 1906, p. 5; Robert Coit Chapin, *The Standard of Living among Workingmen's Families in New York City* (New York: Russell Sage, 1909), 245–50; Caroline Goodyear, "The Minimum Practicable Cost of an Adequate Standard of Living in New York City," *Charities and the Commons* 17 (1906–7): 315–20 (with comment in the same issue by William J. White, "The Facts Considered," 321); and Lee R. Frankel, "The Cost of Living in New York," *Charities and the Commons* 19 (1907–8): 1049–54. For a discussion of the limits to historical uses of cost-of-living estimates, see John F. McClymer, "Late Nineteenth-Century American Working Class Living Standards," *Journal of Interdisciplinary History* 17 (1986): 379–98.

5. Robert Hunter, *Poverty (New York: Harper, 1965 [1904],* 35.

6. Chapin, *Standard of Living,* 245–46.

rising.[7] Added to the loss of income, then, the medical needs that accompanied injury saddled accident victims with a dual economic burden.

Along with lowered standards of living and mounting medical bills, injury brought with it myriad other unwelcome events. In observing 92 families scourged by work injury, McLean found that 26 had suffered "marked deterioration" manifested as "chronic dependency, intemperance not before present, lowering of standards of living, breaking down in health of widow, family broken up, habit of begging developed, savings used up, furniture pawned, [and] first experience of being dispossessed."[8]

Some of these woes reflect the concerns of charity leaders (bad habits, dependency) more than those of the impoverished families. Yet, the extent of trouble and unmet need occasioned by accidental injury still comes through clearly. Serious injuries often became disasters for individuals and families because society made few provisions for aiding accident victims.

The consequences were more devastating in some circumstances than in others. In the trades and general labor where strength, endurance, agility, or dexterity determined the worker's station and continued employment, a disabling injury could render a person unfit to ever return to the same job, causing a downward move from a low-paying to a still lower paying job or even to permanent loss of a job.[9]

That was the concern of George Williams, who broke his leg after a rough 133rd Street sidewalk jolted him out of his wheelchair. Though already disabled, Williams had ingeniously eked out a living in a line of work that his broken leg threatened to take away: "exhibiting himself at various shows, museums and carnivals." This was now endangered

7. One characteristic of the transformation of hospitals that David Rosner found occurring at the turn of the century was the shift from care on a charity basis to a fees-for-services basis. This increased the cost of being injured at a time when hospital care was becoming a typical practice. Rosner, *A Once Charitable Enterprise*, 89–90. For a contemporary review of the city's hospitals, see "Hospital Life in New York," *Harper's New Monthly Magazine* 57 (1878): 171–90.

8. McLean, "Industrial Accidents," 1206.

9. Hunter (*Poverty*, 159) recognized the problem: "Few realize that a very slight injury or breakdown may incapacitate certain workmen from further usefulness in a trade for which they may have been especially trained. A hernia may render a workman employed in moving heavy materials incapable of further usefulness in this employment. Continuous, intense, laborious work demands of the workman a strong constitution and good health." McLean's investigation bore Hunter out; of 350 cases of hernia cases he researched, 60 percent were disabled for over a year, and just under 20 percent had been disabled for ten years or more. McLean, "Industrial Accidents," 1211.

because his injury kept him from "performing the feats which he heretofore performed." For a person in Williams's position, with very few alternative lines of work to turn to, the loss of his special means of earning a living loomed large. It probably loomed even larger after he failed to gain compensation in his trial before Judge John Goff and jury.[10]

What provision did society make for its members who met injury? Where did the injured turn in their time of need? The stories of those who took their injuries to court suggest that they usually called first upon family, neighbors, or close friends to provide sustenance.[11] Other members of the nuclear family took on more work, as Mary Isaac's husband, a disabled veteran, did in the story that opens Chapter 1. Extended family and friends lent money, took in children, provided food and shelter, and occasionally subsidized other needs.

What was happening to this front line of emergency support—family and friends—between 1870 and 1910? In theory, the increasing mobility of the population was disrupting close contact with kith and kin. Transoceanic migration and the constant movement of people between cities[12] did often sever regular connections with extended family, and the constant flux probably did keep many from establishing new networks of people that could be relied upon in times of need.

But was this disruption increasing between 1870 and 1910? There is a tendency to view this era as one of community breakdown, based on the assumption that as cities grew, the close bonds of community were rent asunder. In the strictest sense that is true; the city as one unified com-

10. *George Williams* v. *Mayor et al., City of New York,* 1910 Number W445, N.Y.C. Supreme Court.

11. See Appendix I, "The Temper of the Workers Under Trial," in Eastman, *Work Accidents;* Hunter, *Poverty,* 25–36; and Friedman, *History of American Law,* 428–34. E. Wight Bakke outlined a sequence that unemployed workers tended to follow in seeking sustenance. It is instructive in thinking about where injured New Yorkers (three to six decades before Bakke's observations) looked when faced with the same problem. First, workers used all their own accrued benefit rights, sought commercial loans, put other members of the family to work (those not ordinarily expected to earn), and borrowed on any property they owned because these options did not damage the workers "sense of self-support." The next resort was clan aid or the assistance of friends, both of which impinged on the worker's independence. As the last option, the worker would turn to public or private assistance, but these were assiduously avoided because the involved no possibility of mutuality and were therefore considered too heavy a weight on the individual's sense of independence. E. Wight Bakke, *The Unemployed Worker: A Study in the Task of Making a Living without a Job* (New Haven, Conn.: Yale University Press, 1940), 26–29.

12. Stephan Thernstrom found for Boston in this period that one-third to one-half of the city's population moved every decade. See Stephan Thernstrom, *The Other Bostonians* (Cambridge: Harvard University Press, 1970).

munity was destroyed as it expanded. But in the case of New York, this had happened well before the years of this study. During the span 1870 to 1910 the trend may have actually headed in the other direction, toward greater unification. Seymour Mandelbaum has argued precisely that. Due to transportation and communication barriers, New York in 1870 was a collection of localities loosely tied together. Rather than becoming more fragmented with growth, Mandelbaum believes that the city attained greater unity over time as communications and transportation improvements bound the city closer together.[13]

The oft-employed characterization of the era as one of community breakdown is fraught with problems. Thomas Bender observes that depending upon the historian, the sense of community in the United States was in its death throes in the seventeenth, eighteenth, nineteenth, or twentieth century.[14] If community had died that many times, what ghost of it was left to be dispatched by New Yorkers in 1900?

Bender suggests that the entire concept of linear decline is faulty. Historians have fallen prey to a misbegotten model. Instead of following a line from settlement dominated by face-to-face personal interaction to one where impersonal interaction was the norm, he suggests that New York at the turn of the century was a dual society, with its members leading partly communal and partly extracommunal, or social, lives. Most resided in a community, "a network of social relations marked by mutuality and emotional bonds . . . held together by shared understanding and a sense of obligation . . . rather than the perception of individual self-interest," even while living a good portion of each day away from that community in the larger society.[15]

Just because people became more public, interacting with strangers more often, they did not necessarily lose their communal network. The relation may well have been the converse: Since individuals were forced to spend more time in the impersonal public realm, they might have zealously maintained, even across greater distances, their communal bonds. They may have even strengthened those ties deliberately to reaffirm their roots and bearings and assuage their sense of flux.

The judgments provide some evidence that this was indeed the case. Wounded New Yorkers employed society's increased mobility to draw

13. Seymour Mandelbaum, *Boss Tweed's New York* (New York: John Wiley, 1965), 19–27.

14. Thomas Bender, *Community and Social Change in America* (New Brunswick, N.J.: Rutgers University Press, 1978).

15. Ibid., 7.

upon their extended families' sustenance. Injured ironworker Claude Warren and his wife, for example, crossed two states to find kin they could
stay with, finally moving into a brother-in-law's house in Ulysses, Pennsylvania. Frederick Kindorf also took leave of the city, moving his family
to a kinfolk's small farm in upstate New York "where he did what work
he could about the place." Eva Willets did not have to leave New York,
her family came to her. Her daughter and sister gave up jobs to come live
with her and help run her fourteen-room boarding house.[16]

This evidence does not establish a systematic sense of access to family
and community support over time. But by showing that the first line of
assistance was still operative in 1910, it supports Bender's skepticism
about "community decline" as an agent of causality and throws the burden of proof on those who would argue that community decline heightened need and thereby fostered more lawsuits.

Employers offered another source of support. For 1870 there is not
much evidence of what employers were doing for injured workers, so it is
difficult to establish the trend in employer support across time. But again,
the incidence of support in 1910 apparent in the judgment rolls and state
studies indicates that the practice could not have declined precipitously
over the preceding forty years.

Employers' help was scant and occasional. It appeared most often in
cases of injury on the job. When it was offered, its intent was to help tide
over the injured worker rather than fully compensate her or his losses. In
a few instances, employers continued to pay the workers' regular wages
throughout the course of the disability. Ursula Banks received her full sal-
ary from the city school board for months after twice being hit on the
head by falling light fixtures. Her supervising principal had advised that
she "had better get to the country for a week or two"; the principal would
"see that she gets her money."[17]

More frequently though, employers would hold jobs open or make
work for the injured upon return to the business. They did not do this only
in the case of work injury. Michael Finnie was severely injured on a
streetcar and had to give up his twenty-years experience as a seaman.
Eleven months and three surgeries after his injury, Finnie returned for

16. *Claude Warren* v. *Post and McCord*, 1910 Number P44, N.Y.C. Supreme Court;
Frederick Kindorf v. *Philip Hoellerer*, 1910 Number K72, N.Y.C. Supreme Court; and *Eva
Willets* v. *Central Railroad Company of New Jersey*, 1910 Number W471, N.Y.C. Supreme
Court.

17. Testimony of teacher Katharine Lang, *Ursula Banks* v. *Board of Education of the
City of New York et al.*, 1910 Number B617, N.Y.C. Supreme Court.

work to the steamship line he had worked for as a quartermaster before the accident. The employer tried to make work for Finnie sewing life preservers, but Finnie could not do even that.[18]

Dora Reynolds, too, had an employer who was at least flexible. She had been injured outside work, yet accommodation was made for her upon her return to the Crown Suspender Company. She described her work after the injury: "I did not work steadily during the next year after that. I would go in and maybe work until three o'clock and then go home, and maybe I would put in one day and the next day I was off."[19]

The Hotel Victoria offered a different kind of support to Julia Donegan, who had broken her hand cleaning windows. Her wages had been $12 per month plus room and board. For the first month after the accident, the hotel allowed her to stay on in her room, but she had to purchase her own food.[20] The state Bureau of Labor Statistics found that Donegan and Banks's experiences with employer support were not uncommon, though neither were they typical. In a study of 1,886 employer-reported work injuries in 1899, employers gave the injured workers some support, either for medical expenses or in continued wages, about 20 percent of the time.[21] These were seldom magnanimous benevolences, but injured New Yorkers coupled them with other resources to get by.

In a smaller study that focused on New York City eight years later, McLean turned up exactly the same frequency of response by employers: 20 percent. Whether this signals continuity through time is difficult to tell, because McLean includes employer settlements (given in exchange for releases from liability) in his figure of 20 percent. It is not clear whether the Bureau of Labor study did the same.[22]

In only 13 out of 223 cases did employers actually donate money outright to the injured worker (this excludes settlement deals), making McLean's frequency of employer *assistance* more accurately 5 percent than 20 percent. The donations showed little rhyme or reason: They ranged from $2 given for an unspecified temporary injuries, to $20 and $60 for workers' "brains affected," to $300 given for broken legs. McLean's chief conclusion about employers' payouts (assistance and

18. Finnie v. *Central Park, North, and East River Railroad.*
19. Reynolds v. *Ireland.*
20. *Julia Donegan* v. *American Hotel Victoria,* 1910 Number D261, N.Y.C. Supreme Court.
21. Weber, "Compensation," 577. This is assuredly a higher figure than for instances of work injury that were not reported, or for injuries that occurred outside the workplace.
22. McLean, "Industrial Accidents," 1205–6, 1211–12.

settlements) was that they were capricious and arbitrary. The "veritable crazy quilt of absurdities" patched "generally quite fair" settlements for temporary injuries to "incongruous" ones for more serious losses, as the following amounts given for serious injuries illustrate:[23]

Death	$500	Paralysis	$ 12
Death	$ 50	Legs broken	$300
Fingers amputated	$ 50	Legs amputated	$100

Employer assistance to injury victims was unpredictable but appears to have been constant in its unpredictability through time. Without litigating, injured workers could anticipate only a one-in-five chance of receiving money from employers and then not necessarily an amount befitting the injury. That did not change between 1899 and 1907, the dates of the two studies, and it is difficult to imagine greater consistency in employers' voluntary benefactions and settlements before that time.

There is some evidence behind that skepticism: the silence on the matter of voluntary employer assistance before the 1890s by proponents of workmen's compensation in the first decade of the new century. In hawking their cause, Crystal Eastman, George Alger, and others cast widely for precedents with which to persuade their audience—especially businessmen—of the soundness and rationality of a regular compensation system. If business practices circa 1900–10 had departed significantly from previous practices that had compensated injured workers more regularly, I am certain that those astute advocates would have widely and favorably cited the earlier practices.[24] Without evidence that business sharply reduced support to incapacitated employees between 1870 and 1910, there is no reason to see the low rate of support by employers in 1910 as a cause of the rise of injury lawsuits.

The same pattern of continuity applies to the effect of public and private relief upon Manhattanites' decisions to sue. Public relief laws did not

---

23. Ibid., 1205.

24. An exception that proves the "silence is evidence" argument is McLean's presentation in "Industrial Accidents," approvingly and at length, of the American Manufacturing Company's systematic injury and disability compensation program. While he notes that the "system has been used . . . for a number of years," he refers to it and that of the street railroads as the only "advanced," "scientific and business-like" systems he could find to discuss, indicating the novelty of more regular compensation. The use of "advanced," especially, signifies that in his research he found compensation no more regular previously than it was in his own time. Ibid., 1207–8.

change throughout the forty years,[25] and neither did public ideas about them. In 1870 and 1910 alike, those with any other option open to them avoided relief, which was demeaning and carried heavy social costs. Robert Hunter reported, "In many cases [relief] condemns forever the unfortunate applicants to a position of disrepute in the community."[26] In addition to stigmatizing its beneficiaries, the means and intentions of public and charity assistance were highly unattractive. Long-term assistance was strictly "indoor" relief; the poorhouse was its dispensary. The idea of a stay in the poorhouse was so repugnant, Hunter found, that many permanently injured New Yorkers preferred begging and life on the streets to relief. "What is the cripple to do?" asked Hunter: "He is maimed for life. The only alternative to a life of begging and vagrancy which is offered him is an almshouse, the most dreary, terrible place for a sane man that one can imagine. I know nothing more depressing. . . . Because a man has lost his legs or arms, the prospect for him of an entire life in such surroundings is no more tolerable than it would be to any of us."[27]

By 1900 most assistance to those living at home came from private charity. The charities, led by the New York Association for Improving the Condition of the Poor, had forced this condition. They had campaigned long, hard, and successfully to end all public relief to people not in almshouses, in the belief that relief coddled the recipient and encouraged dependency. In 1877, the city ended cash grants to all except blind adults and did not institute the practice again until 1931. The extent of the success of the campaign against public relief can be seen in the allocation of city relief funds: Of $1.8 million spent in 1903, only $50,000 went to assistance of impoverished New Yorkers outside the almshouse, a sharp drop from the decades before.[28]

---

25. The Poor Law of 1896 (Chapter 225, Laws of 1896), though the first major restatement of the state's Poor Law since 1813, simply consolidated accumulated rules and clarified the distribution of city, county, and state responsibilities in administering the law. New York State Board of Charities, *Charity Legislation in New York, 1609 to 1900*, vol. III of the *Annual Report for 1903* (Albany: Oliver Quayle, 1904), 971; and Martha Branscombe, *The Courts and the Poor Laws in New York State, 1784–1929* (Chicago: University of Chicago Press, 1943), 164–70.

26. Hunter, *Poverty*, 82. Lawrence Friedman, among others, has pointed out that both charity and public assistance were stigmatized, made deliberately onerous to discourage dependency. Friedman, *History of American Law*, 431.

27. Hunter, *Poverty*, 88.

28. David Schneider and Albert Deutsch, *The History of Public Welfare in New York State, 1867–1940* (Chicago: University of Chicago Press, 1941), 46–49, 181; Barry Kaplan, "Reformers and Charity: The Abolition of Public Outdoor Relief in New York City, 1870–1898," *Social Service Review* 52 (June 1978): 202–14; Samuel Mencher, *Poor Law*

So public outdoor assistance, not a particularly attractive option to the injury victim, was fast becoming unavailable. With the virtual elimination of public aid to the injured in their homes, those in dire need were forced to turn elsewhere. Private charity was an alternative, but neither an attractive nor particularly benevolent one. Under the leadership of the charity organizing movement from the late 1880s into the 1910s, the dominant theme among charity activists was to make charity more "efficient," defined as more tightly regulated and difficult to obtain. In practice, this translated to more liberal dispensation of self-help maxims and character-building advice and more miserly allotment of money and material goods. Under this regime, the charities first, upon receiving an application for relief, tried to get the money from the injured individual's personal resources, turning them back on "families, friends, neighbors and others with whom there is personal contact."[29]

Charity leaders need not have worried about enticing New Yorkers into dependency; private charity assistance, when it did come, was niggardly in proportion to need. Among the industrial injury victims in his study, McLean calculated that those who obtained relief got an average of $50, including the value of services received.[30] New York's chief of relief, Charity Organizing Society president Edward T. Devine, offered the most damning assessment of the inadequacy of charity assistance in this era: "Our use of relief has been most sparing and timid. I am inclined to believe that we have caused more pauperism by our failure to provide for the necessities of life, for the education and training of children, and for the care and convalescence of the sick, than we have by excessive relief, even if we include indiscriminate alms."[31]

---

to Poverty Program: Economic Security in Britain and the United States (Pittsburgh: University of Pittsburgh Press, 1967), 282; Branscombe, *Courts and the Poor Laws*, 145, 159.

29. Mencher, *Poor Law*, 291–92. See Kenneth Kusmer, "The Functions of Organized Charity in the Progressive Era," *Journal of American History* 60 (1973): 657–78; Walter Trattner, *From Poor Law to Welfare State: A History of Social Welfare in America* (New York: Free Press, 1989); and Michael Katz, *In the Shadow of the Poorhouse: A Social History of Welfare in America* (New York: Basic Books, 1986). For the best statement of the Charity Organizing program and rationale, by the leader of New York's movement, see Josephine Shaw Lowell, *Public Relief and Private Charity* (New York: Putnam's, 1884); and "A Glimpse at Some of Our Charities," *Harper's New Monthly Magazine* 56 (1877): 441–50.

30. Of the 736 instances of injury, 92 families received aid from charity groups. Forty-nine of those reported that the amount they received added up to $2,647. McLean, "Industrial Accidents," 1205.

31. This is quite an admission of failure; "indiscriminate alms" was the rallying cry in the charity leaders' drive to create the Charity Organizing Society. Devine quoted in Katz, *In the Shadow of the Poorhouse*, 83.

Not only was relief minimal, but trying to get it could be baffling amid the bewildering array of organizations that the injured person faced. There was the umbrella Charity Organizing Society, the Association for Improving the Condition of the Poor, the United Hebrew Charities, the Association for the Blind, the Society for the Ruptured and Crippled, and myriad church-affiliated groups, each attending to a particular constituency and applying its own idiosyncratic rules about the sort of relief to be given (e.g., services, cash) and the conditions for eligibility. The net result of procedural hurdles and low payouts was that charitable aid was an unlikely source of help for the injured. Again, though, public and charity relief was probably not significantly less help in 1910 than it had been in 1870.[32]

Injury victims were acutely aware that relief was minimal and compromised their independence. They avoided it where they could. More of the populace took steps to avert brushes with dependency by forming mutual aid societies and by purchasing commercial insurance. Mutual aid or fraternal societies and union-benefit funds demonstrated popular concern about preparing for the unexpected, but they had real limitations.[33] Unions often provided temporary disability aid, but they served a very small part of the population, probably not even a million people nationally by 1910. Fraternal funds pulled in more participants but typically paid only death benefits.[34] These funds did serve as a resource for brief periods of disability by allowing members to borrow against their contributions.

Supplementing the incipient formal protection programs was the irregular, informal practice of co-workers' collecting money for injury victims. In McLean's work-injury cases, workers gave money to the injured more often than employers did. Typically, the amounts were smaller than employers gave, but not always. In a case of a workman with two broken legs, co-workers collected $125 for the victim; in a case of lead

32. Trattner, *Poor Law to Welfare State*, 73–97; Katz, *In the Shadow of the Poorhouse*, 36–109; "The Ruptured and Crippled Poor," *New York Times*, 14 November 1866, p. 2.

33. For a discussion of union and fraternal self-insurance, see Roy Lubove, "Economic Security and Social Conflict in America: The Early Twentieth Century, Part I," *Journal of Social History* 1 (1967): 61–87.

34. There were New York associations that had disability provisions, the Supreme Lodge of the Knights of Columbia, for example. But the effectiveness of the aid the Knights offered is questionable; member Bernard Geyer had to sue his association just to get an $84 payment he was due for a long illness. That Geyer received his $84 was not guaranteed, because many of these groups had a hard time staying solvent. *Bernard Geyer v. The Supreme Knights of Columbia*, 1890 Number S54, N.Y.C. Supreme Court.

poisoning, co-workers gave $320.[35] Unfortunately, no similar study had been done forty years before with which to compare McLean's 1906–7 findings and determine whether co-worker assistance had diminished or increased over time.

Commercial insurance also began in this period. It grew quickly, from 11,000 policies nationally in the late 1870s to 3.5 million by 1900. This was not accident insurance. Like mutual benefit societies, its payoff was merely a small sum upon death to cover funeral costs. But again, a person disabled by injury could borrow against her or his policy, providing one small source of self-relief.[36]

Accident insurance existed but was not widespread. The first company appeared in the United States in 1864, but the second did not enter the field for another dozen years. By 1890, accident insurers were paying out $3.3 million annually in benefits. This figure, though substantial in the aggregate, amounted to between only 3,000 and 6,000 claims per year nationwide, at a time when New York City alone had over 5,200 accidents "resulting in serious or fatal injury."[37]

No plaintiffs mentioned accident insurance in their injury suits, partly because such evidence was inadmissible in injury cases. Evidence of victims' insurance recoveries was inadmissible because it was irrelevant to the damage caused by negligent acts. Inadmissibility did not deter defense lawyers, who often tried to introduce evidence about plaintiffs' insurance recoveries in the hopes of triggering "jury equity" and reducing verdict size. They did this in suits over fatal injuries, searching for life-insurance recoveries. Judges resisted the ploy, but that some plaintiffs held life insurance remained on the record in the defendant attorney's questions. In the same way, if injury victims had held personal accident insurance, we might expect that fact to have registered at least once in the judgment-roll transcripts. That it did not probably reflects personal insurance's limited presence in New York at the time.

Victims of injury, then, had a few alternative sources of support in 1870: family, community, co-workers, employer, or charity and public relief. Insurance of different types joined that list by 1910 as other sources were leaving; public relief in the home was one option that had all but disappeared by that date. There is no indication that levels of assistance from any of these sources except public relief outside the almshouse were lower in 1910 than levels forty years before. In short, while the economic

35. McLean, "Industrial Accidents," 1211–12.
36. Lubove, "Economic Security," 82–87.
37. Pitcher, "Accidents and Accident Insurance," 132–37.

need of New York's injured was acute, society was not meeting it outside the courtroom any better in 1910 than before, but neither was it doing much worse—at least not so much worse that it forced injury victims into litigation.

For need to have effected injured New York's increase in litigation, not only did New Yorkers have to perceive that alternative sources of aid were disappearing, but the populace had to recognize that lawsuits were a way of filling that void. The first condition was not met, as we have just seen; neither was the second. The injured had few reasons to think that lawsuits would offer a ready source of sustenance in 1870, less still in 1910. Suing did not meet most injury victims' need for compensation because it was chancy—it did not always succeed—and it was becoming chancier over the forty years. Second, when successful, lawsuits typically delivered only moderate sums (though more than charities or employers volunteered), a characteristic that changed only slightly between 1870 and 1910. Finally, when lawsuits delivered compensation, it was not in a timely fashion, synchronous with the needs of the disabled. Examining the general pattern in injury suits' outcomes shows just how far litigation came from filling injured suitors' economic holes.

Invoking legal processes in cases of injury was not the same as successfully invoking them. That comes as no surprise, knowing as we do that tort cases (unlike those involving debt, contract, and property issues) were always contested (see Chapter 1). The question is how frequently the claims of injured New Yorkers succeeded and whether that frequency of success changed over time. Tables 22 and 23 evince that the distinction between suing and suing successfully was significant. As suing (measured by the number of tort suits) shot upward, the rate with which the injured carried their suits to successful conclusions had a different trajectory.

The two tables show that while the number of successful torts—personal-injury suits in particular—grew, they did not grow as steeply as the number of suits filed. From injury victims' point of view, simply put, success fell off over time. Aggrieved New Yorkers were bringing proportionately more tort suits that proved fruitless. In 1870, those bringing personal-injury suits won compensation nine out of ten times (eight out of ten for all torts). By 1890, that rate had fallen to six out of ten (to one out of two for all torts). By 1910, the rate of success had swung against the plaintiffs, who lost five out of nine cases that year; this was true of personal-injury suits and all torts.

While personal-injury claimants met with less success in 1910 than they had in 1870, those who brought property-damage suits fared better

TABLE 22

Outcome of tort cases: Number and percentage of cases

Issue	1870		1890		1910	
	n	%	n	%	n	%
Total tort cases						
Plaintiff wins	25	78.1	82	48.5	321	44.1
Defendant wins	7	21.9	87	51.5	407	55.9
Personal injury cases						
Plaintiff wins	12	92.3	64	57.1	271	45.5
Defendant wins	1	7.7	48	42.9	324	54.5
Property-damage cases						
Plaintiff wins	11	68.7	7	46.7	26	70.3
Defendant wins	5	31.3	8	53.3	11	29.7
Intentional tort cases*						
Plaintiff wins	4	80	12	27.9	34	30.9
Defendant wins	1	20	31	72.1	76	69.1

Source: See Table 4.

Note: The sum of personal injury, property-damage, and intentional tort cases does not equal total cases because suits claiming personal injury *and* property damage are counted in both categories (2 cases 1870, 1 in 1890, 14 in 1910).

*Includes assault, false arrest, defamation, breach of marriage promise.

over time. An initially favorable rate of success for property-damage suits in 1870 gave way to a slightly unfavorable one in 1890, but by 1910, plaintiffs were again winning better than two out of three property-damage cases.

Just as one sort of tort suit fared markedly better than others in the city Supreme Court, so the general pattern of success in personal-injury cases masked variance in success among suits deriving from different causes (Table 23). Two distinct tendencies were at work within the body of personal-injury suits, combining to create the general trend in outcomes of injury suits: Those New Yorkers who sued over work injuries fared very poorly in court, in 1910 as before. However, those who sued over injuries from almost all other causes did much better. Plaintiffs in suits over injuries from railroads, traffic, street railroads, or bad roads and sidewalks won more often than they lost, in 1910 as in 1870. Those who filed suits involving injuries in buildings met with a similar pattern of success, though by 1910 they lost a few times more than they won.

Opposing this was the pattern of failure that work-injury plaintiffs experienced: They fared miserably. They had little success in 1890 (8 suits out of 24 received awards), and though more workers successfully ran the

TABLE 23

Outcome of personal-injury cases

Issue	1870		1890		1910	
	n	%	n	%	n	%
All personal-injury cases						
Plaintiff wins	12	92.3	64	57.1	271	45.5
Defendant wins	1	7.7	48	42.9	324	54.5
–Work-injury cases						
Plaintiff wins	0	0	8	33.3	49	30.6
Defendant wins	0	0	16	66.7	111	69.4
–Traffic-injury cases						
Plaintiff wins	1	100	4	44.4	65	56.5
Defendant wins	0	0	5	55.6	50	43.5
–Railroad-injury cases						
Plaintiff wins	0	0	9	69.2	12	63.2
Defendant wins	0	0	4	30.8	7	36.8
–Street-railroad injury cases						
Plaintiff wins	4	80	19	65.5	49	53.3
Defendant wins	1	20	10	34.5	43	46.7
–Road and sidewalk cases						
Plaintiff wins	3	100	11	68.8	57	51.4
Defendant wins	0	0	5	31.3	54	48.6
–Buildings-injury cases						
Plaintiff wins	3	100	8	50	29	43.9
Defendant wins	0	0	8	50	37	56.1
–Miscellaneous injury cases						
Plaintiff wins	2	100	5	100	10	31.2
Defendant wins	0	0	0	0	22	68.8

Source: See Table 4.

Note: As in Table 22, suits claiming personal injury and property damage are counted in both categories (2 cases 1870, 1 in 1890, 14 in 1910).

gantlet to gain some recompense in 1910 (49 awards for plaintiff, 111 decisions against), their rate of success actually worsened slightly.[38] The difference in outcome between work-injury suits and suits that stemmed from other causes could hardly have been more stark. While work-injury suits were lost causes two times out of three (even somewhat more often

38. New York passed the nation's first Workmen's Compensation law in 1910, but it had no effect on these cases. The new law applied only to injuries occurring after its passage, while the injuries being adjudicated in the city Court in 1910 were typically initiated between 1906 and 1909. See Asher, "Failure and Fulfillment,"; Wesser, "Conflict and Compromise"; and Friedman and Ladinsky, "Social Change and the Law of Industrial Accidents."

in 1910), New Yorkers' suits from other kinds of accidents won two times out of three in 1890 and over half the time in 1910.[39]

Over time, plaintiffs succeeded less, regardless of the sources of their injuries. In 1870 those who sued for injuries saw the court almost universally uphold their claims. In 1890 plaintiffs still won more than they lost of every type of injury suit, except traffic and work injury. By 1910 the injured still won more cases over road and sidewalk, railroad, and streetcar injuries than they lost, but they won these less often than before. For all other types of injuries they lost more than they won.

The general decline in success shared by all categories shows that the change in the overall rate of plaintiffs' success in personal-injury suits was due to more than just the shift in the types of cases being brought. The decline in success was not just a consequence of the growth of the work-injury claims, which were less likely to succeed.

The decline in successful suits was paralleled by a decline in award size. Table 24 shows that the average amount awarded to injury claimants dropped by two-thirds across the period, from $3,357 in 1870 to $958 in 1910. In large part this reflects the great increase in unsuccessful, wholly unrewarded claims. But even when those cases are removed from consideration (Table 24, last column), average awards still declined more than 40 percent, from $3,637 in 1870 to $2,104 in 1910. From 1890 to 1910, the drop was 5 percent, or more than 20 percent in real dollars.

The average personal-injury award was higher than those for other torts, either property damage or intentional, in 1870 and 1890 but not in 1910 (Table 25). By 1910, the average property-damage award was 15 percent higher than its personal-injury counterpart; so too were verdicts in one type of intentional tort, breach of marriage promises, which awarded an average of $2,817 in 1910.

Another way of viewing changes in personal-injury awards is to look at their distribution (e.g., number of $100 awards, $1,000 awards, $10,000 awards) at each point in time. Compared to averages, distributions give a sense of the range of awards and frequencies of occurrence at each level. In Table 26, it is evident that the portion of suits receiving nothing was up sharply. Over the rest of the range the most salient change was the decline in percentage of high awards (above $1,000).

Removing the "no award" cases and condensing the rest into a smaller number of categories (Table 27) reveals that there was, in fact, a trend afoot toward smaller awards. Only a quarter of the cases that claimants won received awards under $1,000 in 1870. By 1910, 55 percent of all

39. For injury suits other than for work injuries, plaintiffs won 56 and lost 32 in 1890 (63% success rate) and won 222 while losing 213 in 1910 (51% success rate).

TABLE 24

Average amount awarded in injury cases

Year	Average Award, all cases	Average Award, cases won by plaintiffs only
1870	$ 3,357 (3,689)	$ 3,637 (3,997)
1890	$ 1,292 (1,656)	$ 2,226 (2,859)
1910	$ 958 (998)	$ 2,104 (2,191)

Source: See Table 4.

n = 13 and 12 (1870, all cases and successful cases), 112 and 64 (1890), and 595 and 271 (1910).

Note: Amounts in parentheses are awards in real dollars, standardized to account for variation in the value of the dollar using Federal Reserve Board Price Index series E-183 from *Historical Statistics of the United States,* I (Washington, D.C.: U.S. Government Printing Office, 1976), 212

injury cases that produced some award yielded less than $1,000. Most of the awards under $1,000 were significantly smaller, for $500 or less. They comprised 38 percent of all awards in 1910, up from 25 percent in 1870. At the other end of the award spectrum, the trend was reversed. In 1870, one-third of the awards exceeded $3,000. By 1910, less than one-sixth of the awards did.

Given the variability of outcome among the different kinds of personal-injury suits, it is no surprise to learn that for some causes awards were higher than for others, and for some, the typical awards changed more over time. The figures in Table 28 show both variance and volatility across the period. Considering all cases (zero awards included), railroad-injury suits generated the largest average awards, four times as large as awards for other types of injury suits. Average railroad awards hovered

TABLE 25

Average amount awarded by type of tort

Issue	1870		1890		1910	
	Average	n	Average	n	Average	n
Personal injury	$3,357	13	$1,292	112	$ 958	595
Property damage	$ 681	14	$ 298	14	$1,146	23
Intentional torts*	$1,255	5	$ 915	43	$ 510	110
All cases	$1,858	32	$1,113	169	$ 897	728

Source: See Table 4.

*Includes assault, false arrest, defamation, breach of marriage promise.

TABLE 26
Personal-injury awards by size

Amount	1870		1890		1910	
	n	%	n	%	n	%
$0	1	7.7	47	42.0	324	54.5
Under $100	1	7.7	0	–	13	2.2
$101–200	1	7.7	2	1.8	26	4.4
$201–400	0	–	11	9.9	37	6.2
$401–500	1	7.7	9	8.0	26	4.4
$501–1,000	0	–	10	8.9	47	7.9
$1,001–1,500	1	7.7	5	4.5	22	3.7
$1,501–2,000	3	23.1	7	6.2	17	2.8
$2,001–3,000	1	7.7	7	6.2	41	6.9
$3,001–5,000	3	23.1	7	6.2	17	2.8
$5,000–10,000	0	–	6	5.4	20	3.4
Over $10,000	1	7.7	1	0.9	5	0.8
All cases	13	100	112	100	595	100

Source: See Table 4.

around $4,400; other suits combined averaged $3,357 per award in 1870 and $851 in 1890 and 1910. Railroad-injury awards fell off by approximately 10 percent from 1890 to 1910; streetcar-injury awards had a net drop of 60 percent from 1870 to 1910, as did sidewalk- and roadway-injury awards. The decline in award size in these categories was at the root of the overall drop in personal-injury awards.

Award size was on the upswing in work-injury cases, where the average award increased 40 percent from 1890 to 1910. The size of traffic-injury awards more than doubled over the same period (after a much

TABLE 27
Personal injury awards by size (For cases where an award was given)

Amount	1870		1890		1910	
	n	%	n	%	n	%
Under $1,000	3	25.0	32	49.2	149	55.5
$1,000–3,000	5	41.7	19	29.2	80	29.5
Over $3,000	4	33.3	14	21.6	42	15.5
All cases	12	100	65	100	271	100

Source: See Table 4.

TABLE 28
Average amount awarded by type of personal injury

Issue	1870		1890		1910	
	Average	*n*	*Average*	*n*	*Average*	*n*
Work injury	—	0	$ 751	24	$1,023	160
Traffic injury	$2,500	1	$ 382	8	$ 977	114
Railroad injury	—	0	$4,650	10	$4,200	19
Street-railroad injury	$2,088	5	$1,331	29	$ 821	92
Sidewalk-roadway injury	$1,700	1	$ 932	16	$ 615	111
Buildings injury	$2,300	3	$ 675	15	$ 836	61
All other injuries	$7,366	3	$1,345	10	$ 641	38
All personal injuries	$3,357	13	$1,292	112	$ 958	595

Source: See Table 4.

higher "average" award from one 1870 case). The average building-injury award dropped sharply after 1870 but rose again by over 10 percent between 1890 and 1910. Despite these increases, 1910 average award levels in work-, traffic-, and building-injury suits remained moderate.

The changes found in Table 29 depart only slightly from award averages shown in Table 28, which included "no award" cases. Considering just the suits where awards were given, average awards increased in the work-injury, traffic (1890 to 1910), building (1890 to 1910), and railroad categories. Average awards decreased continuously for street-railroad, sidewalk-roadway, and assorted other injury suits.

TABLE 29
Average amount awarded by type of personal injury:
(For cases where an award was given)

Issue	1870		1890		1910	
	Average	*n*	*Average*	*n*	*Average*	*n*
Work injury	—	0	$2,002	9	$3,341	49
Traffic injury	$ 2,500	1	$1,020	3	$1,714	65
Railroad injury	—	0	$5,813	8	$6,650	12
Street-railroad injury	$ 2,611	4	$2,032	19	$1,542	49
Sidewalk-roadway injury	$ 1,700	1	$1,355	11	$1,177	58
Buildings injury	$2,3000	3	$1,265	8	$1,961	26
All other injuries	$ 7,366	3	$1,921	7	$1,710	12
All personal injuries	$ 3,637	12	$2,226	65	$2,104	271

Source: See Table 4.

TABLE 30
Term of total disability of personal-injury plaintiffs

Term of disability	1870 n	1890 n	1910 n
Never totally disabled	—	12	7
Up to 1 month	—	1	14
1 to 2 months	1	2	15
2 to 3 months	—	4	22
3 to 6 months	1	3	14
6 to 12 months	—	—	11
12 to 24 months	—	1	6
More than 24 months	3	5	6
Death	2	19	103
Disabled, term unspecified	—	16	218
No mention	6	49	179
Total	13	112	595

Source: See Table 4.

What constituted moderate as opposed to enticingly large awards (large enough to attract to the court those who would not otherwise have sued), of course, depended on one's perspective. The most reasonable measure for characterizing awards as moderate rather than large was the economic adequacy of the compensation relative to victims' losses and needs. Comparing awards to the economic losses wrought by injury—here, considering injury severity, length of disability, and wages in light of contemporary cost-of-living estimates—makes it clear why most awards are accurately characterized as moderate.

The minimal relief these awards gave to injury victims becomes apparent when we take the typical reported experience for plaintiffs in 1910. The average plaintiff, who earned $15 per week (see Table 21), received an award of just under $1,000 (see Table 27, which considers successful plaintiffs only), of which his or her share was $500 (the other half going to the attorney), and was disabled for two to three months (see Table 30). After meeting lost wages or sustaining a family for the period of total disability, the accident victim's share of the typical award left $300 to $350 to cover medical costs (likely if we consider "fracture, teeth knocked out, eye injury" the median level of injury severity: Table 31), a period of partial work loss and occasional recurrences of disability from the injury, any permanent wage decrease owing to reduced work capacity, and pain and suffering. In simpler terms, the typical award yielded roughly seven months of income or expenditures to the typical plaintiff.

TABLE 31
Severity of injuries of injury-suit plaintiffs

Severity of injury	1870 n	1890 n	1910 n
Nervous shock only	—	2	4
Lacerations, bruises, contusions	2	33	168
Fracture, teeth knocked out, eye injury	1	20	128
Digit loss	1	1	5
Internal injury, severe burn, poison, miscarriage	—	7	57
Fracture, permanent ruin of a limb	4	10	34
Loss of a limb	—	6	14
Skull fracture (permanent impairment), multiple limb loss, paralysis, total blindness	1	3	12
Death	2	19	103
Insufficient information	2	11	70
Total	13	112	595

Source: See Table 4.
Note: The injuries are grouped by degree of impairment (from slight and temporary through permanent and severe) rather than by type of injury (e.g., "eye," "arm," "internal").

The final aspect of court-delivered compensation that bears on its fulfillment of the needs of injured New Yorkers is timing: When did injury victims need assistance, and when did lawsuits give it? The fact was that lawsuits were of no assistance in meeting injured suitors' immediate needs. It took time to mobilize the judicial system. The wait for trial took roughly two years in 1890 (29 months, median case) and 1910 (28 months), though by 1910 a new provision for the acceleration of trials in cases of exceptional hardship meant that a portion of people in serious need could get to the court more quickly.[40]

Of course, suing might have provided immediate sustenance by an indirect, less visible route. Loans from family and friends secured by the expectation of future compensation might have mitigated the lag in receiving court-granted compensation, had there been any certainty in the expectation. But as this chapter has shown, uncertainty of outcome was one of the few certain things about the employment of injury law in these

40. There are insufficient 1870 data from which to draw an average time lapse between accident and legal resolution. The 1890 and 1910 median figures were calculated from 103 and 590 cases, respectively, for which information on the date of accident was provided.

decades. Injured plaintiffs won only about half of the time (and that frequency was declining from 1890 to 1910). Even when they won, the plaintiffs' prospect of gaining a sizable award was low and diminishing. Under those uncertain conditions, the prospect of wounded New Yorkers gaining loans (from other than kinfolk) to meet immediate needs seems unlikely.

In sum, no dramatic changes occurred in injured New Yorkers' need for compensation or success in attaining it that would have powered the rise in lawsuits. Need was incessant and urgent but was not made more so across the decades. The frequency, size, and timing of awards delivered by the Supreme Court did not alter in ways that could have encouraged more injury suits.

Considered in combination with the rise in injury suits, the tables on the outcome of suits pose a paradox: More New Yorkers in 1890 and 1910 decided to sue in the face of both diminishing chances for success and the moderate awards that awaited most of those who succeeded. Unremitting need played an important part in the development. Though accident victims faced no dramatic increase in need for court compensation through decline in other alternatives, nothing diminished the constant urgency of victims' need. Accidents straitened the injured in 1910 as in 1870. From our vantage point, lawsuits may appear an unrealistic option for injured New Yorkers to have pressed in the face of weak prospects for success. But their constant necessity made it just as "unrealistic" to sit and suffer stoically.

Need might explain suing but not the increase in suing over the four decades. Need, like access to the law or the incessant incidence of injuries, was party to the rise in litigating but not its cause. Because necessity put constant pressure on injury victims, it cannot account for the timing, shape, and magnitude of the change in their resort to the law.

The paradox itself provides a clue to its own origin and resolution. The pattern of demand made upon the city court (in injury suits) was not the same pattern of response that emerged from the court (in successful injury suits). The difference between trends in numbers of suits, or what the suing populace saw to be legitimate claims, and in suit outcomes, or what the court saw to be legitimate claims, hints that ideas about injury and responsibility might not have been fully agreed upon at the time. It is that possibility—that changes and disagreements in ideas of injury and responsibility propelled the jump in the New York court's injury suits—that the concluding chapter entertains.

7. CONCLUSION:
A CHANGE OF MIND

A reporter for the *New York Times* made a prescient observation in 1866: "Although the law as now established by our Courts seldom enables a man to recover, or even to get his case before a Jury, yet there seems to be no end to the attempts to make railroads responsible for the accidents that are daily occurring."[1]

In the four decades to follow, those attempts would redouble. Victims of accidents around the city sought to make not just railroads but all sorts of others responsible. The rise in their attempts was not due to an increase in accidents (relative to population, there was no growth) or to new, unfamiliar sorts of dangers such as railroads taking their toll. The injuries in the suits came from old dangers as well.

The sudden growth in injury suits cannot be explained by changes in the law, either. Despite legislated changes in injury and safety rules, in application the tenets of injury law operated with great continuity. Injury law changed in practice—lawyers specialized and accepted contingent payments, judges dismissed suits—but these developments worked to discourage as much as encourage suits. With accident victims winning less of their cases over the forty years and receiving smaller awards when they won, it was not any change in the success of those who entered the system that impelled the rise of injury suits.

1. "Another Suit against a City Railroad—Complaint Dismissed," *New York Times*, 11 December 1866, p. 3.

Because legal behavior was changing for no apparent external environmental reason—no physical, social, or legal cause—logic suggests that the explanation lies internally, in the thinking of New Yorkers. James Willard Hurst asserted in *The Growth of American Law* (1950) that a society's ideas must be considered an integral part of the context that shaped the law. The first aspect of law's social environment, he argued, "is what men think: how they size up the universe and their place in it; what things they value, and how much; what they believe to be the relations between cause and effect, and the way these ideas affect their notions of how to go about getting the things that they value."[2]

The tasks of this concluding chapter are to get at what the thinking of New Yorkers had to do with the turn-of-the-century litigation explosion, and beyond that, at what the relationship between the two at that historical moment contributes to our understanding of society and law. To accomplish that, the chapter addresses four topics in turn. First, the nature of the change in the popular conception of liability will be sketched by reference to contemporary observers and by comparison with a contrasting conception of liability.

Second, the thesis will be put to the contextual test to show how it fits with other social and intellectual developments of the day. Third, New York's experience will be called upon to contribute what it can to our understanding of social change's effects on the workings of law. The fourth topic reverses the third: How did the legal developments affect social evolution and order? Considering the trial court as an institution of governance, this section draws upon the developments in New York to look briefly at three interpretations of the court's (and litigation's) role in the state.

The historical record supports examining change in "what men [and women] think," as Hurst put it. The paradox of the increase in suits amid decreases in suitors' success and size of awards, plus the divergence of judges' and juries' conclusions on liability, offer enough suspicious activity to warrant exploring a shift in popular ideas as the chief cause of the rise in lawsuits. What emerges is a public changing its mind about the cause of and responsibility for accidental injuries. The new ideas moved the citizens of New York to see their own injuries as consequences of the acts of other people who were often removed by time and space from the site of injury. The ideas also made those remote other people responsible for their acts. The changed thinking entered the legal system via those

2. Hurst, *Growth of American Law*, 11.

bringing suits and those serving on juries. Changes in "blaming" and "claiming"—the mental processes of transforming injuries into lawsuits—propelled more New Yorkers into the city Supreme Court.[3]

The point that fundamental shifts in a society's ideas led to legal change does not get its first airing here. Recent inquiries into legal ideas, rising at the intersection of the "new" histories and the social and critical avenues of legal studies, have taken Hurst's insight about social thinking a step further: Law is not only shaped by, but can only be understood as ideas, as a matter of cognition. Law is now characterized as "embody-[ing] a set of conceptions—about human nature, property, virtue, freedom, representation, necessity, causation and so forth—that was a unique configuration for its time."[4] When the law of one time, embodying one set of conceptions, encountered a populace in another who held a set of ideas "strikingly unlike" its own, legal conflict and change were likely results.[5]

The emerging attention to popular ideas is a logical extension of the social history of the law of recent years. Years of exploration of concrete, material interests embedded in the law have piqued legal historians' interest in the subtle, less tangible aspects of law, especially the relation of ideas to law's social, political, and economic roles.[6] Where traditional intellectual histories of the law looked typically at the thoughts of leading jurists and their contributions to the evolution of rules, cognition and conceptual patterns—consciousness and ideologies of the law—of the larger populace are now attracting scholars.[7]

3. The terms come from Felstiner et al., "Emergence of Disputes."

4. Gordon, "Historicism," 1021.

5. Walter Lippmann spotted such a process behind the "revolt against the judiciary" in the first years of the new century. The cause of the revolt, he found, was that people were "irritated and constrained by a legal system that was developed in a different civilization." Walter Lippmann, *Drift and Mastery* (New York: Mitchell Kennerly, 1914), 157.

6. Abel, "Redirecting Social Studies of Law"; Gordon, "Historicism," 1017–56; Duncan Kennedy, "Toward an Historical Understanding of Legal Consciousness: The Case of Classical Legal Thought in America, 1850–1940," in Steven Spitzer, ed., *Research in Law and Sociology* 3 (1980): 3–24; and John Brigham, Patricia Ewick, Christine Harrington, Sally Merry, Brinkley Messick, Austin Sarat, Susan Silbey, Adelaide Villmoare, and Barbara Yngvesson, "From the Special Issue Editors," *Law and Society Review* 22 (1988): 629–35.

7. Much of the inspiration for the research into the meaning of law comes from anthropologists, who are still battling over the question of where such meaning resides, within the person or without. Clifford Geertz argues that it must be seen as both cognitive and social, as "conceptual structures or systems of ideas." That definition is consonant with this study's pursuit of popular conceptions as ideas personally conceived, not publicly articulated, yet widely shared. Clifford Geertz and Roy G. D'Andrade, "A Colloquy of Culture

Popular understandings of law—"what the public view[ed] as just and . . . perceive[d as] significant injustice in the operation of law"—are acknowledged not only to have existed apart from the ideas of judges and lawyers but to have shaped law's history.[8] Merging a fundamental lesson of recent social history—that America has been a patchwork of different cultures, divided along lines of class, status (professional or expert standing), race and ethnicity, and gender, among others—with the new understanding of law suggests that at any point in the past, multiple sets of conceptions contended to define the law.[9]

A handful of scholars have taken up the challenge of tracking popular ideas of injury law.[10] David Engel has found them at play in an Illinois county, inciting a rise in lawsuits in the late 1970s very similar to New York's of a century before. Sally Engle Merry has chronicled their distinctive nature and effect on legal behavior in current America. R. W. Kostal tells of the power of popular ideas to define a turn-of-the-century Ontario incident as a matter of fault. But he discovered at the same time limits to the power of these ideas to change law stemming from the people of Ontario's concomitant reverence for the legitimacy of legal institutions. Most comprehensively, Lawrence Friedman has assigned changing popular ideas primacy in producing the twentieth-century expansion of liability.[11]

Theorists," in Richard Schweder and Robert LeVine, eds., *Culture Theory: Essays on Mind, Self, and Emotion* (New York: Cambridge University Press, 1984): 1–24.

Legal ideas have taken on new importance as products of the ideologies of particular groups at particular times. Legal historians are looking anew at the ideologies of judges and the legal profession in different eras, asking how their tenets reflected the beliefs of particular segments of society and how they came to prevail over other strains of thought. See Kennedy, "Toward an Historical Understanding"; and Gordon, "Legal Thought and Legal Practice."

8. Abel, "Redirecting Social Studies of the Law," 928–29.

9. Thomas Bender concludes that history has undergone a "reconceptualization . . . that stresses the interplay of various groups." Bender, "Wholes and Parts," 132. Part of the interplay comes in contesting meanings of ideas and events. The study of meaning has altered intellectual history and made it an integral part of sociopolitical history. William Bouwsma, "From the History of Ideas to the History of Meaning," *Journal of Interdisciplinary History* 12 (1981): 279–93; and T. J. Jackson Lears, "The Concept of Cultural Hegemony: Problems and Possibilities," *American Historical Review* 90 (1985): 567–93.

10. "Handful" because as Felstiner, Abel, and Sarat point out, not enough research has been done on ordinary people as active agents in the making of law and in the defining of legal situations. Studies of use of the law have burgeoned, but "studies of public knowledge and opinion about law . . . relegate the public to a largely passive role as receptor of and reactor to law." Felstiner et al., "Emergence of Disputes," 631–54.

11. Engel, "Oven Bird's Song"; Sally Engle Merry, "Everyday Understandings of the Law in Working-Class America," *American Ethnologist* 13 (1986): 253–70; R. W. Kostal,

The detection of distinctive popular conceptions of law in New York at the end of the century is not only sanctioned by intellectual developments in the present, it is warranted by the observations of commentators contemporary to the city's tort explosion. Judges and like-minded bar leaders were well aware that a conception of responsibility for injury counter to their own was coalescing. They saw it as "popular prejudice," a "mob" idea antithetical to "sageness, virtue, and acumen," or as lawyer Eli Hammond deemed it, "the evil of corrupted public sentiment."[12] New York Supreme Court Judge William Hornblower echoed Hammond's sense of sentiment-powered legal decline. The "great objection to our present general term system [trial courts]," Hornblower warned, "is its liability to yield to local sentiment . . . [producing] erroneous decisions in accordance with the popular idea of the demands of justice."[13]

The effort that city Supreme Court judges expended in their instructions to condemn sentiment reflects their agreement with Hammond and Hornblower's notion. They were deeply concerned that the law was not being applied as they believed it should. But was it really sentiment that they observed? Since judges of this era understood the law and their administration of it as scientific,[14] any disagreement with their views of appropriate outcomes, even when decisions were clearly within the bounds of juries' duties, was interpreted as sentiment. Yet if the "sentiment" that they sensed was, as Hornblower defined it, "the popular idea of the demands of justice," clearly the court was encountering something more thoughtful and reasoned than emotional: a conception of cause and responsibility in injuries that ran counter to the judges' own ideas.

"Legal Justice, Social Justice: An Incursion into the Social History of Work-related Accident Law in Ontario, 1860–1886," *Law and History Review* 6 (1988): 1–24; and Friedman, *Total Justice*.

12. This public sentiment, according to Hammond, was "in favor of looting any public or quasi-public treasury in aid of private suffering or private want." Hammond, "Personal Injury Litigation," 328; and "City Judiciary" unattributed, circa 1870, Charles Daly Papers, Box 18, Scrapbook, p. 23, New York Public Library. Lawyer E. P. Prentice concurred with Hammond, asserting that a return to justice could "only come with a change in public opinion": Prentice, "Where Jury Bribing Begins," 312–19.

13. William B. Hornblower, "New York State Bar Association Minutes," *American Lawyer* 1 (1893): 49. H. T. Smith saw the same force still at work twenty years later in work-injury cases: "Juries are naturally sympathetic and do not care for technical defenses, and with the public at large are inclined to take the view that an employee should be compensated when injured no matter what the judge tells them about the law." H. T. Smith, "Liability Investigations and Adjustments," *Liability and Compensation Insurance* (Hartford, Conn.: Insurance Institute of Hartford 1913): 67.

14. See Kennedy, "Toward an Historical Understanding"; and White, *Tort Law in America*.

Proposing the existence of a popular conception of liability is easier than exposing it. One problem is that a popular conception was never clearly articulated. As Hammond critically but perceptively commented, jurors were probably not even conscious that they were applying their "prejudiced standards" to cases; their "state of mind is such that the process works itself."[15]

The same intuitive thinking can be attributed to the injured as they considered suing. There, too, the process "worked itself" without any formal declaration or clarification of principles guiding the decisions. Students of current legal behavior understand suing as inextricable from legal thought: "The causes a person assigns for an injurious experience will be important determinants of the action he or she takes in response to it; those attributions will also presumably affect perception of the experience as injurious."[16]

The act of suing marks the presence of and reflects the shape of mental workings, such as assigning cause and responsibility. If we view the relationship of idea to act in this way, and find all other forces influencing the act to have been relatively constant, the change in frequency of suing in New York must, then, signify changed "perception of experience[s] as injurious" and changed attributions of cause in those injurious experiences.

At the dawn of the new century, then, the New York City court was riven by two conflicting ideas of liability, one embodied in the rules that had prevailed during the last half of the nineteenth century, the other in the increasing number of injury suits. Most of the city's bench, its elite bar, and its business community subscribed to the former vision. It was characterized by close adherence to the principle of assumption of risk, a low threshold for contributory negligence, and the sense, fostered by the judges' reluctance to see cause beyond immediate interaction, that most accidents were inevitable. As Judge Albert Cardozo put it, injury was often "one of those misfortunes to which all human beings are liable, and for which there is no legal responsibility."[17] The failure to understand that, city bar leader Elihu Root told his confreres, was a prominent source of popular dissatisfaction with judges: "Distorted and exaggerated conceptions [are] disseminated by men . . . overexcited by contemplating

15. Hammond, "Personal Injury Litigation," 329.
16. Felstiner et al., "Emergence of Disputes," 640. See also Kritzer, "Political Culture and the 'Propensity to Sue'."
17. *Doran* v. *East River Ferry*.

unhappiness and privation which perhaps no law or administration could prevent."[18] The judges' reluctance to look beyond immediate causes meant, in practice, construing agency narrowly and setting high evidential standards for proving negligence in less directly caused injuries, such as stumbles on sidewalks and in buildings.

The prevailing conception of responsibility in New York rested in tradition, especially in self-sufficient individualism and a distaste for the strife that litigation expressed.[19] The rhetoric of judges and bar opinion leaders in the late nineteenth century reflects this sensibility. Hammond, for example, scourged emerging popular ideas of liability because they lacked respect for "the barriers [to compensation] found in the ancient law and the repugnance of our ancestors."[20] Judge M. Bruce Linn, likewise, saw troubles aplenty in the new view of the law that was ignorant of tradition: "Its [the law's] influence and power is to-day menaced by those who would completely transform it. They have no regard for its history; no reverence of its traditions; no conception of its obligations; and no appreciation for its ideals."[21]

The popular conception of injury law, too, had its roots in the existing law, as well as in popular mores. The essence of the prevailing rules formed the basis of how most New Yorkers who had occasion to thought about injury liability. The stringent injury law of the mid-nineteenth century began to lose authority in the public eye not because the people of New York rejected the law's central tenet—individual responsibility based on fault—but because judicial interpretations of responsibility and causation in the law were increasingly perceived to be at odds with the realities of the period.[22]

18. Elihu Root, *Judicial Decisions and Public Feeling Address as President of the New York Bar Association at the Annual Meeting in New York City, January 19, 1912* (Washington, D.C.: U.S. Government Printing Office, 1912), 5.

19. Samuel Mencher found self-reliant individualism, or "personal responsibility," the dominant philosophy of late nineteenth-century America. It was a central tenet of the traditional conception of responsibility. Mencher, *Poor Law*, 279.

20. Hammond, "Personal Injury Litigation," 328.

21. M. Bruce Linn, *The Lawyer an Officer of the Court: A Lecture Delivered before the Students of the Albany Law School* (Albany: Albany Law School, 1912), 15. Linn was aiming particularly at lawyers, whom he believed were "imposing upon the ignorant and misleading the unwary." Of course, Linn's attribution of conceptual leadership might reflect his own limits in not being able to conceive of the lay populace departing from judicial ideas without some incitement and misguidance.

22. Harry Kalven noticed that popular ideas of liability in the 1950s—evident in "the jury's polite war with the law"—rested similarly in established legal principles. He was

At the same time, legal roots were only one source of thinking about injury liability. Ordinary people saw only so much in legal terms; the rest they saw in more familiar experience-based terms. That was because "the body of the people," as bar leader John Hale noted, "gave but little attention to what was going on in the courts."[23] Sally Engle Merry has discovered that current popular understanding of injury law also draws more upon common sense than upon recognizable legal precepts.[24]

There were those in law who recognized that the law was drifting away from the surrounding society's sense of "realities." The editor of *American Lawyer* warned that the legal profession was in danger of "becom-[ing] the servant of oppression, . . . discredited in popular esteem and discreditable to itself" by "fail[ing] to meet the requirements of the hour." Law professor O. K. McMurray detected the same trend: "A theory of law which regards it as a sort of semi-inspired revelation . . . , which rejects reason and common sense in a blind worship of authority, . . . [was] fail[ing] of respect in our practical and modern world."[25]

The popular conception parted ways with the prevailing legal version of law over the issues of cause and responsibility, as deeper perception of cause turned the ordinary New Yorker from viewing most accidents as fate to seeing them as the consequence of human acts. Understanding of responsibility shifted from holding the "rugged individual" responsible for all that happened to her or him, to assigning responsibility to the creator of dangerous situations.

The tenets of the popular conception developed along the lines of juries' powers in injury suits. The jury, as we have seen, had among its powers the following two: It was the sole judge of facts in a trial, and it interpreted such terms as "reasonable care" and "negligence." As sole determiners of the facts, the jury set the amount of proof necessary to carry a claim. As members of the body that ultimately defined the general duty of care to others, jurors had to decide what standards of behavior and vigilance they would require of the suitors.

---

impressed that juries' "illegal" reasoning often was law in other jurisdictions, "or at least a reform proposal that has articulate spokesmen in the literature." Harry Kalven, "The Jury, the Law, and the Personal Injury Damage Award," *Ohio State Law Journal* 19 (1958), 168–69.

23. "Trial by Jury," unattributed, circa 1870, Charles Daly Papers Box #15, Scrapbook, p. 9, New York Public Library.

24. Merry, "Everyday Understandings of the Law," 257–58.

25. "Where the Remedy Lies," *American Lawyer* 1 (September 1893): 5; O. K. Mc-Murray, "Changing Conceptions of Law and Legal Institutions," *Proceedings of the Sixth Annual Meeting of the California Bar Association* (San Francisco: Recorder Printing Co., 1915), 35.

Defining reasonable care in each case forced juries to think relatively; "reasonable," after all, was declared by the law to be contextual. Judges gave only broad guidelines and emphasized that "everyday" community norms should provide the answers. What constituted reasonable care and what acts or omissions established negligence depended upon applying those norms to particular circumstances. If reasonableness varied from case to case as circumstances varied, then as circumstances altered over time in a patterned way, it was only logical and consonant with judges' instructions that jurors would find different levels of care acceptable. Operating from the nearly unbounded "everyday measures" charge, New York juries set new standards of reasonable care. By requiring more stringent caution of those who created danger, the new standards distributed the duty for preventing accidents differently than judges intended.

As they altered ideas of reasonable care, juries came to assign cause differently. The populace gained an understanding of cause and effect that included a fuller sense of remote causation—that actors not at the site of an event could create the conditions that cause the event—and began to assess the liability of participants temporally and physically removed from accidents. The scope of the search for liability was pushed beyond immediate contact to outlying areas where those who created the conditions that caused injury worked.

Understanding cause to spring from sources remote as well as immediate, New Yorkers brought suit over injuries from commonplace causes that "ordinarily were never noticed hitherto,"[26] and that had previously been considered the random working of fate. In so doing, they defined anew the "inevitable" event as a compensable injury, conceiving it as the cause and responsibility of someone else.

New ideas of reasonable care also worked to reduce the attentiveness expected of the citizen in ordinary circumstances. This was not uniformly the case; New Yorkers maintained some high expectations of their fellows, holding them responsible for adapting their precautionary abilities and practices to new threats. Juries expected pedestrians, for example, to be able to judge the speed of streetcars and trains and act with appropriate caution. But in general, juries moved toward a relaxed definition of reasonable care for those engaged in the routine activities of everyday life, as in the cases of pedestrians injured by flawed roads, sidewalks, and hallways. The relaxed, flexible care standard contrasted markedly with the rigid traditional judicial conception of reasonable care where the

26. Hammond, "Personal Injury Litigation," 332.

individual "never relaxes his vigilance under the influence of monotony, fatigue, or habituation to danger; never permits his attention to be diverted even for a moment from the perils which surround him, never forgets a hazardous condition that he has once observed, and never ceases to be on the alert for new sources of danger."[27] In so conceiving reasonable care contrary to judges' versions, juries raised the threshold for establishing contributory negligence.

The popular idea of liability that emerged at the end of the nineteenth century built upon the deeper understanding of cause and effect and the altered allocation of duties of care to move away from the mid-century's "rugged individualism" principle of personal responsibility. What it moved toward is a matter for debate. Since in New York, when people were injured they increasingly refused to bear the burden themselves, one possibility is that New Yorkers' ideas of responsibility evolved from self-fault to social responsibility regardless of fault. Such a shift would fit historians' current thinking about change in Americans' ideas in this area. Thomas Haskell and Michael Katz have both noted such a move from individualist to interdependent thinking that balanced interests in these years.[28]

It is difficult, though, to fit interdependence—whether in a version that emphasizes its aspects of progressive, natural, and social efficiency (as Haskell's does), or in one that stresses its defensive, palliative aspects, imposed by an elite (as does Katz's)—onto the budding popular liability

27. E. H. Downey, quoted in Roy Lubove, *The Struggle for Social Security* (Cambridge: Harvard University Press, 1968): 47–48.

28. Thomas Haskell, *The Emergence of Professional Social Science: The American Social Science Association and the 19th Century Crisis of Authority* (Champaign: University of Illinois, 1977), 30–32; and Michael Katz, *Poverty and Policy in American History* (New York: Academic Press, 1983), 174–81. Haskell argues that before 1890, social researchers-commentators could only conceive of causation in traditional "habits of proximate causal attribution appropriate to simple societies." Only after 1890 was the narrow vision of cause transcended, cause extended to environmental factors, and a conception of responsibility based on interdependence developed. Katz makes the important point that the "traditional" vision had not been static throughout time, only to be overturned by an intellectual awakening in the 1890–1910 era. It had been manufactured fresh in the 1870s, and marked a deliberate rejection of other alternatives, just as interdependence was purposely chosen in the 1890s to discredit ideas of class conflict. In fairness to the authors, neither intended his explanation of changing ideas of causation to apply to consciousness of injury law; Haskell identifies the change as a factor in altering a general intellectual response to social problems, and Katz uses his to elucidate the evolution of poverty policy in the era. For a study that attributes altered ideas of cause and responsibility with changing injury-law consciousness toward interdependence ("system blame"), see Daniel Polisar and Aaron Wildavsky, "From Individual to System Blame: A Cultural Analysis of Historical Change in the Law of Torts," *Journal of Policy History* 1 (1989): 129–55.

consciousness in New York. The theories of interdependence assume that the shift in causal attribution occurred in the prevailing (legal) conception of responsibility. They assume (despite Katz's insight that the shift was contested) that the shift in causal reasoning was universal, producing one change, and having a uniform effect on consciousness. Yet in New York, judges and bar leaders staunchly opposed the shift in causal thinking. The emerging ideas of cause and responsibility, rather than producing a uniform effect on a universally supported ideology, promoted division in ideas about liability.

Interdependence also supposes motives that were not evident in New York. The motive of balancing interests, associated with interdependence, was foreign to both the prevailing and popular conceptions of law. In New York interest balancing was later proferred by reformers as a radical departure from the idea of fault to solve the problems created by the conflicts in ideas between judges and the general populace.[29]

If New York's injured suit-bringers did not seek compensation out of a concern for their injurers' interests along with their own, or a sense of mutual interest and benefit between injured and injurer, what did propel them into court? Engel's study of a 1970s tort explosion in an Illinois community presents a more plausible alternative: individualism. Instead of assuming that individualism had to be overthrown for the populace to probe the far reaches of cause and responsibility, Engel found that a different sort of individualism from that which had prevailed in the community promoted suing. The traditional individualism of self-help and personal responsibility had kept people from court; an aggressive, rights-oriented individualism directed people to court when injured.[30] In turn-of-the-century New York the new popular consciousness drew upon just such an individualism, infused with social awareness, to force recognition of others' duties and social obligations.

Assertive individualism fits the evidence from New York. First, it explains conflicting conceptions where interdepence could not. Individualism based on an assertion of rights was in direct opposition to individualism based on personal responsibility; interdependence that balanced interests was not. Second, bringing suit was an individual rather

29. See, for example, Eastman, *Work Accidents*, 119–24. Eastman found workers as responsible (causally) as employers for accidental injuries, yet she believed that compensation was in order because of the hardship caused to the injured worker and her or his family. Compensation was extended not because owners were held to have caused the injury but because it met the needs of the parties.

30. Engel, "Oven Bird Song," 551–82.

than collective assertion of rights. Third, an assertive, individualistic consciousness was historically more plausible and legally more operable than interdependence, because the former drew upon systems of thinking and laws already in existence (responsibility based on fault rather than on an even distribution of costs). Instead of rejecting causal responsibility as a factor in the compensation equation (as interdependence would have required), assertive individualism simply reversed it. From viewing injury as one's own responsibility, it was a smaller step to cast that responsibility onto another than it was to discard the concept entirely for the sake of balancing interests.

The shift in popular conception of injury liability toward one that retained the principle of individual fault, but departed from the "self-responsibility" conclusions of the traditional conception, expanded the range of cause and reduced the realm of inevitability. It reflected general intellectual trends in the United States at the time. The larger society showed a widening recognition of individual and corporate social duties and responsibilities that were closely related to considerations of injury.

Contemporaries perceived the expansion of responsibility. New York City reformer Benjamin Parke DeWitt, for example, found it behind much of the urban reform of the period and thought it "indicative of a quickening community consciousness."[31] Historians, too, have noted the change. Samuel Mencher and Walter Trattner, for example, both discovered fundamental shifts in thinking about poverty in these years, which increasingly asserted others' responsibility in ways that closely paralleled the development of popular ideas about injury liability. The mid-nineteenth-century view that individuals' personal deficiencies caused poverty, and that poor people, therefore, were responsible for their own plight, turned completely around. As social and economic conditions beyond the reach of the victim came to the fore as causes of poverty, others in society (e.g., employers and landlords) were deemed responsible.[32] If, as students of the period argue, ideas of responsibility for poverty and a host of other problems were undergoing radical revision, then the changing conception of responsibility for injury can be seen as part and parcel of the shifting mind of the age.

The roots of change to the conception of responsibility that lay in popular mores, common sense, and experience must have been complex,

31. Benjamin Parke DeWitt, *The Progressive Movement* (Seattle: University of Washington, 1968 [1915]), 342.
32. Mencher, *Poor Law,* 275; and Trattner, *From Poor Law to Welfare State.* Hunter's *Poverty* best illustrates the change in thinking.

given the diverse population from which they grew. Immigrants, for example, injected into the process ideas that also differed from the prevailing legal conception of responsibility for accidental injuries. The thinking of this sizable portion of the populace produced many injury suits and formed part of the popular mind.[33]

Initiating an injury suit was an assertion of rights; its increasing occurrence revealed the emergence of a new idea of responsibility. But the use of the court by recent immigrants raises the possibility that the idea of others' responsibility might not have been wholly new to them. Herbert Gutman's insight that immigrants' cultural baggage was packed with expectations about work and community that differed from those prevailing in their new land suggests that the newest New Yorkers had different expectations about responsibility for injuries. Their ideas probably fit neither the fatalistic, self-responsible individualism nor its assertive counterpart. Immigrants arrived in New York possessing views about social relations that emphasized reciprocal obligations between classes. Though not stemming from an ideology of individualism, the idea of others' obligation or responsibility to victims of accidents would have led injured immigrants to the same expectations that rights-assertive individualism did for other New Yorkers. Adapted to their new environs and new processes for redress of grievances, the old idea of social obligations made it very possible (though there is little evidence to confirm this; see note 33) that immigrants became as frequent court users as the rest of the citizenry.[34]

The point is that the popular conception of responsibility likely had many sources and variations. It was not a sharply defined, unified mindset.[35] Since no place in the world had as diverse a population as New York in 1900, uniformity of thought could hardly have prevailed among

33. The evidence is not complete enough to determine whether immigrant New Yorkers sued as frequently as other New Yorkers when injured, because most plaintiffs did not report their nativity in their complaints or testimony. Enough did, though, to safely say that immigrants sued, that they discovered and were able to use the unfamiliar legal system of their new city.

34. See Herbert Gutman, "Work, Culture, and Society in Industrializing America, 1815–1919," in Herbert Gutman, ed., *Work, Culture, and Society in Industrializing America* (New York: Vintage, 1977), 3–78.

35. This warning issues from Lawrence Veysey's admonition that the historian working with social beliefs be careful not to "upgrade inappropriately the degree of coherence to be found in thought, especially when it is popular thought, so as to invest it with the dignity of social thought." Lawrence Veysey, "Intellectual History and the New Social History," in John Higham and Paul Conkin, eds., *New Directions in American Intellectual History* (Baltimore, Md.: Johns Hopkins University Press, 1979): 21.

the city's inhabitants. Even the idea that immigrants harbored one common view grossly homogenizes the huge differences in culture and intellectual background among the city's newest arrivals.

Yet it is obvious that two general, opposing ways of thinking about injuries were clashing in the city Supreme Court; the opposed conceptions may be thought of as clusters of ideas. Strict adherence to all components in the cluster was not necessary to hold the general view of the cluster; people with different arrays of ideas shared the same general view. Each conception had room for the thousands of individual variants that must have developed in the thousands of minds thinking in the same general ways.

Likewise, the generalization that the traditional idea belonged to judges and the business community and that everyone else held the expanded conception of responsibility is a convenience. Many New Yorkers who were neither judge nor businessman retained the traditional, fatalistic idea of responsibility for injury, just as some judges and businessmen shared the new conception of responsibility. More often than not, the rough categorization works, though it crudely delimits the variety of combinations of social, economic, intellectual, and cultural attributes of the individuals who lived in New York City in the period.

Where did the new conception—the new individualism, the larger net of responsibility, and the deeper idea of cause—come from? In Engel's Illinois study, the potent force of social and economic change figured prominently in the arrival of the new conception; industry and migration swept into stable rural "Sanders" County and almost immediately into its courtrooms. New York was in similar, though much larger-scale, social and economic flux in 1900. Could the changes in New York have wrought similar effect on the load of injury cases in the city court?

Industrialization and mechanization certainly contributed their share of cases to the court docket, but they were not the primary agencies of injury in the rise in suits. This observation, however, should not undermine the measure of industrialization's impact on the law. Industrialization influenced the way people thought about such ideas as individuals' responsibilities to others, the indirect consequences of those same individuals' acts, and their ability to control the environment—all critical components of the shifted conception of injury liability.

What aspects of industrialization, its affiliated social and economic changes, and the numerous other changes rattling New York at the time were the most important to this story? Which had the most effect on the decisions of injured people to seek compensation for their injuries?

Owing to its omnipresence in nineteenth-century matters, it would not be a tough task to tie the change in injury law to industrialization in some tenuous way. To avoid a meaningless attribution of change to formless, boundless industrialization, Thomas Haskell's seminal work on the sources of conceptual change in popular thought can help identify what in the character of that social change triggered shifts in the popular use of the courts.[36]

Haskell has proposed that the spread of capitalism fostered the humanitarian revolution of the late eighteenth and early nineteenth centuries by transforming the way people thought. The spread of the market economy nurtured ideological transformation by altering the way people thought about their responsibility to help others (due to their own indirect causal involvement in the problems of others), their ethical disposition toward helping, and their ability to solve problems, and by making the problem (in this case, accidents and injuries) more visible so that not employing available solutions became unconscionable.[37]

With slight modification, this model outlines just what it was about the complex world of turn-of-the-century New York that prompted the rise in court use by the city's injured. A heightening of a moral sense of duty to others, the same sense that moved so many reformers to action in the period, was one contributor to the shift. A widening view of causality was another. Popular interpretation of causality cast a broader net of responsibility as people pushed causal connections further back into the chain of events.

Growth in knowledge of how to prevent the problems of accidents and injuries and confidence in society's ability to do so converged to provide another important part to the puzzle. The solutions contained in this expanding knowledge, the means to prevent injuries, required no more than ordinary care to implement. This was also critical to the evolution of ideas about the law. If the preventive measures had required extraordinary effort, popular thinking as well as New York courts' rules would have exempted injurers from having to employ them.

36. Thomas Haskell, "Capitalism and the Origins of Humanitarian Sensibility, Parts I and II," *American Historical Review* 90 (1985): 339–61, 547–66.

37. Legal scholar Marc Galanter has developed a similar set of elements to explain the recent rise of injury litigation across the United States. Galanter's list of contributing factors includes two items found on Haskell's list (see previous note)—the increase in "social knowledge about causation of injuries and of technologies for preventing them"—and other factors Haskell did not bring up, such as increased interaction with people outside one's own neighborhood where community sanctions were not controlling. Galanter, "Reading the Landscape of Disputes," 69–70.

The period from 1890 to 1910 brought a great surge in society's sense of duty to others. That surge owed in part to a moral regeneration. The moral imperative to help others, evident in the abolition movement and other reforms of mid-nineteenth-century America, gave way by the later decades of the century to the morality of laissez faire, wherein the advancement of society was held to come from individuals' pursuits of their own best interests. The ethical side of laissez faire did not preclude owing duties to others; Haskell argued just the opposite, that the spread of the market economy based on the keeping of promises fostered the emergence of humanitarianism. But the general ethical thrust of laissez-faire thinking, which was that duties explicitly promised should be rigidly honored, had another side: Individuals were less responsible for acts not explicitly contracted, which comprised general duties. This hierarchy of responsibility was complemented by the belief that social intervention, such as assisting others in need, was futile at best and more likely harmful to society.[38]

Laissez-faire ideas did not go unchallenged for long. Two sources, often intertwined, argued for attention to the duties individuals owed to others. The rise of the Social Gospel, a multidenominational religious movement, gave moral imperative for tending to one's duties to others.[39] That nebulous entity progressivism also advanced the ethic of individual responsibility to society by impelling many social reforms, which vividly demonstrated that the ethos of helping others was practical. Progressivism did not have to dominate popular thinking to have an effect. By simply existing and gaining some public currency, it could justify action by those needing compensation.

The next condition Haskell thought necessary to the ascent of humanitarian behavior was that the protohumanitarian feel "causally implicated in the suffering of a stranger."[40] We can take Haskell's idea one step further by applying it to the change in how injured citizens and their fellows serving on juries causally implicated others in the suffering of a person.

38. See, generally, Sidney Fine, *From Laissez-Faire to the Social Welfare State* (Ann Arbor: University of Michigan Press, 1958).

39. The Social Gospel movement was relatively small but had strength beyond its numbers. It united Unitarian, Congregational, and Episcopal churches with many others, including the Catholic church. The Catholic church was showing its social awareness in the period as well, as the Papal Encyclical of 1891 (on the conditions of the working class) illustrated. See Henry May, *Protestant Churches and Industrial America* (New York: Harper, 1967 [1949]), 170–234; and Ronald C. White and C. Howard Hopkins, *The Social Gospel: Religion and Reform in Changing America* (Philadelphia: Temple University Press, 1976).

40. Haskell, "Capitalism," 556.

Both extensions of perception required that the thinker first conceive of causation in a more sophisticated way by comprehending all the factors that gave rise to an event. In doing so, people learned to see cause in acts that were remote from effects. Haskell has asserted that the spread of the market economy fostered this expanded view of cause and effect because it taught people "to attend to the remote consequences of their actions."[41] Whatever the source, once people saw the effects of their own acts upon others at a distance, it was a small step to recognize the link between remote acts and injurious consequences to themselves.

However, it took more than this altered interpretation of the causes of injury to bring the populace to see other people responsible. Another prime mover was that society was gaining the know-how—what Haskell calls "recipe knowledge"—to prevent injury. Injuries that could have been prevented were easier to think of as someone else's responsibility than those viewed as inevitable.

New Yorkers were gaining such knowledge and believing that with its application, potential injurers could prevent injuries. Railroad-safety laws, traffic-safety laws, and the factory safety legislation are substantial proof that New Yorkers thought danger could be controlled. While the first safety laws antedated the movement, the idea that humans had the knowledge and ability to eliminate society's problems was what progressivism was all about.[42] Oppose this way of thinking to "Social Darwinism"; the difference is stark. Social Darwinism proposed that human society advanced only when the "survival of the fittest" principle was applied to contemporary life and individual competition was not interdicted by "unnatural" reforms and benevolence. The fatalism of that thinking was giving way in the mind of the age to a belief in dynamic human agency. Oliver Wendell Holmes's disagreement with his fellow Supreme Court justices in *Lochner* v. *New York* (198 U.S. 45, 1905) captures the change

41. Ibid., 551.
42. The impulse to effect change worked similarly in the case of a related problem, poverty. Riis's *How the Other Half Lives* began a move to attack poverty by looking at its environment. Hunter's *Poverty*, though concluding on a pessimistic note, nevertheless clearly exhibited the belief that poverty was a social problem that could be overcome. Hunter viewed the poor as "victims of our neglect"; poverty, he wrote, as the product of "the wrongful action of social and economic forces, is a preventable thing." Hunter, *Poverty*, 64. The belief that society could do something to remedy the problem manifested in many ways, in such diverse entities as New York's state Committee on Unemployment and a National Children's Bureau, for example. Ultimately, the same sort of public response emerged to address the problem of injuries in the workplace, offering perhaps the best proof that the people of New York believed that injury was no longer to be accepted with a fatalistic resignation.

in belief about human efficacy. Holmes disputed the majority's basing legal decisions on the principles of "Mr. Spenser's *Social Statics*," because it preached that society could not improve upon the "natural" order of things. Holmes thought differently. That the disagreement came in dissent against a decision to void a New York work-safety statute makes it all the more immediate to this story.

So the people of New York decided that they had the ability to change their environment and used their knowledge to prevent injuries. An important part of their new view of human efficacy was a rethinking of the relationship between man and machine. Ideas about machines changed in a way similar to the shift from Social Darwinism to social efficacy. Technological determinism—that the way people used machines was bound up in the machines themselves—gave way to the recognition that people decided how machines were used. As a consequence, the undesirable side effects of machine use, injury foremost, were no longer considered inevitable. They were now seen as products of human acts. If people were determining how machines were being used, they could decide to use them safely to avoid injury. And it was the owners of machines that had effective control of them; they were much better situated than workers, passengers, or pedestrians to direct the safe use of machines.

The extension of responsibility, the basic conceptual change underlying the change in legal behavior, was not a rejection of technological advance or economic development. The people of New York City were not trying to "repeal" industrialization, they were merely trying to reach a workable accord with the change that raged around them. In fact, Haskell's framework makes it appear that industrialization had a role in pushing the populace to the new conception of responsibility. It is ironic, but in increasing people's awareness of their own power over their environs, industrialization made them all the more attentive to its consequences. Industrialization's lesson about people's power over their surroundings carried over into the rest of society. As people came to realize the extent to which they controlled their environment, they no longer accepted that injuries were only of their own making. Thus, the fastest growth in injury suits came from causes that had long existed but were only starting to be considered legally actionable.

The people of New York City had gained the moral disposition, the belief in the power to bring change, and a way to remedy the problem of injuries that would foster new ideas about the responsibility for injury. Last, they asked nothing unreasonable, no special effort or expenditure, to apply the remedy to the problem. That the remedies required only ordinary acts was important. As Haskell postulated: "The relevant techniques [had to be] so familiar that not to use them would stand out as an abnormality, a suspension of expected levels of carefulness."[43] Not only does this ring true in the sociological sense that Haskell proposed it, that this is the way humans think, but it was a condition for assigning liability under New York law. City court judges Brady, Blanchard, and colleagues would have nodded their assent had Haskell presented this principle as the standard of care that governed cases in their courtrooms.

Carefulness is not a historical constant; it was subject to change. No evidence, though, suggests that the exercise of care declined between 1870 and 1910. New tenements were constructed after 1870 to slightly higher standards, the roadway grade was improved, and the sidewalks were installed where none had previously existed. Conditions, reflecting care, were probably not much better, but it is doubtful that they were much worse.

Like the exercise of care, ideas of care could change. And they did; that is the message of this book. What people thought ordinary and reasonable in 1910 would not have been so perceived in 1870. What happened in the interim was that the populace gradually came to expect greater care of their fellow citizens who were doing potentially dangerous things.

That the exercise of care remained constant (or even improved) in these forty years, but the public's expectation for care rose ahead of that exercise, is consistent with the constant incidence of injury over time and accounts for the rise in injury suits amidst the steady numbers of injuries. What is more, there is an explanation for how this elevation of expectation came to pass.

It revolves around changes in health and health care and the perception of injury. Public health work and modern sanitation practices arrived in New York after mid-century. When they did, the mortality rate from disease began to fall. In fact, the reported mortality rates from all causes save one—violence, including accidents—fell off steadily. That made injury, though occurring at a constant level, appear more malignant than ever.

Meanwhile, the populace was attaching greater importance to health.[44] Advances in medicine (germ theory, antisepsis and anesthesia, making

43. Haskell, "Capitalism," 556.
44. Identifying "concern for the physical and mental health of the community" as one of the leading "social values of the American people," historian Ralph Gabriel states, "This value emerged in the latter half of the nineteenth century when scientific advances enlarged the ability of the doctor to cure disease and made preventive medicine possible."

more complex surgery possible) and its professionalization enhanced public belief in the power of medicine.[45] Hospitals were springing up in unprecedented numbers, 130 new ones appearing in Manhattan and Brooklyn between 1885 and 1915. And hospitals were undergoing a transformation in this period from general care refuges for the long-term ill to acute medical care facilities, more like the hospitals we know today.[46] Medicine was believed to be making inroads into the preservation of life and limb. As Robert Wilson has asserted, "The 'revolution of rising expectations' . . . [found] a counterpart in the great anticipations of the American people for medical efficacy."[47]

Ralph Gabriel, *American Values: Continuity and Change (Westport, Conn.: Greenwood Press, 1974)*, 188–90.

45. Rosner, *A Once Charitable Enterprise*, 2–5; and Martin S. Pernick, *A Calculus of Suffering: Pain, Professionalism, and Anesthesia in Nineteenth-Century America* (New York: Columbia University Press, 1985). The words "public belief in the power of medicine" were carefully chosen, because there is a good deal of skepticism among historians about how much of the advance in health was really due to medicine. See Elliott Mishler, "The Health-Care System: Social Contexts and Consequences," in Elliott Mishler, ed., *Social Contexts of Health, Illness, and Patient Care* (New York: Cambridge University Press, 1981), 195–217. The debate is peripheral to the issue here; what mattered was that people thought medicine was saving more lives, whether it was or not.

46. Rosner, *A Once Charitable Enterprise*, 12; and Charles E. Rosenberg, *The Care of Strangers: The Rise of America's Hospital System* (New York: Basic Books, 1987), 142–165. Sociologist Robert Wilson explains that the hospital's historical caretaking role was "joined by the elegance of therapeutic technique that [made] the institution not just a comforter of life, but a saver and giver of life." Robert Wilson, *The Sociology of Health* (New York: Random House, 1970), 49. Some injured New Yorkers experienced neither elegant therapy nor comfort in their hospital stays. Ursula Banks, a New York City teacher injured in her classroom, left the hospital after "somebody got into the hospital, unobserved by the door attendants, and went from room to room and examined several patients there; [I] was one of them." *Banks v. Board of Education of the City of New York et al.*

Claude Warren spent four weeks in Bellevue, the City Hospital, before he finally left disgusted and still totally disabled. "I was dissatisfied there," he related, "They were doing nothing for me and the food was not just as I was used to." *Warren v. Post and McCord.* Warren might have been lucky to escape when he did. Bernard Ford, a meat-packer, broke his wrist and had it treated at Roosevelt Hospital. He returned twice in the week that followed, complaining that it was not right. Finally he was sent to Bellevue, where he was operated upon the next day. This did not prove successful, as two weeks later doctors took the arm off above the elbow. *Bernard Ford v. Joseph Moses et al.*, 1910 Number F271, N.Y.C. Supreme Court. Bellevue was not held in the highest estimation by the people of the city, it appears. Ironworker Charles Schwartz wound up in New York Hospital after being taken to Roosevelt Hospital and turned away for lack of room. New York Hospital suggested an alternative to their own beds, and the entry clerk recorded Schwartz's response: "He would not go to Bellevue." *Schwartz v. Onward Construction.*

47. Wilson, *Sociology of Health*, 51.

At the same time, injuries continued unabated. The same level of care continued to produce the same number of accidents, but that was no longer good enough. In an age when other disabling causes were in remission, the "anticipations for medical efficacy" and the belief in human agency produced a corollary expectation: that health be preserved and remaining threats to health be reduced by exercising greater preventive care.

If changed thinking of ordinary New Yorkers was the motive force behind the increase in suing, it was not the whole explanation. A necessary complement to the conceptual change was the opportunity afforded by the institutional legal context in which the change occurred.[48] That the new ideas took the form of lawsuits says something about the opportunity and authority that the existing legal process held in the perceptions of New York's people. No matter how dramatic a shift in ideas about cause of and responsibility for accidents, if the legal process had been seen as hopelessly thrown over to the interests of a few, as not dispensing justice in some degree, there would have been no increase in lawsuits. The conceptual change might still have wrought legal change but via a different route, such as legislative campaign or direct popular action rather than lawsuits.

Though unchanging in its general prospect, the legal process carried characteristics that nurtured the new, changed thinking. Residual doctrinal conflicts in the law between principles of strict liability and those of negligence legitimized conflict between the currently reigning and competing visions of liability, especially in extending responsibility as the popular conception argued. The proliferation of ambiguous precedent gave injured New Yorkers reason to think that accidents from a variety of origins might produce legally enforceable claims.[49] And in the jury, those believing in more extensive liability saw their institutional agent. Assuming their neighbors-jurors thought about liability as they did, the injured claimants drew encouragement from the jury's place in the process.

48. Willard Hurst suggested that this would be the case; if ideas were one aspect of the social environment in which law lived, institutions were the other. The two "obviously are inseperable aspects of . . . history." Hurst, *Growth of American Law*, 11. On developments in public responsibility at the end of the century see William Brock, *Investigation and Responsibility: Public Responsibility in the United States, 1865–1900* (New York: Cambridge University Press, 1984).

49. As O. K. McMurray put it, "The very multiplication of authority tends to impair to some extent its force." McMurray, "Changing Conceptions," 40.

The opportunity for inconsistency, for deviance from the prevailing judicial vision, drew the development of the popular conception into and through the courtroom. This irregularity, a failing of the system in the eyes of the legal fraternity, contributed to the legitimacy of the process in popular thinking. It allowed conceptual change to sneak in so surreptitiously as to not trigger immediate detection and eradication. It allowed carriers of the challenging conception to believe their ideas of law the sole operative, universally held ones and to see the courts, therefore, as legitimate administrators of the law.

Two tendencies of the times bolstered this popular legitimization: the scientific reasoning norm prevalent in legal circles and the absence of formal articulation of ordinary New Yorkers' legal ideas. The former meant that lawyers and judges who wrote and spoke of injury law discussed it as timeless, scientific, yet commonsensical, principles. The holders of the popular conception interpreted those terms as affirming their "sole, universal" law as easily as did the bearers of the traditional conception. The lack of a publicly declared challenge to the popular ideas of liability let people of two very different visions continue to enter the courtroom under the illusion that everyone else there shared their vision.

Beyond its immediate effects on injury law and the administration of justice, scholars have detected in changed popular conception and behavior the working of larger social and political forces. The description of change outlined above suggests, for one, the subtle political process of hegemony at work.

A hegemonic vision of New York's injury-liability developments would argue that the powerful elite's vision of law reigned, prevailing over popular expectations that were moving in a contrary direction. Elite law dominated, according to the theory, not through forceful repression of the challenging conception but by successful co-optation of dissent. The contest was played out in a process and institutions where elite authority ruled. Hegemony theory asserts that by entry into such a forum, the challengers conceded tacit support for elite law; outcomes contrary to their interest, foreordained, were legitimized by their participation.[50]

Historians have detected such hegemonic legal development sustaining accident law in other locales of similar circumstances.[51] But hegemony misses what was happening in turn-of-the-century New York, not accurately capturing either the process of legal development or the relative

---

50. For a concise treatment of hegemony, see Lears, "Concept of Cultural Hegemony."
51. See, for example, Kostal, "Legal Justice, Social Justice."

effectiveness of the different participants. While injured New Yorkers operated within a system bound by institutions and rules, they did not acquiesce to those bounds. Instead, they pushed rules and innovated practice constantly, case by case. On the other side of the courtroom, the astute manipulation of the situation that co-optation connotes expects more power and ability of the defenders of the dominant conception than they held. If we read the data from the increased suits/declining success paradox in a different way, we see that in the midst of falling success *rates*, more injured people than ever were gaining some compensation from the court. That certainly was not the intention of the proponents of the traditional restricted responsibility, as evidenced by their lamentations when they discovered the trend. Rather than leading the trend, they were apparently slow to detect the trend's emergence. The judges' response to the emergence, once discovered, further belies co-optation and astute manipulation. On the one hand, they threw out of court as many cases as they could; on the other, they were largely ineffective in preventing awards in many sorts of cases previously uncompensated.

Other scholars suggest that a situation like New York's rise of lawsuits represents, at most, a conservative response to social problems. Marc Galanter has argued as much about 1980s tort-litigation trends. Counter to the litany of explosion theorists who argue that the rise of litigation reflects the disintegration of social institutions, Galanter asserts that the injured's resort to courts was essentially conservative, because it recognized the legitimacy of the existing regime of law and because it submitted almost fatalistically to a process full of adverse rules, arbitrary decision makers, and chance. By implication, suing was also conservative because lawsuits were individual rather than collective acts and aimed only indirectly at rules change, if at all, rather than directly pursing changes in rules.[52]

"Conservative" might accurately label the location of suing on the spectrum of policy strategies in late twentieth-century America, but the present case points out that such an interpretation will not generalize across time and place. To apply the idea to New York circa 1900 would misread the historical situation in at least two important ways. First, it implies that injured New Yorkers had other alternatives available to achieve the same goals, even if their complex goals are reduced to two— recompense and justice. A survey of the field in 1890–1910 reveals that the times may have held great potential for radical social change and that

---

52. Galanter, "Reading the Landscape of Disputes."

people employed a wide array of tactics to change policy in the era—
organized public protest, systematic studies and "muckraking" exposés
of problems, accelerated private and legislative activism, collective self-
help efforts, direct policy-making via the initiative and referendum, and
direct action in strikes, boycotts, and syndicalism. But none of these approaches promised assistance directly on both goals of the individual injury victims.

Second, conservatism suggests that use of a public institution carries
one unvarying meaning through time, rather than having its significance
constantly reconstructed as its established roles and practices struggle
with new demands. If one is to define conservatism by contemporaries'
standards, initiating suit in 1900s New York fell decidedly outside the
definition's bounds. Historians have identified the maintenance of social
order first and pursuit of a more organized, efficient society second as
conservatives' chief goals in the era.[53] Lawsuits, messily erratic and unpredictable, disrupted the organizational impulse of the age. "We are too
far advanced in everything else," the *New York Times* warned, "to continue to leave such important matters to haphazard juries."[54] Moreover,
scads of small battles for individual right and recompense undermined efficiency by increasing public costs of delivering justice. Worst of all from
a conservative perspective, injury suits heightened community contentiousness rather than promote mutual interests and preserve social order.
These by-products of lawsuits, unpopular in most times, were especially
so to the conservative mind of 1900.

Compared, alternatively, to New Yorkers' normal response to injury in
the decades immediately preceding the rise of litigation (that is, not suing) suing appears anything but conservative; it was far more assertive of
rights than "lumping it" or stoically bearing the costs of injury. The same
can be said of suing compared to the policy adopted to replace it in the
most litigious fields over the following decades: no-fault compensation
(as in workers' compensation and, later, no-fault auto insurance).

If a manifestation of neither hegemony nor conservatism, can the
ideas-driven rise in injury suits be read as something more progressive?

53. See Arnold Paul, *The Conservative Crisis and the Rule of Law* (Ithaca, N.Y.: Cor-
nell University Press, 1960); Robert Wiebe, *The Search for Order, 1877–1920* (New York:
Hill and Wang, 1967); Thomas Bender, *Toward an Urban Vision: Ideas and Institutions in
Nineteenth-Century America* (Lexington: University Press of Kentucky, 1975); and Alan
Trachtenberg, *The Incorporation of America: Culture and Society in the Gilded Age* (New
York: Hill and Wang, 1982).
54. "What is the Value of Human Life?" *New York Times,* 1 July 1906, part 3, p. 6.

Social theorist Emile Durkheim reasoned that it should. He argued that suing registered one's solidarity with society; by submitting personal interests to resolution by community norms, one relinquished one's parochial vision in favor of a larger, unifying vision. After studying Boston's use of its courts in the same era as the present study, Robert Silverman reached the same conclusion. Behind a pattern of litigation in Boston similar to the one presented here, Silverman discerned a unifying force of acculturation. Participation in the legal process, he posited, left a diverse populace with "homogenized . . . notions of law, if not of justice." Silverman did not spell out the political consequences of his homogeneity, but he implies that contrary to hegemony, an apolitical, mutually beneficial consensus underlay and was furthered by it. This interpretation has gained the support of William Nelson, who has extended its coverage somewhat beyond late nineteenth-century Boston; he believes that it operated across the whole course of the nation's history. As Nelson boldly asserts, "Law unified American society."[55]

The evidence from the New York court system, though, renders this thesis suspect. What homogenized notion of justice did the injured, suing worker share with the judge who dismissed his suit? The diverging conceptions of liability outlined here could not have done much to promote social unification.

On the contrary, it is just as likely that exposure to law divided rather than unified New York society in this era. In day-to-day life remote from contact with the legal process, New Yorkers were forming the ideas that would convince them to sue if injury were suddenly to befall them. Only injury suit or jury service—contact with the legal process—mobilized latent ideas and forced confrontation with opposing ideas. Before contact with the law, an illusion of unity could reign; awareness that one's conception of law might conflict with prevailing visions occurred only after meeting the law.

Declarations to this effect by jurors or litigants rarely appeared in the historical record, but when they did, they powerfully affirm that law

55. Emile Durkheim, *The Division of Labor in Society* (New York: Free Press, 1964 [1893], 68–69; Silverman, *Law and Urban Growth*, 146; William Nelson, in William Nelson and John Phillip Reid, *The Literature of American Legal History* (New York: Oceana, 1985), 294. For a good overview of the interpretations of changes in courts' work, see Samuel Krislov, "Theoretical Perspectives on Case Load Studies: A Critique and a Beginning," in Keith Boyum and Lynn Mather, eds., *Empirical Theories about Courts* (New York: Longman, 1983): 161–87.

divided as readily as it unified.[56] They are supported by the more abundant testimony to conflict from the other side of the courtroom. As already noted, judges and leading lawyers reported with increasing frequency that their meetings with popular ideas of liability were not unifying but disconcerting beyond simple disappointment at the discovery of conflict. The tone of the testimony reveals that legal rifts reflected, and probably aggravated, fundamental distrust of those who held opposing legal ideas. Instead of seeing reasonable differences and honorable intentions behind the actions of others, those of each vision saw adherents to the opposing one as hypocritical, self-seeking, and corrupt.

Debate over the unifying/divisive tendencies reflected and affected by the law points out that while developments in the larger society shaped the work of the law, effect moved in the other direction as well. Just as social change remade law, changes in the working of the law shaped society. This reciprocity of effect is hardly surprising. If society is understood as a collection of individuals, clustered in communities with unique subcultures, who meet as a society in their public institutions, changes in one institution is going to change the life not only of the individual but of the community and the society. Rising use of the legal process to gain compensation for injuries was such an institutional change. Resorting to the legal process had consequences for those who used it, and the outcomes of that use had effects on the lives of all New Yorkers.

More than semantic pedantry, then, prompts this look at the interpretive possibilities of the rise in injury suits. At root, the review of the prospects for the story's larger meaning raises the issue of the significance of individuals' acts in shaping the course of law and social policy, in other historical settings as well as in turn-of-the-century New York.

Prospects for learning more about injury litigation through comparison with studies of other communities seems promising. David Engel's research hints at the promise. In discovering how important change in a late twentieth-century Illinois community's pattern of thinking was to the course of the community's law use and *de facto* policy, Engel's work suggests broad temporal and geographic applicability of the ideas presented here. On the other hand, projects studying three other locales are revealing limits to that applicability. Popular conceptual shift did not drive turn-of-the-century injury-law developments in California, Colorado, and

---

56. An example of such public declaration was the letter to the editor by an angry coroners' jury whose desire to censure the landlords of a deadly (repeatedly) building was overridden in the coroner's report. "Protest of a Coroner's Jury," *New York Times*, 9 September 1867, p. 2.

West Virginia counties; in fact, none reported jumps in litigation comparable to New York's in the period.[57]

Adding Robert Silverman's study of Boston and Wayne McIntosh's of St. Louis to the comparison suggests that the extent of urbanization of an area affected its residents' legal behavior, at least in the years around 1900. Both studies found their city's courts in the throes of an injury-suit rise suspiciously similar to New York's.[58] That the sources of "suitable" accidents differed in Boston and New York makes the comparison all the more intriguing.[59] It appears to support the broad explanation of conceptual change I have tendered here; despite sharing types of danger, the two cities had in common only the pattern of extending liability to accidents not previously the stuff of lawsuits.[60]

To get a fuller sense of how and why use of the law has changed, the present research on fundamental change in patterns of suing needs to be complemented by a closer look at short-term movements in injury suits. Through year-by-year sampling, Frank Munger discovered that while injury litigation in West Virginia did not show an upward trend, it did fluctuate across time. Wayne McIntosh and Cynthia Colella noted the same sort of fluctuations operating concurrently with St. Louis's long-term rise in injury suits. This reinforces the point that the changed conceptions of ordinary people alone did not determine a pattern of court use like New York's; changes (and stabilities) in context—Munger looks at shifts in economic conditions and legal power, McIntosh at "severe environmental disturbances"—set the pace and degree to which a changing popular conception would be acted upon in court.[61]

Shifts in suing over injury shaped, in turn, policy-making outside the courtroom. The subject of injury and the distribution of its costs were not publicly debated in 1870 or in 1890. Only the increased use of the courts identified the issue as one for debating during the first decade of the new century. The rise in injury lawsuits came at a time when the traditional economic uses of the courts for resolving debt and contract disputes were

57. Engel, "Oven Bird Song"; Friedman, "Civil Wrongs," Friedman and Russell, "More Civil Wrongs," [Alameda Co., California]; Reichman et al., "Social Construction of Duty" [Denver, Colorado]; and Munger, "Social Change and Tort Litigation."

58. Silverman, *Law and Urban Growth*, 99–121; McIntosh, "A State Court's Clientele"; and McIntosh, *Appeal of Civil Law*.

59. The St. Louis study does not report causes of tort suits.

60. See Silverman, *Law and Urban Growth*, table 20, 106.

61. Munger, "Social Change and Tort Litigation"; Wayne McIntosh and Cynthia Colella, "The Social Foundations of Litigation," paper presented at the 1988 Annual Meeting of the Law and Society Association, Vail, Colorado.

declining, making the rise all the more evident. In an era that prized efficiency, the legal elite, businessmen, and even social reformers now considered individual adjudication of problems inefficient in terms of time, money, and predictability. Further, because these most vocal segments of society now considered individual adjudication of problems inefficient in these terms and held it contentious and counter to the harmony of interests that they sought for society, the very visible rise in lawsuits spurred the "discovery" of accidental injury as a public problem.[62]

The opening of injury policy to public debate was not achieved by reformers, nor was it first brought to public light by muckraking investigative journalists. It came only after thousands of injured people decided that they would not shoulder the burden of their injuries alone. The cumulative impact of these individual decisions was to force the issue of injury law and compensation into public consciousness. Attention came because the changes in the number of cases before the courts were so rapid and evident and because the incremental change in the working of the law in these cases was seen simultaneously as too much by one part of society and too little by another.

Because the change came slowly, sporadically, and not always in a straight line toward an agreed upon goal, the period before public debate is often considered one of "drift." Analysis of the drift of injury policy in New York shows that the term masks an elaborate process of policy definition and belies the extent of social engagement in the issue. Because legal policy was ostensibly settled and the challenges to that settlement did not manifest as a collective action, change remained invisible. Yet challenges were afoot, initiated by individuals and individual decisions. The tectonics of social force, the sum of these individual acts, dramatically reshaped the topography of the field.

The challenge to policy by individuals' lawsuits was augmented by juries' decisions. Contemporaries recognized—and many loathed—the power of the jury. The elite bar especially excoriated the institution for its alleged role in fomenting excessive litigiousness and for habitually awarding verdicts to injured parties "contrary to the law." But even its critics were unwilling to dispose entirely of the jury. Much of the jury's support from the legal fraternity was based on its symbolic value and its perceived contribution to legitimizing the legal process among the larger populace. But it also drew support for its traditional role of constantly infusing the community's norms back into the law. Through this time-honored role ju-

62. See Friedman and Ladinsky, "Social Change and the Law of Industrial Accidents."

ries challenged policy during the period of apparent drift, by injecting an alternative, popular conception of responsibility for accidental injury into the legal process.

Transcending the purview of injury law, the popular assertion of this alternative conception bears meaning beyond its effect on legal behavior, its stimulus to social policy change, and its exceptions to our current understanding of how law has developed (specifically, to the hegemony, conservatism, and unifying theses). Its most fundamental historical significance was in its challenge to the entire direction of nineteenth-century law, to what Hurst identified as "the release of individual creative energy" to foster economic expansion.[63] In extending cause and responsibility, bearers of the new conception transformed previously private events into public ones and asserted the public duties attendant upon those engaged in acts in public areas. By this new fundamental belief, individuals, even in the course of their private ventures, owed general responsibilities to their fellow citizens. When people increased the level of danger in society, they should expect to be held responsible for injurious results.[64]

The rhetoric of late nineteenth-century judges promoted the idea that the law rested on timeless principles, remote from vacillating, ephemeral, and self-interested social norms. But the law was deeply rooted in temporal values, ever changing, even if its practitioners could not so conceive it. The events in the New York City Supreme Court show the importance of asking whose values were shaping the law. If the rights- and duty-assertive content of the popular conception was important for the wholesale redirection of the law it would soon sponsor, the agency of that redirection was just as significant. As a society we have long believed, as Simeon Baldwin assured an audience of lawyers in 1903, that "it is the lawyer to whom all men look to tell them of those duties to each other which society demands and enforces."[65] That was decidedly not the case

---

63. J. Willard Hurst, *Law and the Conditions of Freedom in the Nineteenth-Century United States* (Madison: University of Wisconsin Press, 1956), 6.

64. Gordon ("Historicism," 1055) has suggested that exploring active elements of alternative legal traditions constitutes one of the strengths of legal history. It might plausibly be argued, for example, that the reassertion of social responsibilities in the present case represents an activation or persistence of latent republican, civic humanist conceptions among the populace against those supported by prevailing liberalism.

65. Simeon Baldwin, *A Lecture in Legal Ethics Delivered Before the Students of the Law Department of Union University* (Albany: Albany Law School, 1903), 32. Bar leader Elihu Root, astute in his recognition of conditions contributing to conflict between "judicial decisions and public feeling," was as errant as Baldwin in attributing agency for

in New York by 1910. Instead, ordinary people, making demands of the law independent of and often contrary to what lawyers and judges were telling them, set in motion the fundamental change that would so alter the course of American legal development in the century to follow.

---

legal change to the "new conditions" themselves. By doing so, Root implied that change moved itself, inevitably, thus missing the importance of shift in human understanding and of the context that both enabled it to occur and affect as it did. "Judicial Decisions and Public Feeling," 4.

BIBLIOGRAPHY

INJURY SUITS AND INJURY DATA

Dublin, Louis I. *Causes of Death by Occupation; Occupational Mortality Experience of the Metropolitan Life Insurance Company, Industrial Department, 1911–1913, U.S. Bureau of Labor Statistics, Bulletin no. 207.* Washington, D.C.: U.S. Government Printing Office, 1917.

Hoffman, Frederick. *Industrial Accident Statistics, U.S. Bureau of Labor Statistics, Bulletin no. 157.* Washington, D.C.: U.S. Government Printing Office, 1915.

Metropolitan Board of Health (New York). *Code of Health Ordinances and Rules and Sanitary Regulations.* New York: John W. Amerman, 1866.

New York City. Department of Health. *Annual Reports of the Board of Health of the Health Department of the City of New York,* 1870; 1871–72; 1890; 1910–11. New York: David Gildersleeve, 1872; Martin B. Brown, 1890; J. W. Pratt, 1912.

New York State. Appellate Division of the Supreme Court. *Report of the Investigation Ordered by the Appellate Division of the Supreme Court in and for the First Judicial Department, by Order Dated February 7, 1928, upon the Petition of The Association of the Bar of the City of New York, New York County Lawyers Association and Bronx County Bar Association for an Inquiry by the Court into Certain Abuses and Illegal and Improper Practices Alleged in the Petition.* New York: M. B. Brown, 1928.

New York State. Board of Charities. *Charity Legislation in New York, 1609 to 1900,* volume III of the *Annual Report for 1903.* Albany: Oliver Quayle, 1904.

New York State. Bureau of Labor Statistics. *Seventeenth Annual Report of the Bureau of Labor Statistics of the State of New York.* Albany: J. B. Lyon, 1900.

New York State. Department of Labor. *Statistics of Industrial Accidents in 1912 and 1913, Bulletin no. 68.* Albany: J. B. Lyon, 1914.

New York State Senate. *Report to the Legislature of the State of New York by the Commission to Inquire into Employers' Liability and Other Matters.* Albany: J. B. Lyon, 1910.

Supreme Court for the County and City of New York (First Division). Judgments (1870, 1890, 1910). Archives of the County Clerk and Clerk of the Supreme Court, New York.

United States Bureau of the Census. *Historical Statistics of the United States, Colonial Times to 1970.* Washington, D.C.: U.S. Government Printing Office, 1975.

United States Census Office. *Report on Manufacturing Industries in the U.S. at the Eleventh Census: 1890, Part II.* Washington, D.C.: U.S. Government Printing Office, 1895.

United States Census Office. *Report on the Social Statistics of Cities, Part I.* Washington, D.C.: U.S. Government Printing Office, 1886.

Weber, Adna. "The Compensation of Accidental Injuries to Workmen." *Seventeenth Annual Report of the Bureau of Labor Statistics of the State of New York, Part II.* Albany: J. B. Lyon, 1900.

CONTEMPORARY OBSERVATIONS

Alger, George W. "The Courts and Factory Legislation." *American Sociological Review* 6 (1900–1901): 406.

——. "The Present Situation of Employer's Liability." *Charities and the Commons* 17 (1907): 826–28.

——. "Reminiscences of George W. Alger." Columbia University Oral History Collection, New York. 1951–52.

American Lawyer, 1893–1908.

Baldwin, Simeon. *A Lecture in Legal Ethics Delivered before the Students of the Law Department of Union University.* Albany: Albany Law School, 1903.

Chapin, Robert Coit. *The Standard of Living among Workingmen's Families in New York City.* New York: Russell Sage, 1909.

Clark, Lindley. "The Legal Liability of Employers for Injuries to Their Employees." *U.S. Bureau of Labor, Bulletin no. 74* (1908), 1–120.

Daly, Charles. Papers. Manuscripts and Special Collections, New York Public Library.

Deville, Kenneth A. *Medical Malpractice in Nineteenth-Century America.* New York: New York University Press, 1990.

DeWitt, Benjamin Parke. *The Progressive Movement.* Seattle: University of Washington, 1968 (1915).

Donovan, John Wesley. *Modern Jury Trials and Advocates.* Albany: Banks and Brothers, 1881.

Eastman, Crystal. *Work Accidents and the Law.* New York: Charities Publication Committee, 1910.

"The Evolution of the Law Office." *American Lawyer* 2(1894): 78.

"Experiences of a Streetcar Conductor" [anonymous conductor, interview published in the *Independent* LV (August 13, 1903)]. In David Katzman and

William Tuttle, eds. *Plain Folk*. Urbana: University of Illinois Press, 1982, 14–21.

Frankel, Lee R. "The Cost of Living in New York." *Charities and the Commons* 19 (1907–8): 1049–54.

"A Glimpse at Some of Our Charities." *Harper's New Monthly Magazine* 56 (1877): 441–50.

Goodyear, Caroline. "The Minimum Practicable Cost of an Adequate Standard of Living in New York City." *Charities and the Commons 17* (1906–7): 315–20.

Greene, Francis V. "An Account of Some Observations of Street Traffic." *Transactions of the American Society of Civil Engineers* 15 (1886): 123–138.

Hammond, Eli. "Personal Injury Litigation." *Yale Law Journal* 6 (1896–97): 321–32.

Hard, William. "The Law of the Killed and Wounded." *Everybody's Magazine* 19 (September 1908): 361–71.

Hawes, Gilbert. "Letter to the Editor," *American Lawyer* 1 (October 1893): 7.

———. "Winnow the Bar." *American Lawyer* 1 (April 1893): 5.

Hirschl, Andrew. "Personal Injury Actions: The Plaintiff's Standpoint." *Illinois Law Review* 1 (1905–6), 17.

Holmes, Oliver Wendell. "Law in Science and Science in Law." *Harvard Law Review* 12 (1899): 443–57.

Hornblower, William B. "New York State Bar Association Minutes." *American Lawyer* 1 (1893): 49.

"Hospital Life in New York." *Harper's New Monthly Magazine* 57 (1878): 171–90.

Hubbard, Thomas. *Legal Ethics: Lectures Delivered Before the Students of the Law Department of Union University*. Albany: Albany Law School, 1903.

Hunter, Robert. *Poverty*. New York: Harper, 1965 (1904).

"Jurors and Trials by Jury." *American Lawyer* 4 (1896): 200.

Landon, Judson. *Legal Ethics: The Hubbard Course on Legal Ethics*. Albany: Albany Law School, 1905.

Lewis, Loran. "The Law of Icy Sidewalks in New York State." *Yale Law Journal* 6 (1896–97): 258–62.

Linn, M. Bruce. *The Lawyer an Officer of the Court: A Lecture Delivered before the Students of the Albany Law School*. Albany: Albany Law School, 1912.

Lippmann, Walter. *Drift and Mastery*. New York: Mitchell Kennerly, 1914.

Lowell, Josephine Shaw. *Public Relief and Private Charity*. New York: Putnam's, 1884.

McLean, Francis. "Industrial Accidents and Dependency in New York State." *Charities and the Commons* 19 (1907–8): 1203–12.

McMurray, Orrin Kip. "Changing Conceptions of Law and Legal Institutions." *Proceedings of the Sixth Annual Meeting of the California Bar Association*. San Francisco: Recorder Printing Co., 1915.

New York Law Journal. 1887–91.

New York State Bar Association. "Report of the Committee on Contingent Fees." *Proceedings of the Thirty-First Annual Meeting*. Albany: Argus Company, 1908.

Page, Samuel. "Personal Injury Actions: The Defendant's Standpoint." *Illinois Law Review* 1 (1906–7): 27–38.

Pitcher, James. "Accidents and Accident Insurance." *Forum* 12 (September, 1891): 131–37.

Prentice, E. Parmalee. "Where Jury Bribing Begins." *Arena* 22 (September 1899): 313–14.

Richardson, Clifford. "Street Traffic in New York City, 1885 and 1904." *Transactions of the American Society of Civil Engineers* 57 (1906): 181–90.

Riis, Jacob. *How the Other Half Lives.* New York: Hill and Wang, 1957 (1890).

Root, Elihu. *Judicial Decisions and Public Feeling: Address as President of the New York Bar Association at the Annual Meeting in New York City on January 19, 1912.* Washington, D.C.: U.S. Government Printing Office, 1912.

Schmitt, J. P. *History of the Legal Aid Society of New York, 1876–1912.* New York: Legal Aid Society, 1912.

Scott, Henry W. *The Courts of the State of New York; Their History, Development and Jurisdiction Embracing a Complete History of All the Courts. . . .* New York: Wilson, 1909.

Smith, Frank C. "Practice and Procedure." *American Lawyer* 3 (1895): 17–18.

Smith, H. T. "Liability Investigations and Adjustments," in *Liability and Compensation Insurance.* Hartford, Conn.: Insurance Institute of Hartford, 1913.

Smith, Reginald Heber. *Justice and the Poor.* New York: Carnegie Foundation for the Advancement of Teaching, 1919.

Taft, Henry. *Legal Miscellanies: Six Decades of Changes and Progress.* New York: Macmillan, 1941.

Vann, Irving G. *Contingent Fees: An Address in the Hubbard Course on Legal Ethics.* Albany: Albany Law School, 1905.

"Where the Remedy Lies." *American Lawyer* 1 (1893): 5.

White, William J. "The Facts Considered." *Charities and the Commons* 17 (1906–7): 321.

SECONDARY SOURCES

Abel, Richard. "Redirecting Social Studies of Law." *Law and Society Review* 14 (1980): 805–29.

Asher, Robert. "Failure and Fulfillment: Agitation for Employers' Liability Legislation and the Origins of Workmen's Compensation in New York State, 1876–1910." *Labor History* 24 (1983): 198–222.

Auerbach, Jerold. *Unequal Justice: Lawyers and Social Change in Modern America.* New York: Oxford University Press, 1976.

Bakke, E. Wight. *The Unemployed Worker: A Study in the Task of Making a Living without a Job.* New Haven, Conn.: Yale University Press, 1940.

Bender, Thomas. *Community and Social Change in America.* New Brunswick, N.J.: Rutgers University Press, 1978.

——— . *Toward an Urban Vision: Ideas and Institutions in Nineteenth-Century America.* Lexington: University Press of Kentucky, 1975.

———. "Wholes and Parts: The Need for Synthesis in American History." *Journal of American History* 73 (1986): 120–36.

Berger, Peter, and Thomas Luckman, *The Social Construction of Reality*. New York: Anchor, 1967.

Blackmar, Elizabeth. *Manhattan for Rent, 1785–1850*. Ithaca, N.Y.: Cornell University Press, 1989.

Bloch, Marc. *The Historian's Craft*. New York: Vintage, 1971 (1946).

Bloomfield, Maxwell. *American Lawyers in a Changing Society, 1776–1876*. Cambridge: Harvard University Press, 1976.

———. "Lawyers and Public Criticism: Challenge and Response in Nineteenth-Century America." *American Journal of Legal History* 15 (1971), 269–77.

Bouwsma, William. "From the History of Ideas to the History of Meaning." *Journal of Interdisciplinary History* 12 (1981): 279–93.

Branscombe, Martha. *The Courts and the Poor Laws in New York State, 1784–1929*. Chicago: University of Chicago Press, 1943.

Brigham, John, Patricia Ewick, Christine Harrington, Sally Merry, Brinkley Messick, Austin Sarat, Susan Silbey, Adelaide Villmoare, and Barbara Yngvesson. "From the Special Review Editors." *Law and Society Review* 22 (1988): 629–35.

Brock, William. *Investigation and Responsibility: Public Responsibility in the United States, 1865–1900*. New York: Cambridge University Press, 1984.

Brody, David. Introduction to Roy Lubove, "The Tenement Comes of Age." In David Brody, ed., *Essays on the Age of Enterprise, 1870–1900*, pp. 122–23. Hinsdale, Ill.: Dryden Press, 1974.

Carman, Harry. *The Street Surface Railway Franchises of New York City*. New York: Columbia University Press, 1919.

Chambers, Clarke. "Toward a Redefinition of Welfare History." *Journal of American History* 73 (1986), 407–33.

Chandler, Alfred. *The Visible Hand*. Cambridge: Harvard University Press, 1977.

Cheape, Charles. *Moving the Masses: Urban Public Transit in New York, Boston, and Philadelphia, 1880–1912*. Cambridge: Harvard University Press, 1980.

Commons, John R. and John B. Andrews. *Principles of Labor Legislation*. New York: Harper and Brothers, 1927.

Condit, Carl. *The Port of New York: A History of the Rail and Terminal System from the Beginnings to Pennsylvania Station*. Chicago: University of Chicago, 1980.

Daniels, Stephen. "A Tangled Tale: Studying State Supreme Courts." *Law and Society Review* 22 (1988): 833–63.

———. "Continuity and Change in Patterns of Case Handling: A Study of Two Rural Counties." *Law and Society Review* 19 (1985): 381–420.

———. "Ladders and Bushes: The Problem of Caseloads and Studying Court Activities over Time." *American Bar Foundation Research Journal* 1984 (1984): 751–95.

Dublin, Louis I. *Factbook on Man from Birth to Death*. New York: Macmillan, 1965.

Durkheim, Emile. *The Division of Labor in Society.* New York: Free Press, 1964 [1893].

Engel, David. "The Oven Bird's Song: Insiders, Outsiders, and Personal Injuries in an American Community." *Law and Society Review* 18 (1984): 551–82.

Epstein, Richard. "The Historical Origins and Economic Structure of Workers' Compensation Law." *Georgia Law Review* 16 (1982): 775–819.

Felstiner, William, Richard Abel, and Austin Sarat. "The Emergence of Disputes: Naming, Blaming, and Claiming. . . . " *Law and Society Review* 15 (1980–81): 631–54.

Fine, Sidney. *From Laissez-Faire to the Social Welfare State.* Ann Arbor: University of Michigan Press, 1958.

Friedman, Lawrence M. *A History of American Law.* New York: Simon and Schuster, 1973.

——— . "American Legal History: Past and Present," in Lawrence Friedman and Harry Scheiber, eds., *American Law and the Constitutional Order.* Cambridge: Harvard University Press, 1988, 464–73.

——— . "Civil Wrongs: Personal Injury Law in the Late 19th Century." *American Bar Foundation Research Journal* 1987 (1987): 351–78.

——— . "Legal Culture and Social Development." *Law and Society Review* 4 (1969–70): 29–44.

——— . *Total Justice.* New York: Russell Sage, 1986.

Friedman, Lawrence, and Jack Ladinsky. "Social Change and the Law of Industrial Accidents." *Columbia Law Review* 67 (1967): 50–82.

Friedman, Lawrence M. and Robert Percival. "A Tale of Two Courts: Litigation in Alameda and San Benito Counties." *Law and Society Review* 10 (1975–76): 267–301.

Friedman, Lawrence M., and Thomas D. Russell. "More Civil Wrongs: Personal Injury Litigation, 1901–1910," *American Journal of Legal History* 34 (1990): 295–314.

Gabriel, Ralph. *American Values: Continuity and Change.* Westport, Conn.: Greenwood Press, 1974.

Galanter, Marc. "The Legal Malaise; or, Justice Observed." *Law and Society Review* 19 (1985): 537–56.

——— . "Reading the Landscape of Disputes: What We Know and Don't Know (and Think We Know) about Our Allegedly Contentious and Litigious Society." *UCLA Law Review* 31 (1983): 4–71.

——— . "Why the 'Haves' Come Out Ahead: Speculations on the Limits of Legal Change." *Law and Society Review* 9 (1974): 95–160.

Geertz, Clifford, and Roy G. D'Andrade. "A Colloquy of Culture Theorists." In Richard Schweder and Robert LeVine, eds., *Culture Theory: Essays on Mind, Self, and Emotion,* pp. 1–24. New York: Cambridge University Press, 1984.

Gibson, James. "Environmental Constraints on the Behaviour of Judges: A Representational Model of Judicial Decision Making." *Law and Society Review* 14 (1979–80): 343–70.

Gilmore, Grant. *The Ages of American Law.* New Haven, Conn.: Yale University Press, 1977.

Gordon, Robert. "Critical Legal Histories." *Stanford Law Review* 36 (1984): 57–126.

——. "Historicism in Legal Scholarship." *Yale Law Journal* 90 (1981): 1017–56.

——. "Introduction: J. Willard Hurst and the Common Law Tradition in American Legal Historiography." *Law and Society Review* 10 (1975–6): 9–55.

——. "Legal Thought and Legal Practice in the Age of American Enterprise, *1870–1920*." In Gerald Geison, ed., *Professions and Professional Ideologies in America, 1730–1940*, pp. 70–110. Chapel Hill: University of North Carolina Press, 1983.

Gregory, Charles. "Trespass to Negligence to Absolute Liability." *Virginia Law Review* 37 (1951), 359–97.

Grossberg, Michael. "Social History Update: 'Fighting Faiths' and the Challenges of Legal History," *Journal of Social History* 25 (1991): 191–201.

Gutman, Herbert. *Work, Culture, and Society in Industrializing America*. New York: Vintage, 1977.

Halliday, Terence. "Six Scores and Ten: Demographic Transitions in the American Legal Profession, 1850–1980." *Law and Society Review* 20 (1986): 53–78.

Hammack, David. *Power and Society: Greater New York at the Turn of the Century*. New York: Russell Sage, 1981.

Haskell, Thomas. "Capitalism and the Origins of Humanitarian Sensibility, Parts I and II." *American Historical Review* 90 (1985): 339–61, 547–66.

——. *The Emergence of Professional Social Science: The American Social Science Association and the 19th Century Crisis of Authority*. Champaign: University of Illinois Press, 1977.

Hobson, Wayne. *The American Legal Profession and the Organizational Society, 1890–1930*. New York: Garland Press, 1986.

——. "Professionals, Progressives and Bureaucratization: A Reassessment." *Historian* 39 (1977): 639–58.

Hofstadter, Richard. *The Age of Reform*. New York: Vintage, 1955.

Horwitz, Morton. "The Rise of Legal Formalism." *American Journal of Legal History* 19 (1975): 251–64.

——. *The Transformation of American Law, 1780–1860*. Cambridge: Harvard University Press, 1977.

Hurst, James Willard. *The Growth of the American Law: The Law Makers*. Boston: Little, Brown & Co., 1950.

——. *Law and Social Order in the United States*. Ithaca, N.Y.: Cornell University Press, 1977.

——. *Law and the Conditions of Freedom in the Nineteenth-Century United States*. Madison: University of Wisconsin Press, 1956.

——. "The State of Legal History." In Stanley Kutler and Stanley Katz, eds., *The Promise of American History: Progress and Prospects*, pp. 292–305. Baltimore, Md.: Johns Hopkins, University Press, 1982. ˙

Kaczorowski, Robert. "The Common Law Background of Nineteenth Century Tort Law." *Ohio State Law Journal* 51 (1990): 1127–99.

Kagan, Robert, Bliss Cartwright, Lawrence Friedman, and Stanton Wheeler. "The Business of State Supreme Courts, 1870–1970." *Stanford Law Review* 30 (1977–78): 121–56.

Kagan, Robert; Bliss Cartwright, Lawrence Friedman, and Stanton Wheeler. "The Evolution of State Supreme Courts." *Michigan Law Review* 76 (1978): 961–1005.

Kalven, Harry. "The Jury, the Law, and the Personal Injury Damage Award." *Ohio State Law Journal* 19 (1958): 158–78.

Kalven, Harry and Hans Zeisel. *The American Jury.* Chicago: University of Chicago Press, 1971.

Kaplan, Barry. "Reformers and Charity: The Abolition of Public Outdoor Relief in New York City, 1870–1898." *Social Service Review* 52 (June 1978): 202–14.

Karshan, Howard. *Contingent Fees in Personal Injury and Wrongful Death Actions in the United States.* New York: Institute for Judicial Administration, 1957.

Katz, Michael. *In the Shadow of the Poorhouse: A Social History of Welfare in America.* New York: Basic Books, 1986.

——— . *Poverty and Policy in American History.* New York: Academic Press, 1983.

Katz, Stanley. "Law and Economic Development in Antebellum America: A Comment." *Working Papers from the Regional Economic History Research Center* 3 (1980): 90–99.

Kennedy, Duncan. "Toward an Historical Understanding of Legal Consciousness: The Case of Classical Legal Thought in America, 1850–1940." In Steven Spitzer, ed., *Research in Law and Sociology* 3 (1980): 3–24.

Kirkland, Edward. *Industry Comes of Age: Business, Labor, and Public Policy, 1860–1897.* New York: Holt, Rinehart, 1961.

Kostal, R. W. "Legal Justice, Social Justice: An Incursion into the Social History of Work-related Accident Law in Ontario, 1860–1886." *Law and History Review* 6 (1988): 1–24.

Krasity, Kenneth. "The Role of the Judge in Jury Trials: The Elimination of Judicial Evaluation of Fact in American State Courts from 1790 to 1913." *University of Detroit Law Review* 62 (1985): 595–632.

Kretzmer, David. "Transformation of Tort Liability in the Nineteenth Century: The Visible Hand." *Oxford Journal of Legal Studies* 4 (1984): 46–87.

Krislov, Samuel. "Theoretical Perspectives on Caseload Studies: A Critique and a Beginning." In Keith Boyum and Lynn Mather, eds., *Empirical Theories about Courts*, pp. 161–87. New York: Longman, 1983.

Kritzer, Herbert. "Political Culture and the 'Propensity to Sue'." *Institute for Legal Studies Working Papers* 9, no. 1 (July 1988).

Kritzer, Herbert, W. A. Bogart, and Neil Vidmar. "The Aftermath of Injury: Culture Factors in Compensation Seeking in Canada and the United States." *Law and Society Review* 25 (1991): 499–543.

Kusmer, Kenneth. "The Functions of Organized Charity in the Progressive Era." *Journal of American History* 60 (1973): 657–78.

Landes, William, and Richard Posner. "The Positive Economic Theory of Tort Law." *Georgia Law Review* 15 (1981): 851–924.

Lears, T. J. Jackson. "The Concept of Cultural Hegemony: Problems and Possibilities." *American Historical Review* 90 (1985): 567–93.

Lempert, Richard. "Mobilizing Private Law: An Introductory Essay." *Law and Society Review* 11 (1976): 173–89.

——. "More Tales of Two Courts: Exploring Changes in the 'Dispute Resolution Function' of Trial Courts." *Law and Society Review* 13 (1978–79): 91–138.

Levine, Felice. "Goose Bumps and 'The Search for Signs of Intelligent Life' in Sociolegal Studies: After Twenty-Five Years." *Law and Society Review* 24 (1990): 7–35.

Lieberman, Jethro. *The Litigious Society.* New York: Basic Books, 1981.

Lubove, Roy. "Economic Security and Social Conflict in America: The Early Twentieth Century, Part I." *Journal of Social History* 1 (1967): 61–87.

——. *The Progressives and the Slums: Tenement House Reform in New York City, 1890–1927.* Pittsburgh, Penn.: University of Pittsburgh Press, 1962.

——. *The Struggle for Social Security.* Cambridge: Harvard University Press, 1968.

Lurie, Jonathan. "Lawyers, Judges, and Legal Change, 1852–1916: New York as a Case Study." *Working Papers from the Regional Economic History Research Center* 3 (1980): 31–56.

Macaulay, Stewart. "Law and the Behavioral Sciences: Is There Any There There?" *Law and Policy* 6 (1984): 150–56.

McClymer, John F. "Late Nineteenth-Century American Working Class Living Standards." *Journal of Interdisciplinary History* 17 (1986): 379–98.

McIntosh, Wayne. *The Appeal of Civil Law: A Political-Economic Analysis of Litigation* (Urbana: University of Illinois Press, 1990).

——. "*150* Years of Litigation and Dispute Settlement: A Court Tale." *Law and Society Review* 15 (1980–81): 823–48.

——. "A State Court's Clientele: Exploring the Strategy of Trial Litigation." *Law and Society Review* 19 (1985): 421–47.

McIntosh, Wayne, and Cynthia C. Colella, "The Social Foundation of Litigation." Paper presented at the 1988 Law and Society Association Annual Meeting, Vail, Colorado.

MacKinnon, Frederick B. *Contingent Fees for Legal Services: A Report of the American Bar Foundation.* Chicago: Aldine, 1964.

Malone, Wex. "The Formative Era of Contributory Negligence." *Illinois Law Review* 41 (1946): 151–82.

——. "Ruminations on Cause in Fact." *Stanford Law Review* 9 (1956): 60–99; reprinted in Robert Rabin, ed., *Perspectives on Tort Law,* pp. 44–59. Boston: Little, Brown & Co., 1976.

Mandelbaum, Seymour. *Boss Tweed's New York.* New York: John Wiley, 1965.

May, Henry. *Protestant Churches and Industrial America.* New York: Harper, 1967 [1949].

Mencher, Samuel. *Poor Law to Poverty Program: Economic Security in Britain and the United States.* Pittsburgh, Penn.: University of Pittsburgh Press, 1967.

Merry, Sally Engle. "Everyday Understandings of the Law in Working-Class America." *American Ethnologist* 13 (1986): 253–70.

Miller, Richard, and Austin Sarat. "Grievances, Claims, and Disputes: Assessing the Adversarial Culture." *Law and Society Review* 15 (1981): 525–66.

Mishler, Elliott. "The Health-Care System: Social Contexts and Consequences." In Elliott Mishler, ed., *Social Contexts of Health, Illness, and Patient Care*, pp. 195–217. New York: Cambridge University Press, 1981.

Mohl, Raymond. *The New City: Urban America in the Industrial Age, 1860–1920*. Arlington Heights, Ill.: Harlan Davidson, 1985.

Munger, Frank. "Law, Change, and Litigation: A Critical Examination of an Empirical Research Tradition." *Law and Society Review* 22 (1988): 58–101.

――― . "Social Change and Tort Litigation: Industrialization, Accidents, and Trial Courts in Southern West Virginia, *1872* to *1940*." *Buffalo Law Review* 36 (1987): 75–118.

――― . "Trial Courts and Social Change: The Evolution of a Field of Study." *Law and Society Review* 24 (1990): 217–26.

Nelson, William E. *The Americanization of the Common Law: The Impact of Legal Change on Massachusetts Society, 1760–1830*. Cambridge: Harvard University Press, 1975.

Nelson, William E., and John Phillip Reid. *The Literature of American Legal History*. New York: Oceana, 1985.

Paul, Arnold. *The Conservative Crisis and the Rule of Law*. Ithaca, N.Y.: Cornell University Press, 1960.

Pernick, Martin S. *A Calculus of Suffering: Pain, Professionalism, and Anesthesia in Nineteenth-Century America*. New York: Columbia University Press, 1985.

Polisar, Daniel, and Aaron Wildavsky. "From Individual to System Blame: A Cultural Analysis of Historical Change in the Law of Torts." *Journal of Policy History* 1 (1989): 129–55.

Posner, Richard. "A Theory of Negligence." *Journal of Legal Studies* 1 (1972): 29–96.

Pound, Roscoe. "Law in Books and Law in Action." *American Law Review* 44 (1910): 12–36.

――― . *The Lawyer from Antiquity to Modern Times*. Minneapolis: West, 1953.

Purcell, Edward A., Jr. *Litigation and Inequality: Federal Diversity Jurisdiction in Industrial America, 1870–1948*. New York: Oxford University Press, 1992.

Rabb, Theodore. "Toward the Future: Coherence, Synthesis, and Quality in History." *Journal of Interdisciplinary History* 12 (1981): 315–32.

Rabin, Robert. "The Historical Development of The Fault Principle: A Reinterpretation." *Georgia Law Review* 15 (1981): 925–61.

Ransom, Roger and Richard Sutch. "The Labor of Older Americans: Retirement of Men On and Off the Job, 1870–1937." *Journal of Economic History* 46 (March 1986): 1–30.

Reichman, Nancy, and Joyce Sterling. "Constructing Order in the Frontier: The Case of the Missing Defendants." Paper presented at the 1990 Annual Meeting of the Law and Society Association, Berkeley, California.

Reichman, Nancy, Joyce Sterling, and Patricia Wellinger. "The Social Construction of Duty." Paper presented at the 1988 Annual Meeting of the Law and Society Association, Vail, Colorado.

Rosenberg, Charles. *The Care of Strangers: The Rise of America's Hospital System.* New York: Basic Books, 1987.

Rosenwaike, Ira. *Population History of New York City.* Syracuse, N.Y.: Syracuse University Press, 1972.

Rosner, David. *A Once Charitable Enterprise: Hospitals and Health Care in Brooklyn and New York, 1885–1915.* New York: Cambridge University Press, 1982.

Scheiber, Harry. "Public Economic Policy and the American Legal System: Historical Perspectives." *Wisconsin Law Review* 1980 (1980): 1159–89.

Schneider, David, and Albert Deutsch. *The History of Public Welfare in New York State, 1867–1940.* Chicago: University of Chicago Press, 1941.

Schwartz, Gary. "The Character of Early American Tort Law." *UCLA Law Review* 36 (1989): 641–718.

——. "Tort Law and the Economy in Nineteenth-Century America: A Reinterpretation." *Yale Law Journal* 90 (1981): 1717–75.

Schwartz, Gary, and Edwin Perkins. "Tort Law and Business Enterprise in Nineteenth-Century America." *Essays in Economic and Business History* 3 (1984): 218–30.

Silberman, Matthew. *The Civil Justice Process: A Sequential Model of the Mobilization of Law.* Orlando, Fl.: Academic Press, 1985.

Silverman, Robert. *Law and Urban Growth: Civil Litigation in the Boston Trial Courts, 1880–1900.* Princeton, N.J.: Princeton University Press, 1981.

Smith, Samuel O. "Judges and Justice—the Judge's Role in Personal Injury Cases." *University of Illinois Law Forum* 1962 (1962): 172–89.

Sommerich, Otto. "The History and Development of Attorneys' Fees." *The Record of the Association of the Bar of the City of New York* 6 (1951): 369–74.

Stein, Leon. *The Triangle Fire.* New York: Carroll and Graf, 1985 [1962].

Stilgoe, John. *Metropolitan Corridors.* New Haven, Conn.: Yale University Press, 1985.

Thernstrom, Stephan. *The Other Bostonians.* Cambridge: Harvard University Press, 1970.

Thompson, E. P. *The Making of the English Working Class.* New York: Vintage, 1964.

Trachtenberg, Alan. *The Incorporation of America: Culture and Society in the Gilded Age.* New York: Hill and Wang, 1982.

Trattner, Walter. *From Poor Law to Welfare State: A History of Social Welfare in America.* New York: Free Press, 1989.

Trubek, David. "Where the Action Is: Critical Legal Studies and Empiricism." *Stanford Law Review* 36 (1984): 575–622.

Tushnet, Mark. "Perspectives on the Development of American Law: A Critical Review of Friedman's 'A History of American Law'." *Wisconsin Law Review* 1977 (1977): 81-109.

Tweed, Harrison. *The Legal Aid Society of New York City, 1876–1951.* New York: Legal Aid Society, 1954.

Urofsky, Melvin. "State Courts and Protective Legislation during the Progressive Era: A Reevaluation." *Journal of American History* 72 (1985): 63–91.

Uselding, Paul. "In Dispraise of the Muckrakers: United States Occupational Mortality, 1890–1910." *Research in Economic History* 1 (1976): 334–71.

Veysey, Lawrence. "Intellectual History and the New Social History." In John Higham and Paul Conkin, eds., *New Directions in American Intellectual History*, pp. 3–26. Baltimore, Md.: Johns Hopkins University Press, 1979.

Walker, Claire. "A History of Factory Legislation and Inspection in New York State, 1886–1911." Ph.D. dissertation, Columbia University, 1969.

Walker, James Blaine. *Fifty Years of Rapid Transit, 1864–1917.* New York: Law Printing Company, 1918.

Wesser, Robert. "Conflict and Compromise: The Workmen's Compensation Movement in New York, 1890–1913." *Labor History* 12 (1971): 345–72.

Wetzel, Kurt. "Railroad Management's Response to Operating Employees' Accidents, 1890–1913." *Labor History* 21 (1980): 351–68.

White, G. Edward. *Tort Law in America.* New York: Oxford University Press, 1980.

White, Ronald C., and C. Howard Hopkins, *The Social Gospel: Religion and Reform in Changing America.* Philadelphia: Temple University Press, 1976.

Wiebe, Robert. *The Search for Order, 1877–1920.* New York: Hill and Wang, 1967.

Wilson, Robert. *The Sociology of Health.* New York: Random House, 1970.

Yellowitz, Irwin. *Labor and the Progressive Movement in New York State.* Ithaca: Cornell University Press, 1965.

INDEX

Library of Congress Cataloging-in-Publication Data

Bergstrom, Randolph E. (Randolph Emil), 1956–
    Courting danger : injury and law in New York City, 1870–1910 /
    Randolph E. Bergstrom.
        p.   cm.
    Revision of thesis (Ph. D.)—Columbia University.
    Includes bibliographical references and index.
    ISBN 0-8014-2607-3 (alk. paper)
    1. Personal injuries—New York (N.Y.)—History.   2. Accident law—
New York (N.Y)—History.   I.   Title.
KFN5311.B47   1992
346.747'10323'09—dc20
[347.4710632309]   92-52744

»▶ »▶ »▶ »▶ »▶ »▶ »▶ »▶ »▶

THE BATTLE OF THE LITTLE BIGHORN

★ ★ ★ ★ ★ ★ ★ ★ ★

GREAT BATTLES OF HISTORY SERIES

HANSON W. BALDWIN
GENERAL EDITOR

MARI SANDOZ

»▶ »▶ »▶ »▶ »▶ »▶ »▶ »▶ »▶

THE BATTLE OF
THE LITTLE
BIGHORN

★ ★ ★ ★ ★ ★ ★ ★ ★ ★

J. B. LIPPINCOTT COMPANY
PHILADELPHIA & NEW YORK

"I heard the alarm, but I did not believe it. I thought it was a false alarm. I did not think it possible that any white men would attack us, so strong as we were."

—Account of Custer fight by Low Dog, Oglala Sioux chief.
Leavenworth Weekly Times, August 18, 1881.

»▶ »▶ »▶ »▶ »▶ »▶ »▶ »▶ »▶

CONTENTS

★ ★ ★ ★ ★ ★ ★ ★ ★

»▶ »▶ »▶ »▶ »▶ »▶ »▶ »▶ »▶

THE BATTLE OF THE LITTLE BIGHORN

★ ★ ★ ★ ★ ★ ★ ★ ★

»▶ »▶ »▶ »▶ »▶ »▶ »▶ »▶

1 DEPARTURE
FROM THE
YELLOWSTONE

★ ★ ★ ★ ★ ★ ★ ★

There was little to suggest the usual heat and dust of June in the Yellowstone River country this noontime. The sky hung low and gray. The northwest wind, still raw from the hailstorm of the night before, swept over the sagebrush and blew the manes and tails of the horses as the bearded Brigadier General Terry* and his staff, Colonel Gibbon and Major Brisbin, rode out to a ridge and waited. Off below, at the bivouac of the 7th Cavalry, the trumpets sounded "Boots and Saddles," the call thin and fading but golden against the wind.

The command of twelve troops approached, the head of the column rising out of the bottoms, led by Lieutenant Colonel†

---

* Full names and ranks of the military men mentioned in the text are listed at the end of the text, pp. 183–184.

† Current official rank is used in the narrative here, as in all official communications, references, and signatures. Custer (Major General, USA, 1865, by breveted temporary rank) is lieutenant colonel of the 7th Cavalry under Colonel Samuel Davis Sturgis. In

George Armstrong Custer in buckskin and a whitish, flat-topped plains hat, his adjutant, Lieutenant Cooke, beside him, the huge Canadian with long side whiskers swept back by the wind. Behind them rode the standard-bearer, pushing hard against the staff of the swallow-tailed banner—red and blue with the crossed silver-white sabers of Custer's personal emblem—whipping against the sky. Saluting, the commander of the 7th reined up beside the waiting reviewers. The chorus of trumpets broke from the bottoms, the forked guidons streaming over the faded blue of the column that moved smartly up the rise in fours, the shod hoofs already stirring dust from the drying earth. The trumpeters swung their gray horses out beside Custer and halted, their shining song to escort the regiment as it passed.

First came the scouts, headed by the young West Pointer, Lieutenant Varnum. With him rode two well-known plainsmen, Mitch Bouyer and Charley Reynolds. The swarthy Mitch, who was in half-Indian dress, knew every Sioux camp ground, every lodgepole trail from the Musselshell down to the forks of the Platte River. Lonesome Charley Reynolds, who had carried Custer's news of gold located in the Black Hills to the world in 1874, was promised another message of great import on this expedition. So he joined, too, even with an infected hand—his gun hand—in a sling. Behind them jogged a group of other civilians, among them Herendeen, the courier that Terry sent along to bring a scouting report back to him; the two official interpreters, bewhiskered Girard and the Negro Isaiah Dorman, both long in the Missouri River trade; and two realtives of Custer's—he was really sneaking them past—a brother, Boston, listed as quartermaster employee, and the seventeen-year-old nephew, Autie Reed.

The Indian scouts rode in a body, sometimes passing each

---

narrative reference the qualifying "lieutenant" is usually dropped; in conversation the complimentary highest rank attained by an officer is commonly used.

other or drawing back, the men still chanting from their usual circling ride before any departure to a fight. The ponies varied in color from dun to bay and black, some spotted like the hail drifts that had still gleamed in the breaks when the sun rose, some of the horses painted and feathered for war. Custer's favorite scout, Bloody Knife, wore white-man shirt and pants, his loose hair held down by a twist of flannel about the head, with three feathers rising from the back. The other two dozen Arikaras looked much the same, all dark-faced and moody ever since they reached the mouth of the Rosebud on the Yellowstone, so far from their earthen villages on the Missouri, so deep in the country of their powerful enemy, the western, the Teton Sioux, and in the time of the great annual gathering from all the Plains.

The six Crow Indians were taller and gayer, more carefree, perhaps because they were headed toward their own country, where they knew every canyon and snakehead gully that led to home. There was a correspondent along, too, although specifically forbidden by Sherman, General of the Army. It was Terry's duty to enforce Sherman's order in this as well as in the refusal, practically to the last minute, to let Custer go with his regiment, yet somehow the general permitted the newspaperman, Mark Kellogg, to slip past on his mule.

Behind Varnum's men came the rhythmic thud of shod hoofs, the creak of leather, the jingle of bit and thump of slung carbines as the blue stream passed, two and two, troop by troop, followed by a small herd of extra horses and finally the dainty-footed mules of the pack train, their inexpertly tied loads already slipping, the animals straggling along, one nipping a bit of grass here, another there, some stopping entirely or deciding to run back to their wagon mates left at the river, the noncoms of the train guard sweating with effort and embarrassment, the civilian packers unconcerned and insolent.

Once more the trumpets came up to send their call to the

·wind and to glisten as they were lowered. Then the Gray Horse Troop moved forward into the column headed off on the five-day scout ordered by Terry. The route laid out was up the Rose-bud Valley to verify the direction of the Indian trail that Major Reno had just located for Custer and to scout Tullock's Creek and the upper Tongue River, heading off any Indians trying to escape southward. This was also to give Gibbon's infantry time for the march from the Yellowstone by way of the Big Horn River and up the valley of the Little Bighorn, meeting Terry late on the 26th or on the 27th. From the headwaters of the Tongue, Custer was to turn northward across the divide to the Little Bighorn and move down the stream to the junction with Terry on the 27th, the fifth day of the scout. Between the two forces the hostile Sioux would be cracked like a nut in a vise, or, as one of the friendly Sioux scouts said, "Maybe like the weak little flea between the fingernails," his eyes looking far away as he spoke.

When the regiment was gone—all except a couple of the pack mules running down a washout—the colonel clasped the hands held out to him there on the ridge and wheeled his horse to overtake his command. Gibbon called out after him, "Now, Custer, don't be greedy. Wait for us!"

Custer lifted his gauntleted hand in acknowledgement. "No!" he shouted back, "I–I won't!" his stammer very slight, the ambiguity left hanging like a puff of pipe smoke over the shoulder as he galloped off, the wind whipping the color of his standard behind him.

The clouds thinned and drifted apart in the dying wind. The sun burned down on the column moving in sections along the broad valley, fragrant here and there with wild roses still a pink cascade in late-blooming patches. Blackbirds sang in the rushes and now and then an awkward shitepoke rose from a marshy bend, or perhaps a deer started up a slope, looking back. The scouts burned to take up the chase, to make money as they had on the trail from Fort Abraham Lincoln on the Missouri to the Yellowstone encampment: two dollars apiece for the hind-quarters, a dollar for a forequarter or a saddle—fresh meat for the command. The scouts had earned hundreds of dollars on the way, but now there was to be no shooting at all, not even the pistol's casual bark, except at the enemy. None carried the silent bow, and besides, game would be scarce up where the large Indian camps had been. Perhaps one of the Arikaras, the Rees, would make a bow to get venison for Colonel Custer, who liked it roasted over the coals, as Young Hawk understood so well.

The march of this June 22, 1876, was a weary one, even up the pleasant Rosebud Valley. Last night had been like the usual eve of a military expedition's departure on the Plains, many of the men, particularly the officers, getting little or no sleep. Besides, half of the troops and many of the horses and mules were worn from the long scout under Reno, returning downstream only day before yesterday, and already back on the trail again.

When the bluffs began to push in closer upon the small, clear-watered creek, the command slowed and finally halted on an open bottom along the left, the night-wind side of the creek, where the prevailing west wind blew the mosquitoes to the far bank. They made camp in a patch of timber at the foot of a steep shielding bluff only eleven or twelve miles out, but this, as Reno had reported, was one of the last lush stretches of grass before they reached the deserted campsites of the Sioux, where the valley, the bluffs, and the upland were cropped bare by the vast pony herds of the Indians, the lodgepole trail leading up the creek wide and deeply worn.

There was deadwood for the squad fires here, and the fine smell that even army coffee can send far out to toll the hungry.

Thin streaks of smoke clung along the bluffs an hour before the lagging pack train was finally whipped in—strung out over a mile, goods and most of the expedition's ammunition handy for any Sioux charging out of the willows with waving blanket and stinging arrow. But somehow none seemed around anywhere today.

After the early supper the men scattered over the ground, many napping or already asleep when the shadows crept out of the cuts and canyons to push the sunlight back. A trumpet blew officers call; men rose here and there, some from their troop bivouac, some stretching wearily as they moved through the shadows to the low fire at Custer's tent, the only tent except pup halves in the command. The men settled around the colonel's bed, everybody there from Major Reno down to the greenest second lieutenant—including some who had charged the enemy at Custer's side before and perhaps even had their winter tents burned when their haste did not equal the commander's urgency.

To the older campaigners, Custer seemed less elated this evening than usual by tracks of an enemy ahead, certainly less overflowing with assurance and self-sufficiency than on his strike against the Cheyennes at the Washita eight years ago. There seemed unease about him standing there, even flanked as he was by his brother Captain Tom Custer and his brother-in-law, Lieutenant Calhoun, with Boston Custer and the nephew off to the side, and his favorites around him. Cooke, in the adjutant's position, was at his elbow, Keogh nearby and the Michiganders too—Weir (like Custer, earlier from Ohio, and a strength to him when rebellion against Custer broke out in the 3rd Michigan Cavalry in 1865); Yates, also from the Michigan Volunteers; and, farther over, the young and imaginative Harrington, his strained face often kept in shadow.

One civilian always up close was Mark Kellogg, to catch every

word and report it to Bennett of the New York *Herald,* long a
backer of the bold commander of the 7th Cavalry who had
proved an even bolder commander of the pen, not only for
the *Herald,* but, some said, as the author of the May 4 New
York *World* attack on Grant for his treatment of Custer. According to the *World's* account, the Secretary of War and
General Sherman had gone to the President to protest his treatment of the colonel, Sherman saying that Custer was the only
man fit to lead the expedition against the Indians. At Grant's
angry demand for an explanation, Sherman wrote a long disclaimer of the whole story. Such a protest had never been made,
nor had he ever expressed or intimated the sentiments attributed to him. He believed the army possessed hundreds who
were competent to lead the attack on the Indians. As General
of the Army he was well aware that Terry had already been
appointed to head the expedition.

Now at his tent on the Rosebud, and even though topped
by his big adjutant, Custer looked very tall in the firelight creeping up the fringed buckskin to his intense, wind-burned face
with its reddish bristles. The sockets of his eyes deepened in
the shadows as he gave out directions about troop distribution
and formation if the camp were attacked, directions so elementary they clearly hid some more significant purpose, particularly
in a regiment that had campaigned nine years with practically
the same officers, without one such rudimentary council or
instruction. The review seemed more proper to a green regiment out on a more dangerous mission than scouting. Perhaps
it was for the benefit of Kellogg, the young law student serving
as war correspondent, but the older officers looked uneasy.

Then suddenly the tone of the commander changed, his
stammer more evident. He was always willing to accept recommendations from even the junior second lieutenant of the
regiment, but such recommendations must come in proper

form. He was perfectly aware that his official actions had been discussed and criticized to the Department staff by some here. Now such criticism must cease or proceedings would be initiated against the offenders as provided in the army regulations.

There was a moment of embarrassed silence among the men not of Custer's family or favor, particularly with civilians present —a stunned silence among the newer officers. The tenth-year men, those with the regiment from its first summer, realized that the charge probably lay upon them, no telling where. Finally Captain Benteen of the cropped gray curls spoke up. As everyone knew, his relation to the colonel had not always been the warmest, but as everyone also knew, he was a soldier who did a soldier's duty.

"General,"* he said, "will you not be kind enough to inform us of the names of the offending officers?"

The commander had his reply ready, speaking deliberately, his stammer almost entirely hidden. "While I am not here to be catechized by you, Colonel Benteen," he said, "I take pleasure in informing you, for your own gratification, that you are not among the officers alluded to."

Yet somehow this did not seem enough under the bright evening sky of the shadowed Rosebud, and Custer pushed himself on to the unusual, the unprecedented extreme of explaining himself, asking cooperation from the troop commanders in measures obviously their minimal duty, such as husbanding the rations and conserving the strength of their horses and mules. The command might be out much longer than the five days planned, he said. He intended to follow the trail until they got the Sioux, even if it took them "to the Indian agencies on the Missouri River or in Nebraska," including the latter—although all the men realized that General George Crook, commander

* Complimentary use of former highest rank in conversation, as Custer calls Benteen colonel.

of the Department of the Platte, had been out south of the Yellowstone country since winter and was surely somewhere around the headwaters of the Tongue or the Rosebud right now with his fifteen troops of cavalry and five companies of infantry. Neither Custer nor his officers knew that five days earlier, Crazy Horse, with only part of the hostile Indians, had driven Crook back from the upper Rosebud—Crook, who had whipped the Apaches and sent part of his force to destroy Two Moon's Cheyenne and Sioux camp on the Powder River last March. What most men listening at Custer's fire must have realized was that only Terry's intercession with the infuriated President Grant had restored the colonel to his regiment at all, and at least one knew that Custer in his immediate elation had told Captain Ludlow of the Engineers (with him to the Black Hills in 1874) that he would cut loose from Terry now as he, Custer, had got away from Stanley in the railroad survey of the Yellowstone in 1873.

To his frank determination upon a personal Indian chase even as far as Nebraska, Custer added that there would be no more trumpet calls. "Boots and Saddles" would be at five, each troop commander responsible for his men in all but the start and the camp selections. Then the colonel offered his staff one more surprise: he asked for suggestions that might expedite the march. Once more the men before him moved in uneasiness, puzzled, particularly those who understood the accumulated desperation of the last few months and realized that the coming glories of this centennial summer, this 100th celebration of the Declaration of Independence, promised no shining place in the nation's finest show for George Armstrong Custer. The image of the adored young hero of 1862 and 1868 was now, in 1876, so tarnished that Custer could be ordered to go smell out Indians for the success of Terry and even Gibbon. There were some here on the Rosebud who realized that Custer must feel trapped in the confining dimensions of the scout laid out for him, as trapped as a great winged eagle forced into a cage, making wild and desperate thrusts against the confining bars, breaking plumage, talons, and beak.

Few of Custer's staff would risk making suggestions, even to his public request. Afterward they walked back to their troops, alone or in twos and threes—silent mostly, a few in low, sparse talk. Lieutenant Wallace, regimental recorder and only four years out of West Point, fell in beside Captain Godfrey, an old-timer with the 7th.

"I believe General Custer is going to be killed," the young man finally said, his voice barely rising above the swish of boots through the grass. "I never heard him talk that way before."

At the Indian camp, on a little rise to catch any night breeze that might carry a remote sound to their ears, and away from the sour smell of the sweaty white men, some of the scouts were gathered around a handful of coals for a thoughtful smoke. Custer's Bloody Knife, the Ree-Sioux, and Half Yellow Face, the Crow, were bridging the language gap with sign talk, considering what might happen, what seemed certain to happen. As Godfrey came by, they inquired if he had ever fought the Sioux. To his show of confidence in the regiment, one of the Crows reminded him this was the foe who had wiped out the arrogant Fetterman about ten years ago and less than one day's hard riding to the southward.

Even Mitch Bouyer was not convinced that the 7th could whip the Sioux. "One goddamn big fight," he predicted, with a Frenchman's shrug of the shoulder, and went out to look along the bluffs for the day scouts, yet to come in to the late supper.

The disquiet among the officers lasted long after they left Custer's tent. Several little knots of them were still talking low and seriously when the thin horns of the new moon settled into the hazy west. Many of them had not slept at all the previous night. The *Far West*, the shallow draft stern-wheeler steamboat carrying the headquarters of Terry's expedition, was anchored in the Yellowstone near the mouth of the Rosebud. Tom Custer and Calhoun had played poker on board until dawn with Keogh, the Irish soldier of fortune. They left IOU's behind, although the paymaster, at Custer's orders, had accompanied the command to the first camp out of Fort Abraham Lincoln.

"To avoid the whisky sellers getting the two months' pay," was Custer's explanation at the time, but his feud with the post trader was well known. Besides, there were whisky sellers all along the route and several around last night to grab what was left of any loose pay, from the new recruit's thirteen dollars a month on up. Much of the money had been sent back to Fort Lincoln and beyond by the mail couriers from the camps on the way west, or spent with the trader wagons along the Yellowstone, for hunting ammunition or big hats against the sun, but mainly for whisky. The army poker players usually kept their money handy, particularly in the 7th, with enough recklessness in the regiment to bring complaints against Custer for permitting, even encouraging, the gambling that was the ruin of many young officers.

But not everyone on the *Far West* spent last night at poker. Some of the officers made their wills, the adventurous Keogh among them. Others left verbal instructions for the disposition of property and mementoes if they did not return.

Custer had been in conference with Gibbon and Terry on the boat when the hailstorm struck the regiment, whitening the prairie like winter snow and leaving the air chilled into the next day. The men in the cabin of the *Far West* had understood the military, political, and financial nature of the problem very well: the hostile Sioux under Sitting Bull and Crazy Horse refused to leave their ancient and treaty-sanctioned hunting ways for life on the reservations. Now these Indians must be driven from all the Yellowstone country, swept out to clear the way for the Northern Pacific Railroad, which had been stopped at the Missouri by lack of funds in the panic years of the early 1870's. Custer's 1874 expedition had been intended to locate the gold known to be in the Black Hills, and to bring in a rush of railroad investors and gold seekers. The gold was found but the investors did not come. Still, removal of the Indians would bring them and release the railroad snorting impatiently at the Missouri. With the Sioux gone from the Yellowstone Valley, the way would be open to the gold mines of Alder Gulch and Virginia City, Montana—open for new gold strikes, too, and new range for the Longhorn herds bellowing their way north from Texas. Chiefly, however, the urgency was for the gold and its magic with the centers of powerful finance, American and European.

General Terry had seen the reports sent around the Departments of Dakota and the Platte in April and early May, verifying that there were three thousand lodges of hostile Indians in the Yellowstone country. He knew this meant 3,500 to 4,000 warriors at the least, more against an attack, with every male from twelve to eighty a fighter in defense of the villages. Terry understood the starvation on the reservations that drove the Indians out to the buffalo ranges as soon as the ponies strengthened with new grass, even if no courier reached him with the late May report that the Sioux agencies down in Nebraska were almost deserted, that eight hundred to a thousand agency warriors had secretly gone north to join Crazy Horse. Every old-timer in the region, red and white, knew that more Indians would go for the summer sun dance and great annual Teton Council, including all the western Sioux. Anticipating such powerful numbers had justified General Crook's move out of the south to the upper Tongue River country with a force of well over a thousand men when winter still held the Indians. Custer's activities in the East had delayed the command from the north; but now, four months late, Terry and Gibbon with their strong forces were to reach the Little Bighorn late the 26th, while Custer scouted the Rosebud and the Tongue.

After the conference on the *Far West*, Terry and Gibbon had accompanied Custer to the bivouac, the night white as with snow, the hail crunching under their boots. At his tent they shook hands and left, wishing him good luck. Custer was irritable and apparently full of apprehension, although both men had been as helpful as possible. Gibbon, despite his own command's needs, gave up his best guides, including the Sioux breed, Bouyer, and six of his Crow scouts, men of the Yellowstone country who had hunted and fought Sioux all over the region.

General Terry had been generous all spring. He had requested that Grant let Custer return to his regiment for the expedition against the Sioux, despite the President's anger over Custer's volunteered testimony in the army tradership investigations, which were planned, many thought, to give the Democrats their first chance to elect a President since the Civil War. Even the investigators labeled the Custer testimony hearsay, with no firsthand information. Although the Secretary of War had already resigned, Custer did emphasize Belknap's gag rule against army officers and cited the "banishment of Colonel Hazen to Fort Buford, 1,000 miles up the Missouri," as punishment for his protests against farming out post traderships and the profiteering on the common soldier.

There was some surprise at this praise of Hazen, for Custer had shown animosity against him ever since, as Officer of the Day, Hazen had placed young Custer under arrest at West Point for one of his many infringements of the rules. Besides,

Hazen was sent into the Black Hills in 1867—seven years before Custer, who since 1874 had publicly prided himself as being the first into the Hills. In addition, Hazen was General Terry's choice to lead the expedition against the Sioux if Custer had not been permitted to return to his post. Intentional or not, Custer's charge that Hazen had been banished for protesting graft in traderships summoned him before the investigators, too, and held him in Washington when he should have taken command at Fort Abraham Lincoln.

More infuriating, however, to the President than Custer's charges of graft and rake-offs against the already disgraced and departed Belknap were the accusations, also hearsay, against half a dozen prominent army men and Grant's own brother, in addition to other charges against Lewis Merrill, major of the regiment, and even Sturgis, colonel of the 7th Cavalry. The President was certainly aware that Custer was involved in the New York *Herald* articles denouncing Belknap and the whole Administration, some perhaps actually written by the ambitious Custer during this presidential election year, when it seemed that practically any Democrat might be elected. Besides, Grant must have known that Custer himself stood accused, by hear-say, of graft and attempts at graft through post traders all the way from Texas to Fort Lincoln and beyond. It was a time of graft, insubordination, and disobedience.

But with May upon them, and General Crook in the field for months, the expedition from the north must move, the 7th Cavalry, commanded by Major Reno while Sturgis was on detail duty in Washington, with it. Custer was urged to go directly to the President. But Grant refused to see him, either while arrogant or after some awkward attempts at a halfhearted penitence. So Terry suggested that Custer wire the President, begging to be spared the humiliation of seeing his regiment march without him. To this Terry appended a note and received a reply from General of the Army Sherman saying that he could take Lieutenant Colonel Custer on the expedition if he wished, but adding: "Advise Custer to be prudent, not to take along any newspapermen, who always make mischief, and to abstain from personalities in the future . . ." It was a few hours after Custer received this news that he told Captain Ludlow he intended to "cut loose" from Terry. Ludlow immediately spoke of this to fellow officers, perhaps uneasy about the campaign and angry at Custer's arrogance toward a superior who had gone to such lengths to restore him to the regiment.

After the disastrous months just passed, Custer knew it was time to place himself above his enemies. With the convenient memory of the ambitious, he apparently recalled the extravagant praise of the winter and made something of the usual toast to "a future president." And why not? Such ambition was the privilege of every native male, intensified by the serious political interest common to every high officer of the army in these uncertain years. Custer's interest in national politics was an old one. In 1860, while at West Point, he wrote at length about the presidency.* Then in 1866 he had ridden Johnson's train in the President's hopeless campaign to win support for his Reconstruction plans and a favorable Congress. Custer had spoken from the rear platform and heard the applause of the crowd. Often enthusiasm was much greater for the young major general than for Johnson, and sometimes shrill shouts demanded

* Letter, May 5, 1860, to a friend at New Rumley, Ohio, discussing the coming presidential election: "It . . . will result in the utter defeat of the Republicans and I hope in the complete demolition of the Republican Party. Although I am far from being a Douglasite I believe he would make a good president, there are others I would prefer to him, I would like to see either Dickinson of this state, Lane of Oregon or Hunter of Virginia receive the nomination. I am satisfied however that the party will yet unite on a good man and that man is destined to be the next president . . ." signed GA Custer. (Reprinted with permission of Michael Ginsberg.)

Grant and Custer instead of the President. And then came last winter's entertainments by the newspapers and railroads, and the flattering, if perhaps hollow, suggestion for the national ticket this election year—not Grant but Custer.

So last night, June 21, Custer had returned to his tent from the *Far West* and prepared to march in the morning. Still nervous and irritable, he abolished his own recent division of the regiment into two six-troop wings commanded by Reno and Benteen. From now on, every troop commander would report directly to him. This reduced Benteen to his one troop and left Reno, less than a month ago commander of Fort Abraham Lincoln and the 7th Cavalry, with no unit at all, only his personal striker and a cook, both from Keogh's I Troop.

A pool of around 155 or 160 mules had been selected from the wagon train (left behind at the Yellowstone) with each troop assigned twelve animals to pack the rations, enough for fifteen days instead of Terry's planned five. Each trooper would carry 100 rounds of ammunition for his carbine and 24 for the pistol in addition to 12 pounds of oats for his horse. The extra regimental ammunition—24,000 rounds—was packed on the twelve strongest mules.

Some of the commanders questioned these loads for the fast pace Custer outlined. The mules from Reno's long, swift march up beyond the forks of the Powder, over to the Tongue and down the Rosebud, and just in yesterday, were worn. Overloaded, they would break down.

Custer had cut the complaints short. "Gentlemen, you may carry what supplies you please. You will be held responsible for your companies," he said, and elaborated on the arduous route and pace he planned. Then, as he entered his tent, he turned his head back to advise the men they had better carry an extra supply of salt. "We may have to live on horsemeat before we get through. Probably mule meat, unless some men are left to walk or many saddles are emptied."

After the conference the officers scattered, mostly to the *Far West*, some to a night of cards and whisky, some to stories and song. Once Reno and the lieutenant of the boat's guard stood together, arms around each others shoulders, singing "Larboard Watch."

Custer also returned to the boat. Major James S. Brisbin, commanding Gibbon's cavalry and considered an officious old blatherskite by some, complained to Terry about "the insufferable ass, the wild man" that the general was turning loose up the Rosebud in pursuit of the Sioux, and urged that the four troops of his 2nd Cavalry be added to the 7th, Terry to go as commander of the combined column.

The general refused. Custer smarted under a rebuke from the President, he said, and wanted an independent campaign and a chance to do something.

When Brisbin still persisted, Terry stopped his protests. "You don't seem to have confidence in Custer."

"None in the world," Brisbin replied. "I have no use for him." Yet he received permission to approach Custer with the idea. Custer refused, saying he had everything he needed in his regiment. As a homogeneous body it would accomplish as much as the two commands combined. Plainly, he welcomed no superior along, not even General Terry.

To Brisbin's offer of Low's battery of rapid-fire Gatling guns Custer agreed, but an hour later he returned to say, bluntly, "I won't want Low. I am afraid he will impede my march with his guns."

Aware that the general was sending Custer farther around to delay his arrival at the Little Bighorn to meet Gibbon's infantry coming up the river, Brisbin urged Custer to reconsider. Without replying, the colonel went to Terry with his refusal of the Gatlings. They were drawn by condemned cavalry horses, much to slow to keep pace with his troops, he said.

Apparently the general was unwilling to push the need for

delay or was convinced that the guns wouldn't slow the march. Probably he was still humoring his ambitious subordinate for private and unexplainable reasons.

Now, after the short march of June 22 to the first bivouac on the Rosebud, it was clear that even condemned cavalry horses would have kept up with the ragged, disintegrating pack train and that the Gatlings would have been useful in holding off a fast warrior charge that could sweep away the poorly protected mules strung out miles behind the command. But Custer's decision stood, no matter how gnawed over by the officers, like coyotes worrying an old buffalo skin.

Finally the last uneasy officer settled down to the stir of insects and the weary snores in the patch of timber. Few privates, except the sentries, lay awake tonight, not even for the coyotes, very noisy, with the high, thin yip of young ones among them, or for the farther, deeper howl of the prairie wolves, nor even to listen for Sioux war whoops that would surely be heard soon—perhaps at dawn tomorrow, or before. Several men who wandered off to the latrine area went beyond, slipping horses out past the weary guard. Perhaps they were afraid of Indians, but more probably they were drawn to the gold boom over southeast, in the Black Hills. Like earlier deserters, back near Custer's old trail into the Hills, they knew that Deadwood Gulch was full of motley miners where a man could lose himself as easily as he could kick his cavalry mount in the belly, send the horse running into the timber, or perhaps even trade it to brand blotters, as he could trade his pistol for a pair of civilian pants.

Custer had scouts out in twos and threes, searching the night, but the Ree, Bloody Knife, had gone alone, unofficially, missing soon after supper. No one admitted he knew where the Knife had gone, although several realized he had obtained a flask of whisky, either from Mark Kellogg, who stopped him earlier to ask questions, or from one of the officers wishing to cheer the expert scout out of his growing gloom. Plainly the liquor must be taken away from the camp, and so Bloody Knife disappeared to his horse and into the hills, perhaps to think about the long-time enmity between his parental peoples, the Rees and the Sioux, and about the annual Teton council, of the seven divisions of western Sioux that had met at Bear Butte near the Black Hills until last year, until driven off by the miners of Deadwood. He knew that this year the call gathered them somewhere south of the Yellowstone, both the hostile and the agency Sioux with thousands of warriors. Surely he thought about Custer and about the colonel's talk to the Rees at Fort Lincoln and later at Young Man Butte, the seventh camp on the expedition. Both times Custer told them this was to be his last campaign and so he must win a victory. A victory now, even if only against five or six lodges of the Sioux, would make him the President, the Great Father in Washington, and he must turn back as soon as he had won. He would take Bloody Knife to Washington with him and then send him home again to a fine house built for him. All the Ree scouts would have plenty to eat for all time to come.

". . . you and your children," he had told them.

But now it was plain that this white-man war chief was leading them not against a few lodges but upon the great annual summer gathering of all the Teton Sioux, the people whose power the Rees had felt so often. With Custer were the scouts that Bloody Knife had encouraged to come along. Perhaps because the load of this knowledge—the danger he had put upon his brother Rees—was too heavy, Bloody Knife had slipped away, welcoming the forgetting in the whisky, not to return until after dawn, stumbling, leading his horse, still too drunk for the saddle.

As ordered, there was no reveille for the regiment the 23rd. At three o'clock the horseguards fumbled around in the dark shaking the troops from their sleep. The scouts—Ree, Crow, and white—w.re already gone with Varnum. At five the column moved out, Custer leading, followed by the two color sergeants. The reorganized pack train was massed near the end of the command, with Benteen and three troops bringing up the rear to collect the straggling and straying mules, pick up the scattered packs.

By now the bluffs pushed in close upon the Rosebud. Within the first three miles the command made five crossings of the thin string of water, often with deep mud and marsh in the bends. Finally the valley opened out once more. Five miles on, brush and timber spotted the pleasant bottoms, crowded in around the feet of the bluffs, and trailed up the deeper ravines. Custer found some of his scouts waiting here, at the Rosebud trail and one of the campsites that Reno had seen on his scout. There were many packed-earth circles where lodges had stood and many remains of wickiups—bent ribs of willow sticks and brush still tied together at the top and once covered with robes or blankets—the low temporary shelters for extra youths and warriors. Some of the troops, the recruits raw to the country, even a few of the officers, thought these were shelters for dogs, perhaps misled by all the tracks of wolves and particularly coyotes, the scavengers of any deserted camp. Many of the men did not understand the difference between the Missouri River tribes and other reservation Indians, with their rabble of dogs, and the Indians out on the prairies, where one bark could betray a small camp to an overwhelming enemy. The troopers might have noticed the reaction of the scouts with the column. Dark and stony-faced, their moccasins soft on the worn earth of the camp, they moved from the large central circle where the council lodge had stood to the skeleton of the farthest wickiup in the brush. They examined the thick scattering of bones, particularly the larger ones, cracked for the marrow. They kicked these aside to send the bugs scurrying, talking quietly about the number and kinds; they considered the earth under the fire spots for the length of burning.

The scouts out ahead reported that the grass was eaten off short for miles around, the earth dotted with the droppings of thousands of horses, droppings beetle-worked and dry. At the upper end of the camp the tracks converged into a broad trail, cut deep by unshod hoofs and raked by thousands of dragging lodgepoles, all headed upstream.

Custer gathered the scouts to him and listened to what he might detect beyond the interpreters, beyond the sign talk, his bearding, sun-flushed face skeptical. Afterward he sent the scouts ahead in two parties and then talked to Varnum alone.

"Here's where Reno made the mistake of his life," the colonel said. "He had six troops of cavalry and rations enough for a number of days. He'd have made a name for himself if he'd pushed on after them."

Yes, if he had pushed on after the Sioux, but it would have been against orders, for he was on a scout, his finding to be reported.

Some distance beyond the first Indian camp the column passed more such sites, one in practically every creek bend, all about the same age, as though the Sioux had moved many times in one day and somehow burned the wood and grazed the hills as well as ate the tons of meat once on the scattered bones. Surely the Rees, the Crows, and the Missouri Sioux, like White Cloud, as well as Mitch Bouyer and Charley Reynolds, knew that these were different villages, different bands, gathering to a great conference. Some of the more observant noticed that as the campsites increased, the Indians with the command began to turn the heads of their horses toward each other, faces set, only the eyes moving, sliding quickly from one to another in secret knowledge, apparently not reassured by the evidence that these camps all seemed to be at least three weeks old and that the Indians might be scattered long before now. Plainly there was uneasiness among the scouts—not only in the taciturn Bloody Knife but in all the traditional enemies of the Sioux who were with him.

Custer hurried on, his dust-reddened eyes focused on the far bluffs up the Rosebud, his ears closed to the warning of his scouts. He forded the creek when necessary and pushed ahead like a hungry wolf on a hot trail. After making thirty-three miles, the command crossed to the right bank and camped at about four-thirty, early enough for the grazing that the horses needed badly. Across the stream the hills rolled back, lightly timbered, with deep ravines that might cover an ambushing enemy, even an attacking Indian army.

Out of the general uneasiness a man was sent back down the Rosebud to hunt for Benteen, somewhere far behind with the pack train. It had taken an hour and a half to get the in-expert outfit through the first crossing. By then Custer's column had been out of sight, at least six miles ahead of the reserve ammunition. With over 150 mules scattered out for almost a mile, Benteen, an experienced Indian campaigner, realized that a handful of warriors whooping out of the nearest canyon could stampede the mules as easily as they could a flock of sheep. They would get at least part of the train, probably the ammunition, packed on the mules that were plainly the best.

With his eyes on the rim of the creek bluffs much of the time, Captain Benteen decided he must have better control of the mule train than from the rear, as ordered by Custer. He sent one troop to flank the head section of the pack string, one to protect the center, and remained with the third, riding guard around the rear. Through increased orderliness he made better

progress, but in concentrating on the mules, he came near losing Dr. Lord, one of the regimental surgeons. The doctor grew
so seriously ill that he fell behind the packs, far out of sight,
and barely managed to drag himself into camp after dark. His
ailment was not the only such case in the command. There
were few without some sign of trail colic, for which whisky was
the accepted palliative, if not the specific. The infection was
widespread. On the *Far West* up on the Yellowstone, Gibbon
lay stricken with the infection, unable to join his plodding infantry until the 26th.

Benteen managed to cover the day's march four hours behind the column. While Cooke, the regimental adjutant, with
his long chop whiskers bristling at the tardiness, designated the
camp space for the train and its guard, Benteen told him of the
troubles with the mules and the packers, and the changes he
had made in the disposition of his troops to protect the train.
He asked the adjutant, a favorite of Custer's, to report the
liberties he had taken with the orders of the morning.

"I will not tell General Custer anything about it," Lieutenant
Cooke replied with his usual brusqueness. "If you want him to
know, you must tell him of it yourself."

Fires were ordered extinguished immediately after supper,
most of the men asleep before the late twilight was gone and
the stars clear. At daybreak the 24th, the Crow scouts reported
to Custer that they had found fresh sign of Indians, only three
or four horseback and one man afoot, but the trail ahead was
broader and fresher too. Excited by the news, the commander
did not hold himself to the pace of even the main column but
struck ahead with two companies* that were still fairly well
mounted. As he rode past the bivouac of the mule guard, Ben-

* The terms "troop" and "company" were used interchangeably
to designate the same tactical unit until 1880.

teen reported what he had done about the pack train and its supplies yesterday.

The commander seemed to take it calmly, in his larger preoccupation. "I am much obliged to you, Colonel Benteen," he said. "I will direct the officer who relieves you today to guard the train in the same manner."

Then, with his colors fluttering in the rising breeze toward sunup, Custer headed on up the stream, riding very fast, the recruits among his men understanding as never before why their commander was called Hard Backsides, understanding with admiration. Many stationed along the dull Missouri River posts for several years were eager for the first Sioux war whoop.

The stable sergeants had their constant worries over forage for the stock of the command, well over eight hundred head, not counting the horses of the various civilians, and this with the grass eaten into the ground. The Indians and other scouts were worried too: their horses had to cover substantially more miles than those of the regiment. Six Indians were sent out to hunt up remote low spots and bottoms for grass for their hungry ponies, grass preferably rich in seed to be gathered into their blankets and bundled tight with the lariats.

There was a continued scarcity of game too; even the blackbirds were gone from their nesting marshes, with little sign of life anywhere except for the magpies scavenging the old campsites and a buzzard or two circling. The greenness of the broken branches around the camps, the growing freshness of the pony droppings, and the wind-blown ashes of the fires told the scouts and even some of the troopers how swiftly Custer was overtaking the Indians. Finally the column reached a large, grazed-over stretch, the grass eaten bare for many miles out over the low hills and along the pretty valley of the Rosebud. Plainly, the camp here had been occupied for some days. Out on the bottom stood the bare frame of a large circular sun dance arbor, the pine boughs browning and brittle, the center pole still up with some tatters flying at the top where the buffalo image and other ceremonial objects had hung. On a stick thrust into the ground was the dried scalp of a white man, perhaps of the one 2nd Cavalry trooper killed sometime ago during Gibbon's march down the Yellowstone to the meeting place. It was taken to Custer and then passed around the angry men of the command, and ended up in Sergeant Jeremiah Finley's saddlebags. He was one of the older line sergeants of the regiment and perhaps was given first right.

There were other things more disturbing than one scalp to the scouts, both Rees and Crows, and certainly to the Sioux, who understood much of what had happened here from what was left behind. On a sand bar they found pictures drawn with a stick, perhaps a message for Indians to come past that way. The Sioux scouts slumped in their saddles a long while, speaking low, making signs.

"The pictures say an army is coming . . ."

In one of the dismantled sweat lodges, much like the remains of the low wickiups but with stones that had been fire-heated and then doused with water, sand had been heaped in a long ridge and pictures drawn along it, shod-hoof prints—meaning Custer's cavalry, the scouts thought—on one side, the pony tracks of the Sioux on the other. Between them lay many dead men, their heads toward the tracks of the Indians.

The Rees, of a small sedentary tribe long raided by the powerful Sioux, were very disturbed, certain that the enemy medicine was too strong for the soldiers and that they would all be defeated. This was fortified, they said, by stones left in another sweat lodge—three stones painted red and set in a row, meaning in Sioux sign language that the Great Powers had promised them victory and if the whites did not come for them, the Indians would search them out. In thanksgiving for these assurances, four upright sticks held a buffalo calfskin that had been adorned with cloth and other articles of value as gifts to the Great Powers, White Cloud, the Sioux scout, explained.

Probably none of the officers gathered in a curious half-circle on their horses at the sun dance place knew it was Sitting Bull who had danced here for guidance, for the wisdom to stop the white man pushing in with guns destroying the buffalo and miners digging up the sacred earth of Paha Sapa, the Black Hills. Now the white man's fire wagon that tore through the silence across the Platte country of the south was roaring its impatience at the Missouri, the path already laid out to the gold fields of the western mountains up along the Yellowstone, the final arrow to pierce the heart of the Indian country.

Certainly the scouts—at least the Sioux—knew from the symbolic pictures that the dreamer was Sitting Bull; that here, after giving one hundred bits of skin from his arms and staring into the sun for two days while he danced, he had received the vision pictured on the sand ridge of the sweat lodge: soldiers falling head first into his camp—many, many soldiers. This news had surely been signaled to the last of the young men on the agencies, from those in west Nebraska to those of the upper Missouri—a special inducement to obey the call to the great annual Teton council even though it was away from the sacred Bear Butte. More would slip away, as their fellows had been doing all spring, eager for the promise in the Hunkpapa medicine man's vision, certain now that the move of the council from the Sacred Bear near the Black Hills to the Little Bighorn was sanctioned as good.

So the trail up the Rosebud had grown even wider, deeper, as a river grows when fed by many springs.

Nor did Custer or his Indian scouts know that barely a week

ago a war party of these Indians had faced General Crook's army only a few miles up the Rosebud and that, for the first time in history, the Sioux had attacked in something like an organized battle charge, led by a war chief whose name, Crazy Horse, was scarcely known up around Fort Abraham Lincoln. Some may have heard of him almost ten years ago, when he led the decoy party that brought the end of the willful and disobedient young Lieutenant Fetterman.

There were darkening looks and low, angry words among the Rees, too, as they realized where the great enlarging trails led. For perhaps 150 years the Sioux had met at Bear Butte, just above the Black Hills. Since Custer's report of "gold at the grass roots," two years earlier, miners ran like ants over the rocks and burrowed into the earth of the Hills, many so near that, with the wind right, the loud whoop of a gold strike around Deadwood Gulch could be heard at the Butte of the Crouching Bear. Until last year, for two summer weeks the rolling hills around there lay dark as in brooding cloud-shadows with the twenty–thirty thousand ponies of the Sioux, while thousands of lodges stood in the forks of Bear Butte Creek in the seven circles of the Tetons. Many tame Indians, those from the trader forts and the agencies, came too, taking their traditional places for this ancient ceremonial, this ancient counciling that the Tetons brought west. It was a time of excitement, with racing, wrestling, dancing, singing, drumming, and always the formal ceremonials in the great center lodge made with poles eighteen feet tall from the deep canyons of the Black Hills. Here in this vast lodge, the chiefs of all the Tetons met to plan the year for the entire nation.

Now, since they were driven from Bear Butte, they were gathering somewhere up ahead in all their power, with many allies as guests, many Northern Cheyennes, some Arapahos, and perhaps a band of eastern Sioux, too, old Inkpaduta and his small following of Waist and Skirt people.*

Custer ordered coffee boiled and summoned his officers to where the guidon was stuck into the earth, whipping in the hot southerly wind. Once more it was an awkward conference, possibly because the commander was irritable and unsure, perhaps because he felt disapproval in the air. Many of the officers were jumpy, perhaps certain they were involved in open disobedience to Terry's orders. They knew about the early-morning Crow report of what looked like smoke over the ridge at Tullock's Fork, the creek that General Terry had ordered Custer to scout, with Herendeen along to carry the news of the findings back to the general from there.

The men listened to Custer's description of the trail ahead, freshening hourly, he said, but the scouts still found no scattering anywhere, none of the bands leaving for a hunt or perhaps a raid against the Crows or the Shoshonis. Instead, the trail that increased like a burgeoning river was now fed by a deep new one of many riders, their tracks thick and plain over the older lodgepole furrows that headed toward the ancient route across the divide to the Little Bighorn, the Greasy Grass of the Sioux. The trail was six inches deep in fine dust and half a mile wide in places, with the tracks of vast pony herds, and surely more of these farther out, for grass.

Dismissing the sign over Tullock's Creek as morning mist and ignoring Terry's orders to scout the region, Custer commanded the regiment to take the trail ahead but to proceed with increased caution, each troop to march a slightly different route to cut down the dust that would be so detectable from far off.

As the officers started toward their men, the wind blew

* A division of the Sioux.

Custer's standard down, toward the rear. Captain Godfrey re-covered it, only to see it fall toward the rear once more. A second time he rescued the banner from the dust, this time digging the staff into the baked earth, supporting it against a sturdy sagebrush. The flag stood now, its swallowtails sagging; but Godfrey, from Custer's native Ohio and a stalwart admirer, was disturbed by the double fall rearward, as were others who saw it—an omen of defeat at this crucial time.

Custer led his force out, ignoring the warning and the grow-ing sullenness of his scouts—both Crow and Ree, including Bloody Knife, his long-time friend and trusted wolf, as a supe-rior scout was called. He paid no attention to the quiet caution of Charley Reynolds or the louder complaint of Mitch Bouyer. Spurring on, he kept the column strung out behind him, mov-ing as fast as the weary horses could manage, the lagging pack train once more miles behind, the packers and the trooper guard stopping, with sweat and curses, to gather up the scattered packs, to whip the mules on, now that the Indians seemed closer every hour. Probably few of the raw recruits thought of anything beyond the ache of their burning saddle galls, the soreness of their swollen, blistered faces. The doctors did what they could to keep the men comfortable in spite of dust and alkali and buffalo gnats, swarming and tiny as circling dust particles, biting the eyelids until they swelled half-shut, the ears until they were thick as florid saucers. Old-timers knew that the Indians smeared themselves thick with bear grease and ashes against the pests and that freighters and hunters spread bandannas under their hats with a spot of coal oil on each flapping corner.

Even without deer flies to drive the horses crazy, and the gnats, the march would have been hot and dusty, with repeated halts necessary to let the scouts keep ahead. To Custer's ex-asperation, his Indians traveled more and more slowly as the trail freshened. Some looked back from one rise after another, anxious to keep within range of immediate support, even support whose adequacy they plainly doubted. The sun burned down through the sweated gray-blue shoulders of the troopers, although the buckskin of Custer and some of the other officers was even more airless, the soft surface thick with dust in spite of the staggered order of march.

Around four o'clock several of the Crows returned. They had been out on some of the stronger army horses and reported another trail, only a day or two old, of a large band of Indians from the south. These had not followed the regular route from the Nebraska agencies—down the Tongue—but crossed the Rosebud above the sun dance site and struck the trail where it turned toward the Little Bighorn, which was not over thirty miles ahead, moving with precision as though by guide or very accurate direction.

Custer, with his orderly carrying the guidon, took the information to the Ree camp. The Indians were sitting in a half-circle, the pipe of council going around. Custer joined them, resting on one knee, and asked about the report of the Crows, speaking, as always, with less impediment to the Indians.

"They tell me there are large camps of the Sioux," he said. "What do you suppose will be the outcome?"

Stabbed, the adviser, the medicine man among them, jumped up and hopped around in a bullet-dodging dance to show how the Indian saved himself while the troops stood still to be shot down like buffalo calves. Other officers came to listen at the smokeless little council fire, hearing Custer tell the Rees that all he expected of them in the fight was to capture as many Sioux horses as they could get, all for themselves. He ended by repeating his promise to befriend the Rees in Washington if the campaign was successful, the promise that he had elaborated to Bloody Knife and the others of the tribe long ago.

About five in the afternoon Custer led the regiment forward once more, across the Rosebud, the stream's left bank ridged by uncountable lodgepoles. The trail grew steadily deeper, with fresher, later travel. About seven forty-five in the evening, after twenty-six miles for the day, the command halted below a steep bluff, hidden as well as possible from all but the early croak of the frogs and the far howl of the coyotes, starting very early, the Rees remarked, as before a big hunt, a big meat-making. The troopers were ordered to keep their fires small as the scouts' little nest of coals, and soon dead. The mules were left under packs, the horses saddled, some trying to roll in the dust to rid themselves of the day's sweat and weariness, the recruits of the horse guard struggling with them under the curses of their sergeants, trying to keep them from scattering so swiftly to the first real grass they had found—grass now because here the Indian trail went on and on, without a stop.

A whisper ran through the bivouac like a little night wind talking to itself: the scouts were hurrying out on the trail beyond the turn toward the Little Bighorn, where the command was to meet Gibbon and Terry, maybe the day after tomorrow. Old campaigners predicted that, if the trail really crossed the divide, the regiment would march tonight. Major Reno, still without a troop to command, was silent, almost an outsider, less than a bystander with the regiment he had led so recently.

After the frugal and hasty meal, Captain Keogh and his lieutenant, James E. Porter, had come over to Benteen's bivouac, where four–five officers were sitting around listening to Lieutenant De Rudio's yarns in his heavy Italian-English, yarns of campaigns in other wars in other lands. Benteen brushed the dust from his curly graying hair, set his saddle up for a pillow, spread the saddle blanket, and notified the rest that he was going to pick up a little sleep, for surely they would not be camped here all night.

Around ten o'clock an orderly from regimental headquarters came to call the officers to Custer's tent. By now the sliver of early moon was gone; the night was darkened by the pattern of fireflies off toward the creek, the sound of arrow hawks falling upon their prey loud in the silence between the creak of saddle leather and the nose-clearing snorts of the stomping horses.

Benteen directed his first sergeant to see that everything was ready for an immediate march, and joined the other officers stumbling through the tangle of brush, with snoring troopers stretched out anywhere. At Custer's tent they were told that the Crow scouts had come in to confirm the expected direction of the fresh trail that they estimated at about four hundred lodges, with, counting those in wickiups, perhaps 1,500 warriors. Custer passed the figure on with no reference to the Indians of the earlier trail or to the Ree warning of the great annual Teton gathering up ahead. The march was to be resumed at eleven, to get as near as possible before daylight, with time to select the best possible concealment for the day.

Lieutenant Hare and his K Troop were put on duty with the scouts. The other officers aroused their bivouacs, calling the sergeants, low at first, then raising their voices, and finally receiving shouted replies from the darkness off along the bluffs. Horses stomped and whinnied; mules brayed: the peculiar carrying qualities of the hee-haws would attract wide notice to an army in the region.

It took Keogh, in charge of the pack train, an hour and a half to get the mules across the swampy bottoms of Mud Creek in the darkness, the column held impatiently on the other bank while he tried to curse and pound efficiency into the mules and the packers. He was greatly disturbed by the confusion and by the vagaries of the loose pack animals wandering in the dark. Benteen went back to help a little, advising Keogh to take it easier, that nothing short of a howling, arrow-pricking Indian charge could run off one of those mules. Some of the badly tied packs might slip down and be left behind, but these could be recovered at daylight.

When Varnum came in from a long scout, the big man stiff and worn for sleep, Custer told him that the Crows spoke of a high hill about twenty miles ahead, with a pocket on the slope, one big enough to hide the scout horses. The point, called the Crow's Nest, was on the divide.

"At daylight one can see by the rising of the smoke whether there are Indians on the Little Bighorn or not."

But for this important scout the colonel wanted an intelligent white man to go along to verify what the Indians saw and send word back to him.

Wearily the lieutenant nodded to himself. "I guess that means me . . .," he said, and climbed into the saddle. He selected the quiet, reserved, and experienced Charley Reynolds, even though his infected trigger hand was still swollen, and added Bouyer and several Crows, all men who knew the country, every moccasin track of it.

Through Girard the commander explained his instructions to several Rees he was sending along as a further check on the Crow scouts, who were, after all, Gibbon's men, not Custer's of solid acquaintance and promise, as the Rees of the Missouri River were.

Finally the column began to move, and although the stars hung clear and bright, the dust rose in a gray, furry haze that shut away even the dark masses of the troops as they turned from the pleasant minty bottoms of the Rosebud and headed westward, up along the breaks of Davis Creek. The sections of the command had a difficult time keeping anywhere near each other, let alone following the troop ahead. The jingle and creak of equipment and the snort of the horses helped. Hoofs, soft in the dust, sounded louder on the stretches of baked earth where their shoes struck sparks from the flinty gravel. Gradually the dust lessened on the rising trail to the Little Bighorn and communication became easier as the night turned toward the morning of June 25.

»▶ »▶ »▶ »▶ »▶ »▶ »▶ »▶

2 OVER
THE DIVIDE

★ ★ ★ ★ ★ ★ ★ ★

George Armstrong Custer led his 7th U. S. Cavalry through the pitch dark, Girard, the former trader and now the official Ree interpreter, riding beside him. Half Yellow Face, leader of the Crow scouts, knew every break and ridge and washout over the Little Bighorn, but he kept close, too, sometimes barely keeping up even with the commander's strong horse, although he was supposed to be out ahead, picking the trail.

The clouded night hung low and unbroken, the occasional flicker of lightning low in the northwest too far away to light even a silhouette of the rising hills called Wolf Mountains. Behind Custer the stinging alkali dust was riffled now and then by a light breeze that sprang up like a bird fleeing before a coyote. Then the little wind was gone, the temporary billowing of the dust cloud sensed more by the nostrils, even through a bandanna drawn up over the nose, than by the eye in the darkness. The horses within the troops still had trouble following each other; the van of the units was sometimes forced to halt and listen, hand cupped to the ear, to catch the direction of those ahead, perhaps guided by the signaling taps of a tin cup or a canteen against the saddle as the command felt its way. Now and then a section might be caught in a little box canyon or snakehead draw, the men compelled to turn upon themselves to get out, and yet always the thrust was upward toward the divide, awkwardly but with determination toward the divide between the Rosebud and the Wolf Mountains. Sometimes Custer himself was stopped while one of the Indians got off to feel the earth for a turn or swerve in the worn lodgepole trail they tried to follow around bluff side or canyon. Even with all the caution, now and then some weary horse stumbled on a washed-out buffalo trail, stepped into a badger hole, or lost its footing at a cut bank, to struggle and fall. The rider, perhaps thrown out of a saddle sleep, awoke, cursing and shouting to stop those immediately behind, the horse, up, grabbing hungrily for a mouthful of grass or weed through bitted teeth.

Keogh, with Lieutenant Mathey of the pack string, was far back along the trail, struggling, with the mules—naturally sharper-eyed and surer-footed than horses, but hungry enough to stray badly now—and the packers were cursed out as an unskilled, shiftless lot. Each time they were gathered up, the mules brayed their lonely desolation, their weary protest usually answered from up ahead, where Mark Kellogg rode—the repeated brayings surely the signal of an approaching army to any hostile Indian within five miles. Even without the noisy outbreaks, any Sioux could feel the cadence of so many hoofs with his palm, his fingertips, laid to the bare earth. Not that there was danger of a night attack from the Sioux. Night fighting was considered unlucky, with the dew-softened moccasins vulnerable to any rosethorn and cactus, the wet bowstrings stretched so they refused to send the arrow against an enemy. But dawn would come, the time of Indian ambush and attack—and where the

Sioux chose. Still no one dared suggest a halt to Custer, although he knew from his scouts, white and Crow, that he could not hope to find a protected bivouac beyond the divide, no safe place to hide a mounted regiment until the next night, while the Indian camp was located and the troops made ready to meet General Terry.

It was a slow, weary march, and several times one troop commander or another dropped back to talk the situation over, or to keep himself awake by recalling that day after tomorrow, the 27th, the Democratic Convention* opened at St. Louis, the nominee, with all the scandals around Grant, given the first good chance against the Republicans since the Civil War. How would such a victory affect the officers stationed over the South, and in the Plains Army, and the whole Indian extermination policy—all sponsored by Republican administrations? What of the career men in the army?

Out—practically everybody out—most thought, except those who knew of Custer's optimistic prediction to his Ree scouts. He would surely try.

So a painful eight or ten miles were covered, the horses and men both worn, the scouts who had been in the saddle most of the nights up the Rosebud sleeping on their horses while they could. Then, as the grayness began to creep into the clouds overhead, the movement in the van suddenly stopped, the troops spreading out as they came up to a flattish bottom under a bluff that was still more to be felt than seen in the darkness. The thirsty horses broke for the thin thread and the stinking pools

* In a box of Custer battle souvenirs loaned by the Sioux of Pine Ridge Reservation, S. Dak., to John Colhoff, the author's interpreter with the old buffalo hunters, to show her, was an unidentifiable fragment of notebook with the following entry: "June 24. The political discussions are still going on. Kellog [sic] gets in a real sweat as do some others. There's a lot hangs on what's done at the conventions. St. Louis will tell whether the army is cut, rumors report."

of upper Davis Creek; but they snorted and threw themselves back from the water that was so alkaline that the coffee from it was undrinkable.

Most of the stock was left under saddle, but some of the older troopers slipped them off for a few minutes, rubbing the sweat-scalded backs of their horses with twists of weeds, and reluctantly set the leather back into place, leaving the cinches loose, the bits out of the mouths so the tethered animals could eat the little grass available. The recruits and young Boston Custer and Autie Reed tried to ease their own saddle gall and the sting of the alkali, while the hardened campaigners sprawled on the ground, snoring the dust from their nostrils.

But Colonel Custer had other concerns than the gray coffee or even the weary horses and men. He was anxious for news from his scouts. With his brother, Captain Tom, and Adjutant Cooke he waited while the younger members of the Custer family slept, for all their excitement.

Scouts had gone out in several groups from the last camp on the Rosebud, in addition to Bob Tail Bull away wolfing alone for sign since the noon before. The Crows with Lieutenant Varnum knew all this country and led him directly toward the high lookout butte called the Crow's Nest. The party stopped twice to smoke. The Indians shielded the small point of light in the bowl and made some quiet talk among themselves. There was uneasiness in those who had been out ahead to examine the warming trail of the Sioux.

"The Indians are very, very many," Varnum was told, but with the low, flat tone used to one known to be totally deaf, whether deaf to their warning by his choice or that of his commander. They were embarrassed by this because they liked the big-nosed, broad-mustached young officer. He had endurance, and was not working to get himself ahead.

"Yes, there are very many Sioux," the Rees agreed, making the signs. "All the Tetons from all over . . ."

When the pipe was put away, the scouts headed up the rises toward the lookout butte. At about two-thirty they stopped in the pocket the Crows had described, and unsaddled. Varnum was worn out from his scouting since yesterday, thirty-six hours without sleep or even rest, on top of almost continuous work since they left the Yellowstone. He stretched his long body awkwardly in the darkness for a little sleep while two scouts, including Hairy Moccasin, the smallest and most alert of the Crows, climbed to the peak of the Nest.

After an hour or so there was an owl's hoot from up on the point, vaguely touched on the east by the coming dawn. It wasn't a loud hoot, but clear, and in meaning too, apparently, for the Rees around Varnum began to sing their death songs until silenced by the scouts coming down from the lookout. Through signs the two Crows reported Sioux tipis ahead. Varnum, awakened by the voice of Hairy Moccasin, saw him standing among the scattering of dark trees against the gray sky and went to lead the clamber up to the point. On either side the earth fell away; the slopes of gray rock, sage, and sparse grass were dotted with the green-black of cedar and jack pines coming out of the foggy morning haze. Far down the eastern slopes there was the bluer drift of smoke from the regimental fires creeping up across the daybreak.

"Does Custer think the Sioux have white-man eyes?" the Crows demanded sourly, their thin lips curling in contempt.

Northwestward the land descended in broken steps to a shallow valley still in darkness but where, the scouts said, they could see tipi smoke and horse herds. Varnum pulled the spyglass out long and looked, then watched the Indian faces as the light grew, showing the timber-shielded Little Bighorn snake across the prairie and dip down behind a row of bluffs. One by one the

Indians exclaimed and pointed northward, to where the mist seemed denser, darker, and under it the sense rather than the sight of movement, a confused and widespread stirring. The Crows spoke among themselves in awed voices.

Charley Reynolds took a look through the glass and remarked mildly, "That's the biggest pony herd any man ever saw together . . ."

"Biggest camp, like every summer," Bouyer amended, with French emphasis and Indian directness. "Far too big."

As the light spread out of the east through the cover of clouds, Varnum strained his eyes, blurred and bloodshot from the seventy hours of dusty scouting, first with Reno, now Custer.

"Look for nest of worms," Mitch Bouyer suggested. "Big pony herd far off look like tangles of fish worms."

Still Varnum saw nothing, but he realized from the excitement that the others did and knew that their findings would be sound. He wrote a note to Custer saying that the Sioux had been located, and started Red Star, a young Ree, off with the message a little after four-thirty. The Indian stopped to tie up his horse's tail in the sign of war and headed down toward the regiment, Bull going along with the verbal report for double security but lagging because his horse was worn and weak from travel and too little feed and water.

Up on the Crow's Nest, Varnum and his scouts saw six enemy Indians* leave cover near the hill. Four rode off into the sparse clumps of timber, but two slipped down a dry coulee that cut in ahead of Red Star and Bull. At first Varnum thought of trying to overtake them, kill them; but firing shots now, with the enemy apparently very close, would betray the whole regiment, destroy the last hope of a surprise or even a close approach.

* Little Wolf's Cheyennes, on their way from Red Cloud to the summer conference.

Motioning for silence, he listened, a cupped hand to his ear, the glass searching for a blue puff of black powder smoke; but there was no gunshot, and arrows seemed unlikely against the carbines of the scouts if Bull's horse didn't drop out entirely.

Apparently the couriers weren't discovered at all, and when Red Star came in sight of the blue-clad sentries he gave the whoop of success and rode his horse zigzag back and forth on a rise, meaning, "Enemy found!"

Several Rees hurried out to meet him, escort him into camp just as the early sun found a rift in the clouds. Bloody Knife and Stabbed, the holy man, hurried up with praise that Red Star had been chosen to carry the message. There was a pipe to be smoked, and a little thanking ceremony to be made at this honor to their young man. In the meantime another party of scouts came in and had to hear the news.

Ah-h, then probably everybody would have to hurry out for more spying on the Sioux, the leader remarked thoughtfully.

"Yes, but let us get breakfast first," someone said. "If we must go to the happy hunting ground of the missionaries we should go on a full belly."

But even with this nearness to a fight, some of the scouts just in were too worn to eat, and the others swallowed their food as fast as they could, their eyes on the little knoll where Custer's tent stood.

Most of the soldiers were still stretched on the ground, asleep, but the officers were moving around and saw Red Star return. When Custer heard about this he didn't wait for the news to be brought to him in the formal Indian way but came with Girard to interpret, Captain Tom Custer along and Mark Kellogg edging up. The colonel settled to his usual posture, leaning on his left knee, and made signs to Red Star, asking about the Sioux. The young Indian was still cooling his tin cup of coffee, and answered by drawing Varnum's note from his pocket. Then he took cautious sips of the cup while Custer read of the scout findings at the Crow's Nest, his bristly, sun-raw face growing jubilant.

By now, more Indians had come to squat in a sort of circle before Custer; the dozen pairs of expressionless eyes on him apparently pushed him to a feeble attempt at humor. By signs to Bloody Knife he pretended it was not the Indians who were afraid but his brother, Captain Tom.

"His heart flutters with fear at this news of the Sioux," he said. "When we have whipped them, he will be a man."

This seemed puzzling foolishness even after Girard tried to interpret it. Custer was only half listening, his weary face lined, his eyes focused far away. Something in Bloody Knife's serious reply jerked the colonel's attention back to the circle of Indians.

"What's that he's saying?" he demanded.

Slowly, formally, Bloody Knife rose to repeat his words, taking advantage of his position as favorite scout of the commander. "There are too many Sioux over there," he said. "All the Tetons come together. It would take many days to kill them all."

Custer laughed at the brown faces about him, suddenly elated once more by the prospect of an early encounter and a victory that would astonish these Indians who had never seen a real general in action.

"Oh," he said casually, "I guess we'll get through with them in one day."

He said it confidently as he had told a luncheon given for him by an associate of Jay Gould that his 7th Cavalry could whip all the Indians on the Plains. And it was a good time now for a military victory, only nine days to the Fourth of July and the national centennial, a hundred years since the Declaration of Independence was signed. It was an excellent time to defeat the warring Sioux, and today the best time of all, with the Democratic Convention opening the day after tomorrow, and

James Gordon Bennett of the New York *Herald* or his lieutenants surely prepared to stampede the convention for his friend, General George Armstrong Custer. Or Jay Gould of the New York *World* and the western railroads might be as effective. Victory now would leave two days and three nights to get the news to the telegraph office and to the Convention at St. Louis. Charley Reynolds, who had carried Custer's news of gold in the Black Hills out to the world, could reach the telegraph office at Bozeman in less than two days with a terse account that Custer would write. There would be additional messengers for insurance, Herendeen and others, each taking a different route, Bouyer to spur down to the telegraph at the North Platte River, with Custer himself probably making the run to the Missouri River—Custer for this run and Mark Kellogg. A victory telegram read at the Convention the morning of the 28th would do it, so he must succeed by sundown this evening, even if the defeated were only a small camp, only the "half a dozen Sioux lodges" that he had told the Ree scouts would make him the Great Father, the President.

In his elation Custer leaped to the first horse he reached, and rode at a gallop bareback through the command, the fringes of his buckskin sleeves flapping as he shouted orders to prepare for marching at eight. Behind the dust of his running horse the officers hurried into knots of three and four for a hasty breakfast and some guarded talk about the colonel's excitement and what lay ahead as they tried to wet down their dry food with the alkalied coffee or the dregs from stale canteens. The horses were still without water, a few trying to break away, many with heads down, their tongues so parched that the oats they tried to eat fell dry from their muzzles. By now the news had spread through the troopers: the Sioux camp was seen on the Little Bighorn, twelve–fifteen miles beyond the divide that lay before them.

A little after eight, without orders or bugle call, the advance troop began to move behind Custer, in a clean gray-blue shirt now, and buckskin suit and his broad whitish hat. The rest of the command followed, one troop after another, the pack train still in the rear and lagging. For about two hours and a half the regiment crawled up the hostile slopes, many of the rolling foot-hills topped by bald knobs of gray rock under the pale sky. They moved slowly through the lower cuts and passes, parallel to the deep Indian trail, but trying to keep to sod or stone to decrease the dust that was so trying to the thirsty stock and the burned-lipped men. Still it plumed upward where the regiment had passed, a war signal to even a far-off Indian. The windrows of thin clouds cut off the direct scorch of the sun but not the heat, so the men sweltered under the sultry, whitish sky, the horses wild to reach some creek, or plodding in weariness and exhaustion. After the march of about ten miles to the foot of the Crow's Nest, the command was hidden as well as possible to wait until the colonel returned from his ride ahead to the lookout.

When Custer first climbed the peak of the Crow's Nest, Charley Reynolds pointed to a spot for observation. With field glasses to his eyes, the colonel stared a long time into the bluish haze that was creeping over much of the lightly shadowed heights and hollows. He looked and said he was unable to distinguish what others called lodge smoke or even the movement of the enormous pony herds, probably on the way to water or returning to the grassy hills beyond the Little Bighorn. Despite the certainty of the scouts and the efforts of Reynolds and Bouyer, Custer insisted he saw nothing.

"I've been on the Plains a good many years," he reminded them. "My eyesight is as good as yours and I can't see anything that looks like Indian ponies."

Charley Reynolds held his usual silence but Bouyer's black-bearded face grew furious. "If you don't find more Indians in that valley than you ever saw before, you can string me up."

"All right, all right; what good would it do to hang you?" the colonel exclaimed impatiently.

Perhaps to bolster his public contention that there was no Indian village ahead, Custer claimed no hostiles could have seen the command. He rejected Varnum's report of the Indians at the foot of the hill earlier and that they must have noticed the fresh tracks of shod horses, at least of his and the white scouts'. Surely they saw the dust spreading back where the column had marched.

Curiously, the commander seemed opposed to Half Yellow Face's urging for an immediate attack, saying he planned to wait for night, although no one around believed this. Mitch Bouyer, who had worked with the trader whisky wagons among the Sioux and Northern Cheyenne camps for years, knew their power and the size of the Teton summer councils that were driven from Bear Butte by the miners. He had one suggestion for Custer: "Get your outfit out of the country as fast as your played-out horses can carry you."

There was no reply to this, barely an acknowledgment. Not that Bouyer could have expected a response to any protesting voice, or voices, all plainly less than the shake of a cottonwood leaf in the wind today.

The scouts talked gravely among themselves, glancing off toward the Little Bighorn and then toward their homes, none of them convinced that Custer really intended to hide out to dusk, most of them certain that he would not hold back. True, men like Reynolds and the older officers of the 7th knew that Custer's one successful encounter with Indians was his attack on the Southern Cheyennes on the Washita. That had started with a charge out of a frosty winter dawn, with Chief Black Kettle just back from a talk with their agent, Colonel Hazen, to the camp on their reservation, supposedly safe. There, as at Sand Creek, the Cheyennes were shot down running from their winter sleeping robes and as they were last March when Crook's force struck them in the Powder River country.

The Sioux had managed to elude all such early-morning attacks. Their one real defeat by the army was in daylight during the old peace days, before the tribe realized they were in a war. Harney had approached them under the pretext of friendly counciling and when Little Thunder's band was surrounded, the guns and cannons began to boom.

As Reynolds, Bouyer, and the Crows knew, and particularly Bloody Knife and his Rees, the Sioux over there on the Little Bighorn were not a single band under a peace chief but practically all the Tetons of war age; their chiefs, war leaders like Sitting Bull, Crazy Horse, Big Road, Crow King, and Gall. Besides, Custer had no cannon like Harney—not even the Gatling guns that Brisbin had offered, even urged.

Down in the ravine the hidden regiment was close-packed; men and horses jammed together, airless and burning hot, mouths parched, tongues swelling. While loosening his girth, Sergeant Curtis discovered he had lost some clothing from his saddle roll on the awkward uphill march. He got permission from Captain Yates to slip down along the trail to search for it but came galloping back, spurring as fast as his horse could run. He had found a box of hardtack dropped from one of the mule packs with several Indians squatting around it. They fled to their horses and headed toward the Little Bighorn when they saw him come—all but one, who stopped off on a ridge out of carbine range, but with a rifle glinting across his saddle. He waited, looking, certainly understanding, what the deep, fresh trail of shod horses meant, the trail of many, many iron-hoofed cavalry horses barely past, even if he and the others hadn't actually seen the dusty regiment and the long train of mule packs that surely contained ammunition, coffee and sugar, too— but best of all, the long-forbidden ammunition.

Custer was told this when he came riding down a draw from the Crow's Nest to gather his officers around him. He reported what they all knew: that the Crow scouts insisted they could see tipi tops on the favored campground of the Sioux, the Little Bighorn. Lots of ponies too, and dust and smoke. But he had looked through the binoculars himself, and said that he saw nothing and did not believe anyone else did either. How many of the men standing before him believed that his words were sincere could only be guessed, but certainly they all understood his agitation, the burning of his dust-reddened eyes, the stutter trapping his excited tongue.

The Ree scouts had stepped aside from the scouting here and from the lookout because it was Crow country. But now there was to be shooting, and so they prepared as well as they could against their ancient and most relentless enemy, the Sioux—this time in overwhelming numbers, fresh warriors on fast war horses, while the Rees were very few, mostly on thirsting and worn-out ponies.

After awhile Custer came to them and said if they would not fight they might at least hurry ahead fast to take all the Sioux horses that they could. At this order Stabbed, the medicine man, rode out before his tribesmen and, turning his horse back and forth, exhorted the young men to keep up their courage. The battle today would be a hard one, and many of his brothers were raw and inexperienced, going into their first real shooting. Then the medicine man dismounted and, opening his large painted bag, took out bits of clay to rub between his spit-moistened palms, singing a little, a thin, high song for power against the enemy. Finally he called the young men to him so he could rub the good medicine on their bodies against arrow, spear, and bullet.

The scouts lined up with none of the joy and anticipation usual before a good fight with horses and other booty possible, not even in the most eager youths. There was nothing now except Stabbed's silent painting with the clay and the plaintive song of one of the Rees off on a hillside, his arms lifted to the sky. One man after another the scouts stepped up to the medicine man, holding their dusty, faded shirts away from their brown bodies for the daubing with clay, even the older men whose chests were scarred from warrior ordeals.

Bloody Knife, in command of the Rees, asked to make a little talk with Custer. Through Girard he recalled that once before he had nearly touched death while with the colonel, on the Black Hills expedition. The wagons had got stuck and because Long Hair* thought it was Bloody Knife's fault, he aimed a carbine shot at him.

"Later I asked you to come back," Custer reminded the scout, "and apologized."

"Ahh, that is true, and I said it was not a good thing, this that you had done. If I, too, had been possessed by madness, you would not have seen another day."

The Rees murmured in concern, many hearing of this shooting at their head man for the first time. But Custer paid no attention to them, apparently concerned with deep plans and preparations. Bloody Knife spoke again, as out of some inner compulsion, and very gravely. "I am going home today, not the way we came, but in spirit, home to my people."

The commander of the 7th Cavalry smiled a little, his burned

* Common Indian name for Custer before he—along with the rest of the regiment—was ordered to cut his hair in 1876.

lips thin under the red stubbling, but his mind was plainly too engrossed for much show of scorn or even concern for this fear of a bunch of wild Indians, or for a repetition of the promise to take Bloody Knife to Washington when he had made himself the Great Father.

After a fireless breakfast of raw bacon, hardtack, and stale canteen water the command moved. The heat of the coming noonday lay over the high ground of the divide as the command started up the last slope. On an open place where grouse panted behind the scattered clumps of weed, Custer halted the regiment and ordered each troop commander to send a noncommissioned officer and six enlisted men back to take charge of the pack mules of his unit and help Lieutenant Mathey protect the train. Then the colonel turned to the formation of his column for attack, announcing that the first troop commander to report his pack detail completed and each trooper carrying the proper 100 rounds of carbine ammunition and 24 rounds for the pistol would receive the advance position.

There was no telling the commander's preference for this important and honored place but Benteen had his men right there behind him and it was impossible not to volunteer without implying that the officers of H Troop were a lax and unsoldierly lot, so he spoke up, certain that his unit was in order as a matter of course.

Custer accepted the salute. "Then, Colonel Benteen," he said, his stammer noticeably increased by the agitation of the day, "you have the advance, sir."

McDougall, the last commander to report ready, was detailed to help guard the pack train as penalty. With the regiment standing in columns of fours, Custer notified Benteen to move his troop to the right, but before long he galloped up to say that the captain's pace was too fast. Taking the front himself, Custer

led the 7th out across the heavily traveled saddle of the divide
and toward the Little Bighorn, twelve–thirteen miles away, the
Crows said. If anyone recalled that Custer was to locate the
Indians, scout their numbers and movements to prevent any
slip southward to Crook's department, with an outranking for
Custer if he met the general's force, apparently none spoke of it.
Or that tomorrow evening or the next day they were to meet
General Terry on the Little Bighorn with the information
gleaned in the scouting. Certainly none would have dared mention such ideas, or remind the commander that Gibbon's last
advice as the regiment started was, "Now, Custer, don't be
greedy."

After awhile the column was halted and dismounted for a
breather. Custer, with his adjutant, drew off a few yards in the
advance, just out of earshot, to plan and make notes on what
looked like a memo book or scratch pad. After fifteen minutes or
so, Cooke came galloping back to Benteen with orders from the
commander. He was to mount D and K Troops in addition to
his H outfit and proceed left at an angle of about 45 degrees
west-southwest to the line of march, going to a ridge of high
bluffs about two miles off, and apparently on and on. He was
to keep a well-mounted officer and ten men in advance, be prepared to pitch into any Indians he could find, and notify the
commander at once of any encounter.

With Lieutenant Gibson and ten troopers in the van, but
with no Indian scouts—not one man with Benteen who knew
anything of the country—the captain led out toward the rough
breaks of the Wolf Mountains, off to the left. He moved
through foothills from one steep ridge to the next, knowing
from his years on the Plains that the trail he left behind was of
eight, ten, or even fifteen thousand Indians who must be on the

Little Bighorn—surely where the scouts saw the lodges and the great pony herds. Yet, if any Sioux were ahead of him, even a thousand or two, his orders were to "pitch into" them with his force of 120 men. But with no turn-off on the trail, no sign of hoof or moccasin anywhere, it seemed he was sent chasing a bunghole bugle, a wind trumpet, sent on a fool's errand like any green looey come west.

As he passed Reno, still with no command, the major called to Benteen, asking where he was going.

"To those hills over there, to drive everything before me," the captain replied sourly as he led Weir and Godfrey and the three troops off across the dry canyons.

About a mile on, Custer's chief trumpeter was sent to Benteen with the commander's compliments and additional orders. If nothing was visible from the far ridge, he was to go to the next. Later the sergeant-major of the regiment galloped away to Benteen with further instructions from Custer: go to the next line of bluffs and on to the valley beyond, and, by implication, on and on. The orders, altogether, were almost like a sort of lopping-off of his men, as a branch is cut from the tree, from the living fluid of the trunk.

In the meantime Custer had made further division of his command and sent the bearded Cooke on to Major Reno. "The general directs you to take specific command of Companies A, G, and M."

When there was no clarification, no order of specific disposition, purpose, or objective, Reno asked, "Is that all?"

"Yes," the big adjutant replied and, wheeling his horse, was gone.

So now the 7th Cavalry was once more organized into battalions. Reno had made such division at Fort Lincoln while Custer was away in Washington; but when the commander returned, he immediately divided the regiment into wings, Reno in command of the right, Benteen the left; and then at the Yellowstone camp he had reduced it to individual troops under his own firm hand. Now, facing a fight, Custer returned to the battalion unit—three instead of Reno's four.

Varnum and Hare pushed the protesting and apprehensive scouts out ahead of the two columns hurrying along the Indian trail, but never got them far beyond the guns of the troopers. Boston Custer, Autie Reed, and Mark Kellogg rode together, close to the commander. Like the troops, they were silent now. The bluffs with stunted evergreens shut out all sign of the Little Bighorn and its own protecting ridges, while far behind somewhere McDougall was trying to hurry the pack mules along.

From the dry head of Ash Creek the evergreens began to thin and vanish, but the Indian trail clung to the narrow valley that led far off to the river. There were several cracked and dried mudholes, and then swampy spots from seepages gone dry with summer, one with the warning stink of some animal caught in the bogs—a buffalo; only the balding head out above the dried scum over the mud, the eyesockets a writhing of worms. The water-desperate horses tried to plunge into the bogs, too, but were held back with bit and quirt and spur.

While Custer pushed on along the right side of the shallow canyon, Reno started down the left, Lieutenant Hodgson galloping back to instruct each company to ride a little to the side of the one ahead, to keep the betraying dust down. Both battalions moved parallel to the wide Indian trail that had been increased once more by a branch, this one apparently from higher up the Rosebud—a war trail, with no tracks of lodgepoles, no colts, no sign of lagging old mares.

Suddenly the advance scouts slowed, pointing ahead openly,

not as to an enemy discovered but with more excitement than for a deer or even a buffalo. It was a tipi, painted and alone, standing out on a widened little bottom of Ash Creek, dried now, but with water in the spring.

Custer stopped, spoke to Girard, who signaled to the Rees, calling out, "The chief says for you to run!"

At this Strikes Two gave a war whoop and charged in, the first to count coup on the tipi, his riding whip popping against the dry hides. Young Hawk, just behind, jumped from his horse and with the long knife from his belt slashed the lodge open from top to the ground. Inside was a dead smell from the scaffold with a body* wrapped in a beaded buffalo robe, a feathered shield with bow and quiver, and a pipe and fire bag beside him; meat and even a wooden bowl of soup lay at the foot of the posts. Although it was plain that part of the Sioux had camped here very recently, no one of Custer's command seemed particularly interested that the Indian had died of bullets, of war wounds. None could know that eight days ago warriors from here had gone to attack Crook on the Rosebud, not far above Custer's turn-off at Davis Creek; but others besides the scouts must have discovered this, at least recognized the new trail coming in from the left as that of a very big and triumphant war party, multiplying the danger ahead at the river.

Reno stood high in his stirrups looking out over the rising ground and outcroppings of striated, weathered old sandstone on both sides of the little valley. As he expected, there were Indians, off some distance, watching; twenty men, perhaps even forty or a hundred hidden in an ambush; those in sight sitting on their horses with no sign of surprise or alarm at all these soldiers. They were just out of carbine range, as though inviting

---

* Old She Bear, wounded in the Rosebud fight, June 17. He was the brother of Circling or Turning Bear.

pursuit, but when the major and his scouts followed them a short distance, they still kept just ahead, the hoofs of their ponies spurting up dust.

By the time Reno returned to his troops, some of the scouts had whipped back to Custer, who ordered them to follow the fleeing Sioux, attack them. Silently the Indians refused, so now here was the showdown that all had felt coming from the first alarmed report that the Rees had made, far back down the Rosebud.

"We are scouts, to find the Sioux, not to fight them," Girard and Bouyer finally interpreted for the Indians, Crows as well as Rees.

Custer snorted, stammering in his anger. "Take the guns and horses from them!" he shouted. "Let them run home to their women!"

The scouts still refused to move, silent again under his common insult to their women. They looked away, around the closed-in horizon, finally speaking among themselves of the scattered command: Benteen far out of sight in the broken country, Reno up ahead. They gathered in little knots, some with army horses turning them over to the stable sergeants and mounting their own ponies, determined to hold to Custer's earlier promise that they need not fight, just take all the Sioux horses they could. So together they returned to Varnum and Hare.

Custer sent Adjutant Cooke loping after Reno with the news —the admission that there was a Sioux village at the river, said to be not more than two miles away, and that the Indians were running away.

"General Custer directs you to take as rapid a gait as you think prudent and charge the village, and you will be supported by the whole outfit."

The excitement of the men close enough to overhear the

order ran through the whole three companies, weary as they were, they and their horses. Lieutenant Wallace, recorder of the regiment, fell in beside Reno's adjutant, Lieutenant Hodgson, both reining close behind the major as he led off down the left side of the dry run that became the southwest side of Ash Creek. Reno was on the wide, worn lodge trail that followed the curves of the bed of sand and stagnant pools, with Custer's force off to the right, the pack train far behind somewhere, only a faint rising of dust any indication that it existed at all. There was no sign of Benteen, marching at the 45-degree angle leftward, no telling where in the rough breaks of the Wolf Mountains, or some valley beyond.

And ahead of Reno, through a cut, the men saw the tops of a few trees—the Little Bighorn. A cheer broke from them as they spurred ahead.

»▶ »▶ »▶ »▶ »▶ »▶ »▶ »▶

3 RENO
ON THE
BOTTOMS

★ ★ ★ ★ ★ ★ ★ ★

During his nine years out of West Point, Major Marcus Reno had been in the dragoons, the cavalry, and the Freedman's Bureau, served as acting inspector-general, on such boards as Retirement and Small Arms, and commanded Fort Totten and Fort Lincoln. His Civil War record was excellent, with several brevets, including a commission as Brevet Brigadier General of the U. S. Volunteers in 1865. It was perhaps characteristic of the man that neither he nor anyone else often thought of him as a general or very often called him that.

Now the afternoon of June 25, sometime between one o'clock and two-thirty—a difference between a guess at the sun's height and the watches running on the Chicago time of Fort Lincoln— Major Reno looked back over his dusty, march-worn battalion standing in twos. He drew his broad hat to his black eyebrows, turned his stocky body in the saddle, and struck out at a gallop down the drying creek for the Little Bighorn, leading his force of 112 men and the scouts, promised by Custer they need not fight.

The major soon slowed his pace to avoid winding the tired horses. By then Adjutant Cooke and Captain Keogh had crossed over from Custer's battalion to ride beside him for a while, their purpose not clearly defined. In the meantime Custer was slacking his pace too, lengthening the distance between the two columns. He had the young Crow breed, Curly, and Mitch Bouyer to scout for him, both men familiar with every break and canyon in the region. Most of the other Indian scouts had been ordered to Reno's force with the interpreters Girard, Dorman, and Billy Jackson, as well as Charley Reynolds and Terry's courier Herendeen, never sent back to the general. Even Bloody Knife, Custer's man, was with Reno in a sort of banishment. From the start the Indians had lagged, either deliberately or because their ponies were gaunt and worn by the long, thirsty travel and the lack of feed. Some trooper stock, too, fell back in spite of raw and bleeding sides roweled by spurs.

As the Indian trail crossed over to the wider bottoms on the left side of the little creek, Reno drew his horse in to keep the column closer together. By now all sight of Custer's men was cut off by an intervening tongue of rise; but ahead of the major there were glimpses of brush and trees, a glint of water too, and a great wall of dust climbing to the cloud-streaked sky of the northwest. Then suddenly the valley of the Little Bighorn opened before them, the dry, rolling, sunburned bottoms left of the stream, with a rimming of higher ground beyond, while on Reno's side, below the trail ford and the mouth of Ash Creek, steep, yellowish bluffs, gashed and torn, rose abruptly from the river bank and followed it, apparently for two–three miles.

As the smell of water reached the horses many that had lagged became wild, rearing, trying to run, those of the recruits breaking unchecked for the river, with officers spurring after them, shouting orders and caution.

"Don't let the horses jump off the high bank!"

"Don't let them bloat themselves, make themselves so logy they can't run . . ."

"Don't let them founder, die right under the saddle!"

But even so, many took the bit and plunged into the stream, throwing water high, thrusting their burned muzzles deep into the current as they drank frantically, refusing to break out of the river for whip, spur, or profanity. The men drank as thirstily, many too much, in spite of all the warnings. Then the canteens were gathered up.

"Fill them to the top! We're going into a hard fight!" the sergeants warned.

In the meantime the Rees had stopped on the far bank, refusing to cross at all. They listened, sullen and unmoved, to Lieutenant Varnum's exhortations. A few edged their horses off to the side and vanished into the breaks.

By now there was more dust down the tree-patched snake bends of the Little Bighorn indicating where the great Sioux village probably stood, and that warriors, many warriors, must be running their horses back and forth for that second wind that would carry them through a good fight. Besides, a great dust shielded not only their activities and numbers but any ambush planned.

Reno glanced anxiously back for Custer, for his support, as he worked the command across the Little Bighorn and out upon the bottoms. Cooke and Keogh were all that was visible of the Custer battalion. They sat their horses, watching awhile. Then they shouted "Good luck!" and turned back.

Girard, coming down from a bluff overlooking the river, called out that there were many Indians under the stirring dust and many, many more were whipping up along the bank from farther down. He hailed Cooke and explained what he had seen. The adjutant listened, promised to report it all to Custer, and set off rapidly back up the creek trail.

While Reno labored to form his battalion into some order, Varnum was still on the far side of the river, frantically shouting his contempt against the stubborn Rees, who understood few of the words but all of the meaning. When Girard returned, the lieutenant called to the interpreter, who hurried in to lash the Rees in their own tongue, roaring like a haranguing war chief. Finally a dozen or so did cross the river with him and Varnum, Hare, Charley Reynolds, and Isaiah Dorman, the Negro interpreter, but reluctantly looking back to Stabbed, their medicine man, rooted on the far side.

In the meantime the bellowing noncoms had reduced some of the confusion. With the girths tightened, the troopers forced their dripping horses into place, perhaps rearing and bucking, or plodding, head down. The command, finally solidified into troops, faced a stretch of about two miles that was mostly prairie-dog town and empty sage-dotted second bottom to a thumb of brush and timber extending leftward from the river bank. It was beyond this protection that the cloud of dust lifted upward, with faint whoops now and then carrying against the light cross-wind. Reno looked back over his water-spattered column to the ford that was still empty, even the dust of Cooke and Keogh's departure thinned away, and no sign of a dashing figure in a wide white hat leading five troops to the fight. Anxiously, Reno beckoned his striker, McIlhargy, of Keogh's Company I, which had served under the major on the Canadian border survey back in 1873–74. Supplying the private with one of the stronger horses left, Reno sent the shrewd, resourceful man to hurry to Custer, probably off somewhere behind the line of steep bluffs across the river by now and with no ford for miles down the stream, as both Curly and Bouyer must have told the colonel.

It was an urgent call for the promised support. "I have everything ahead of me and the enemy is strong."

The major turned in the saddle to watch the courier cross the river and vanish around the bluff up the little creek. Then, rising in his stirrups, he ordered two of his companies forward, the third, under Lieutenant McIntosh, to remain back in reserve. Spurring ahead, Reno led the charge down the dry bottoms, the men in fours behind him, the horses jumping the prairie-dog holes, shying at the audacious barks, and, beyond the dog town, stirring up the smell of sage in the hot, still air. After a mile or so, the lathering, the laboring of his horses and the sign of increasing force at his front decided Reno to form the two companies into line, the reluctant scouts under Varnum well off to the left, toward the rising ground, with Girard, Herendeen, Reynolds, and the other civilians between them and the troops but not taking much part either, beyond firing a long shot or two, watching the fight start. When the Indians began to shoot, the scouts rode down to the patch of timber extending out of the snake bends of the river and left the horses near a natural clearing in the center. From there they scattered out casually through brush and weeds to see where the encounter was going and then slipped back, one after the other, for their horses.

By now the Sioux ahead were firing more frequently and whooping louder as they charged up, stripped to breechclout, more and more of them painted for war, but still breaking easily into retreat—too easily, as the old campaigners on the bottoms knew. Plainly, they outnumbered Reno several times over, knew their terrain, hidden by the dust, and had their village, their women and children, to defend. Yet they made no real effort to check the advancing troops. It could only mean an ambush.

With still no support from beyond the river, Reno sent Adjutant Hodgson to bring up Lieutenant McIntosh and his G Troop. In the meantime he started Mitchell, his cook, also from Keogh's Company I, with a more urgent message to Custer. From the bottoms Girard thought he caught a glimpse of the Gray Horse Troop riding hard along the ridges beyond the river, but perhaps it was only the nine Rees who had remained on the other side with a small bunch of village horses, probably the women's, pastured in a pocket over there to keep them from drifting away. In addition, Lieutenant De Rudio insisted that Custer himself appeared on the heights directly across the stream, waving his hat, apparently in approval. But that point was far below any crossing to support Reno, as Curly and Bouyer must have told Custer, and, as nearly as any from Reno's force could see, very far above other crossings that might be useful.

After Reno's battalion had advanced in the line for about a mile, they seemed to be nearing a shallow ravine, or dry wash, one reaching all the way down from the lowish bluffs on the left to the river, cutting across the entire bottoms in a sort of natural breastworks. Occasional puffs of wind lifted the dust momentarily, exposing the ravine edge here and there, with lines of Indian heads visible beyond the charging riders, the low ravine surely full of Sioux. Plainly, this was a time for caution, with too much eagerness growing among Reno's troops. Both horses and men were excited by the stink of living dust and gun powder, by the whoops and war cries, particularly the recruits, men who did not know about Indian ambushes or that Indian fighting was to the total death, as surely as the attack against them was intended.

Major Reno decided to deploy his force as skirmishers between the arm of timber from the river and the rises to his left. Even before this could be done, two horses became unmanageable and bolted ahead, carrying their riders through the Indian line and the shallow ravine into the Hunkpapa, the Sitting Bull village, the uppermost of the great camp, and were torn from their horses there.

Apparently the Indians considered these men the forerunners of a powerful charge, the two troopers bold as warriors might be bold, riding through the enemy to gain honors or death, and to break the fighting courage and will for an overwhelming attack. So the Sioux hurried their own charge in great force, coming on their finest horses, painted, the tails tied up for war, with feathered manes and jaw ropes. Their spearheading attack was not toward the soldiers but against the scouts along the low bluffs on the left flank, forcing back the section held by their old, old enemies, the Rees. These Indians recognized the power of the coming charge, understood the number of warriors along the Little Bighorn that day, and fled, most of them whipping clear back across the river where the eight men under Stabbed were gathering and trying to hold the small bunches of Sioux horses.

Even with his left flank collapsed, Reno realized that the Sioux should be fighting harder than this so near their standing village, and he dared not proceed without strong reinforcement. There was no support anywhere in sight, Benteen probably fifteen miles up the river and Custer—who could guess where Custer was now? Certainly not any man who knew that he did not support Major Elliott and his men on the Washita, had not even tried to rescue their bodies.

With the dubious aid of the Indian scouts gone—all except Bloody Knife, who had been out gathering up three loose Sioux horses, and one or two Rees lost somewhere in the dust and smoke—Varnum and Hare were left with the crumbled flank and a handful of men. Reno ordered G Troop thrown into the gap now that the Sioux were advancing and firing more daringly than ever in the shielding dust, and retreating to lure the troopers into ambush. Reno thought of the trails that led to the river here, trails of at least five thousand fighting men or more, the scouts had said. He had believed them, and now he was faced by at least five–six hundred warriors with little over one hundred men, since the two were carried into the Indian camp and the two couriers were hurried out to Custer.

Plainly, the major's position was desperate, and yet he felt he must try to hold the bottoms a little longer for the promised support to come, and so he flung up his hand, setting his horse back on its haunches. "Halt!" he ordered the troop commanders, "halt and prepare to fight afoot!"

There was some confusion as the men dismounted and the horse-holders, all veterans, grabbed the bridles, four each, and galloped the horses into the timber toward a central clearing. The thin line of foot soldiers wavered at first and shrank from the crack and whine of the bullets about them and the pale zing of arrows, but they steadied and began to fire at the whooping warriors sweeping up and wheeling in the billowing yellow dust and blue powder smoke, the Indians clinging to the far side of their horses. One warrior, stripped, had wrapped a company banner around his body and raced his war horse five times past the line of troopers, drawing bullets like hail about him and getting away untouched.

In response to a rallying, the line of troopers slipped forward 100 yards or so, one man after another, led by veterans crawling, dodging from hollow to weed to sage clump to prairie-dog mound under the shielding smoke. They stopped as a little wind lifted the cover of dust and gunfire for a moment and

showed a solid wall of racing and whooping horsemen and beyond them the blackened pole tops of skin lodges thick as a
forest. The line halted and began to fire rapidly from knee and
belly. Almost at once a sergeant was killed and a couple of
other men hit as the Sioux swooped in, shooting point-blank.
They got what they wanted: an excited and blinding roar of
guns, the ammunition largely wasted in the dust, the firing so
fast that the barrels of the carbines heated and the swollen
cartridges jammed in the breeches, the cursing men hacking
away at the empty casing with their knives so they could fire
again, perhaps compelled to go to the pistol.

Reno had moved up and down the line to calm the men—
over 15 per cent under their first fire—to slow their need to
shoot at any distance. He was near Captain Moylan when word
came from the timber that the Sioux were massing on the far
side of the river and slipping across to the timber to get at the
horses. Leaving Lieutenant Hodgson to keep him informed of
the situation on the firing line, Reno risked taking G Troop—
the smallest, under thirty-five men—to the brush at the river
bank. From there he got a good view of the upper lodges and
could see the Indians scattered all along the stream, coming
and going in painted, dusty swarms, some guarding the women
and children fleeing down the river, fresh warriors whipping
up, apparently from camps lower down.

But there was no way to stop the Indians still creeping in
through the underbrush and dust past G Troop to infiltrate
the horse-holders, pricking a couple of the best animals with
arrows, making them break away, to be swept off by yelling
youths. It was a desperate moment, for in ten minutes the
troops could all be set afoot and run down like rabbits fleeing
through the grass. Major Reno hurried out upon the open
bottoms, trying to get beyond the dust, to make a last search
of the horizon for his support, any support. There was nothing,

only the roar of battle back around the timber, and far bullets spurting around him as Sioux sharpshooters tried to pick him off. He signaled for his adjutant. Hodgson came galloping up, his young face dirt-streaked and disturbed: The Sioux were passing around the left of the firing line with little opposition and gathering behind it.

They couldn't hold out long here, the young lieutenant had to say.

The major nodded, wiping the stinging dust from his eyes and the sweat from his mustache with a bandanna. Once more he looked back to the river crossing, past the hanging dust blued by gunsmoke, and beyond, where Sioux charged out to recapture some horses that the Rees were running off into the breaks. But there was no blue-britched battalion in sight, no support, although it was practically an hour and half since he had struck the Little Bighorn, and his two couriers were either lost or ignored. By now Custer might be five–six miles down the river. Perhaps he had discovered the half-dozen "Sioux lodges," enough lodges whose defeat would make him, as he had promised the Rees, the Great Father. Perhaps he was on the way to a telegraph office himself by now, to Bozeman or the Platte with the news of a victory to stampede the Democratic Convention, either through the rumored inside track he had with James Gordon Bennett's men there, or with those of Gould's World. Then there might be friendly delegates from Michigan, in spite of some apparently leaning toward Hendricks. Surely someone in the home delegation was waiting in St. Louis for the news of victory.

Even so, there should be some sign of McDougall and the pack string, at least the ammunition mules belonging to Reno's three troops, with the troop escorts. Perhaps the Sioux had finally decided to capture the strung-out train, as the major had feared every day since they left the Yellowstone, or Mc-

Dougall might have been ordered straight to Custer. Even without orders, he would probably follow Custer's trail, the heavier, plainer one, and leave Reno surrounded by yelling Sioux and his guns empty.

It was a time beyond the bitterest profanity. Only the scattering of veteran sharpshooters among the troopers were holding the Indians off now, and soon their guns would be empty if the battalion wasn't overrun before. Reno and his subordinates knew by now that he would have to proceed as though there wasn't another soldier in the whole country, and clearly he would have to act soon or he would lose at least the depleted troops of the firing line. Temporarily, he could draw them into the thickets around the spreading cottonwoods that sheltered the horses, but there was no telling how many Indians had worked up the arm of the brush to the timber, creeping as quiet as bullsnakes as they did elsewhere, through rushes, weeds, and sagebrush, not even a grasshopper aroused to jump and betray them as they passed.

Out at the firing line, Lieutenant Wallace, who had heard Cooke's orders to Reno after the division of the command, was desperate too. He had remained out when Lieutenant McIntosh withdrew his G Troop to guard the horses. Seeing Captain Moylan through the smoke, Wallace shouted that another courier should be sent to hurry up Custer's promised support.

But who? Not Terry's courier Herendeen, with a good horse but not familiar with every cut and canyon as the courier must be—preferably an Indian who could strip and be a Sioux in the dust. Unfortunately, the few Indians remaining with Reno were strangers to the country, and too much afraid. There was, however, Billy Jackson, breed scout, with friends among the hostiles.

Jackson agreed that the situation was desperate and that a

messenger to Custer was imperative. Then he pointed off toward the river crossing, shut off now by a wild racing of Indian warriors who had turned the left flank, with surely many more hidden along the bank and in the silvery buffalo berry thickets.

"Nobody get through," the scout said, shaking his shaggy head. "Nobody . . ."

The men within hearing looked to each other. He was right.

By now too many troopers were being hit in the thin and scattered firing line, bold warriors charging their horses through it, perhaps to fall and be dragged away by the lariat around the horse's neck, but more coming, always more. Soon the line would be overrun entirely by a determined attack, the Indians clinging to the far side of their mounts by a toe over the back and a hand in the mane while they shot through the flying cloud of hair above the withers or under the neck of the galloping ponies.

Abruptly Major Reno decided to order the men into the timber. They came, stooping, running, faces blackened by dust and powder soot, sweat- and blood-streaked, some going down from bullet or arrow as the warriors whooped them along. A couple of the wounded were gathered up and carried on the run, others helping themselves as well as they could, the dead left behind to be struck with quirt, spear, or bow as the young warriors counted their coups on the bodies, dead or alive.

There was confusion in the timber, too, the officers losing contact with their men in the tangle of thorny rose and plum brush around the scattered cottonwoods and box elders, the whole timber now filled with the roar of panic shooting, and the thickening stink and sting of black powder smoke augmented by fire set along the river by the Indians to eat its slow way toward the brush. Troopers shouted, Indians whooped, whistling bullets ripped the foliage, thudding as they struck wood or flesh, the horses plunging and screaming—his troopers surrounded by four–five times their number, and more warriors constantly arriving from down the river.

Surely Charley Reynolds realized there must be at least five thousand fighting men in the great camp. He knew the southern Oglalas and Brules, the scattering of Minneconjous aligned with them, from his years scouting around the North Platte region. He knew those of the Missouri agencies, too, but less of the hostile Hunkpapas, although he recognized Gall, Crow King, and Knife Chief when they rode in. Gall, usually a peaceful man, had his hair ragged and new mourning striations bleeding for the wife and child he found killed just now when he returned from down near the great central council lodge. Young Black Moon, warrior society leader in the charges against Reno, was killed soon after the troopers were deployed and now Gall and Crow King took over. Reynolds also knew Red Horse, another chief of the great council lodge, and Kills Eagle, from the Blackfoot Sioux up north. He saw the brother of Feather Earrings, a Minneconjou, fall and be dragged away as Red Horn Bull, the famous Oglala runner, led the charge.

Once a great shouting went up for a swarm of warriors from the camps farthest down the river. Reynolds saw them enter the fight, still unbloodied: a great party of Oglalas and Cheyennes led by Crazy Horse, with Hump, head warrior of the Oglalas, riding beside him. He couldn't know that the Oglala war chief had organized the attack on Crook the 17th of June, the first organized Sioux attack in history, strong enough to drive the general from the field. But Reynolds knew Crazy Horse, and knew the attack would take on a new daring, a new wildness, and a new solidarity, with slier attempts at decoying Reno farther on, far enough to surround and overwhelm him.

With the ammunition getting low, Reno drew his defense back from the river bank too now, into a broken circle in the

timber. But he knew he must not try to hold out here either—
unless he and his men were to remain forever. He could no
longer hope for reinforcements. So far as the major or his officers knew, there had been no battle plan, and by now the
7th Cavalry was apparently hopelessly scattered, Benteen and
McDougall, perhaps even Custer, in possible difficulties elsewhere, or surely someone would have brought Reno an order,
if not support.

Hoping to unite the regiment, as seemed absolutely necessary
in the face of the overwhelming enemy, to save his own men
from total annihilation, perhaps even the entire regiment of
approximately 650, Reno decided to move across the river to
the ridge. There he could be seen and he could dispose of his
force to hold out until reinforcements, Benteen or McDougall,
he hoped, might arrive. And they must come soon, even up
there. The men had started with 100 rounds each for the carbines, half in their belts and half in the saddlebags, but the
hot exchanges had brought this dangerously low.

The fires in the dead rushes along the river bank had spread
both ways into the ripening June grasses of the bottoms and the
buffaloberry brush. Now it had reached straight ahead into the
higher, drought-withered weeds and burned more rapidly, making a great smoke as it crept along the dusty, dried brush tops
in the light northeast wind, blazing up in the tent caterpillar
webs, leaving the green wood smoldering, the fire smoke setting
even the seasoned, gun-broken cavalry horses wild. Here and
there one tore loose, the horse guard leaping into the saddles
of the wilder ones, to hold them if possible. On the river side
the scorching head of flames drove the troopers back, so the
defense was collapsing there, in spite of Reno's frantic efforts
to bolster the resistance long enough for an orderly movement.
He shouted assurance that no naked Indian would come creeping in from that side, not through the smoldering brush; but

his voice was lost in the roar of guns and the snap and pop of the fire.

Sweat-streaked and powder-smoked, the major hurried around the broken circle of his troopers in the timber, trying to be heard, cautioning that the Indians were stealing in under the rolling smoke from downwind, one not over five feet away when a bullet finally drove him into the earth. More horses were struck, screaming as they went down. The men were forced still farther upon themselves. Several more were wounded, one from M Troop so badly that the doctor was found and hurried through the underbrush.

Reno caught a glimpse of interpreter Isaiah Dorman and then of the sooted, resigned face of Charley Reynolds, who had come along on Custer's scout although his gun hand was swollen and infected. Then he had realized the overwhelming number of Sioux sure to be gathered here for their summer conference and angered the colonel by saying this. Girard told Reno he had given Charley a drink of whisky to cheer his gloom, but it didn't help and now there seemed only one purpose left in him. Methodically Charley Reynolds thrust cartridges into the breech of his rifle, and, ignoring the pain in his hand, watched with his customary patience for a warrior charging in close or for the slow, gentle shake of brush that revealed a stealthy Sioux approach. Then he pulled the trigger, ejected the smoking shell to the scattering around him, and threw in another. Bloody Knife, too, had the calm face of the resigned, bending forward, peering through the brush and smoke, his gun ready. The major stopped beside the Ree to ask by sign where the Indians would concentrate their thrust, to help him plan the run for the river and the heights beyond.

Before the scout could answer, a new burst of bullets ripped through the torn foliage. One of them struck Bloody Knife, blowing his skull open and spattering the handsome black silk kerchief with blue stars that Custer had given to his once-favorite scout—spatterings that reached Major Reno standing beside the Ree.

For a moment the hardened campaigner was as sickened as the rawest recruit. Plainly the Indians were everywhere, penetrating everywhere, so many of them that even two–three times the number of his battalion would not hope to hold out in this patch of timber. Perhaps not even the entire 7th Cavalry, with all the ammunition of the pack train, could hold out. Plainly, he must act fast if he was to save any of his deserted force, save any at all, even at the sacrifice of leaving the dead behind.

Waving his pistol, the major shouted his orders to repair to a new position beyond the river, on the bluffs. In the central clearing he gave the order to mount and form in columns of four to Moylan and McIntosh himself and sent Hodgson on to Captain French, but with the crashing of gunfire, the whooping, the thunder of hoofs, no order by voice could be heard two yards away. Dust, smoke, and burning brush made communication by signal impossible and Custer had forbidden trumpets.

Furious at the desertion of his force by the commander, Reno watched the men come running out of the thickets to the horses, hoping that all those scattered in the underbrush had been reached with the order before it was entirely too late, and that the few wounded could be helped to mount. The dead had to be left behind, the dead and near-dead, for the withdrawal could not wait, with the Indians firing into the troopers from the timber around the clearing. Some men, well hidden, took the opportunity to avoid the run for the river, Lieutenant De Rudio of Company A among these, and several soldiers as well as Herendeen, Girard, Jackson, and other scouts.

Then a trooper was picked off from the middle of Company

M, crying out as he was hit, to slide dead from his horse, the riderless animal loose and crashing through the brush. Now Reno knew they had to move quickly, not wait for the rest. He spurred to the head of Company A to lead the desperate run from the timber and out across the bottoms swarming with Sioux. He realized he would lose many men, but some could be saved this way, the only way, with the predicted overwhelming number of Indians all around him, and the failure of the support promised by Custer, even the failure of the battalion's reserve ammunition. It was a hard choice for a man with four brevets for gallant and meritorious service, now to be hung up like this, where he must watch his men being slaughtered.

Before the charge of the troops toward the river, the Indians parted, catching the column between a cross fire of bullets and arrows from both flanks, particularly from the right, shutting Reno away from the good crossing, forcing him down the river to a narrow one-pony-wide ford cut through the high earth bank down into the soft quicksand of the channel with the same narrow, steep climb out on the far side. Indians afoot were dodging from tree to tree over there and from cut bank to bush, getting into position; while on the mile and a half bottoms that Reno had to cross six–seven hundred mounted Sioux whooped and shot. The troopers replied with their pistols as they spurred ahead, but the expert warriors were sliding to the far side of their galloping ponies, deliberately emptying the army saddles, while others, mostly youths, gathered up the loose cavalry horses. Then, as the hand guns were silenced, the warriors closed in, swinging war clubs, wrestling men from their wild and rearing mounts. Reno emptied one pistol into the Indians and then the other as he tried to hold them off, and to pay them for the men he was losing—particularly the proud Lieutenant McIntosh, of Indian blood too, who went down at the edge of the timber. For this one man alone Reno's fury would have been great—the good soldier sacrificed on this foolish venture today when tomorrow they would have had an army, an army with whom the Sioux could have been "popped like a louse is popped between the thumbnails."

But instead the Indians were free to push in upon his little force, half lost in the new cloud of dust and stinging powder smoke, lost and trapped like a herd of buffaloes, the warriors crowding in, cutting the men down like so many fat yearlings.

At the ford Reno shouted commands to cross single file, but no one could hear him now—not those in front, ridden down by the frantic horse behind, not those behind, driven on by arrow and lead. The stampeding horses plunged forward into the narrow pony crossing, two, three, and more wedging themselves, the water ahead full of men fighting for the yard-wide outlet up the high bank on the far side, indeed like buffaloes caught in a narrow water gorge. Some daring young warriors leaped into the churning stream with knife and war club. After the first troopers lucky enough to get out, the bank sides became slippery from the wet horses and began to break down under the desperate pawing of the ironed hoofs. Men and animals died there under the hot Sioux fire. Lieutenant Hodgson, Reno's adjutant and a favorite of the regiment, tried to avoid the pile-up and leaped his horse off the high bank, but it was struck by a bullet and fell dead in a mighty splash of water, the lieutenant hit in the knee. Grabbing the stirrup of Sergeant Culbertson, he was towed across, only to be shot down after they got out on the far side. Dr. De Wolf managed to reach the far bank too, and then was killed from the bluff above. Davern of Company F, lost his horse to a bullet, but he had kept one cartridge in his pistol. With this he shot the Indian from his pony, leaped upon the bare back, and spurred after the van of troops heading up the old buffalo trail into a draw that narrowed to the ridge, the horses taking the steep rocky climb by heaves and jumps. The troopers who made it felt their lives had been returned to them by sheer luck. Sergeant Ryan of Company M looked back upon the hazed and swarming bottoms and was certain that in a few minutes more down there and not a man would have lived to escape. On the bluff the weary Lieutenant Varnum, hat gone, looking tall as a tree, was holding up his hands to stop the troopers appearing over the steep edge.

"For God's sake, men," he shouted, "don't run. There are officers and men killed and wounded down there and we must go back to get them."

Perhaps some heard him, but plainly it was not voice or command that held most of the men—particularly the green ones, those new to the Indian wars. Only the failure of their horses kept them from fleeing as most of the Indian scouts had fled.

On the broken, unfamiliar ridge Reno tried to find a high spot visible to any scout or courier from far off, and yet offering the best defensive position. He selected a knob topped by a sort of shallow depression to hold the horses and protect the wounded that Dr. Porter was gathering to a shot-torn banner drooping in the hot air. Ten of these had been able to get to the hill mounted. Most of them were from A Troop, which had led the column. Reno turned the care of the wounded over to Captain Moylan, to make them as comfortable and secure as possible. Then, with still no sign of the pack train anywhere, the major sent a man to find McDougall and bring the ammunition mules in on a gallop.

By now some noticed that Reno had also lost his hat in the run for the hill and tied a red bandanna around his head. His mustache and beard were thick with the pale yellow-gray dust caught and crusted in the sweat. Hurrying around on the hill, the major deployed his men, as well as he could at the low depression, to dig into the gravelly, hard-baked earth with all they had—knives and tin cups. The major's dirty face was still streaking with tears over the loss of his adjutant, Hodgson, and over McIntosh and the rest as he tried to take stock.

Three officers were dead, including Dr. De Wolf, and twenty-nine enlisted men and scouts; seven had serious wounds, and fourteen soldiers and scouts were missing, some probably behind in the brush and thickets of the bottoms. Reno and the rest had a fair idea where Lieutenant De Rudio would be, and Herendeen and Girard, too, the latter particularly noted for taking care of his own skin. He and most of the other scouts didn't consider themselves hired to fight; really none except Charley Reynolds, who was either completely disabled or dead, or he would be here. The Rees, probably all except the dead Bloody Knife, had vanished over the ridge toward the mouth of the Powder River—and justifiably so, many thought. They had tried to tell Custer just what would be found here on the Little Bighorn—the great summer conference of the Tetons. Probably twelve to fifteen thousand Indians, they had said, with perhaps twenty thousand horses and at least five to seven thousand fighting men.

As Reno worked out a place of defense, some of the Crow scouts began to slip in out of the canyons. The major welcomed them, hoping to make the best of what remained in men and scanty ammunition—less than five rounds per man, Varnum said. He hoped, too, that the scouts might help hold the Indians off the bodies of Hodgson and De Wolf and the troopers killed on the steep climb to the hill.

It was not too soon, for the Sioux, doubly angered at the killing of High Eagle, a chief of the great council lodge, were beginning to drop bullets in upon them from some of the surrounding ridges. Next it might be prairie fire; although there was very little grass, it was dry. Besides, the hordes of Indians could drag up dead rushes and timber from the river bottoms, push the burning stuff in upon Reno as soon as the wind rose a little, to panic the horses and the green recruits, blind everyone in the smoke, and cut them down.

But one had to hope for the men here on the ridge. Somewhere there were three more sections of the great 7th Cavalry—nine troops more and the pack train with the ammunition so desperately needed. Of these Custer and his five companies had surely passed them by—as the fresh trail of shod horses off on the right beyond Reno's hill showed very clearly—although Moylan tried to believe that the colonel was still in the rear and would come to their assistance.

With a moment to consider their position, the major and his officers spoke about the rumors that firing had been heard far down the river somewhere while the battalion was piled up in the pony crossing of the river. They listened now, with hands cupped to ears, but there was no sound other than the Indians shooting and yelling around them, nothing else except the faint whooping from the village below, still largely hidden by the rise of brush- and grass-fire smoke on the bottoms, although the dust down there was drifting away over the prairie. Women were all over the fighting ground, their knives glinting occasionally in the pale sunlight—women hurrying here and there, like small running specks, hacking and then running again.

The Indians around Reno seemed in no great hurry, perhaps depending upon time: lack of ammunition and thirst could do the job without the loss of another warrior.

»▶ »▶ »▶ »▶ »▶ »▶ »▶ »▶

4 RENO ON
THE HILL

★ ★ ★ ★ ★ ★ ★ ★

The consultation of Custer with his adjutant, their weary horses standing quietly together while the men worked over the notebook, had produced a battalion of three companies for Benteen, and his orders to strike off on a valley hunt, as he called it. The captains of the added troops were Godfrey and Weir, both fellow Ohioans of the Custers. Weir was a particular partisan of the commander from his four years, to a lieutenant colonelcy, in the 3rd Michigan Cavalry—the unit that had mutinied against Custer in 1865—and had testified for the colonel in the court-martial of 1867.

Weir and Godfrey looked back to their colonel as the new battalion was being set up. Then they fell in behind Benteen as he led out, trot and walk, from one line of high bluffs to the next, seeking an unknown valley harboring Indians and holding himself ready to "pitch into" any he could find. The terrain along the breaks of the Rosebud and the Wolf Mountains was unfailingly rough and rocky, largely bare of grass, sage, or weeds,

with no sign of hoofprint anywhere, pony or buffalo, or even
a prairie sparrow to rise before the marching column. No one
with the battalion had ever been anywhere near the region, and
although the six Crow scouts of the regiment knew every knob
and canyon of the country, as did Jackson, Bouyer, and even
Reynolds, none of these was sent with Benteen.

But the captain with the thick thatch of gray curls darkened
by the fine dust of the day's march was an experienced Plains
campaigner and experienced, too, in the ways of his commander.
It was not the first curious detail assigned to him, but perhaps
the most curious, with trails of a great camp ahead of the regiment—trails of far too many Indians for the whole 7th to face,
if the scouts were right. In the meantime Benteen had been
sent off to the left into the lifeless wilds, with a fourth of the
force.

As the battalion drew farther and farther from the command,
the captain knew he had to come to some decision. There was
no Indian sign anywhere and no sign or smell of water for the
thirsty men and horses, while the trail Custer was following had
offered plenty of both. Judging by the lag in both the Weir
and Godfrey companies, nobody wanted to be left out of the
coming fight somewhere behind them. Besides, the help of his
three troops, with the lowest per cent of recruits never exposed
to gunfire, might be welcome, even crucial.

Benteen had considered his orders militarily senseless from
the start, whatever Custer's personal reasons for sending him
far from any possible action by the regiment. Now he decided
to ignore the instructions to hunt that unknown valley. He
recalled his advance guard and struck diagonally across to the
probable direction of Ash Creek and Custer's march, hoping by
speed on the easier downslope of the general terrain to make
up for the precious time lost in the futile valley hunt. Riding
well ahead of his force, Benteen reached the trail with the scant

droppings of Custer's horses still drying, but with no mule tracks except those of Mark Kellog's animal and of the one assigned to the Ree, Stabbed, when his pony gave out. At the boggy place Benteen spent perhaps fifteen minutes trying to water his thirsting animals a little. Just as the battalion lined out again, the advance mules of the supply train thundered up at an awkward gallop, packs pounding and flapping, the guards trying with yell and spur to head the animals, but unable to keep the leaders from plunging straight into the bogs, some going down to their packs in the mud.

Benteen looked back but he couldn't spare the time to help in the extrication, which was the responsibility of the train escort, large enough for all such contingencies if not for a stand against the Sioux. He followed the fresh trail along the left of Ash Creek. A mile or so below the lone tipi, still smoldering, Sergeant Kanipe came riding in from Custer with Cooke's written orders to the commander of the mule train to hurry the packs. Benteen sent the man on to McDougall, some miles back by now. As Kanipe passed the column he shouted, "We got 'em, boys!" seeming to imply that Custer had attacked the village and captured it. But the message increased Benteen's uneasiness about serious trouble, and with his orderly he hurried on, riding four–five hundred yards ahead of his battalion to draw them along, the eager Captain Weir about midway between him and the column.

Before long, Benteen saw another man come whipping up the trail. It was Trumpeter Martin, his lathered and worn horse staggering along as fast as it could go. The man handed over a scrawled and abbreviated message from Cooke: "*Benteen Come on Big Village Be quick Bring packs W. W. Cooke*" and a postscript, difficult to read: "*Brng Pacs.*"

Benteen looked down the trail in alarm, but all he could see was a riderless horse, perhaps played out and left behind.

"What is happening?" he demanded.

The Indians were skedaddling, abandoning the village, Martin told the captain in his broken Italian-English—natural from the immigrant Martini enlisted under the Anglicized name of Martin. It had taken the trumpeter three-quarters of an hour to get from Custer to Benteen, and about fifteen minutes since he looked down into the river valley and saw the fighting there. But Benteen, not knowing of Custer's later division of his force, did not ask about Reno, and Martin volunteered nothing of the fight. He said that probably Custer had made a charge through the Indian village by this time.

This limited information seemed to reduce the urgency. There was no sound of firing, so instead of hurrying back to the pack train himself, Benteen gave Martin a note to McDougall. By then the trumpeter had been issued another horse. His was not only played out, but it had picked up a bullet in the hip somewhere along the route.

"You're lucky it wasn't you!" Benteen told the courier.

But the bullet was tangible evidence to underline the need for the packs. The captain waited until Weir came up and showed him Cooke's message, asking no questions and receiving no volunteered advice. By this time Benteen felt he had some sense of the situation. If he went back for the packs, which could be moved only so fast after the long marches, valuable time would be lost getting his battalion to Custer, who at least needed his ammunition. If he halted to wait for the packs, there was no gain except protection for the train from Indian attack, unlikely now. So he took the trot along the fresh trail of what seemed part of Custer's force and gradually raised the vibration of far gunfire. The sound of shooting grew distinct as Benteen neared the Little Bighorn along the lodgepole trail that was surely headed for a crossing. Once his horse pricked up its ears and looked off toward the breaks to the right, but it was only the breed Curly, one of Custer's scouts, slipping away as most of the Rees had done.

The sound of battle grew louder and more continuous, more pronounced and insistent. The captain ordered a gallop with drawn pistols, expecting to see the enemy around every bend, the Sioux being driven toward him by Custer.

Benteen was forming a line to meet the fleeing enemy when he came into full view of the Little Bighorn and stopped his troopers. The river valley was full of dust and smoke from the powder, and from the grass that the Indians had fired. The field glasses showed a scattered engagement about two miles down, with gunshots and moving specks visible through the glass, fleeing specks, friend or foe, strung across the river and up the steep bluff on this side. With the high ridge rising there and pushing close to the stream for some miles—bluffs difficult to climb under fire if he were driven out too—Benteen hesitated to charge over into the milling Sioux.

Several Indians appeared back behind the bluffs to the right of the river, stopped their horses to look, and then whipped up with a small herd of captive ponies. They were Crow scouts; one of them shouted, "Many Sioux!" to Benteen and made the signs of "big fight." Another pointed back along the top of the river ridge where some soldiers were coming together, bent low on their horses, kicking them to keep them going. More appeared over the steep rim of the bluff, some stumbling up afoot, perhaps dragging at their blown horses. Here and there a trooper looked back and fired against some enemy hidden in the breaks below, the puff of smoke a blue explosion, and then moved to a point where a man—not Custer, but Reno—was gesturing toward a planted banner, gesturing direction and haste.

Benteen lowered his glasses and deployed his force into a skirmish line along the river side of the steep bluffs, hoping to hold back the Indians swarming up from the bottoms. When Reno's troops gathering on the hill saw Benteen's battalion, loud cheers went up from them—cheers intended for Custer's five companies, come to the rescue at last. The pursuing Indians stopped at sight of the new troops, whoever they were—four or five hundred Indians on the highest point of land about a mile away, surprised in the attack on the little knot of troopers, with about nine hundred more warriors still milling around on the bottoms and stringing over the river.

Major Reno came riding down to meet Captain Benteen. He was still hatless, with the red bandanna around his head against the heat and the vagrant sun, his face, his mustache and bearding caked with dust. He was excited, and furious at what he called the betrayal of his men by the commander's failure to support them. He greeted Benteen most gratefully; his arrival was a damned welcome surprise. When he last saw the captain he seemed headed off beyond the Rosebud Mountains on some long, long route.

"Where is Custer?" Benteen asked, unaware even now that the command had been divided once more after his departure. To Reno's explosive, "I don't know!" the captain produced Cooke's message to bring the packs. It seemed Custer had forgotten about the order to go valley-hunting, and if Benteen hadn't finally decided to ignore, to disobey, the command, he could have been twenty, even twenty-five miles from the packs and the trail when Martin came to find him, pushing his horse, already failing, as far as it could go.

But Reno and his men knew even less about Custer's whereabouts than the order for the packs suggested. From French, Moylan, Varnum, and Wallace, stopping by at intervals to welcome Benteen, there was anger and curses, for their colonel—running off and leaving them hanging after he ordered them to attack the village. It wasn't that he didn't know exactly where they were, not after he sent Cooke and Keogh along as far as the river crossing, where the rising dust of the Sioux warriors was plain to see. And when the Indians, far too strong, pressed hard, the major had sent two couriers back, at intervals, for the promised support. Nothing had been heard of them or of any reinforcements. Reno had seen nothing of Custer since several miles back, although some of the men said they caught a glimpse of him on a bluff down the river, from their position on the hill here, and some told him now that they heard firing from down farther. Reno assumed that was Custer, as Cooke's message to Benteen and Martin's words seemed to corroborate. But there was no sign of the pack train and Reno's ammunition was dangerously low, even for a stand up here, where he could be seen, be reached by McDougall.

On Benteen's asurance that the mule train could not be very far away by now, Reno asked Lieutenant Hare, acting as his adjutant in Hodgson's place, to go hurry the packs along as much as possible. But young Hare's horse was spent. Offered a choice of Benteen's force, the freshest remaining because he might have to outrun a lot of Sioux, the lieutenant slipped down to shake hands with Captain Godfrey, his commander in K Troop, and to accept his horse for the attempt.

"We had a big fight in the bottoms and got whipped," Hare called back as he spurred away.

Captain Benteen divided his practically untouched ammunition supply with Reno's men, particularly with the 15 per cent of itchy-trigger-fingered recruits. Yet Lieutenant Varnum, wild with sorrow when he discovered that his friend Hodgson was dead, had blazed away at Indians hopelessly out of reach even with a borrowed rifle for its range over the carbine. Reno had fired the same hopeless shots because so many men had been lost, particularly his brave young adjutant, lost by the miscalculations of his superiors. All that could be done for Lieutenant Hodgson now was to try to keep the Indians from where his body probably lay.

Benteen, grim at what he saw on the ridge, with so many Indians swarming to the attack, hurried to help form the defense. No one could tell how powerful or protracted the attack might be, with the semicircle of higher ridges blocking out most of both the village and the Little Bighorn farther down. He looked around the men, the shaken survivors, and realized that even with his three fresh companies, all of Reno Hill could be overrun here in the next twenty minutes, perhaps with guns from the pack train, which would have to break through the tightening circle of attack.

Facing this nightmare that had confronted Reno one way or another since he led his troops in a gallop across the bottoms, it was decided to keep most of Benteen's fresh force along the bluff face below the major's position. There the troops could see two–three miles of the bottoms with part of the river ridge and surely detect any large body of Indians creeping up from the stream. But those coming up behind the heights, from above and below, could not be detected until they caught the little circle on Reno Hill in their cross fire. Besides, there must be reinforcements ready, stout and resolute men, to go help the pack train through the gathering siege. The gunfire was already breaking into bursts of drumming roar around the hill, some of the bullets whining as they struck the loose rock and pebbles, to ricochet dangerously. But here, too, the bow was a telling weapon in the hands of the few expert warriors who managed to creep near and drop arrows among the horses and the wounded without lifting a dusty head to sight.

For a necessary moment several officers collected in a pocket at the edge of the bluff, to plan as they peered over into the valley full of thinning haze, with fresh dust and smoke creeping across the snake bends of the river farther down, surely from some other engagement. There were still many Indians down the river, some collected in standing knots along the bottoms, some whipping back and forth or stopping in rows to look up toward the heights downstream, some of them so far away they seemed bits of burned grass blowing along, lodging here and there and drifting again toward the river and out of sight.

Up on the heights the Indians were sharpening their attack on Reno, pushing in from every side, even along the bluff face. More young warriors with their paint caked in yellow-gray dust moved like bullsnakes toward their prey, creeping slowly, imperceptibly, from hollow to little cut bank, to weed clump, driving a silent arrow into any careless movement. More, too, farther out, were lifting their bows upward and letting the sharp iron points fall into the little circle of men and horses.

Yet the overwhelming charge expected any moment did not come, giving the diggers who tried to throw up small breastworks from the hard-baked and rocky soil a little time while the sharpshooters watched to hold the Indians back. The officers kept returning to the one question that had no answer. Some asked it laudatorily, as Captain Weir, who had lost no men, had no blood and brains splattered over him; some who had charged unsupported into the waiting horde of Indians on the bottoms profanely: Where was Custer?

Captain Moylan, a veteran in Plains warfare, was heavy with the weight of the injured upon him, many too wounded to flee as the Indian scouts had done, even if there were enough strong horses left to carry them beyond the Sioux. He offered one remark: "Gentlemen, in my opinion, General Custer has made the biggest mistake of his life not taking the whole regiment at once into the first attack."

There were dark looks from the Custer partisans, but Varnum the white linen hankerchief still around his head, recalled now that when he was trying to hold the Indians off the dead and wounded down toward the river he had heard some far-off firing—just a hard burst, not a volley, but a short hot exchange lasting a few minutes. Lieutenant Wallace was beside him at the time, and he had said, "Jesus Christ, Wallace, hear that— and that!"

It seemed some miles off and Varnum said he thought that Custer was having a warm time of it, but before long the shooting was done.

Others repeated now that they had seen Custer and Cooke on the ridge while Reno was fighting down on the bottoms, with some disagreement about the actual time and the exact point and whether his field glasses reflected a momentary bit of sun through the thin clouds. Still, even without the glasses, he could see the skirmish line by the puffs of smoke and all the Indians massed at the front and understand how badly the fight was going. Bare-eyed, he surely saw that the valley was full of smoke and dust and alive with thousands of Indians like fierce ants disturbed at a new nest.

Benteen considered these stories carefully and decided that Custer's appearance on the ridge was about the time Trumpeter Martin was sent back with the message to bring the packs. The repetition of the scrawl "Brng pacs" seemed to indicate that at least the writer, Cooke, was excited or wanted to assure special protection for the mule train. From the point where Custer had stood, miles of river valley were visible, with large camp circles and thousands of riding Indians. Now he must have realized something of the desperate situation his scouts had predicted ever since they saw the first of the gathering trails. But perhaps not. He had, after all, told luncheon guests in New York that his regiment could whip all the Indians on the Plains . . .

Possibly Captain Weir, too, began to understand something of the power of the Sioux here; more probably he was anxious to be in the fight beside his old commander in the 3rd Michigan Cavalry for the glory of it. There were some words with Reno, impatient words, Weir insisting that the force push down to where Custer must be. But there was not enough ammunition for a protracted stand, not enough to risk leaving such protection as they had here before the mule train arrived, let alone to break through the Indian encirclement. Surely Custer expected to be short himself, judging by the anxious messages he sent out for the packs. Besides, Reno's troops had gone through a terrible battle, his men and horses both exhausted, and with many stretcher-wounded who must be carried afoot.

Angrily, Weir went to find his lieutenant, Edgerly, while in the little depression behind him Dr. Porter and his aides were working with the wounded, to stop the bleeding, ease the pain, and protect them as much as possible from the firing from a height off northward, more bullets and arrows dropping among the horses too. In the meantime the troopers were getting the range and spying out gullies and little ravines where the Indian bowmen were hiding. There had been no movement down where Sergeant Culbertson said Hodgson's body probably lay. The firing of Reno and then Varnum seemed to have kept the Indians off until Benteen arrived. Now, with the capable captain to take command, even if his major should not return, Reno decided on a little foray to save at least the body of his loyal adjutant and to get some of the canteens refilled for the wounded, fevering in the swelter of windless heat, Moylan begging for water for them. Armed with carbine and pistols, he gathered a small party of volunteers—ten or twelve draped with strings of empty canteens—and with Culbertson, at whose stirrup Hodgson had crossed the river, the major started down the ravine, running low, dodging to bank and washout. The guns of the Indians hidden along the bluffs broke into an echoing of explosions, the steep slopes suddenly bursting with puffs of blue smoke, the Indians slipping from behind puffs before the troopers could reply, earth and broken sand rock spurting up around Reno's little party strung out along the draw. For a while a couple of the Indians hid their location by shooting through rawhide sacks slipped over the guns and extending well past the muzzles to catch the smoke as it erupted. They wounded two troopers, but were no more dangerous than several bow warriors who got up close, the arrow betraying neither its man nor its direction by sight or sound.

The water detail had to cross an open stretch of bottoms, running low, one man hit, the others dropping flat at the edge of the stream. They crept around a dead trooper sprawled down the bank and, with bullets throwing up mud and water over them, tried to fill the canteens that an Indian sharpshooter with a bitter sense of humor punctured or knocked from the hand. Too many men were struck, and reluctantly the party was ordered to retreat to cover, the bullets from the carbines above attempting to hold the Indians back, out of range.

Culbertson had located Hodgson, his sweat-streaked, sooted young face turned toward the sky and already grayed in death. The lieutenant's watch and chain were gone but not the West Point class ring, and in the midst of bullets and flying gravel, Major Reno stooped to work the ring from the dead man's finger. He searched the pockets and located some keys, his men shouting warnings to him of Indians creeping close and the bullets striking all around him. Reno buttoned the findings in his pocket, then, with his broad mouth clamped tight in the dirty stubble of bearding, he ran through the bullets that tore up the ravine as it had been torn during their earlier struggle for the top. Once he looked back, but he could not ask any man to help carry Hodgson's body up through this, could not make himself risk more men.

Further on, a G Troop man came creeping out of a brushy

wash not far from where he had lost his horse on the climb from the river. But perhaps he should have remained hidden, for in spite of the desperate measures of Benteen's men to keep the Indians back, it seemed neither he nor Reno or the rest could live to reach the hill. Then the attack seemed to slacken a little as they neared the top, or perhaps it was the fire from the Weir and Edgerly troops, who had moved around to the northward, that helped drive those Indians back. What seemed more probable was that the Indians were running out of ammunition, scarce ever since the sale to them was prohibited long ago. Reno, on the upper Plains most of the last three–four years, was aware of the desperate attempts the Sioux made to get the outlawed arms and powder from traders, from the Red River breeds of Canada, and even from a medicine man who claimed he could build guns and ammunition by magic.

When Reno got back to his command, Lieutenant Hare was coming in with two pack mules loaded with ammunition, a couple of men for each animal, one ahead jerking the mule along in a slow, awkward lope that was maintained by a trooper riding behind, whipping the narrow dusty rump, whipping and cursing. One of the troopers was crying in his fury at the stubbornness of the breed, though the mule was worn out, as many of the horses were, as his own mount was, the animal's sides bloody from the roweling of the spurs to keep up the staggering run. Lieutenant Hare was embarrassed by the hoarse cheers his arrival brought, saying that they had less trouble getting through to the command than seemed possible when he left. Where were most of the Indians from back of the ridge going—heading northward?

It was true that the firing was slacking off on the other sides too. The warriors remaining to guard Reno were going to picket their horses out of reach of gunfire down where there was grass. But many rode away, and as the lull increased, the men on Reno

Hill listened for far gunshots, but there had been none that anyone could hear for certain since that violent burst mentioned by Varnum and some of those along the ridge a while ago.

It was just as well that the Indian attack had cooled, for now a few men from each side left their positions and ran openly to the two pack mules for ammunition for their fellows. Some pried at the lids of the heavy wooden boxes, but one corporal had a hatchet at his belt and with this he chopped a box to pieces and doled the cartridges out by the double handfuls.

While Major Reno was out with the water detail, Weir, who had never fought the Sioux, started off along the ridge downstream, riding alone. Lieutenant Edgerly, thinking the captain had Reno's permission to go, followed with D Troop from Benteen's battalion. When the major saw Weir and the company off on a knob to the north, he sent Hare to him with orders to communicate with Custer if possible. As soon as the pack train was safely reunited with the troops and the wounded cared for from the pack pharmacy, he would leave the hill and follow.

As soon as the pressure decreased, Edgerly started on again, down a ravine and along the ridge that ran parallel between the river and Custer's trail, plain now, off to the right, along the far slope. But from his higher point Weir could see a large force of Indians head for the lieutenant to cut him off from behind. He signaled the danger and orders to change direction. Edgerly moved over to the high point near Weir's men and remained there, not seriously molested. They could see Indians riding back and forth a couple of miles farther on, and shooting at something or at least shooting now and then.

Finally, around five o'clock or a little later by most of the watches of the outfit, McDougall came up with the pack train. Reno talked to French about burying Hodgson and some others along the bluff and the river while the ammunition and extra campaign hats were being distributed and the wounds treated. With two spades from the packs Varnum started down to help. By this time the Indians along the river and the bluff face seemed practically gone, so that thirteen men and Herendeen, the courier who was to have been sent to Terry from Tullock's Creek, came out of hiding down in the timber. They were fired on by five Indians still watching the river, but managed to drive them off and hurried up to rejoin the command. They all had good explanations: they had lost their horses in the stampede for the river, and hid, largely because there were several wounded men among them.

By the time Reno's arms and ammunition were back to battle standard there was another volley, far off downriver, either combat or a unison firing to celebrate a victory. The major recalled the burial detail and led his command out in a column of twos, heading down toward Custer's supposed position, hoping for a reunion of the entire regiment before the Indians returned to the attack, as they surely would. Hare, with his orders to Weir to open communication with Custer delivered, returned and met the command coming down the river, even Moylan, encumbered by the wounded carried in horse blankets by six men each and moving very slowly. The pack train was coming too, although still farther behind.

Gradually the weary and worn troopers lined out, sharpshooters keeping off any snipers who might remain, the two battalions moving along the heights, clearly visible from far off. On the highest bluff about a mile out Reno and his men stopped, looking past Weir's point to the twisted ridges and ravines down the river. They could hear nothing, but the air ahead was full of dust and smoke, with a spreading cloud above it like a transparent disintegrating thunderhead. About two miles off, knots of horsemen stood together here and there, some moving enough so they could be identified as Indians, but no one understood what they were doing.

Suddenly someone noticed a curious expanse off left of the river. The gradual slopes of grassy prairie looked as though fire had scorched the foliage of a vast stretch of brush, moving brush. Finally some of the men realized what it was: an immense pony herd such as none here had ever seen, heading perhaps to water or to new pasture. The one herd must have been a large part of the twenty thousand head that the Rees had predicted would be brought together here in the annual summer council of the Teton Sioux.

Twenty thousand head of horses they had said and perhaps eight–ten thousand warriors, counting all from thirteen to eighty years of age, and all the usual visitors.

By now some of that warrior force had seen the troops watching on the ridge, and several thousand, it seemed, began to swarm toward them in long strings coming up the slopes. Reno was certain neither Weir's position nor his could be defended, the first wave of warriors threatening to roll Weir back upon the rest, perhaps roll them all together like an Indian woman rolling up a lodge skin. Even Weir saw the impracticality of going farther, and Lieutenant Hare, realizing the danger, used Major Reno's name to order the advance units to return. When the heavy firing began, Weir hurried his withdrawal, leaving an injured man behind crying, pleading not to be left for Indian revenge. Godfrey's company acted as rear guard, taking the heavy fire of the Sioux attack as Weir and the others retreated, some passing Moylan and his wounded in their hurry to regain the scant protection of Reno Hill.

»▶ »▶ »▶ »▶ »▶ »▶ »▶ »▶

5 THE MAN
AGAINST
THE SKY

★ ★ ★ ★ ★ ★ ★ ★

The morning of June 25 the scouts had drawn a map of the
Ash Creek region with a weed stalk in the dust for Custer,
showing the terrain all the way from the saddle between Davis
Creek and the upper dry wash of Ash to the bluffs pushing
up against the Little Bighorn. Carefully they marked the ancient lodgepole trail down the creek to the river, indicating
where the first live water would be found.

When Custer's chestnut-sorrel, Vic, saddle-sore and weary
too, began to faunch at the smell of water ahead, the colonel
signaled for a stop to let the stock drink a little, turning back
in the saddle to glance over his troopers, men picked for his
purpose this crucial day and its afternoon. Benteen was far off
in the breaks somewhere, ordered left at an angle to the line
of march, to seek out one valley and then the next and the
next, although there had been no sign of trail or track that way.
Reno was some distance ahead of the colonel, following along

the far left side of the little valley of Ash Creek, with orders to make all prudent haste to the river and to charge the Indian village beyond, with the promise of full support.

The colonel let his horse drink too, but pulled the animal back, warning his commanders against too much water, the thirst-frantic stock of the five troops given turns at the little pools, to nuzzle the greening scum away and drink to the muddy bottoms, or to suck up the thin thread of flow in the summer creek. For about five minutes the commander rested, then he was back in the saddle, his face gaunt and wind-burned, his eyes bloodshot from dust and loss of sleep. But he started briskly, followed close by his color bearers and his orderly, not down the creek with the spreading trail of cavalry dust along the far side. Instead he turned right, behind a low ridge that shut him and his men from the sight of Reno, and up a shallow ravine to the rougher, barer heights back from the river.

With Custer rode the dash and color of the 7th Cavalry, the men who had given the regiment the aura of far adventure so envied by the millions caught in lives of hopeless mundanity. Besides the colonel only three were Military Academy men— Lieutenants Porter and Harrington (the latter one of Custer's favored Michiganders), and Second Lieutenant Sturgis, son of the regimental colonel, of last year's class—three Point men in the whole five troops. Benteen, the ranker sent off up the river, had two in his three troops and Reno, sent over to attack the Sioux camp, had five in his three, including the major himself. Custer had the soldiers of fortune: the swaggering Irishman, Miles Keogh, apparently from the French Foreign Legion and the Papal Guard; Cooke of the "Queen's Own" of Canada; and the cripple-armed Smith of the Gray Horse Troop. Young Captain George Yates, Custer's favorite from his home town of Monroe, Michigan, was the brother of Frank Yates, trader at Red Cloud Agency, down in Nebraska, the trader who was

still charged with graft in moving the Spotted Tail Agency
four years ago. Back in February, young Captain Yates had
ordered ammunition directly from the Chief of Ordnance, War
Department, Washington. In April he wrote again, demanding
the requested ammunition immediately for Custer's expedition
going out May 1. He was informed that the order had not been
received and that his lettter was being referred to the Department of Dakota, with a chilly reminder that there was a commanding officer, Major Marcus Reno, right at Fort Lincoln,
and the usual chief of ordnance in the Department itself. Mark
Kellogg, along against Sherman's explicit orders, carried a romantic aura as a writing man, a correspondent. Even Trumpeter
Martin, detailed from Benteen's H Troop as orderly to Custer,
was said to have been drummer boy for Garibaldi. Then there
was the Custer family: the dashing Lieutenant Colonel George
Armstrong himself; the roistering Captain Tom; the sickly young
civilian Boston; Autie Reed, the favored nephew; and Lieutenant Calhoun, the pampered brother-in-law.

Once away from Ash Creek and the other battalions, Custer
led out at his usual gallop, up along the far slope of the ridges
that Mitch Bouyer and the Crow scouts told him lay like the
backbones of a bunch of ancient mares between them and the
Little Bighorn, a mile and a half or two away. Custer had sent
White Swan and Half Yellow Face off to the river ridge to see
what the Sioux were doing. They went, but joined Reno's
scouts and did not return. Later the colonel dispatched the four
Crows left to him, including the youth Curly, with similar
orders. In the meantime the command moved slowly, but
hurried on again after the scouts returned with confirmation of
lodges stretched for a long way down the river valley, the
upper end full of mounted Indians charging back and forth,
shooting at Reno's column moving over the bottoms toward
them.

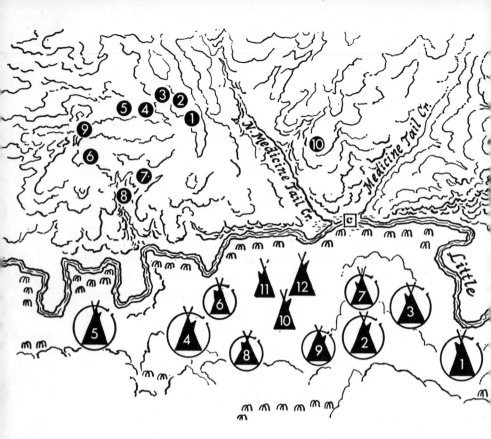

BATTLE OF THE LITTLE BIGHORN

June 25-26, 1876
(Map Based on U.S. Geological Survey, 1891, and Military and Indian Accounts)

 HIGH POINTS: A—Custer lookouts over Reno fight.
B—Reno Hill. C—Weir Point.
D—Probably farthest Reno advance.
E—Indians commanding later attacks on Reno.

 CUSTER BODIES: 1—Calhoun's command. 2—Lt. Jas. Calhoun.
3—J. J. Crittenden. 4—Capt. M. W. Keogh.
5—Keogh's command. 6—Commands of Capts. Yates and Custer. 7—Dr. G. E. Lord. 8—Lt. Smith's command. 9—Custer Hill: Col. G. A. Custer; Lts. W. W. Cooke, A. E. Smith, W. V. W. Reily; Capt. T. W. Custer nearby. 10—Sgt. Butler.

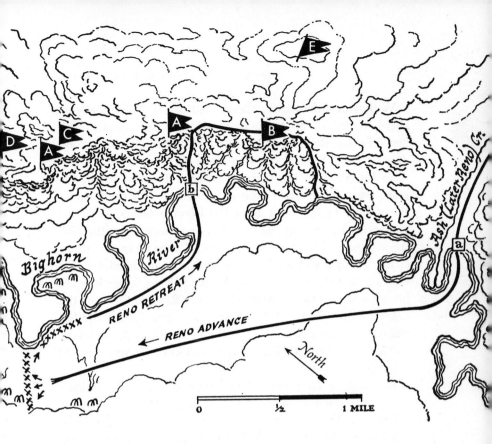

 CROSSINGS: (a) Ancient lodge trail and buffalo ford.
(b) Steep, narrow pony ford. (c) Marshy pony ford.

INDIAN CAMPS: (*In village circles here, due to lack of ground
space, instead of usual great circle at Bear Butte, S.D.*)
1—Hunkpapa. 2—Minneconjous. 3—No Bows. 4—Oglalas.
5—Northern Cheyennes, guest tribe. 6—Brules.
7—Blackfoot Sioux. 8—Yanktons. 9—Santees.

LODGES:
10 and 11—Warrior societies guarding council lodge.
12—Great lodge of annual council, poles 18 feet long.

 WICKIUPS and shelters for young warriors

With this information Custer started off again, spurring ahead, trailed by his troopers, the shallow depression he followed behind the river ridges so windless that the rising cloud of dust hung thick enough to make the Gray Horse Troop seem like a gap in the hurrying column. The clothing of the men, even the blue-gray trousers, darkened with sweat under the soiling. Lather burst from the laboring horses, some beginning to lag—for all the bloody spur rakings across the ribs, lagging and falling far back. Those with Custer on earlier Indian chases feared a violent explosion from the commander as the horses gave out, the sunken flanks like bellows, heads hanging toward wavering knees, some going down flat. But this time the colonel didn't even look back when his young brother Boston was off and trying to whip his horse back to its feet, the scouts passing him there, their smaller ponies running very hard to keep up.

Gradually a far sound of bunching gunshots thrust itself above the pounding of hoofs on the baked earth and through a low place the troops caught a momentary sight of the dust-filled river valley. Vague specks that were riders raced through it, the sharp cut of far carbine fire following the puffs of blue powder smoke. A cheer broke from the troops, the recruits letting their excited horses get out of control, some plunging ahead of the commander.

The colonel rose in his stirrups and shouted after these men, "Hold your horses, boys! There are plenty Indians down there for all of us!"

Then Custer touched his spurs lightly to Vic's lathered sides and led out in a gallop again, dodging behind the higher ridges, out of sight of the enemies in the valley. More horses played out, not only those of the green men but that of Sergeant Finkle too, dropping him back from his position close to his captain, Tom Custer, back to where the Crows and Mitch Bouyer were whipping along.

Sergeant Kanipe, on a stronger horse, was up close and so received the call to carry the commander's orders instead of Finkle. "Go to Captain McDougall," Tom Custer instructed. "Tell him to bring his pack train straight across country. If packs come loose, cut them and come on. Quick! There's a big Indian village ahead. If you see Captain Benteen tell him to hurry up."

Then, as if to emphasize the urgency, the captain repeated, "A big Indian village . . ."

Kanipe turned and with his neckerchief drawn up over his mouth and nose he spurred back along the trail. The column started ahead at its fast gait. By this time Adjutant Cooke was back in his place from the river with Keogh where they had watched Reno cross and then charge toward the Indians kicking up the shielding dust with their ponies.

As Custer rounded a big bend of a hill, the firing off to the left was suddenly louder. Motioning to Cooke, he led toward the edge of a high point in the river bluffs and looked down upon an Indian village circle where only women and children seemed around, and exclaimed something that the Italian trumpeter, Martin, thought was, "We caught the Indians asleep," but was more probably that they had caught the Indians napping. Even that would have been a facetious remark, for Custer was visible to some of the men on the river bottom and so he could surely see Reno's skirmish line bloom into puffs of blue in a hot fight, with the haze of smoke and dust over hundreds of milling, charging Indians, and the horde creeping up that Reno could only suspect.

Custer jerked off his wide, light-colored hat and gave a cheer. To his men he shouted, "Hurray, boys! We'll get them and as soon as we have them we'll go back to our station."

Then he set his spurs and turned right, off the ridge that was ending against the river three-quarters of a mile down. He headed along the back of the second rise and across the point of a draw that cut the broadening slope to the river a diagonal mile away, with more villages plain on the far side. As the Indian scouts and Bouyer had warned, there was no ford for some miles below the mouth of Ash Creek, where he had been expected to cross in the support of Reno. But there was the dust of charging warriors at these lower villages too, and more Indians hurrying up from below and now some coming from above, too, still on the far side of the river but looking, gathering, signaling with mirror flashes and flapping robes.

The colonel stopped, Cooke beside him. The adjutant motioned Trumpeter Martin up and started to give him verbal instructions. "Take this order to Captain Benteen—" but then he pulled out a notebook and laying it against his leg, wrote the message to bring the packs.

With the note buttoned into his shirt pocket, Trumpeter Martin started across the three–four miles of ridges to Ash Creek, the way Kanipe had gone. The courier looked back from a rise and saw the command headed into a low, wide gulley in three sections, the middle one Smith's Gray Horse Troop, almost lost, like a gap in the line, still nearer to the color of the bald knobs and the rising dust. As they galloped on, the column swung leftward a little as though to strike diagonally for the river and the camps beyond. Martin heard firing behind him and glanced around. Parties of Indians were suddenly at the flank of the column and ahead of one section, too, afoot, as though rising out of the ground, some whooping and waving buffalo robes to stampede the horses, some shooting.

They had been hidden in ambush, waiting.

Martin tried to hurry faster, spurring his worn horse already panting open-mouthed, head dropped, stumbling at any clump of weeds or loose stone. A little farther on he saw a man coming toward him on a hard run: Boston Custer. He had managed to get his exhausted horse back to the pack train and replaced it with a fresher one. He slowed down to shout this and to ask Custer's location. Trumpeter Martin grinned, pointing back over his shoulder toward the gunfire, and young Boston hurried on, eager not to miss the best of the fight.

When Martin passed the point where Custer had stopped to look down into the valley of the Little Bighorn, he saw through the increased dust and smoke that Reno's force was surrounded by hundreds of Indians, the troopers falling back.

There was no time to watch, for now the pack train and Benteen had to be found in a hurry. Besides, some Indians saw the courier and they might try to intercept him.

Ever since the morning sun came to stand on the heights east of the river the scouts of the great Sioux camp were reporting soldiers in the country, but no one would have believed that they were so close and would actually attack in daylight, or even dare to ride against the vast Sioux conference at all. Then suddenly there was dust rising above the river crossing, and bluecoats charging in double file across the bottoms against the Hunkpapa lodge circle—soldiers falling into Sitting Bull's camp as his vision in the sun dance had foretold. By then the warrior society policing the camp that moon hurried out to whip their horses into the second wind for a good fight, and to raise a protective dust. In the meantime other Indians were running to help. Drummers hurried out to spread the alarm, mirrors flashed pale signals from the veiled sun. The one-feather men, members of the Teton council, hurried from the great lodge in the center of the three-and-a-half-mile stretch of village circle, the Hunkpapas Sitting Bull and Gall whipping to their camp, all the war leaders working desperately to prepare for the attack, to save the women and children helpless before the coming soldier guns. At the great conference lodge the guards stripped the painted skins from the eighteen-foot poles, rolled them up in sections, and, loaded on pony drags, whipped off westward to hide the skins in draws from the eyes of an enemy.

Back at the villages, criers ran around the lodge circles shouting that every young man was to get his horse and his weapons. The war chiefs were already riding through the camps with their bone whistles and their chantings, even in the villages far down the river, the Crazy Horse Oglala Sioux and the Cheyennes. Some men didn't wait for their fighting horses to be brought in from the prairie but took any mount available, whether the handsome ceremonial horse tied behind some chieftain's lodge or an old travois mare to be whipped into the fight. In the meantime the women ran gathering up their children and the trophies of their warriors while the older men directed their escape, whether temporarily or for a long flight if that should become necessary.

Then the two Reno troopers on their runaway horses had come charging into the Hunkpapa village and were brought down and cut to pieces. But their coming—that they could penetrate the strong warrior line—scattered the women and children running for the river, to swim where they must but to get to the east side, put the high-banked stream between them and the enemy. Then they saw the Ree scouts on that side, and so they fled downstream through the thin brush, women, any woman, dragging children by the hand, the babies on their backs bobbing hard.

The young Indians who were herding a few village horses in the pockets against the steep bluffs east of the river found themselves helpless with only their bows against the gun-armed Rees. They fled for the brush and the rushes too, letting the scouts sweep away the small bunches. But some of the warriors attacking the soldiers on the bottoms heard the shooting. Leaping their ponies down the river bank, they cut back part of the herds and hurried the Rees on with their guns. By that time swarms of war horses were being whooped in from the high prairie west of the river and soon the soldier fight was moving back toward the Little Bighorn.

As soon as the shooting was gone from the timber and across the bottoms, travois poles came rattling and jumping over the rough ground behind the old mares gathering up the wounded to be hurried to the medicine men. There were many to be carried away, for the soldiers, cornered, had fought hard. Women who lost men in that fighting ran out to avenge them on the bodies of the soldiers and the scouts, particularly Bloody Knife, with his Sioux half-sister there to help. His head was cut off in the ancient manner of the tribe, the custom long before they learned about scalping from the warriors who had gone east to fight in the French and Indian Wars.

While there was still the thunder and roar of a fight at the river and along the bluffs, Indians, mostly boys and older men, hunted the brush of the bottoms for live soldiers, and the dead too, to strip bare. Suddenly a man from the Cheyenne camp raised a cry. He was holding up a blue shirt with the 7th Cavalry insignia on the collar tab. This he had seen before, on the soldiers who had killed his mother and his wife on the Washita.

"This day my heart is made good!" he shouted, tears running down the grooves of his dusty face. Waving the shirt like a captured banner, he whipped through one camp after another, crying his news all the way to his own village, the farthest down the river.

But before now another messenger had come riding through the villages and on to those searching the bottoms, his arm pointing off across the river and beyond the bluffs that pushed against the stream. He was shouting something about more soldiers seen, many, many more—a long string of them riding along the far side of the hills. Instead of going to help those first ones, those being driven in a hard fight across the river, the column of bluecoats was heading along the second ridge and probably for the crossing near the lower Indian camps, where so many of the helpless ones, the women and children, the sick and the ancient, had run. But as they, too, saw the new soldiers, they turned back across the river with their children, shouting of troops even when the blue riders were still hidden from the camps.

"More horse soldiers are coming! They are on the sacred hill of the wild peas!" the women shouted.

It was true that troopers were riding over the little hill that was all in bloom, the recumbent loco weed like a painted robe under the feet—white, pale pink and lavender, rose, vivid magenta, and deepest purple. The long row of bluecoats on sorrel horses, and gray and brown, was crushing the flowers into the gravel—flowers that had always ripened to a mat of buffalo beans for the women to gather and boil in the meat kettles. Now enemies rode there on the hill of peace, come against them in plain daylight, coming along the pretty hill that had never shielded anything larger than the ant and the little gray jumping mouse, the horses cutting the bloom with their iron hoofs, their manure defiling the sacred place where youths went for their puberty dreams.

Suddenly the bluecoats broke into a gallop, the forked-tail flags ahead, the double row of riders followed by the long dust that rose from behind the hills—more soldiers riding hard to fall into the camp as Sitting Bull had envisioned.

Those around Reno at the river and along the bluffs couldn't see Custer, but four Cheyennes who had been hunting the bottoms for injured warriors were halfway to their own lodge circle at the north end of the great camp when they heard the alarm of the new enemy coming. They pushed their horses down the steep splashing jump into the river and climbed dripping out the other side. From there they moved in a formal row around the point of the river bluffs and up the open slope of ravines and draws that fanned out from the far, high ridge where the dry heads of the two Medicine Tail Creeks started. Bobtail Horse led the Cheyennes, all four singing their death songs and shooting their weapons, mostly bows, lifting the arrows into the air toward the troops, who were like a row of far trees against the grayish sky. They were too far away to hit, but the Indians hoped to slow the string of soldiers hurrying along the broken heights that turned toward the lower part of the Sioux camp and ended in a point across from the Cheyenne lodge circle. The cloud of women and children who had fled there were running again, away from the new danger. The older men led them up the low rises to the left of the river and out upon the gullied prairie, to scatter there like quail.

From up the stream, hidden by the first line of ridges, rode Gall, the Hunkpapa, with Crow King beside him, their followers strung out behind. Gall had been leading a charge to cut off Reno's retreat to the bluffs with the fierceness of a wounded grizzly, the man wounded, too, in his most vulnerable spot: his wife and children dead in the Hunkpapa village. But one of Gall's warriors on a high point had signaled to hurry down the river. Another, a bigger, bunch of soldiers was riding fast against the lower villages and had already crossed the dry little valley that was South Medicine Tail Creek. Turning in fury, Gall whipped his horse along, his mourning tatters flying out behind him, his rifle across the withers of his lunging horse, ready.

Other warriors were hurrying across the river now, many putting their horses over the steep river banks, then to vanish into the ravines. Seeing these things, Custer's Crow scouts lagged more than ever, their horses worn out or deliberately held back as they had been on the hard run from Ash Creek. Finally the scouts stopped on a high point and looked, dark-faced, toward the great Sioux camp and then to Smith with his Gray Horse Troop going down South Medicine Tail and Custer hurrying along the slope northward—the scouts just sitting, making no words.

Mitch Bouyer reined over to the seventeen-year-old Curly, the handsome, wavy-haired Crow breed.

"You are very young," Bouyer said to him. "You don't know much about fighting. Go back, keep away from the Sioux, and go to those other soldiers, there at the Yellowstone. Tell them all of us here are killed."

Curly looked down upon the spreading dust of the warriors, warriors of the Sioux, that most powerful enemy of his mother's people, gathered here in such numbers as he had never seen before. Although their war whoops were still far off, the sound carried easily against the barely perceptible wind. He looked over the river once more, and then kneed his stockinged, bald-faced pony into a run southward along the still-dusty trail. From a high point he peered back under his palm. Bouyer was riding toward Custer, who had halted the command to let the men tighten the saddle girths for a hard fight. Then the colonel led off diagonally across the head of upper Medicine Tail ravine. Many Indians moved along the bottoms now, some openly, more hidden in cuts and draws and washouts, ready to rise.

The young Crow turned his horse off deeper into the hills and struck out for the Yellowstone and General Terry. He swung far around the Sioux attacking where Reno was digging in on the hill, and around Benteen, coming up along the bluffs from near Ash Creek.

The other three Crow scouts still with Custer had warned him as sternly as the Rees and Bouyer. All of them had said flatly three days ago that the enemy would be too many, far, far too many. Now, seeing the Sioux camp strung for miles along the river and the warriors moving in spearheads up the slopes, the scouts stopped again, stony-faced, holding themselves aloof, plainly with no further concern here; and so they were told to go, get out.

"Save yourselves!" Mitch Bouyer called back as he kicked his horse into a run to overtake Custer, angrily forging ahead without his Indian scouts.

Once the Crows stopped to watch the colonel's command for a moment. They saw Smith and his Gray Horse Troop trotting diagonally across the ravined slopes, gradually thrust sideways by an occasional bullet spitting up earth and gravel around them, the horses jumping back as from rattlesnakes or rearing and plunging as the sting of the lifted arrows sent them sideways into the dust of the company ahead, higher up the slope. Together the Crow scouts kicked their weary horses into a dog lope toward the lodgepole trail along Ash Creek five miles away, circling far around the Sioux coming from the back of Reno Hill. Judging by the hard fire they had heard against the major, all his men must surely be dead by now anyway. But Benteen saw the three scouts and signaled them over to help dig trenches with their long knives, at least for a while. They came, their faces sullen, but they came, dodging the Indians left hidden to keep these troops pinned down for a later return to the attack as one held a buffalo herd until the hunters were ready. The finish here would be easy; the troops on the hill were exhausted, encumbered by many wounded and by empty cartridge belts.

The warriors from the Reno fight rode against the new soldiers with the power of victory in them, their paint furred with dust. Some had bloody scalps at their belts, some with blue shirts on their backs and captured carbines in their hands, perhaps even with cartridges heavy in the pipe bags or breechclout flaps tied up for pockets, the two warbonnet men proud that no bullet had come through the feathers to reach them.

While the Indians from the east and northeast of Reno Hill

went along the back slope of the heights toward the spreading dust of Custer's men, those from the river side of the bluffs were led by Gall in a swing low down around on the left, to cut the troopers off from the river and the camp circles beyond. The warriors farther down were crossing anywhere, many at the pony ford near the mouth of Medicine Tail Creek, some to spread upward, like the sharp, raking claws of a hungry grizzly reaching up for a row of small and imprudent mice along the rise. The Indians slipped into ravines or cut banks or washouts, mostly leaving the horses hidden, creeping in upon the enemy. A few did charge boldly in the open, but not in the usual single recklessness against which Crazy Horse, Gall, and others harangued. This was not the day for mere coups and honors, as in wars far from the villages and the helpless women and children. This day they must strike hard, strike to destroy this enemy who dared attack their great summer conference, something that had never happened before. No army had ever come shooting against a Sioux camp of any size except upon the band of Brules under the peace chief, Little Thunder, twenty years ago. For that, too, there must be punishment today.

Some of the more daring of the young Indian women, boys, and older men gathered on rises to watch the soldiers who had stopped their horses in a long, segmented row strung out for three-quarters of a mile along the heights. They watched the officers spur together up there with gestures and shouts, arms pointing toward the river and the Indian camps beyond, field glasses turned upon the warriors streaming along the slopes. Some of the young Indians went up closer now, whooping, waving robes, stinging an occasional horse by a lucky shot, to plunge and rear.

Now there was a hesitant stopping and starting in Custer's movement along the high backbone to where the ravines of the main Medicine Tail started. He led down to the dry gullies and across toward the ridge that ran parallel to the river, about half a mile from it. More Indians swarmed over the stream, and from above. They swept some of the horses of the rear troops against those ahead, against the Grays, while more warriors came up toward the rugged ravine that led to the nose of the ridge ahead of Custer and still clear of dust.

The first solid return of fire by the troopers was from the saddle, and brought two warriors down and several Indian ponies, driving the foremost warriors back for better cover, to snake themselves forward again, up draws, from bank to sage-brush. They dropped arrows among the soldier horses, soon too excited for steady aim or for a good stand, plunging even from the whoops and the waving blankets of the occasional daring young Indian eager for coups, leaving here and there an empty saddle, the trooper hit or thrown. Then suddenly the pale sun-light glinted on shining instruments held to the mouth as a group of Smith's Gray Horse troopers blew a battle song. The sound cut clear and thin over the far valley and the farther ridges, perhaps to hurry the pack train and Benteen, if the cap-tain hadn't obeyed Custer too closely and was not too many valleys away.

The fine sound startled the Indians a moment and brought young women riding out of their watching places. Then the warriors saw that it was like their own battle songs, and they began shooting again, the soldier horses rearing and running. The trumpets were hastily replaced by carbines spitting rows of new smoke. The Indians did not break and retreat, and many of the soldiers dismounted, as Calhoun's and Keogh's troops were doing against Gall and his warriors moving along the slopes from the southward, and those behind them too, now also from the Reno fight. Every fourth soldier held the horses and tried to take them to protected ravines and gullies, but not too far away, while the men, both on the rise and down the slope, fired from the knee for careful aim or what was hoped would be careful.

Indians were hit in the repeated volleys, but more came in the growing charges, some riding on horses captured from Reno, with blue coats to get up close. Finally the soldiers began to go backward, retreating up the slope, helping two wounded men along, trying to make little stands, not only to hold the enemy back, but to keep the troopers who had never fought whooping warriors from breaking into a run that could not be stopped. The Indians on the river side signaled those behind the ridges for cross fire, safe for the warriors, with the troops on the backbone above them, the few bullets whistling overhead. They were determined to prevent any from escaping, as Crook's men had managed to withdraw at the Rosebud eight days ago. But Crook's horses were not tired out and his infantry had their good long guns, his force altogether, so many more than here. Besides, these looking down into the valley of the Little Bighorn had come against the women and children and must be punished hard, punished for that as well as for attacking a Teton conference.

Lieutenant Sturgis with a platoon of the Gray Horses had moved into a deep gully leading toward the river, perhaps to locate a crossing; but almost at once Crazy Horse and his followers pinned them down, the Indians anxious to protect even the poles of the great conference lodge from the first enemy attack against it as well as to keep the shooting from the helpless ones. Creeping up, the warriors lifted their arrows to fall among Sturgis' men and horses. The gully walls were cut and broken, and it seemed the inexperienced young second lieutenant might hold out until the Indians were driven back. But elsewhere the troopers were retreating, some no longer kneeling to shoot or

even leaning forward against the kick of their guns. They just
fired and ran, each soldier trying to get to his horse, ready to
flee. Most of the animals were wild with terror now that the
steadying hands of the troopers were failing them. Some plunged
back, rearing, going over backward in their panic even with seasoned troopers, the best, finding their guns jerked with the
finger in the trigger guard. Some of the troopers hurriedly
rein-hobbled their horses by tying one rein short to a forefoot.
These the warriors charged whooping through the dust, particularly the Cheyennes with Lame White Man from the Reno
fight, leaving the troopers little time to untie their horses or even
to cut the leather, so that some fell still reaching for the rein,
the gut-shot horses screaming, the stink lost in the stench of
powder.

By now the shooting was hot from the back of the ridge
where Calhoun's men were trying to make a stand, the dust
and smoke so thick that it was hard to tell a trooper from a
warrior. Only two men were plainly visible. One was a soldier
left behind in the small retreats, his horse played out, the man
brought down by arrows and a war club as he ran, his shirt dark
with blood. The other was an officer boldly riding back and
forth trying to direct the fight and hold the men firm. It would
have been a fine coup to pick him off, but always he seemed to
be lost in the dust as the sights came upon him.

In the meantime Gall's warriors were moving in large numbers toward the knob held by Calhoun. Those afoot worked
their way up the slope. Jumping high in the haze of the fight
to let their arrows go and then dropping down out of sight, they
drew soldier fire and a waste of soldier ammunition. The bold
officer was still riding around there in the dust and smoke, trying
to rally his men. Finally one of the many whose aim was upon
his horse brought it down, to stagger up again; but the man

had sprung to another mount as agile as any young Sioux set afoot in a war charge. He rode on but somebody got the brave one at last, because suddenly he was not seen any more.

Farther back, Gall and the judicious Crow King massed their mounted warriors and drew in several other parties. When the high, thin call of Gall's war flute cut through the roar of the fight, the Indians rose together with a great whooping. Those afoot worked like sharpshooters while the mounted warriors whipped their horses into a charge that carried them clear over Calhoun's men, the shouts and cries of the troopers only empty mouths working as the horses were upon them, the war clubs swinging, leaving dead and wounded scattered behind. But a couple of important Sioux went down too and, infuriated, the warriors charged on northward to Keogh's men, getting some who hadn't scattered out to run along the ridge toward Custer. Even then they had trouble turning their excited war ponies far out in a swing back to the slopes. But good warriors had been left behind, unhorsed, perhaps, and flattened like trembling cottontails in the scraggly scatter of grass and sagebrush, but with the shielding dust and smoke to sting their eyes and lungs. The wounded and the dead were to be dragged away, sometimes by a rope around the pony's neck, the end tied to the belt of the warrior's breechclout so the running animal took him out of the fight, dead or alive. More often it was some bold relative or friend or warrior brother charging into the fight to carry him off.

By now the riderless horses breaking away from the soldiers had stampeded in every direction, some running toward the stock of the troopers along the ridge ahead, toward Custer. Most, even the wounded still able to run, fled down the slopes, many with reserve ammunition untouched in the saddlebags. The loose horses were caught up by youths and young Cheyenne women coming across the river. Several of the tribe, including two of the women, rode through the thick of the battle darkness clear up and over the rise where Custer had passed on his way toward the point of the ridge that ended half a mile from the river, and not much farther from the Cheyenne camp. The fighting, too, had moved out along the narrow backbone, and the young riders passed unchallenged among the scattered dead of Calhoun's and Keogh's troops looking for wounded Indians. On the way one of the young women swung off leftward close to the fighting along the slope where her husband was leading an attack. She fired a few shots with her pistol and when the soldiers made a small countercharge, she carried off a young Indian whose horse was killed under him. With him behind her she whipped her pony away through the stinging murk and the whine of carbine bullets.

The dust and smoke thickened over the almost windless battlefield, so dense and shielding that the troopers, driven toward Custer's position, were fleeting shadows as they ran, mostly afoot, dodging from dead horse to hollow and weed, hurrying on toward the head of the column or going down, face in the torn gravel. But the same battle darkness hid much of the concentration that was closing around the men in the cuts and ravines between the nose of the ridge and the river and closing around Custer Hill, where a scattering of troops from the heights were gathering. But their commanders, the Custer brother-in-law, Calhoun, and Custer's favorite, Keogh, both lay dead on the far rise. Keogh, who had come out of the Foreign Legion and the Papal Guard to a ridge in Sioux country, lost one of his side whiskers there, stripped off as an unusual scalp.

With ocasional glimpses of the thousands of Indians swarming up from the river and along the slope, and no telling how many creeping up close for a sudden overwhelming, it is improbable that George Armstrong Custer remembered his remark a few months earlier: that his 7th Cavalry could whip all the

Indians on the Plains. There was desperation now, and the bravery of desperation. Suddenly a lone rider with three stripes on his sleeve, Sergeant Butler, spurred out of the dust over North Medicine Tail ravine and started across the slope, riding hard through breaking clouds of smoke, straight into groups of startled Indians who let him disappear, perhaps thinking for a moment he was an Indian in the clothes of a trooper he had killed. But realizing who he was, they charged him, whooping their signals of an enemy fleeing. Butler shot back a time or two, although mostly he clubbed his horse along with his carbine, straight ahead, determined it seemed to get through southeastward, probably to the pack train or Benteen or to carry the message of disaster to the outside, to some telegraph office that Custer had hoped to reach himself before another day. The sergeant covered over half a mile through bullet and arrow but on an open slope he was finally brought down, the Indian who killed him praising his bravery in song.

Back behind Sergeant Butler, Lame White Man was leading a strong force of Indians, mostly from the upper camps, against the troops of Yates and Tom Custer while more Sioux were creeping up to the siegers holding the Gray Horse troopers in the deep gully. Lame White Man had had a good day and was wearing a blue coat he found tied behind the cantle of a captured saddle. But in the battle clouds over the slope it was difficult to recognize anyone and so the bold war leader from the Southern Cheyennes was killed by a Sioux who thought he was one of Custer's Indian scouts.

Lame White Man was soon avenged. His followers, doubly furious now, made repeated charges against the troops in the ravines, killing or stampeding what seemed the last of their horses and then charging them, afoot and mounted, until all were dead or running for the last hill, Captain Custer, Yates, and even Smith of E Troop fleeing too, the officers somehow

mostly still with horses, Mark Kellogg with his mule, he to fall
not far from the circle at the top of the ridge. Boston Custer
and Autie Reed didn't make it to the hill but fell on the slope
from the river. An officer on a sorrel horse was the last to retreat
toward the hill. A Sioux wearing a scalp shirt rode at him and
was killed, and then a Cheyenne. Brave Bear was the third, but
his bullet brought the officer from his horse.

In the meantime Crazy Horse was leading his Oglala Sioux
up the slopes in one attack after another until his horse began
to fail. Then he swung back to his village for a fresh battle
mount. From there he rode down the river leading many Sioux
through the Cheyenne camp past the lodge of the Sacred Buffalo Hat, the holy object of the Northern Cheyennes. The little
tipi was open, the Sacred Hat surely carried out upon the
prairie for safety from enemy contamination. More and more
warriors on fresh horses gathered to Crazy Horse as he crossed
the river with the drumming back among the helpless ones
throbbing like spring in the ground to his ears. His Winchester
ready in his hand, the Oglala led his warriors around the end of
the Custer ridge, heading toward the ravine behind it to cut
off the escape he feared, particularly since he lost Crook's men
last week. As Crazy Horse rode, more and more Indians came
up behind him until the fresh war horse was the point of a
great arrow, growing wider and longer, the dust of it joining the
cloud standing like a thunderhead into the sky.

They reached the upper ravine just as the Indians from the
river side pushed the soldiers up to the end, the nose of the
ridge. With a great whooping the fresh warriors charged the back
of that blue stand, using mostly arrows, spears, and clubs, hot
for the close combat. The roar of the soldier guns seemed little
more now than the popping of the winter ice going out of the
Yellowstone in the spring. In the wild riding attack the ponies
jumped a Sioux who fell among them, jumped him like so much

sagebrush or stone. The first charge by the Crazy Horse warriors broke over the top of the ridge and circled the troopers on Custer Hill, the cluster of men fighting from behind their horses, dead now, the warriors cutting off any who might be fleeing there from the slopes. At the next charge a few Indian horses were hit, another man or two, nothing to count in this fight of a summer day on the Little Bighorn to protect the great conference lodge and the helpless women and children. Hundreds of warriors circled and charged and circled again, more than hundreds, clotting together in the dense smoke and dust from the battle whose roar was deafening to the ear in a darkness as of evening.

There were some good men on that hill, some still trying to shoot carefully from the knee even as the Indians closed in, but the circle was getting smaller, men piling up behind the dead horses as their carbines stuck, the roar of their revolvers choking in their hands. No Flesh killed the standard-bearer and tore the banner from his faltering hand, while another bold warrior rode straight through the little circle of troopers, his pony jumping the dead horses and men. He was followed by a whole charge, and so the soldiers went down under hoof and spear and war club until it seemed nobody could be alive in that bloody pile. But there were a few. Jumping up together, they headed off through the haze of smoke and dust down the slope toward the brush of the river, so very far away, the whooping warriors running them down like newborn buffalo calves, striking them to the ground, looking for more, until suddenly there were no more.

While the warriors sat around on their horses, not believing this easy victory, two young Sioux came back from the breaks, disappointed that the fight was over so soon. They had chased an officer who escaped in the smoke on horseback and were cheated because he put his revolver against his head and all they got was the killed-himself one, and couldn't even strip him, as a suicide. By now even the horses here were gone, all rounded up down along the river. The animals had been so worn out they were not afraid of Indians, as trooper horses usually were, but just stood, heads down, as the youths came to gather them up, and the women passed, some with travois, some singing victory songs. Spreading up the slope, they ran over the battleground seeking out their dead and wounded, keening as they found the dead ones, avenging themselves on the bodies of troopers nearby, stripping the white men to the skin.

Next came hundreds of boys and youths riding out to the battlefield to sit their horses and think about this victory that was already bringing alarm to the faces of the headmen over the punishment to come. But who was to punish the great Sioux nation? the foolish boys asked each other. Many of the youths had found carbines and revolvers or were loaned them by relatives to fire volleys into the dead soldier bodies, as in the old days they would have shot hundreds of arrows. When every brush patch and washout had been whipped through for hiding troopers, the war leaders rode back to the ridge of the dead. By now they were stripped, naked and white as buffalo fat where the clothing had kept off the sun, looking so pitifully weak and helpless. These were the men who had killed so many women and children, the Cheyennes told each other in wonder.

But they had killed no helpless ones except Gall's family, not on this day long to be remembered.

Now the warrior societies formed in individual lines and, crossing the river, charged into their villages shooting, whooping, singing victory songs, to be met by the women who had fled to the upland with the small children, all running back, only now feeling safe. But some at the upper camps looked uneasily toward the knots of troops on the ridges across the river. Still, they sang their warrior welcoming songs.

But there was the uneasiness among the councilors, those who knew something of the white man's numbers, and even among the war chiefs who feared the day of retribution when they had so few arms and so little ammunition while the soldiers had the roaring wagon guns, the cannons. Some pointed to those soldiers up on the hill, still alive, the ones who had struck first against the great camp and killed even Gall's stepson besides several good men. Those soldiers must not escape either, and so, with whoops and battle songs, the leaders headed the thousands back toward Reno, and saw that those soldiers had all moved out and were bunched at the edges of some high points like lead buffalo cows smelling out a changing wind. Plainly, they were also as blind as the buffalo and would be as easily scattered as those soldiers already dead, and would die so easily.

In St. Louis, as the later Democratic delegates were gathering on the afternoon of the 25th, New York's Tilden seemed to be strongly favored over General Hancock; Hancock to become another soldier-president if he won. But this time he would be the responsibility of the Democrats, who had been howling about the corrupt administration of a greater, if Republican, general. Yet surely the high tide of anger that had been raised against a soldier-president could be diverted. There was the popularity of the romantic fighters against the Indians, and while General Hancock was not the dashing figure of a Custer, he also had burned a Cheyenne village.

Yes, if Hancock came up as a dark horse and the circumstances were just right, he might win the nomination, if no more attractive figure appeared.

Three days before the opening of the Democratic Convention there were the usual last-minute scandalous rumors, this time against New York, the state's Colonel Church charged with having "some unhappy pecuniary relations with a female descend-

ant of 'The Father of His Country,' " followed by the antici-
pated public brawling between the pro- and anti-Tildenites.
There were rumors, too, of something brewing among the
Michigan delegates, without a suggestion of its nature. The
New York *Herald* carried an editorial on Crook's defeat:

> Some time ago we knew of certain regiments going into the
> Yellowstone region. Why they went is not clear. . . . Critics
> of the administration will say that if General Grant had not
> removed that superb Indian fighter Custer to avenge Belknap,
> we should not now be mourning ten dead and twenty
> wounded soldiers. . . . He (the Indian) has been plundered
> and starved. We have hunted him as a bear or a panther.

June 26, the *Herald* asked "Is Hancock the Dark Horse?" although the paper was still speaking for Bayard. June 27, more
corridor brawls were reported and the *Herald* complained about
"The gallant Custer in the role of a guide" in the search for
Sitting Bull.

Anyone in St. Louis expecting the triumphant telegram from
Custer that the colonel had hoped to send abroad to the world
had to receive it no later than the 28th.

» » » » » » » »

6 RETURN
TO THE
SIEGE

★ ★ ★ ★ ★ ★ ★ ★

Under the thin gray streaks of dust and smoke, so high they seemed a part of the whitish mare's-tails across the sky, some of the Indians still sat on their horses in scattered little knots along the slopes. They had been looking off northward, firing an occasional gun in their victory exultation. Then there was a gesturing back to the soldiers coming along the ridges and finally the stopping to look. At a whooping and a rough, wavering blast from a trumpet, the warriors wheeled their horses, first here and then there, to start in prongs up the ravines toward Reno's hesitating groups of soldiers on the far points. The fighters from their victory charges through the villages came too, crossing at the pony ford near the mouth of Medicine Tail Creek, or, impatient, spread out along the river, leaping their horses from the bank, throwing water high, and, clambering out, whipped up the steep bluff sides. They cheered and whooped each other on, for if those soldiers up there ahead died as easily as the ones left white and naked scattered along the open, unshielding ridges and slopes down the river they might miss the fight altogether.

"Nobody is to be reckless and get hurt. The soldiers can all be killed by no water," the war leaders cautioned in one way or another. But the young warriors were hard to hold. Sweeping toward the soldiers, they began firing their new guns and ammunition, although some were a mile away and more, some swinging out to cut off the nearer, the bolder, and more foolish of the troops. Captain Benteen watched them come. He had moved out beyond the rest to a point where he hoped to see some sign of Custer and his battalion. There was only the thin spread of dust cloud and the warriors moving along the slopes, but across the river, villages were strung out as far as he could see, perhaps 1,800 lodges and certainly hundreds of the small wickiups for the young men—at least four or five thousand warriors.

By the time Reno and a small detachment reached the high point farther on than Weir, he could see swarms of Indians—thousands. The major told Adjutant Hare that their position was not a good one to make a stand, not with the Indians beginning to pour into the shallow gorge that led up behind Benteen and behind Weir's men, too, and the scattering of other troopers, gathered in dark little rims along the edges of the ridge points. Plainly the command must be consolidated, and quickly. As the roar of guns came closer and closer, even Weir, in spite of his partisanship to Custer and Reno's orders to open communication with the colonel, had to see the danger as his men began to waver before the bullets that sent the horses, particularly those of the recruits, plunging and rearing, wild to escape.

The small knots of troopers began to fall back from the various points, following Reno's lead. He was hurrying, with Moylan's wounded and the pack train to be protected. Benteen planted a guidon on Weir Hill when he passed, as a signal and a guide and cheer to any scattered men or detachments who might come in sight. French, who had already felt the Indian charges on the bottoms and to Reno Hill that afternoon, was retreating fast, too, and so Weir fell in behind him, the troopers spurring and whipping the worn horses. When they neared Reno, Weir sent Hare to report that he had found the whole country ahead of him covered with Indians and that they had been getting around his position.

As more troops fell in behind the common retreat, Edgerly of D Troop was trying desperately to mount his frantic horse, wild from the whoops and the shooting, with several Indians charging in from the sides. He made it just as the first warriors came up over the bluff within rifle range but riding flat against their ponies, difficult to hit by the troopers shooting back on the run. The Indians aimed mostly for the cavalry mounts, not to kill so much as to graze, drive them wild to escape their riders, who could be cut down with war club and ax, the horses rounded up by the herders. One trooper was wounded in the saddle but clung there while several others were set afoot, running through the dust and smoke to catch a stirrup or even a flying tail. One of Weir's D Troop slid to the ground and lay there, bleeding. As Edgerly passed, he called out to the man to get to a hole and he would form a skirmish line and come back to get him. When Edgerly managed to reach Weir to tell him of the promise and ask for a line, the captain refused. Orders were to get back to the hill of the earlier stand.

It was true that the Indians, on their fresh horses, were gaining fast, sweeping down the saddleback and up toward Reno Hill. Godfrey saw that such close pursuit would throw the whole command into confusion and fright, perhaps start a real rout, particularly among the men who had already had their units decimated by the power of the Indians that afternoon.

With his fresh troops dismounted and deployed, he made a stand to cover the retreat. Lieutenant Hare, on the way back from Reno, who was hurrying on to his hill with Moylan's wounded and the pack train, decided to stay with Godfrey, even though he was the adjutant and perhaps needed elsewhere. With the Indians sweeping around toward both sides of Reno Hill, Godfrey sent the led horses ahead to the command, while his troopers flattened into small depressions and behind clumps of sage and gumweed to slow the Indians, shoot some down so the rest would hunt cover. But although his men brought some of the horses down, the warriors clung to the far side until they actually fell and then slipped into the charging Indians, to be dragged away, the thundering mass of warriors no thinner but sweeping in by the hundreds—the thousands, it seemed—so that Godfrey was ordered to fall back rapidly while he could. Keeping up the firing, the troopers ran, stooping low under the dust and blue puffs of smoke from bank to weed to hollow, falling spraddle-legged, ready to fire. Bullets struck all around the men, spurting dirt and gravel over them, the *ping* overhead ever more demoralizing.

When they reached the ridge before Reno's position, they found the men there dismounted and being set around the shallow depression, the horses and the pack train corraled and a picket line thrown out, mules tied to it and unpacked. Dr. Porter gathered the wounded in the bottom of the shallow hole, protected as much as possible with pack saddles set in a barricade around them.

It was a well-maneuvered retreat, as the experienced Plains soldiers like Benteen realized, with only one man lost, although there were wounded to add to those fevering and thirsting from the earlier fight. In spite of their own precarious situation, several of the officers, and the older troopers too, talked among themselves about Custer.

Perhaps he had had an encounter and withdrawn to the Yellowstone and General Terry . . .

But mostly the men worked fast to prepare for the attack to come, surely planned to overwhelm them, ride through them. The Indians already darkened the heights and began to sweep down in hard charges that called for staunch defense. Finally they surrounded the hill entirely, the firing general all along the line, very fast and at close range. The Ree scouts who hadn't started for the Yellowstone hid behind the east ridge, watching. Some of the warriors saw them and took up the chase. The Rees scattered and flattened to the earth. The Sioux, afraid they would miss the fight and the plunder on Reno Hill, gave up the search, and when they were gone Young Hawk climbed to a high point where he could see Reno's flag far off, along the river ridge. He cut a stick, tied his white handkerchief to it, and with the Rees gathered up, several afoot, but the wounded on horses, Hawk led off to Reno. They met a lot of Sioux swarming up around back of the ridge and had to run. The soldiers saw the scouts coming and began to shoot too, past them into the chasing enemy. Near the hill the Hawk's horse went down but, still waving the white flag above him, he raced for the troops, through the continuous roar of the attack on Reno. Panting, Young Hawk fell into the little hollow, grabbed a hardbread box, and flattened himself behind it while the wounded Rees were dragged down to the little breastwork protecting the other injured ones, and where a keening went up at the news that Bob Tail Bull was dead.

By this time the outline of Reno's position was roughly a wide circle, with the southeast, the upstream, side cut off flat and open. This, Reno ordered closed by some of Mathey's hardbread boxes set in a low barricade, making the whole defense line an irregular horseshoe, with the end barred. The ground fell away there for some distance, but with a high point beyond from which the Indians dropped arrows and bullets into the depression.

Benteen had left one company back on the ridge to hold it at any cost, but when the Indians struck those troopers, they came running in as fast as any others. He sent Captain Godfrey's men to another rise to hold the Indians off as long as possible and ordered Wallace to place his troops in a weak spot. Wallace pointed out that he had only three men left in his Company G, and was sent anyway, with a promise of support. He would need it, with at least 2,500 warriors surrounding the command, the firing hotter than the troopers could be expected to face for long.

Reno was making the rounds of his defense and Benteen fell in beside him awhile, the two men moving stooped down as they talked. The show of a hat or a head or anything lifted on a gun barrel brought a volley of arrows and bullets through the slow-rising smoke. They directed the tightening of the defense line. The horses and pack animals were corraled more securely in their circle, the reins of a dozen tied together and anchored to the legs of dead horses. Moylan's company covered these from behind the pack saddle breastworks Mathey had set up for the wounded. To Moylan's left were Weir and Godfrey, then French, Wallace, and McDougall, with the latter's left resting on the downriver bluffs. On the upstream side Benteen's line stretched along a higher knoll offering a farther sight area and, consequently, farther exposure. By then it was about five-thirty in the afternoon, perhaps later. No one had time to look at a watch, certain to be on Chicago time anyway. As the firing sharpened, every man hugged the dry, dusty earth, making himself as thin as possible, none with the time to dig in if there had been more shovels, those flattened down behind sagebrush hoping that it was neither transparent or bullet-welcoming, the whole command—particularly Reno's battalion—in no condition for hard work or for a protracted wait without dozing off in the desperate need for sleep.

The Indian circle around Reno's position was about 4,000 yards in circumference, the warriors at varying distances, from knots of headmen observers at 1,200 yards to warriors as close as 30 feet—young warriors making records for great boldness before they were detected and brought down for their daring, but not before they took a heavy toll, their memory to be honored in song and story.

Somehow the Indians seemed to have more guns or ammunition than down on the bottoms, good guns that carried far. The troop to the right of French's Company M lost several men, killed within a few minutes by fire from a high ridge. One of the Indians seemed to be a genuine sharpshooter. French's men saw this and flattened even closer to the earth, waiting their turn while they tried to spot the culprit in spite of the Indian's usual quick jump away from the betraying spread of his gunsmoke. Yet for all the attempts to stop him, the sharpshooter worked into M Troop and down along the line. He killed the fourth man from Sergeant Ryan, hit the third and struck a second, who jumped back down among the wounded to the doctor. Captain French and the sergeant, both certain that Ryan's turn was next, leaped up with half a dozen of their men and instead of firing straight ahead as before, they wheeled suddenly to the right and put a deadly volley into the heights, and while they could not see any effect through the stinking smoke, the Indians ran and the sharpshooter fired no more.

Gradually the sun receded and dusk came. Now the red spurts of gunfire exposed the exact point of discharge, but creeping Indians could move up close without detection through the shadowed low places almost within spear's reach of the troop line—spear and arrow that created no betraying fire. The situation looked more and more desperate. Darkness was coming fast, to cover united charges that could surely overrun the thin circle of soldiers. There was perhaps more confidence against this possibility in men like French, Moylan, Benteen, and Reno, who understood the Indian's conviction that fighting after dark was bad luck, a survival from the old days when night dews not only softened the moccasin sole to the rock and the thorn but—worse—stretched the bowstring so it refused to send the arrow into the darkness.

The firing slackened as the clouded night fell, sometime between nine and ten o'clock in that region, but there were signs of sentinels left to guard the besieged soldiers, with the frequent sound of hoofs on the hard earth, sound of horsemen coming and going. Even half a dozen creeping Indians could be a great menace to troopers who had had almost no real sleep the last three days, with hard, weary marches and bloody fighting. The younger men particularly fell asleep at the first lull.

Several times Reno tried to get a detail to water, but the Indians were most watchful along the river bluffs, with piles of dry grass ready to blaze up at the least sound or movement, exposing the creeping troopers to the pitiless glare, and the bullet and arrow.

The men of responsibility on the hill, as well as the packers and other civilians, wondered about Custer, with no courier from him, no signal by day or night. Many believed that he had probably been defeated and driven down the river. Yet his horses were worn out, with even Boston Custer having to return to the pack train to replace his. The Indians, as all who had seen the great moving herd knew, had endless horses, tough and fresh, for relays in the chase. Still, Custer, wily and known for fool's luck, probably had his men with General Terry this minute, to return to the Little Bighorn with him; instead of Custer meeting Terry and Gibbon coming up the river tomorrow evening or the next day, when Custer's whole force was to be in from his scout, then with all the 7th Cavalry alive and well.

But mostly the troopers thought about Terry because even tomorrow might be too late for them here, and no telling what Custer reported to the humoring general if he did go there. Benteen and some of the others remembered the desertion of Elliott on the Washita, even the bodies unrecovered. Who could say why he didn't trouble to support Reno as promised? There were several men here whom Custer could spare from his regiment without much regret.

It was a time of bitterness, of darkness not entirely of the night. Besides, some knew of the promise Custer had made to Bloody Knife: that a victory over even half a dozen Sioux lodges would make him the Great Father. Who could say what small camp might have been discovered by the Crows or Bouyer for Custer to destroy, and that he was not hurrying a message to a telegraph station this moment for the Democratic Convention gathering at St. Louis?

By now the question, "What is the matter with Custer?" was receiving increasingly impatient replies. Whatever else tomorrow or the 27th might bring to the men besieged on the hill, there would be hordes of howling redskins around them before dawn, and now was the time to prepare for the attack, prepare as well as could be managed. And if anyone forgot, there were the little red glow spots of enemy scout fires reflected against the clouds overhead, fires of Indians watching them on every side, with occasional hoofbeats of horsemen coming and going, perhaps relief for the sentinels, with now and then a wolf howl or an owl's hoot that the scouts and the old-timers recognized as entirely too natural—surely Indian signals.

During the evening fight it was planned to send a messenger

out as soon as possible after dark. He was to locate Custer or go on to Terry coming up the river, deliver a paper telling of their troubles here. Forked Horn agreed it should be done, but he was a Ree and unfamiliar with the region. Unfortunately, Goose, a Crow who knew every gully and badger hole within fifty miles, was wounded. Anyway, several couriers should be sent out, mounted on the strongest government horses remaining, all to ride hard, pay no attention if any of the others were shot. Both Reno and Varnum of the scouts emphasized this: one of the men must get through. Anyone who fell wounded was to pull out the message paper so any soldiers who might find him would see it.

At a scout's suggestion, the farrier removed the iron shoes from the horses so they could run better, Forked Horn said, with less noise or sparks from stones, and leaving no tracks behind to betray them as soldier couriers for any skulking Sioux. With best wishes but without trumpet blast or fanfare three Rees, including Young Hawk, Custer's favorite meat broiler, started. At the last, Goose, even though wounded, insisted on going too, for he knew the country, Goose and a white sergeant. They eased their horses cautiously out along the darkness of the ravines, but it was not like a man creeping. The Sioux heard and fired on them, so they all whipped back.

Reno, weary from the hard marches and the three bloody encounters of his men with overwhelming forces in one day, was very disheartened. He tried to get some of the civilians who knew the country to carry a message out. They refused. Varnum himself volunteered, but Reno pointed out that the lieutenant had no knowledge of the region, so even at best it would be suicide. He could not let a man with no chance at all go out. Perhaps toward dawn they would try again, when their Indian scouts were more inclined to travel, less certain of bad luck in anything of war in the nighttime. But they were all of tribes who understood the power of the Sioux, and preferred to stick close to the little hole on Reno Hill.

The older campaigners knew that Indians were notoriously close-fingered with fuel; but as the night darkened, the fires in the villages across the river blazed up high, even those far out of sight casting light against the thin clouding overhead, the figures dancing around the nearer flames making gigantic leaping shadows in the light that flared up against the bluffs and ridges along the river where Benteen's men particularly could see them. Desperate for rescue, it was easy for the fevering wounded to imagine columns of troops here and there below, and others too. Once, many thought they saw the shadowy duskiness of troops moving over the hills and ridges, with the dull thud of iron hoofs, the command of officers coming from far away, and even a proper blare or two of a trumpet. Stable call was sounded by one of Reno's trumpeters, shots were fired in signals of friendship. Every hope possible gave itself form: a civilian packer leaped to the bare back of a horse and galloped along the line in the darkness, shouting.

"Don't be discouraged, boys!" he kept repeating. "Crook is coming!"

Crook . . . the only general who had ever succeeded in an attack on a substantial village of these northern Indians, and then not the Sioux but only a part of the small tribe of Northern Cheyennes. But he had struck and destroyed the village out of a cold dawn last March, not in the heat of summertime and not against the great summer conference of the Teton Sioux. There would have been even less optimism if the men in the circle on Reno Hill could have known of Crook's fight up the Rosebud eight days ago. It had required only part of the gathered warriors to drive back General George Crook, the graying Indian fighter, and with a much stronger force than the entire scouting regiment, Custer's 7th, all together.

Soon it was plain that General Crook was not coming, nor anyone else; and gradually the men, even the frightened romantic recruits, had to give up their dream of a storybook cavalry rescue and start digging rifle pits as fast as they could in the baked and stony earth, working in groups of threes and fours through the danger of creeping figures in the dark and the unusual amount of howling northwestward from wolves under the thinner, higher, more hysterical yip and cry of the coyotes. At the start Benteen had sent to the packs for spades, but there were none there. Sergeant Ryan of French's M Troop had a couple of small ones and in addition used boards from the hardtack boxes for digging. A few of the troopers had hand axes and hatchets, others used their knives and even the forks from their folding mess kits, as well as tin cups and halves of battle-punctured canteens.

Reno made a hurried round of his position, stumbling into the fresh holes in the darkness, and over legs sprawled out. Worried, he was driving the men, knowing that dawn would bring a concerted attack beyond anything his force had yet endured, even those who had been on the bottoms with him. There was some talk of slipping away, secretly in little groups, and openly, the whole command going, even leaving the wounded behind. But with the worn men and animals and the Indian watchers to signal any movement, ready to bring overwhelming pursuit, it could only end in a disastrous running fight or a stand in a much less defensible position than here, and with no water anywhere or even the hope of it. Reno moved cautiously among the dusky figures of the wounded where Dr. Porter worked by touch, with even a momentary matchlight bringing swift bullets. The blood and woundings were already a sweetish stench, some of the men talking wildly, begging for more water than the mouth-wetting from the lightening canteens being saved for them. Several were no more than boys, city boys away from home in a wilderness teeming with Indians and thirst and pain.

When the commander came to the packs protecting the wounded and the animals he found a great many skulkers there, some packers known through the regiment for their thieving and some other civilians too, perhaps thinking they might as well take now, for there might be no tomorrow, puncturing the few tins of canned fruit with their knives, drinking the juices—juices and fruit Reno was trying to husband for the wounded through what might be days of siege. He had already fired Girard, missing since the fight on the bottoms but not considered dead by anyone, such were his wily ways. Reno had thought he was stealing from the government and refused to sanction his employment further. Now the commander drove the packers and the other civilians away from the supplies, but he had to return to do this several times, finding packs broken open, half the contents gone, particularly the fruit. Roaring out that the horses and mules were safe and did not need these men, who had no business there now, Reno demanded of one of the more troublesome what he was doing among the packs and received an insulting reply. This, on top of all the day's trials and sorrow, infuriated the commander so he struck at the man and shouted out what many said was a threat to shoot him if he was found among the government goods again. Benteen was angry too. He had had to drive some of the packers from the goods at the bivouacs all the way from Fort Abraham Lincoln, drive them out like thieving dogs.

As the night drew on, the fires flared higher in the villages along the river, with a roaring of songs and drumming pierced by yells and gunshots. To those who knew the Indians this seemed a lot of victory-dancing for Reno's soldiers lost—even for Bloody Knife, the traditional enemy who had led Custer into the sacred Black Hills two years ago. Besides, he had brought the soldiers here to their summer conference, after it was driven away from Bear Butte by the miners that his guiding had tolled to the place called Deadwood. Still, there seemed excessive jubilation in the vast Indian camp, even counting the two troopers whose panicking horses had carried them into the Sioux village, the village of Sitting Bull, the man whose dreaming had been pictured at the sun dance site back on the Rosebud.

"Soldiers falling head first into his village . . ." the Sioux scouts had said the signs meant.

Some of the troopers less schooled in Sioux warfare thought of prisoners being tortured in the camps, as in the old stories of the Iroquois and French Indians flaying and burning their captives two hundred years ago. True, some of the Sioux remembered their early custom of decapitating their enemies, the heads carried through the victory-dancing and then impaled on the poles of their fortified villages in the upper Mississippi country. Inkpaduta and his small group of Santees who had fled to the Tetons after the troubles in the Spirit Lake region were probably the only practicing decapitators in the camp. Lieutenant Hare and some of the others did recall Lieutenant Harrington's gloomy foreboding that he was to be captured and tortured. Back early in the expedition he had made sketches of himself tied to a tree with naked savages dancing around him. It seems he sent these back by mail courier, not to his wife but to a friend, and yet he had not been easier in mind.

There were several light sprinkles during the night, the raindrops making light running sounds over the dry earth, like timid mice. But there was not enough to wet one parched tongue or to soak the grass piles of the Indians watching the way to water. Besides, there was repeated heat lightning, re-vealing all the ridge and its bluffs in rosy glare. Toward dawn, ammunition and rations were distributed for the coming fight, dry rations with not even alkali water for coffee, the whole-bodied, too, suffering from thirst although the Little Bighorn was only three–four hundred yards away.

Relays of short rests had been arranged, some of the troopers sleeping while the rest dug rifle pits or built breastworks with the boxes and the bags of bacon, hay, and oats. Pack saddles were set up in rows, some with pads and blankets hung be-tween them, offering protection from the eyes of the enemy when dawn came if not against his bullet, arrow, spear, and even knife and tomahawk, for it would surely come to that if the command was not relieved soon.

Only Reno seemed not to rest or even to nap. "Great God, I don't see how you can sleep!" he told Edgerly on the lieu-tenant's awakening.

Toward dawn the fires and noises of the villages lessened so that Benteen's men along the bluffs could see the interlacing of fireflies in the valley below and hear the fall of the arrow hawks upon their flying insect prey, a peaceful night sound as though there were no men dead below them, and none still to die not far away. Several times the Indian scouts and the old plainsmen put a naked ear to the ground to detect faraway sounds of regular hoofs—cavalry or even Crook's infantry marching—but there were only irregular vibrations, perhaps a little late dancing below, and surely of Indians coming and going from their guard points.

With the first graying in the east around two-thirty or three there were two rapid shots from the Indians splitting the dark sky together, apparently a war signal. Some of the troops were still digging when the attack opened and sharpened as the light silhouetted the tops of the ridges. Spits of fire revealed the

Indian circle, with puffs of powder smoke spread almost imperceptibly in the pale light, followed by the lagging boom of the farther guns. They were answered by the troops, but with caution now, many of the wildly shooting recruits of yesterday's fight on the bottoms either dead or grown into veterans in twelve hours. All the men of the circle except the side against the Little Bighorn had some shelter as the light crept down over them, at least if they lay flat and kept their heads down. But Benteen's men were guarding the broken canyons and ravines that led from the river directly to the bluff top, into the entrenchments. To watch these cuts and breaks the men had to expose themselves and gradually some managed to slip away under the smoke to Reno's hole, to hide among the packs. Benteen went to run them out, his voice harsh with dust and fury. He made them drag down some of H Troop's pack saddles, bacon bags, and hardbread boxes for a redoubt to protect his wounded until they could be moved to the hill.

As the east grew lighter and reached in reddening streaks up the clouded sky, it spread a flush over the gray, dusty men on the hill and then moved down the slopes and finally over all the bottoms. Down along the river, morning fires sent twists of smoke out on the prairie where horse herds were sweeping in from the western upland. Indians gathered in swarms along the river—mounted, warrior Indians, apparently reserves waiting for space in the attacking circle. Buzzards hovered over the Reno bottoms, drawn by the dead men and the bloating horses. Some were flying off northwestward too, most of them beyond clear view even with the field glasses, disappearing, dropping down out of sight as several eagles soared in fast and high, like swift bits of black hair against the graying clouds.

The attack sharpened, the Indians drawing all the fire they could, to wear out the ammunition and make the cartridges stick in the heated carbines as they had done yesterday, but there were ramrods from both the supply packs and willows cut by some of the old-timers on the bottoms. Here and there warriors poked up mats of dark buffalo hair on the end of their guns or their coup sticks, buffalo-head mops, with feathers stuck in them, like the top of Indian heads. The bolder ones jumped up high and dropped down, drawing the fire of the recruits who believed they could guess where the men would drop. In the meantime a small knot of sharpshooters gathered on the high point out of range of the Springfield .45 carbines, using infantry rifles mostly captured from Crook last week. They hit the horses and mules in the shallow depression, setting them wild, their empty saddles flapping a little, the Indians hoping to stampede the stock out across the prairie, young warriors ready to round them up.

Benteen's men also suffered from these guns, with their section open to the long-range firing from the northward too. After a long roaring of shots from all around, the flashes paling in the brightening day, the mounted charge that all experienced Plains fighters dreaded came. With their horses whipped into a high run in their second wind, the warriors clung flat to the heaving sides as they headed straight for the little circle on the hill, hundreds of Indians it seemed, firing. In spite of the warning to keep cool, take careful aim, some of the Indians got clear into Reno's defense line before they were turned aside. Some were dropped, perhaps the horses going down headfirst or slowing, stumbling. Others ran free, their riders gone, perhaps to be dragged away by the neck rope tucked under the rider's belt or carried off by a fellow warrior.

As the advance scattered in the dust and smoke, the officers hurried among their men, here and there one hit, perhaps in the head, finger still on the trigger, to be lifted out of the way before the next charge. By now Benteen realized that his position was the key to the whole defense and that he would probably receive the next onslaught. His ammunition was getting very short, some men down to four–five cartridges, and no relay of boxes possible to them over the exposed bluff crest that was in the sights of Indian sharpshooters. He was disturbed, too, by his growing number of wounded, who could not be moved to protection or to Dr. Porter, still working without sleep to ease and comfort the desperate condition of the injured now that the water was gone. Yet if the Indians made a determined rush, retreat of Benteen's troops was inevitable, with the collapse of the entire bluff line and the probable loss of his disabled, perhaps all of Reno Hill and the men dug in there.

Ordering Lieutenant Gibson to hold on, under no circumstances to fall back, Benteen, under such cover as his best marksmen could give him, slipped up a shallow ravine to find Reno. He discovered that all the defense was hard-pressed, with earth and gravel spurting up over the defenders, the whine of bullets ricocheting from pebbles and rock loud above the thud of lead on flesh and the sobbing of some of the wounded. He found Reno up at Weir's position, lying low, his head once more covered by a dusty blue kerchief, lifting up now and then to survey the area and ducking as the shooting multiplied.

"The Indians are doing their best to cut through my lines and it will be impossible to hold it much longer," Benteen reported to the commander.

Reno pointed out that the whole defense was in great danger, but when Private McDermott came snaking up a cut under the smoke, bringing Gibson's report that the ammunition was almost gone, Reno had to consider the problem. Unhappily, the fight was growing even hotter all along the line, the bowmen becoming very expert in raising arrows high to fall among the horses and the wounded. Still, he could not afford a break-

through from the river, so he ordered Captain French with his
M Troop over to the southerly side. He and his men at least
knew something of the terrain there, from the retreat.

On the way back, Benteen, his curly hair powdered with
gray dust, gathered up some more men from the horse detail
and hurried down, just in time. The fight was almost hand to
hand now: a hundred men, it seemed, against every one of
Gibson's, all ready to charge in upon them bodily. One warrior
shot a trooper from so close that with one plunge forward he
touched the body with his short coup stick. The man was killed
by an alert trooper and lay there in his dusty, bloody paint and
breechclout, the only Indian casualty left in sight anywhere
because he was too close for even the most daring rescue. The
warriors moved around, but there were always some on high
points out of range, watching and directing, generaling the fight
by signals to the many hidden behind ridges and cut banks and
in ravines two hundred to five hundred yards off in a continuous circle around Reno's command, at one place sometimes less
than thirty yards from the troops. After the hot exchanges the
Indians seemed to think the besieged were so hurt and disorganized that it was the time to charge again. They came once
more, under the smoke and dust, sticking flat to their horses,
those afoot dodging from ridge to hollow to weed, perhaps
arching their silent, unbetraying arrows into the soldier hill.

By now there were no spoken questions about Custer, only a
rare meeting of eyes and a bitterness worse than alkali on the
cracked and blistered lips.

French agreed that the men scattered around the bluff face,
unprotected, visible from at least one side or the other or from
below, must be kept there at any cost. Benteen wanted the
Indian boldness repaid with a charge of the two companies.
Reno slipped down to lead it, the firing a roar of steady thunder, the smoke clinging to the breaks as the troops moved afoot,

creeping, running, falling. Somehow they pushed the warriors back from one protective ravine and draw to the next, some almost to the river. But the Indians had endless reinforcements to take the places of their wounded and dead as a counter-charge was built up.

The attack was costly in ammunition to Benteen's men and in casualties. They were gathered to the shelter of a ravine, all but Private Tanner of French's M Troop. He was hit far out on an exposed knob and unable to drag himself out of arrow shot. At a hurried call for volunteers Sergeant Ryan grabbed a blanket from a saddle and with three men ran to the wounded Tanner, rolled him upon it, and, stooping low, with bullets and arrows, even a spear or two striking around them, the flying gravel sharp against their faces, got the man to the ravine of the wounded. In a few moments Tanner was dead, but it heartened the men to know that their injured were rescued as daringly as any Indian.

Captain French's favorite horse, the best buffalo hunter in the command, was among the held ones near the wounded men. The animal received a long-range shot in the head and began to stagger around, setting the other horses to rearing and plunging, trying to break loose. Private Voight of M Troop started to lead him out of the way and got his brains spattered over everything, as Bloody Knife had down in the bottoms, when Reno stood beside him.

Soon the firing commenced in greater fury, most recklessly from the southeast, evidently to cover an attack gathering else-where. Reno gave Benteen permission to make up a short charge from D, G, and K Troops.

At the captain's shouted order, "Give them hell! Hip, hip! Here we go!" the men leaped out, carbines ready to fire at will.

Only one man stayed behind in his little pit, crying like a child. In their run over the ridge, Benteen's men could see a large body of Indians gathered at the foot of one of the hills to the north. As the short foot charge moved toward them, firing as the men came, the Indians broke and scattered. All the troopers returned. The only serious casualty was the man who had remained in the rifle pit, crying. He was dead, apparently by a bullet from his own pistol.

By now the men on Reno Hill were ordered to keep down, to save themselves and their ammunition, for they must somehow last until Terry and Gibbon arrived. It was the first real admission that Custer was no longer expected to join them. The men flattened down low in their shallow holes and trenches and behind dead horses, the buzzing gases in the heat bloating the bellies up high until hit by bullets. Any that struck bone released not only a terrible stench but blew the rotting flesh over the men hid behind them. Even less fortunate were the troopers lying beside corpses swarming with flies, those dead since yesterday bloating like the horses, with maggots beginning to work in the blackened mouths and eyeballs, the sight even more horrible than the stench.

The horses and mules up around Dr. Porter's patients were so wild for water that their rearing against the picket lines endangered the wounded men unable to escape. Even the horse guard was liable to injury, the number doubled for safety, although the Indians were driving holes in the outer line. The whole command was desperate for water, the thirst aggravated by the sultry heat of the summer day where the thermometer often went above 110 degrees. The occasional spatter of rain running over the grass was only a tantalization, the smell of water driving the horses to wilder plunging. Even so, the dust was never laid, gritty and burning in the dry mouths of the able as well as the burning and delirious wounded. The men were forbidden the comfort, and the drying effect, of a smoke or a cud of tobacco. Some put pebbles into their mouths; some tried to chew grass. Those whose hunger drove them to gnaw at a little hardbread found that it blew out of their mouths like flour in their breath. A few raw potatoes offered a little relief, but there were so very few. Several times volunteers started over the bluff rim for water and were always driven back or left flat on the broken earth. Now and then a recruit who would be a hero slipped away without authority—none of those who had been on the bottoms with Reno: they knew. Sometimes the daring one got back through a costly cover of bullets to hold the eager Indians back, and face the scathing, dry-mouthed profanity due a fool in war.

Benteen, with the best view of the river and the bottoms, estimated there were two thousand Indians around the hill and as many as a regiment waiting along the river for their turn to enter the fight. A formal file of Indians on good horses, a couple of the grays almost as well matched as Smith's, came to watch from a remote point. In the center group was a white-patched golden buckskin that the troopers with Custer in 1873 declared belonged to Crazy Horse. Whoever the Indians were, they gathered, with the horse heads close, apparently in consultation, and then dismounted and settled in a circle for a smoke, with signals from mirror flashes, bannered spears, and hands. It looked like a concerted charge was coming, the depression on the hill to be overrun by the very number of the enemy. But apparently it was put off, for now the warriors in the attack no longer exposed themselves, although a few got close enough to send rocks and spears into the circle by hand and to count coup on a dead trooper within Benteen's line. They dropped arrows into Weir's and Godfrey's men too, and had to be driven out by a charge like Benteen's once more led by Reno. There was a suspicious lack of real resistance and after the

troops were withdrawn the Indians slowed their attack, apparently waiting for the thirst to do their work, as the troopers
told each other sourly. No use losing more warriors.

By now most of the men on the hill had had no water for
sixteen hours, the horses for twenty. Dr. Porter came stumbling
with fatigue to say he must relieve the thirst of his patients.
His wounded were dying, more from the lack of water than
from the injuries. So the desperate attempt must be made;
somehow they must reach the river. A skirmish line was arranged, to be put out as soon as there seemed some hope of
success, Benteen ready to offer all the protection he could give
to the water detail. A party of volunteers draped with empty
canteens and carrying camp kettles crept out, to run from rock
to bush to bank into the steep ravines that led to the bottoms.
But from there they had to make a rush across the open space
to the river, much like the spot where Reno's men had suffered
such casualties. Those who made it with the kettles dipped
them and tried to race back to the ravine to fill the strings of
canteens hanging from the carriers like vines of flattened fruit.
Indians, hidden in a nearby brush patch fired on every man
making the run. Some of the soldiers went down, their kettles
spilling; others tried it a second time, with kettles spurting
water from bullets and arrows. As the wounded accumulated,
there was the additional need to rescue them, with more men
endangered. But the water relay went on somehow, the smoke
of gunpowder clinging over the brush and rising upward in
parallel streamers, while the arrows from bushes and hollows
left no betraying trail.

By noon the shooting up around the hill had quieted, the
troops saving ammunition, the Indians probably stopping to eat
and sleep a little as was their custom in even the hottest fight.
But the river was still closely guarded and there were still sharpshooters on a high knoll, out of range of the carbines. One of

the sergeants, handling a fifteen-pound .45 Sharps with telescopic sights, fired a few times to get the range and then put several bullets into the sharpshooters' nest to quiet them a little.

Sometime in the early afternoon an appalling number of Indians suddenly appeared out of the draws to make a fast charge all around the command. Leaving their horses out of range, they crept up and drove the troops down into their pits and trenches once more. Once more it looked like the end, this time by generalship. McDougall was ordered to make a little charge against the creeping Indians. He covered about sixty yards, until the firing got so heavy from the right and then across his position that he had to retreat.

But the Indians seemed to be withdrawing too. Reno came over to look.

"Where are they going?" he asked, peering under his shading palm.

"Downstream," McDougall replied, from what he had seen outside the depression, and fell into step beside Reno as he circled the line.

There were still small groups of Indians on the higher ridges, but some from the bottoms were trailing away downstream, too, leaving smoke to rise behind them from patches of grass and sagebrush, the smoke pearling upward. Slowly the Indians withdrew from the heights too, and those surrounding the hill.

An hour passed and another without more than an occasional arrow's fall, with no crack of Indian gun all that time. Gradually the troopers got up to stretch, wiping the dust and soot from their red-rimmed eyes, the dirt from their gaunt, stubbled faces. More men slipped down for water, creeping cautiously out of the ravine, looking toward the brush patches, some of them afire with a green-wood smoking and smudge. There was no crack of rifle or silent flight of arrow. While a detail helped Dr. Porter soak the stinking bandages from the wounded, the first smell of coffee brewing in the kettles crept over the weary men. Bacon was frying, perhaps on sticks over the coals, the hardbread catching some of the sputtering fat. The prairie fires along the bottoms had spread, moved off in the wind, leaving their black trail behind, but watched by few except the sentinels and the officers, out on points, looking.

By seven in the evening someone of the second relay of guards lifted his hoarse voice in an involuntary hurrah. From behind the trailing smoke, blown aside now and then, he could see an immense moving mass starting up the low breaks to the prairie on the west, the left side of the river, apparently heading toward the mountains. One after another the men forgot all danger and gathered in close groups on the ridges to watch under their palms, shielding their eyes against the late sun. Even the officers forgot the danger from skulking snipers left behind and passed the field glasses around. Although the movement was miles away, it looked like one of the vast buffalo herds that once marched those prairies; but they were all gone and besides this was not so dark. It was the great camp of the Indians in a solid, moving flow of riders and family travois with their lodges and belongings, the poles stirring up dust that drifted slowly away, curiously golden in the evening sun. The horse herds were along too, generally off to the side—many, many horses, probably the twenty or twenty-five thousand that the Rees had predicted would be there as part of the great Teton summer council with their usual allies and guests. The creeping blanket stretched out for miles, some thought as far as three or even five miles over the evening prairie.

"Thank God they gave up the fight!" someone said, and although "giving up" didn't seem quite the right words, almost anyone from Reno Hill might have said it, for certainly that many Indians could have overrun the hill any time they were willing to take the casualties, or they could have waited in safe and comfortable relays of watchers for the thirst to finish the work.

Then someone expressed the disturbing possibility that the Indians might just be short of meat and grass—very convincing in such a vast camp—and were moving the families to some buffalo range the hunters had located, the horses to fresh pasture. Afterward the warriors could sweep back to overwhelm Reno's command in close combat. For the first time the troops and most of the officers realized the full power of the Indians —enough warriors to overwhelm Reno's command with no more than knives and war clubs—understanding finally what the scouts really meant when they told Custer that the Sioux were too many, and the sense of Bouyer's suggestion to him: "Get your outfit out of the country as fast as your played-out horses can carry you."

It was true that the Indian scouts might have detected Terry and Gibbon coming up the river, but suppose that Terry did not come and the Indians returned; suppose that the warriors, all the warriors of so great a camp, managed to prevent the general's march up the Little Bighorn?

The dead men and horses in the hot June sun were drawing flies, carrion beetles, and some of the circling vultures from down the river. Reno decided that his command must move nearer to water, away from the stench and the health hazard, but to a position that could be defended if they were attacked again until they could retreat to the pits on the hill. The move was made slowly, well guarded and carefully, along the rugged ravine to assigned positions. The horse guard under McDougall was watering the frantic stock, a few at a time at the narrow pony ford, permitting only a half a dozen quick swallows, then to be whipped out to the grassy plots, most of the horses unsaddled for the first time in forty-eight hours, to let the animals roll in the dust. Later they were watered again and then a third time.

The rest of the men were caring for the wounded or digging pits and a protected area for the fifty-two who had to be carried very gently, with a couple of amputations necessary as soon as the doctor dared to perform them. For the present, they were all shielded from the sun's glare and the dust as much as possible, Dr. Porter, worn and without sleep, working to save lives that might still fall to an Indian war club or knife. By dark the eighteen men lost on the hill had been buried as properly as possible in the baked and stony earth.

That night Lieutenant De Rudio, Private O'Neal, Girard the loud-mouthed interpreter, and Jackson the breed scout came slipping up to the new position. Many had assumed that they had fled with the Indian scouts or even been killed, they and some other troopers who sneaked up too now. Several had expected De Rudio to look out for his own skin very well, and certainly Girard would take no part in any dangerous activities. He had the trader's instinct to keep out of other people's fights. The men all had their stories ready. Left behind in Reno's retreat, they had found it safer to hide in the brush up the valley, in the direction the fleeing scouts had taken.

Night sentries were set, some far out, trustworthy men, with frequent relief. Tuesday morning, June 27, brought reveille without morning guns and the first real meal for the men since the camp on the Rosebud. The stock was watered again, fed and rubbed down, the scalded and galled backs washed and treated. But Reno, the man of all the 7th Cavalry who had faced the most Sioux, was not giving up his caution now. He anticipated a possible trap and renewed his orders that every man be ready to take to the pits at a moment's command, even though the lookout with field glasses couldn't see an Indian, nothing except a few ponies grazing down the valley, apparently loose and deserted.

"The worst sign in Indian country is no sign at all," one of the old-timers offered sourly.

Trumpeter Martin sounded retreat, recall, and march, to draw in any of the command who might be hidden out somewhere. He went to the highest point around and blew his trumpet again, the instrument gleaming in the sun, blew it loud and clear to carry for miles.

There was a growing uneasiness about Terry. Where was the army? Could it have been held up, waylaid, ambushed by the men of that great moving camp? Or had Reno and Benteen been deserted as Elliott was on the Washita? Perhaps they should move out tonight while the region seemed clear, cut their way through; yet that might mean losing the wounded in a running fight. Still, for the moment anything seemed better than to wait for the Indians to return.

Although couriers had been sent to find Terry or Custer—at least Custer's trail—it seemed they had found nothing or they fell to the Indians. Then, midmorning, someone detected a pale cloud of dust streaking the horizon far down the river in the opposite direction from the Indian march. The trumpeter sounded assembly, the horses were put into the protected area, the kettles and canteens filled, and then there was nothing but more waiting. Reno, Benteen, and others went to high points to look through the time that seemed to stretch forever but was actually about an hour. The slow advance of the dust seemed proof of troops, including infantry. Surely no Indians moved like this, so it must be troops—but whose? Anyway, Lieutenant Wallace was sent out to show Terry or Custer or Crook how to get to the Reno position.

As the march neared, no one could pick out a Gray Horse Troop with the glasses, so it was not Custer's force, or Terry's either, for Custer must surely be with him by now. It must be Crook. Cheers went up for him, for old Braided-Beard, as the Indians liked to call him.

Then a white scout, Muggins Taylor, came spurring ahead to the sentinels who crowded around, barely letting him speak. He bore a message from General Terry to Custer, dated the 26th, stating that two Crow scouts had reported that the 7th Cavalry had been whipped and nearly annihilated. Terry had not believed them but was hurrying anyway, with medical assistance. The scout said he had tried to get through to Reno's lines the night before but the Indians had driven him back.

Yes, that was very probable.

By now Lieutenant Bradley of the 7th Infantry rode in asking for his friend Godfrey, who hurried up, demanding, "Where's Custer?"

"I don't know," Bradley admitted. "I suppose he was killed. We counted a hundred and ninety-seven dead bodies back there. I don't suppose any escaped."

Bodies! A hundred ninety-seven bodies! The command was dumfounded. It was not only the first intimation of Custer in real trouble, but even the first suspicion that he might not have escaped that overwhelming body of Indians.

The men hurried to Reno and his officers, carrying the news, some stumbling in their shock and weariness.

When General Terry arrived, his face grave, gray above the bearding, was enough to verify the news, the appalling news. With tears standing on his lean, dusty cheeks, he told what had been found.

»▶ »▶ »▶ »▶ »▶ »▶ »▶ »▶

7 THE
RENDEZVOUS

★ ★ ★ ★ ★ ★ ★ ★

Terry's march from the Yellowstone started uneventfully. The only immediate problem seemed the summer sickness of Colonel Gibbon, who had to be left behind on the *Far West* while the infantry marched on ahead. Still, Custer's 7th Cavalry was not due on the Little Bighorn from the long scout until the 26th or even the next day.

The real concern about the delays over Custer's return from the East all spring was not only about the command of the expedition out of Fort Lincoln but, less openly, the fact that General Crook, up from the south with his Sioux scouts, was in the field for months. He had a real advantage and would surely try to locate and destroy the enemy before Terry's force could contact them. It was, in a way, a race between two commanders of military areas—Terry of the Department of Dakota and Crook, head of the Department of the Platte. After the orders to attack all Indians not on the reservations by January 31, Crook's force had taken the field early and managed to strike a Cheyenne village in March; in the Department of Dakota everything was held up by Custer's eastern junket—Custer feted by the Northern Pacific Railroad and the New York *Herald* and offending his superiors by his hearsay testimony before Clymer's Committee in the Belknap exposures—and by further insubordination, with no one of Terry's command moving against the Sioux.

Custer's scout high up the Rosebud and over to the Tongue should reveal something of Crook's activities as well as the whereabouts of the Indians, but so far no couriers had arrived, not even Herendeen, sent with Custer particularly to carry back news of any Indians on Tullock's Fork. Terry had arrived at the mouth of the Fork the 24th and lingered the next morning. When no courier arrived, he marched a few miles up the valley, hoping to meet Herendeen. Finally the general stopped and sent Lieutenant Bradley with his mounted infantrymen farther ahead. The Crow scouts refused to go on—getting more and more agitated about the powerful Sioux—and Custer had been given all the white or breed guides, men like Bouyer and Jackson, who knew the country.

Terry and the four troops of the 2nd Cavalry that Custer had spurned at the Yellowstone four days ago arrived at the mouth of the Little Bighorn very late the night of the 25th and camped. The next day Bradley and his mounted men saw three Indians that the Crow scouts hailed as friends. The three sign-talked and shouted over the swollen waters of the river about a great battle on the 25th in which Custer and all his men were killed. Then they whipped their horses homeward, suddenly followed by Bradley's alarmed Crow scouts.

The desertion of the Indians added some weight to the story, and yet neither Terry nor Gibbon, both inexpert in Sioux tribal matters such as ceremonials, conferences, and great councils, would believe the Indians could gather enough power to involve Custer in more than an engagement. With the shoes of

Gibbon's infantry spurting up the dust, the column followed the Little Bighorn to about twelve miles below Reno Hill. As they camped for the night, hundreds of mounted warriors gathered on the benchlands to the southwest. Now and then some bolder youth raced his pony daringly between the bivouac and the river, but no shots were fired and by dark all the Indians were gone.

At reveille the 27th not an enemy was in sight anywhere. The column started out early, marching along the even bench west of the river valley while Bradley and his mounted men scouted the breaks and ridges along the right side of the stream. From a highish point they noticed strange objects scattered over the hills rising far ahead—buffaloes, probably an Indian hunt, the whitish carcasses, skinned to the tallow, the dark not yet touched. But curiously there was no movement, no butchering women and children running from one animal to the next, no men packing the meat on horses, no one standing guard.

Terry halted when the glasses showed the first signs of the deserted Indian camp—the Cheyenne village, the ribs of the wickiups and bare, gaunt lodgepoles like clumps of weed sticks in the hot sun. There were more dusky patches farther on, as though a great Indian encampment had stretched in scattered villages up along the river for miles. But not one twist of smoke rose in the air, nothing that could be identified as a movement anywhere, except an eagle flying, or buzzards dropping to the far ridge where it seemed there had been a buffalo hunt.

The column was moved down into the bottoms behind a detachment riding fast through the first deserted camp circle to search out any hidden enemy, stopping to examine a burial lodge or two standing firm and neat in the midst of chaos that signified swift departure. Inside lay men in full paint and regalia, warriors and chieftains plainly honored for bravery in a recent fight.

During the short stops some of the soldiers, particularly infantry men, managed to slip into the death lodges, grabbing whatever they could—moccasins, beaded shirts and blankets, quivers, handsome bows and lances, anything. Outside, they tried to scavenge a little through the great scattering of goods over the campground—brass kettles that no woman discarded without desperate urgency, dried meat, clothing, robes and blankets, even the scarce hoop iron for arrow points.

The horse droppings, the freshly worn pony trails to water from the upland prairie, were beyond anything Terry or Gibbon had ever seen, speaking of great herds, many, many thousands of animals. Through all this sign of an overwhelming force the column was kept moving in uneasiness, the old campaigners certain they were being watched by hidden Sioux scouts, with no telling how many of the warriors of this great camp might be waiting in ambush in some timber patch ahead, some narrow canyon.

The bearded Terry slumped in the saddle, his eyes alert, his dusty face sweat-streaked in the early-morning heat of the sun, the regimental colors sagging in the stillness of the air. On the ridge across the river a mile or more away, Bradley and his men were riding among the dark objects, going from one to the other, but apparently without haste, even dismounting. Someone with Terry thought he detected another movement through the steadied glass—this one far ahead—a lot of dark specks on the bluffs also along the east side of the river, specks moving around but not marching, with no trail of dust rising, as over Terry and Gibbon's men, and no faint spreading haze from earlier travel hanging in the sky. Then three men appeared on a point across the river from Terry, apparently troopers in what seemed uniform through the glasses, and on cavalry horses. They were the volunteers from Reno, come to investigate this mass of men moving up the river bottoms with orders to escape somehow to Terry if it was the Indians returning.

By now Bradley, pale under the dust and sunshine, and silent, had plunged through the flooded stream and hurried to Terry. Saluting with parade-ground formality, he approached to report that they had examined the strange-looking objects along the hills to the east: 197 dead men of Custer's force, stripped to the bloated, discoloring skin, most of them unrecognizable, the dark objects their horses, all dead for days, two–three days.

A Terry scout out a long time searching for sign of Custer's force finally saw the three Reno troopers hurrying back to their command with the good news of Terry and Gibbon's approach. From the ridge the battle-worn men of Reno watched the column march up a little beyond the unburied dead on the bottoms, drag away a body or two and some horses, some already torn apart by the wolves, and go into orderly camp. Some of Gibbon's men were sent over to Reno's defense circle to skin the horses killed there yesterday, the hides to be dried for travel slings to carry the wounded down to the *Far West*. With no tents in the Terry command, men were hurried out to gather bundles of diamond willows for wickiups to be covered with blankets against the boiling sun of day and the chill of the night. The first shelters were ready for Reno's wounded by the time they were carried across the river to needed medical supplies and a doctor less hollow-eyed for sleep. One man of that first desperate water detail was suffering from a shattered leg whose spreading gangrene demanded immediate preparation for amputation when he reached the new camp.

Reno, gaunt and bristle-faced, remained to see about his wounded and then went to make a full report to Terry, from his first crossing of the Little Bighorn with Custer's orders to attack the great Sioux camp and his promise of full support. With their adjutants close behind, the men rode across the bottoms that had been grazed by the village horses of the Indian, the earth torn now by all the bare-hoofed charges of two days ago, the grass roots so cut up that the Indian fire had barely crept out of the dead rushes and timber patches. They paused at Reno's first stand and the ravine ahead of it, marked and scraped by the bodies of hundreds of men who had hidden there in ambush to toll the troopers to their death. They rode on to the Hunkpapa village not far below the ravine, where several blackened and burned lodges were left standing. Among these they located the mutilated bodies of the two men carried into the village by their stampeding horses, and finally the head of Bloody Knife.

Benteen got permission to take his troops across the battle-field to identify as many of the dead now, while it could still be done, and perhaps to understand something of the disastrous fight. He followed down the low gorge where it was assumed Custer had marched and was surprised that there was no deep trail, no trail of shod horses at all. Sergeant Kanipe moved off to Benteen's right, covering the ground he had crossed with Custer's message the afternoon of the 25th and seeking out the body of Sergeant Finkle who, but for his exhausted horse, would have been the messenger sent to McDougall, and Kanipe, still with Custer, would have died. As the troopers passed the points reached by Reno, Weir, and Godfrey the evening of the 25th, Benteen and some of his men stopped at the farthest of these heights, afraid to look ahead, afraid of what they would see, of what they might have missed then. But there was still nothing, no sign at all of combat, only the empty slopes where the knots of warriors had stood looking northward firing guns now and then against nothing—firing in victory as all the old campaigners should have understood. It was from there that the Indians had seen Reno's men gathered along several points and charged them, the warriors riding hard enough to cool even Weir's heat for battle, though he had not yet felt the force that Reno and his men understood.

The men of H Troop spurred across the slopes to a far, high

place, where suddenly the battlefield lay before them. It was like a great leaf, dead and fading in its straggly and browned June grasses and sagebrush, like a leaf crumpled into ravines and shallow gorges of dry waterways, with slopes rising along the ridges that were the broken midrib. Over the farther reaches lay dark objects—horses, bloated, the legs sticking out stiff as wood. Then they saw the naked bodies, in little rows, in knots and singly, dead men scattered like handfuls of pale Indian corn flung over a rumpled tawny robe in a children's game. There was no indication of battle lines or of orderly skirmishes except where five–six horses lay in a sort of string up a rise. Ahead of them were five–six dead men spaced about the same, as if they had run when the horses were shot, and were brought down too. They lay not far from Calhoun's body, all apparently running for the ridge that held one of the few clumps of troopers that had somehow gathered there and been brought down—perhaps twenty men killed not far apart—while off on higher ground, four–five more lay within twenty–thirty yards. But it didn't seem a stand, only a sort of sweeping together, perhaps with Indians creeping up the back slope too. The only real stand seemed on the far end of the ridge that pointed like a thumb at the river, below the last Indian camp. Here Custer had fallen with most of his officers within a barricade of dead horses, surely not killed so long as flight seemed possible, killed only in the last desperate moments to delay the end. Off southwestward in a ravine perhaps seventy-five yards from the river lay twenty-two bodies. Most of them seemed to have been killed with stones and war clubs. Perhaps they were the wounded taken there for protection, but more probably they had run there to hide, and were overwhelmed by warriors creeping up to the edge of the draw.

Benteen counted seventy horses and two Indian ponies dead on the field, indicating what every Plains campaigner knew: that the Indians usually fought on foot, crawling up, running, dodging, falling in protected spots, always free to grab any loose enemy horse. Riding over what was really a compact piece of bloodied ground, it seemed to the troopers that Custer's force had probably let their horses be stampeded in a panic of man and animal. The whole scene spoke of a rout, and a swift one, most of it lasting perhaps not half an hour.

Deliberately, Benteen returned to the nearest spot that any of Reno's force had reached the evening of the 25th. From there he and his lieutenant tried to see the battle slopes and ridges, and from the point where he had planted the guidon as a signal to Custer of Reno's position. The nearest of the dead was Sergeant Butler, a soldier of many years of experience and unquestionable courage. He was lying all alone on a slope, far from his company, as though he had somehow escaped at the last minute or been sent as a desperate courier to Reno, or more likely as a sort of final messenger from Thermopylae. But there was no miracle for him, and he went down with empty cartridges all around him.

Only three of Custer's officers were found with their companies, so apparently the fight was not by units. All but Keogh, Calhoun, and Crittenden were on or near the final hill near their commander or missing. Harrington's body was not with his C Troop, nor with his captain, Tom Custer, who lay up toward the stand made near the point where his brother died, nor found anywhere else. As the officers of the 7th talked this over, there were the uneasy recollections about Harrington's notion that he was to be captured and tortured, but close examination of the deserted Indian camps produced no sign of captives and none of torture, including no indication of the romantically horrible burning at a stake or tree that Harrington had envisioned in his sketch of himself.

Reno listened to Benteen's report, shaking his heavy head. He had sent both his striker and his cook to their deaths in his effort to get Custer to keep his promise of support. Perhaps he should have realized from the first the support would never come.

Early the morning of the 28th Reno ordered Captain Mc-Dougall and his B Troop to the Indian camps to search out implements to bury the dead. With what he could scare up—very little—the captain crossed the river in the bright morning sun. Someone noticed a movement in a small brush patch nearby—a horse. It turned out to be Keogh's favorite, called Comanche, with seven wounds but still alive. McDougall detailed a man to look after the animal and went on, as ordered, to bury E Troop of the Gray Horses—men he had commanded for years. Spreading his force out in a sad skirmish line, he moved up from the river, searching through hollows and clumps of sagebrush. They found them, most of the men dead in the ravine. From a distance it was plain they had used the upper sides of the cut bank as a sort of breastwork, sliding down as they were struck. Bloated and blackened as the naked bodies were—the faces like the wounds, puffed and swollen, oozing and flyblown—few were recognizable. The captain had a record kept of those who could be identified, pathetically few, although he had known many of the troopers for years. One definite identification was a sergeant because he had one sock on, with his name still plain.

But in the heat and stench the men trying to examine the decomposing bodies began to vomit so violently that Mc-Dougall finally had great chunks of earth and sod cut from the banks of the wide draw down upon the dead of Company E, covering them as well as possible, filling in much of the ravine's depth for all time, changing and obliterating much of the site.

Elsewhere, other burial details moved over the ground, men looking for some special friend going along, as Moylan went to see where Calhoun, his brother-in-law, lay. The bodies were all in similar condition on this third day of heat. Most of the dead were completely naked, many scalped and hacked, although it was no longer always possible to distinguish the wounds of actual combat from later mutilations. Custer's stripped body had been found in a sort of sitting position between two troopers in the low pile of dead behind the breastwork that was a tangle of stiff horse legs sticking out, and great bloated bellies, the gases stewing and whistling in the climbing heat of the sun, the rushing sound of maggots busily gnawing, great dark flies crawling heavily over it all.

Tom Custer's body was face down, most of his scalp gone except some tufts of hair at the nape. The skull was crushed, with several arrows shot into it and into his back. Godfrey had the body rolled over for identification. The features, pressed into the ground, were flattened and decomposed, unrecognizable, but on one arm, broken by a shot, were the tattooed initials TWC with the goddess of liberty and the flag.

There were 42 bodies and 39 dead horses on Custer Hill. Altogether, according to Godfrey's memoranda, they buried 212 bodies, bringing the dead, with the missing and those of Reno, to 265, including 16 officers, 7 civilians, and 3 Indian scouts. Without proper tools to dig the hard-baked and gravelly earth of the Custer ridge, the bodies were not buried in the usual deep graves or trenches. They were covered, but so thinly that those who knew the swift gully washers and cloudbursts of the dry country realized that some of the bodies would surely be washed out before fall, or covered by fill-ins beyond all finding, many of the poor markers set up at the graves of the officers certain to be swept away.

The men, ordered to destroy the Indian camp, to burn all that was possible, gathered up even the lodgepoles into rude blazing piles, the long ones from the conference lodge with the rest. They found the pocket instrument case of Dr. Lord, and perhaps realized that some woman must have been in great haste, leaving all those instruments with fine steel edges, sharp and keen, behind. The men also found the buckskin blouse of Porter, and some underwear with the name of Sturgis on it, both bloodied and shot full of holes. Young Sturgis' end seemed a particularly ironic one. Son of the colonel of the 7th with whom Custer had had a long-time feud, the young second lieutenant had been with Benteen at Fort Rice until two, three months ago. One of the lieutenants at Fort Lincoln was transferred East, and Gibson of Rice was offered the position. It was really a promotion but Gibson's young wife refused to let him take it, feeling an unreasoning foreboding against it. So young Sturgis asked for the opportunity to apply for the transfer and, perhaps because he was the colonel's son, although less than a year out of West Point, he was given the position, which put him into Smith's Gray Horse Troop on the Little Bighorn. Now Gibson was alive with Benteen, and not even a recognizable body remained of the son of the colonel.

Terry had planned to leave the battleground the evening of the 28th, but the doctors insisted that the disabled men needed another day of quiet and strengthening food before starting the long trip to the Yellowstone. The long, slow column started the 29th, when the lowering sun began to cool the broiling heat that had been so difficult for the wounded and the sick even in the shade of the wickiups. Each litter was carried by four men afoot, stumbling over the uneven prairie in the pale light of the growing moon. They had to stop every fifty or seventy-five yards to rest. The setting down and lifting was so painful that the carriers were doubled. After six or seven miles the command camped. Many of the troops went bathing in the evening river, but chiefly to slip back to the deserted Indian villages in the moonlight, and even to climb up to the stinking place where Custer's men had fallen, the fattening buzzards refusing to rise into dark flight, even the coyotes standing, looking, too lazy to run.

The stunned pall of the annihilation still lay upon the command, many of Reno's men and even Benteen's realizing the luck of their battalions. There was quiet talk among the officers of Terry and Gibbon's forces too. What a difference the 2nd Cavalry would have made on Custer Hill, or Low's Gatling guns. Or abiding by the arrangements—to send Herendeen to Tullock's Fork where Terry waited, Custer to scout farther up the Rosebud and the Tongue and meet the command coming up the Little Bighorn on the 26th or 27th. Many of the 7th recalled the stern admonition of the scouts—the Rees, who knew of the great summer council of the Teton Sioux and said there were too many Sioux up ahead. Even the trusted Bloody Knife had spoken with no more effect than the wind over the buffalo grass, his headless body down in the brush of the bottoms, the promise of a trip to Washington never to be fulfilled. The words of Charley Reynolds had been unheard as those of the Rees, as were those of Mitch Bouyer, both dead now, and gone to their death knowing it would be so.

The next night the wounded were carried in mule slings made of the horsehides, with the mules tied between the two poles of each sling as between shafts, one mule ahead of the patient, one behind. So Terry finally reached the mouth of the Little Bighorn and found that the captain of the *Far West* had managed to work the shallow-draft steamboat that far up the Bighorn River. The wounded were carried aboard and made as comfortable as possible, with a detail of their own 7th Cavalry men their nurses.

Then the moorings were loosened, the *Far West* swung slowly around and down the Bighorn to the Yellowstone and Fort Abraham Lincoln, bearing the news of the second wipeout of United States troops by the Sioux and their allies within ten years.

»▶ »▶ »▶ »▶ »▶ »▶ »▶ »▶

8 RESUMÉ

★ ★ ★ ★ ★ ★ ★ ★

The Indian wars on the Plains differed from the usual military conflict, whether civil or between nations, in most aspects except one. As always, there were people who did not consider the warring inevitable. This time they could point to Canada, who took over her entire region without one battle with her Indians by the simple expedient of keeping her treaties. If more territory was to be appropriated from the natives, new treaties were negotiated, without subterfuge, force, or coercion. The United States broke most of her treaties before the ink on the Indian's X was dry.

The situation on the Plains was complicated by the wholesale destruction of the buffalo, the commissary of the Indians. Because the great herds, on Indian lands, were not only his sustenance and his religion but ethically, at least, his property, his anger was understandable. In the meantime the land-hungry pushed in for homes, the cattlemen for grass, the gold-seekers for treasure. Then in the early 1870's the depression dried up the financing of railroads headed into the west and Indian country through Kansas and the Dakotas. It was hoped that new gold strikes and railway access to old ones would lure reluctant investors. Besides, since the Civil War there was further intensification on the only remaining field of conflict—the rivalry for officerships in the shrinking army and the necessity to keep the Indians stirred up not only for war profits for the manufacturers and contractors but to advance the careers of the military.

From 1865 it had been clear that the Army of the Plains would be short-lived, with ambitious officers driven to jockeying for honors and victories to raise their rank and position, at least to hold their standing when the inevitable cuts came, and to further financial and business opportunities on retirement. To this end by 1867 the Plains had become a gaming field, a hunting ground for military trophies—victories over the Indians, particularly over bands with women and children, for warrior parties were difficult to locate and more difficult to strike, to defeat. Even with the avowed Extermination Policy of the government, there was usually some protest over the slaughter of helpless Indians and demands that the real culprits, the hostile warriors, be punished. Because peaceful villages were always easier to find, closer to the forts, trails, or agencies, unprepared for defense, and with fewer of the wilder, more daring young warriors, it was the peace Indians who were struck, with efforts to make them look like hostiles.

Out of this complicated Plains situation grew a sort of general disobedience of Plains officers, from colonels down the scale, usually with loud newspaper and magazine applause. Most of the men who hoped to further their ambitions in Indian warring, from Fetterman in 1866 through Reynolds the spring of 1876, were accused of disobeying orders. Royall, accused earlier, was charged with disobedience at the battle of the Rosebud only eight days before the Custer fight, and Mer-

ritt soon after the news of the Little Bighorn fight got out.
He ignored General Crook's specific orders to hurry directly
to him from the North Platte with supplies and reinforcements.
Instead, he put off facing the hostile Sioux by swinging up
around Red Cloud Reservation to intercept an older, more
peaceful group finally driven out by starvation to take the
treaty-guaranteed summer hunt. It happened to be a band of
tame Cheyennes, mostly women and children and old men,
a band peaceful enough to have remained this long around
the hungry agency. Merritt's disobedience was aggrandized by
King in his *Campaigning with Crook*, which the author had
to withdraw for libel of a newspaper correspondent whom he
called a coward, the reissued volume containing an abject
apology, and admission by King that he had written from hearsay. He wasn't there at all.

With such Plains records, particularly Custer's own, including his suspension in 1867 and his arrest by Stanley on the
Yellowstone in 1873, Terry could not have expected anything
but the customary disobedience.

As for Custer's plan of battle, there is little to be said about
that. The wide and worn trail should have warned so experienced a man that there were probably six to eight warriors
for every trooper he had, warriors on fresh horses, fighting on
their own terrain, for their homes and families. Further, Custer's scouts had tried to warn him of the great annual gathering
up ahead and surely he had heard of the summer conferences
at Bear Butte, so long a matter of common knowledge. The
Medical History of Fort Laramie records that in 1834 Bull
Bear brought one hundred lodges down from Bear Butte to
trade at the new post on the North Platte River. In 1849,
traders reported that the seven great council fires of the Teton
Sioux were gathering there, and in 1857 word reached Washington that the great Teton council was meeting at Bear Butte

to decide what must be done against the whites for Harney's attack on Little Thunder (now that the Indian year of mourning was over, as the Sioux told this author). In 1868 the commanding officer at Fort Laramie wrote of uneasiness about the big council of the Sioux, Northern Cheyennes, and Arapahos called to meet at Bear Butte. As usual even the Loaf About the Forts left Laramie to attend, anxious this year to discuss the government's request that the Loafers join the breeds on a reservation on the Missouri River, where all the Southern Tetons—the Brules and Oglalas—were eventually to go. The obligation of every band to be present at the great summer council while Custer pushed into the Black Hills in 1874 accounts for the lack of real resistance to his approach. The conference was always a time of counciling, from the smallest band to the chiefs of the seven divisions. Full attendance was encouraged, no war parties were permitted out.

So it was on the Little Bighorn, late June, 1876, now that there was no peace at Bear Butte any more. Everyone was to be there, no war parties were permitted against Crow or Shoshoni or Assiniboin, not even raiders against the gold-seekers heading to the Black Hills.

In the face of the evidence of the great trail before him, the advice of his scouts, Indian and white, and the knowledge he should have had of the ancient summer conference, Custer's division of his small force into three parts is inexplicable, unless one assumes that it was of overwhelming importance that neither Benteen nor Reno share in any victory. How the fight would have ended if the command had not been divided must remain pure speculation.* That the Indians were powerful

---

* Lt. Gen. P. H. Sheridan, C.O., Military Division of the Missouri, 1877, with account of Red Horse, Sioux in Custer fight, says if Custer had joined Reno and Benteen at the ford he "could have held his own, at least, and possibly defeated the Indians."

enough in numbers and in determination to defeat the entire force cannot be doubted; whether the worn horses of the troops were strong enough to carry any beyond the reach of the pursuing warriors is debatable. At best the carnage would have been appalling. The unit was, after all, planned for scouting, not for combat without reinforcements by infantry, more cavalry, and Gatling guns.

The charge that there was a great deal of whisky among the troops on the Little Bighorn, either in Reno's pocket or with the soldiers of Custer's battalion, seems untenable. It was probably limited largely to hip flasks and the medical stores. Girard seems to have had the most. According to rumors he, as a noncombatant civilian employee, carried whisky in his saddlebags instead of ammunition, whisky that he sold except, perhaps, the drink he gave to Charley Reynolds in the timber on the bottoms. The report that the Indians said Custer's men were drunk probably originated in the Sioux way of getting an abstract idea across, the result of misinterpretation by the literal-minded. Probably the Indians told the interviewers what was often said in the hearing of this author—that the troops acted drunk, meaning they acted excited and unreasoning. That there was whisky in the canteens seems unlikely too. This must have been another error of interpretation—the Indians probably meant the metal flasks that many of the troopers, particularly the officers, carried. It was customary for most men, even nondrinkers on the summer Plains, to have some whisky handy because it was considered a sort of specific for bowel cramps—either the so-called summer cholera or dysentery—as well as for snakebite. There were high possibilities of both in late June weather. Colonel Gibbon had an attack of something like dysentery on the Yellowstone. Rattlesnakes were common all over the Plains, and a particular menace to men fighting running foot battles, ducking into hollows, dropping behind bushes or banks with no time to look the ground over. The author found a rattlesnake skin on Calhoun Ridge as late as 1930.

As for Reno being drunk the night of the 25th—that story didn't get around until about 1879. Most army officers were drinkers of varying degree. The fact remains that Reno saved most of his force, no mean feat for a sober man, as the bodies strung out along the ridges and slopes far beyond him testify. One might argue that the passionate Custer partisans denigrated the regiment by their efforts to prove everyone but their hero guilty of the debacle on the Custer battleground. They even went to the extreme of gathering up a false affidavit from Mary Adams, colored maid of the Custers. In her statement she claimed to have overheard General Terry tell Custer at the mouth of the Rosebud, "Use your own judgment and do what you think best when you strike the trail, and whatever you do, Custer, hold onto your wounded."

It is highly unlikely that the illiterate Mary Adams would have remembered the exact words as late as January 16, 1878, the date of the affidavit. Besides, it has been proved that she was not at the mouth of the Rosebud at all in 1876, but had remained with Mrs. Custer at Fort Abraham Lincoln. There were dozens of other concocted stories, some inspired by Custer adherents, many of those seeking self-aggrandizement, including the seventy men who claimed to be survivors of the Custer fight that E. A. Brininstool, writer on Sioux and Custer topics, collected. The exaggerations, the violent partianship, did help push one section of the 7th Cavalry into the most barbaric conduct fourteen years later, when they mowed down women and children with Hotchkiss guns at Wounded Knee in 1890, shouting, some reported, "There's another blast for Custer!"

The 7th of the Plains was a great regiment and the common

trooper of it deserved a better reputation than he sometimes receives.

That large sums of money were taken by the Indians from the bodies of Custer's men is another fantasy. It is true that the colonel had prevented the paymaster from delivering the two months' pay at Fort Abraham Lincoln, apparently to keep Seip, the post trader, from getting it. Instead, the paymaster was ordered to accompany the expedition to the first camp, on Heart River, designated as Camp One. It was a sort of last farewell for some of the officers and their wives. Mrs. Custer and several others had come out with picnic hampers and camping equipment. The next day the mail was sent back by the returning escort, and no telling how many troopers sent money to families, friends, creditors, or to banks. At Camp Eight, two scouts were sent back with the mail. One of them, Red Bear, brought many letters and newspapers out a few days later, the first of several of these mail round trips.

It is known that a mail bag went in from the Powder River June 10 because it included a letter from Custer to his wife, with the usual outsider's remarks about the region. Certainly any man as long on the Plains as Custer knew better than to say they were in country that had never been visited by white men. It is clear that the Verendryes were there in 1742–43, and both Spaniards and Frenchmen long before them, with small trading posts at various nearby sites for a hundred years by 1876. Still, it is a revealing remark from the man who could never bear to be second.

By the time the column reached Camp Twenty on the Yellowstone, with the *Far West* anchored in the river, James Coleman had set up a large trader tent well stocked with the usual supplies requested by an army in the field. There was a large quantity of liquor, and apparently considerable sale.

Troopers drunken enough to warrant detention in a guardhouse were herded out upon the prairie and sobered up there. At frontier tent-saloon prices, the enlisted man's base pay of thirteen dollars a month would not cover much more than one good drunk.

Many bought so-called dry goods from Coleman—the large hats to keep the hot sun off and extra kerchiefs against the dust besides the little luxuries and necessities like salves, raisins, cigars and chewing tobacco, and candy.

To be sure, the gamblers of the 7th clung to some of their money for the games that had brought the 7th Cavalry some notice. These included several of the young officers who stayed up all the night of the 21st before the start along the Rosebud the next day.

There is substantial difference in the amount of distant firing reported by the men of Reno and Benteen, including Godfrey and Benteen, Varnum and Reno. One wonders if it was not more temporary war deafness on the part of one group and a refusal to understand the actual power of the Indian on the other—between the Reno men who had faced that power and were concerned with bare survival and those who came up after the bloody fight on the bottoms and the river and bluffs was about done, and understood nothing of the situation. Benteen, as an old campaigner, had some discernment, of course, and one could expect young Varnum, only four years out of West Point, to have ears as sharp as Godfrey's—except that Varnum's rang with the close gunfire that had scattered his scouts and wounded and killed his friends in the first hot encounter of his life, while Godfrey had been off on a quiet valley chase with Benteen. There was also the difference in sounds from as far off as four and a half miles, cut by river breaks, particularly with a cross-wind, no matter how light.

Besides, there was the urgency of the Indian attack, as well as differences in the interpretation of what was heard and exactly when. Those who argue against any validity in the Indian reports of the Custer battle because they vary a great deal should try to bring some agreement out of the white-man accounts. On even so elementary an aspect as the time of day, there is as much as four–five hours' difference.

So long as men of the time of Custer with the 7th Cavalry were alive, it was common out on the Plains to hear such conjecturing: Suppose Custer had managed a victory over a few Sioux June 1876, and got word of it to the Democratic Convention at St. Louis. How would Custer have run against Hayes for the presidency? Generally the verdict was that he would have made a better showing than Tilden. Custer was well aware that the nation gave the presidency to such men as Washington, Taylor, and Grant because they won her wars. Surely the man who ended the twenty years of Plains wars with the Indian would be no less rewarded. Besides, in 1876, aspiring to the presidency was still considered the privilege of every native male, not only the man with millions or high political position, but also the man with no money or political position as well. There was probably never a better year to stampede a political convention than at St. Louis in 1876, and who ever voted against a national hero?

There is a recurring interest in the presidency in Custer's juvenile letters and utterances from before West Point on, augmented powerfully by the colonel's success as a speaker from Johnson's presidential train, where he heard the cry not for Johnson but for Grant and Custer. Well, old Ulysses S. had his round, and now it was Custer's turn. He had listened to the suggestion several times in the fulsome praise of newspaper and railroad owners. Now the sense of destiny that often appears in youths intolerant of discipline and restraint was upon him, a sort of desperate destiny. The mood permeates all the speeches and flattery of the luncheons and dinners the winter of 1875–76 in New York. The later corroboration by the scouts in Libby's *The Arikara Narrative* came as no surprise to anyone who had followed the stories of the Indians and the white men of the Plains, or Custer's own writings. The *Narrative* is the story of the Ree scouts with Custer to the Little Bighorn, and contains their firsthand accounts of Custer's promises to Bloody Knife when he was made the Great Father, the President, if he could win even a little victory over a few Sioux.

Custer was very well aware that no one voted against a national hero.

»▶ »▶ »▶ »▶ »▶ »▶ »▶ »▶

APPENDIX

★ ★ ★ ★ ★ ★ ★ ★

(This list includes the names of enlisted men, as far as can be ascertained, with many of them illiterate and some hiding their identity.)

Benteen, Capt. Frederick W.
Bradley, Lt. James H.
Brisbin, Maj. James S.
Butler, Sergt. James
Calhoun, Lt. James
Cooke, Lt. Wm. W.
Crittenden, 2nd Lt. John J.
Crook, Brig. Gen. George
Culbertson, Sergt. Ferdinand A.
Curtis, Sergt. ———
Custer, Boston
Custer, Capt. Tom W.
Davern, Sergt. Edward
De Rudio, Lt. Chas. C.
De Wolf, Dr. ———
Edgerly, 2nd Lt. Winfield S.
Elliott, Maj. ———
Fetterman, Capt. Wm. J.
Finkle, Sergt. August
Finley, Sergt. Jeremiah

French, Capt. Thos. B.
Gibbon, Col. John
Gibson, Lt. Frank M.
Godfrey, Capt. Edward S.
Hare, 2nd Lt. Luther R.
Harney, Gen. Wm. S.
Harrington, 2nd Lt. Henry M.
Hazen, Col. Wm. B.
Hodgson, 2nd Lt. Benj. H.
Kanipe, Sergt. Daniel
Kellogg, Mark
Keogh, Capt. Miles W.
King, Lt. Charles
Lord, Dr. G. E.
Low, Lt. Wm. H., Jr.
Ludlow, Capt. Wm.
McDermott, Priv. ———
McDougall, Capt. Thos. M.
McIlhargy (or Ilhargey),
   Priv. Archibald

McIntosh, Lt. Donald
Martin, Trumpeter John
Mathey, Lt. Edward G.
Merrill, Maj. Lewis
Merritt, Col. Wesley
Mitchell, Priv. John
Moylan, Capt. Myles
O'Neal, (or O'Neil), Priv. Thos.
Porter, Dr. H. R.
Porter, Lt. James E.
Reed, Armstrong (Autie)
Reno, Maj. Marcus A.
Reynolds, Col. Joseph J.
Royall, Maj. Wm. B.

Ryan, Sergt. John M.
Sherman, Gen. Wm. T.
Smith, Lt. Algernon E.
Stanley, Gen. David S.
Sturgis, 2nd Lt. James G.
Sturgis, Col. S. D.
Tanner, Priv. James
Terry, Maj. Gen. Alfred H.
Varnum, Lt. Charles A.
Voight (or Vogt, Voit),
　Priv. H. C.
Wallace, Lt. Geo. D.
Weir, Capt. Thos. B.
Yates, Capt. Geo. W.

SELECTED BIBLIOGRAPHY
for the General Reader

Bourke, John G. *On the Border with Crook*. New York, Charles Scribner's Sons, 1891.

Brill, C. J. *Conquest of the Southern Plains*. Oklahoma City, Okla., Golden Saga Pubs., 1938.

Brininstool, E. A. *A Trooper with Custer*. Columbus, Ohio, Hunter-Trader-Trapper, 1926. Vol. I.

———. *Fighting Red Cloud's Warriors*. Columbus, Ohio, Hunter-Trader-Trapper, 1926. Vol. V.

Bureau of Ethnology, *Annual Reports*. Fourth and Tenth.

Byrne, P. E. *The Red Man's Last Stand*. London, 1927.

Clymer, Hiester. "Report on Management of the War Department, Rep. Hiester Clymer, Chairman of Committee," *House Reports* No. 799, 44th Cong. 1st Sess. Serial No. 1715 (1876), Vol. 8.

Custer, Elizabeth B. *Boots and Saddles*. New York, Harper and Brothers, 1885.

Custer, George A. *My Life on the Plains*. Chicago, Lakeside Press, 1952.

DeLand, Charles Edmund. *The Sioux Wars*. South Dakota Department of History Collections, Vols. XV and XVII. (Pierre, S.D.)

Dustin, Fred. *The Custer Tragedy*. Ann Arbor, Mich. Privately printed, 1939.

Finerty, John F. *War Path and Bivouac, or the Conquest of the Sioux*. Chicago, Donohue, Henneberry & Co., 1890.

Fougera, Katherine G. *With Custer's Cavalry*. Caldwell, Idaho, The Caxton Printers, Ltd., 1940.

Frost, Lawrence A. *The Custer Album: a Pictorial Biography of General George A. Custer*. Seattle, Wash., Superior Publishing Company, 1964.

Gibbon, Colonel John. "Last Summer's Expedition against the Sioux," *American Catholic Quarterly Review*, Vol. II (April, 1877).

———. "Hunting Sitting Bull," *American Catholic Quarterly Review*, Vol. II (October, 1877).

Graham, Colonel William A. *The Custer Myth: A Source Book of Custeriana*. Harrisburg, Pa., The Stackpole Co., 1953.

Grinnell, George B. *The Fighting Cheyennes*. New York, Charles Scribner's Sons., 1915.

Hawley, Paul R. "Did Cholera Defeat Custer?" *International Abstracts of Surgery*, Vol. 84 (May, 1947).

Hazen, W. B. *Some Corrections of Life on the Plains*. Norman, University of Oklahoma Press, 1962.

Keim, De Benneville R. *Sheridan's Troopers on the Frontier*. Philadelphia, David McKay, 1891.

King, Charles. *Campaigning with Crook*. New York, Harper and Brothers, 1890. [Reissued with apology for libelous material in earlier editions, 1891.]

Kuhlman, Charles. *Did Custer Disobey Orders at the Battle of the Little Big Horn?* Harrisburg, Pa., The Stackpole Co., 1957.

———. *Legend into History: The Custer Mystery*. Harrisburg, Pa., The Stackpole Co., 1951.

Libby, Orin G. (ed.). "The Arikara Narrative of the Campaign Against the Hostile Dakotas," *North Dakota Historical Collections*, Vol. VI (Bismarck, N.D., 1920).

Luce, Edward S., *Keogh, Comanche, and Custer*. St. Louis, Mo., J. S. Swift Co., Inc., 1939.

Maguire, Edward. "Explorations and Surveys in the Department of Dakota, 1876–'77," *Report of the Chief of Engineers for Fiscal Year ending June 30, 1877*. Appendix.

Marquis, Thomas B. *A Warrior Who Fought Custer*. Minneapolis, Midwest Book Co., 1931.

——. *She Watched Custer's Last Battle* [Katie Big Head]. Hardin, Mont. Privately printed, 1933.

Menninger, Karl. "A Psychiatrist Looks at Custer," *International Abstracts of Surgery*, Vol. 84 (May, 1947).

Merington, Marguerite. *The Custer Story*. New York, Devin-Adair Co., 1950.

Merril, Edward. *Auld Lang Syne*. Privately printed, n.d.

Mills, General Anson. *My Story*. Washington, D.C. Privately printed, 1918.

Neihardt, John G. *Black Elk Speaks*. New York, William Morrow & Company, 1932.

New York Herald, June 1 to August 31, 1876. [What one newspaper published.]

Parsons, John E., and DuMont, John S. *Firearms Used in the Custer Battle*. Harrisburg, Pa., The Stackpole Co., 1953.

Remsburg, John E., and George J. *Charley Reynolds*. Kansas City, Mo., H. M. Sender, 1931.

Reno, Marcus A. (defendant). *Reno Court of Inquiry: Abstract of the Official Record of Proceedings*. Preface by W. A. Graham. Harrisburg, Pa., The Stackpole Co., 1954.

Sandoz, Mari. *The Buffalo Hunters*. New York, Hastings House, 1954.

——. *Cheyenne Autumn*. New York, McGraw-Hill Book Co., Inc., 1953.

——. *Crazy Horse*. New York, Alfred A. Knopf, Inc., 1942.

Schmitt, Martin F. *General George Crook: His Autobiography*. Norman, University of Oklahoma Press, 1946.

Scott, Hugh L. *Some Memories of a Soldier*. New York, Century Company, 1928.

Sheridan, Phil H. *Records of Engagements with Hostile Indians, 1868–1882*. Washington, 1882.

Sturgis, Thomas. *Common Sense View of the Sioux War*. Waltham, Mass., Sentinel, 1877.

The Tepee Book (1916 and 1926, etc.)

United States War Department. *Annual Report, 1876:* Report of the General of the Army.

———. *Annual Reports, 1874, 1875, 1876, 1877:* Reports of the Secretary of War.

Van de Water, Frederick F. *Glory Hunter: A Life of General Custer.* Indianapolis, Ind., The Bobbs-Merrill Company, 1934.

Vestal, Stanley. *Sitting Bull: Champion of the Sioux.* Boston, Houghton Mifflin Co., 1932.

———. *Warpath: True Story of the Fighting Sioux.* Boston, Houghton Mifflin Co., 1934.

Wheeler, Homer W. *Buffalo Days.* Indianapolis, Ind., The Bobbs-Merrill Company, 1925.

Whittaker, Frederick. *A Complete Life of Gen. George A. Custer.* New York, Sheldon, 1876.

INDEX

★ ★ ★ ★ ★ ★ ★ ★

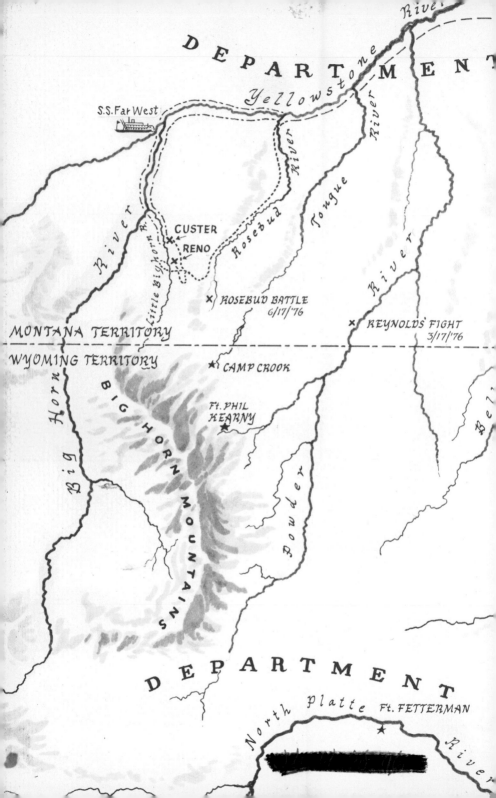